Kantian Dignity and its Difficulties

Kantian Dignity and its Difficulties

KARL AMERIKS

Great Clarendon Street, Oxford, OX2 6DP,
United Kingdom

Oxford University Press is a department of the University of Oxford.
It furthers the University's objective of excellence in research, scholarship,
and education by publishing worldwide. Oxford is a registered trade mark of
Oxford University Press in the UK and in certain other countries

© Karl Ameriks 2024

The moral rights of the author have been asserted

All rights reserved. No part of this publication may be reproduced, stored in
a retrieval system, or transmitted, in any form or by any means, without the
prior permission in writing of Oxford University Press, or as expressly permitted
by law, by licence or under terms agreed with the appropriate reprographics
rights organization. Enquiries concerning reproduction outside the scope of the
above should be sent to the Rights Department, Oxford University Press, at the
address above

You must not circulate this work in any other form
and you must impose this same condition on any acquirer

Published in the United States of America by Oxford University Press
198 Madison Avenue, New York, NY 10016, United States of America

British Library Cataloguing in Publication Data
Data available

Library of Congress Control Number: 2024932997

ISBN 9780198917625

DOI: 10.1093/9780198917656.001.0001

Printed and bound by
CPI Group (UK) Ltd, Croydon, CR0 4YY

Links to third party websites are provided by Oxford in good faith and
for information only. Oxford disclaims any responsibility for the materials
contained in any third party website referenced in this work.

For Geraldine

Contents

Acknowledgments	ix
Note on Sources and Key to Abbreviations and Translations	xi
Introduction: On the Very Idea of Kantian Dignity	1
1. The Distinctiveness of Kantian Dignity: Its Meaning and Relevance	16
2. Dignity as Universal: Herder, Diversity, and Development	49
3. Dignity as Unconditioned: Race, Religion, and Fascism	71
4. Dignity and Democracy: Missed Connections with the United States	94
5. Dignity Beyond Price: Kant and His Revolutionary British Contemporary	117
6. Dignity Lost and Regained: Thomas Mann's Elliptical Path, Part I: Background	143
7. Thomas Mann's Path, Part II: Intellectual Foundations in German Philosophy	156
8. Thomas Mann's Path, Part III: Back to the Early Romantics and Kantian Dignity	181
Afterword	196
References	201
Index	221

Acknowledgments

The acknowledgments on this page reflect only a part of my deep indebtedness to numerous philosophers—teachers, students, colleagues—ever since my first courses in the subject in 1965. There are many more relevant names than, at this age, I can sort out without the fear of accidentally forgetting to mention others who are also very important. The motivation for this latest project has been especially connected with the international background and interests of our family, my ever-encouraging wife Geraldine, and her many fascinating relatives. Unfortunately, this book was not finished in time to share with Henry E. Allison, whose friendship was always much appreciated and whose work remains an enormous help for all scholars of modern philosophy.

For ideas regarding the final structure of this book, I am heavily indebted to Peter Momtchiloff and anonymous reviewers for Oxford University Press, whose suggestions helped me to expand it into its final form. As always, the Notre Dame philosophical community, including its interdisciplinary institutes (the Notre Dame Institute for Advanced Studies, the Nanovic Institute for European Studies, and the Center for the Philosophy of Religion), has been exceptionally supportive. My study of current approaches to Kant's practical philosophy is much indebted to an NEH summer institute organized long ago by David Hoy and Jerome B. Schneewind, and to several later events involving Onora O'Neill and my longtime Notre Dame colleague Alasdair MacIntyre. For recent help and enlightening discussions that bear on the book's philosophical and historical issues, I am especially indebted to Karl Martin Adam, Lucy Allais, R. Lanier Anderson, Robert Audi, Noell Birondo, Tobias Boes, Elizabeth Millan Brusslan, Sarah Buss, Thomas Cantone, David Carranza, Andrew Chignell, Colleen Coalter, Alix Cohen, Stanley Corngold, Janelle DeWitt, Meredith Trexler Drees, C. Stephen Evans, Wolfgang Ertl, Naomi Fisher, Richard Foley, Manfred Frank, Paul W. Franks, Patrick Frierson, Kristin Gjesdal, Lydia Goehr, John E. Hare, Desmond Hogan, Otfried Höffe, Vittorio Hösle, Andrew Huddleston, Anja Jauernig, Patrick Kain, William Kinderman, Patricia Kitcher, Jane Kneller, Katharina Kraus, Markus Kohl, Charles Larmore, Béatrice Longuenesse, Jacqueline Mariña, Colin Marshall, John McGreevy, Melissa Merritt, Michael Morris, Samuel Newlands, Robert E. Norton, Robert B. Pippin, Buket Korkut Raptis, Arthur Ripstein, Fred Rush, Steven Naragon, Karl Schafer, Tamar Schapiro, James Schmidt, Sally Sedgwick, Sandra Shapshay, Susan Meld Shell, Allen Speight, Samuel A. Stoner, Dieter Sturma, Clinton Tolley, Owen Ware, Eric Watkins, Aaron Wells, Howard Wettstein, Huw Williams, Allen W. Wood, Günter

Zöller, Rachel Zuckert, Ariel Zylberman, and philosophers at gatherings at the University of California San Diego and Riverside campuses, the University of North Carolina, Mugla, Turkey, Cardiff, Wales, and at the 2019 national meeting of the German Studies Association and the 2022 national meeting of the American Society for Aesthetics.

Chapters 2–5 are slightly revised and significantly expanded (but without any noteworthy philosophical changes) versions of essays that appeared in an earlier form in the following publications and are reprinted (in part) with permission, and their publishers are thankfully acknowledged: "History, Progress, and Autonomy: Kant, Herder, and After," in *Kant and the Possibility of Progress: From Modern Hopes to Postmodern Anxieties*, ed. Samuel A. Stoner and Paul T. Wilford (Philadelphia: University of Pennsylvania Press, 2021), 137–51 and 262–6; "The Fate of Dignity: How Words Matter," in *Kant's Concept of Dignity*, *Kant-Studien Ergänzungshefte* 209, ed. Yasushi Kato and Gerhard Schönrich (Berlin: De Gruyter, 2020), 263–84; "Kant and Dignity: Missed Connections with the United States," in *Proceedings of the 13th International Kant Congress 'The Court of Reason' (Oslo, 6–9 August 2019)*, ed. Camilla Serck-Hanssen and Beatrix Himmelmann (Berlin and Boston: De Gruyter, 2021), 27–47; "Dignity Beyond Price: Kant and his Revolutionary British Contemporary," *Kant Yearbook* 13 (2021), 1–27. https://www.degruyter.com/journal/key/kantyb/html?lang=de

Note on Sources and Key to Abbreviations and Translations

References to Kant's works use the abbreviations below, and details on translations, all from Cambridge University Press editions, are given in the list of references at the end of this volume. References cite, in square brackets, the volume and page of the Academy edition: *Kant's Gesammelte Schriften*, Ausgabe der Preussischen Akademie der Wissenschaften (Berlin: de Gruyter, 1900–), except that references to Kant's *Critique of Pure Reason* are given in the standard way by citing KrV and pages of the first ("A") and/or second ("B") edition.

List 1: Kant's Writings, Listed by Abbreviation

Anth	*Anthropologie in pragmatischer Hinsicht* [1798] [7: 119–333], trans. in Kant (2007).
Auf	"Beantwortung der Frage: Was ist Aufklärung?" [1784] [8: 35–42], trans. in Kant (1996a).
Basedow	"Zwei Aufsätze, betreffend das Basedow'sche *Philanthropinum*" [1776-7] [2: 447–52], trans. in Kant (2007).
Bem	*Bemerkungen in den "Beobachtungen über das Gefühl des Schönen und Erhabenen"* [1764-5], ed. Marie Rischmüller, Hamburg: Meiner, 1991, corrected edition of [29: 1–102], trans. in Kant (2011b).
Beo	*Beobachtungen über das Gefühl des Schönen und Erhabenen* [1764] [2: 207–56], trans. in Kant (2011b).
Br	*Briefwechsel* [10]–[12], trans. in part in Kant (1999).
Earthquakes	"Fortgesetzte Betrachtung der seit einiger Zeit wahrgenommenen Erderschütterungen," [1756] [1: 465–72], trans. in Kant (2012b).
Ende	"Das Ende aller Dinge" [1794] [8: 327–39], trans. in Kant (2018).
Feyerabend	"Naturrecht Feyerabend" [1784] [27: 1319–94], trans. in Kant (2016).
Fort	"Welches sind die wirklichen Fortschritte, die die Metaphysik seit Leibnitzens und Wolff's Zeiten in Deutschland gemacht hat?" [1804] [20: 257–332], trans. in Kant (2002).
GMS	*Grundlegung der Metaphysik der Sitten* [1785] [4: 387–463], trans. in Kant (2011a).
Idee	"Idee zur einer allgemeinen Weltgeschichte in weltbürgerlicher Absicht" (1784) [8: 17–31], trans. in Kant (2007).
KpV	*Kritik der praktischen Vernunft* [1788] [5: 1–164], trans. in Kant (1996a).
KrV	*Kritik der reinen Vernunft* [A 1781, B 1787], trans. Kant (1997a).
KU	*Kritik der Urteilskraft* [1790] [5: 164–486], trans. Kant (2000).

xii NOTE ON SOURCES AND KEY TO ABBREVIATIONS AND TRANSLATIONS

MdS — *Die Metaphysik der Sitten* [1797–8] [6: 205–493], trans. in Kant (1996a).

MK — *Immanuel Kant's Menschenkunde oder philosophische Anthropologie* [1781–2?], ed. Johann Adam Bergk (1831) [25: 853–1203], trans. in Kant (2012a).

MPC — "Moral Philosophie Collins" [1774–7?] [27: 243–471], trans. in Kant (1997b).

Nachschrift — "Nachschrift zu Christian Gottlieb Mielckes Littauisch-deutschem und deutsch-littauischem Wörterbuch" [1800] [8: 445], trans. in Kant (2007).

Nova — *Principium primorum cognitionis metaphysicae nova dilucidatio* [1755] [1: 385–416] trans. in Kant (1992).

Ped — "Uber Pädagogik" [1776–87] [9: 437–85], trans. in Kant (2007).

Phys Geo — *Immanuel Kants physische Geographie*, ed. Friederich Theodor Rink [1802] [9: 151–436], trans. in Kant (2012b).

Pöl-Rel — *Philosophische Religionslehre nach Pölitz* [1783–4] [1817] [28: 993–1126], trans. in Kant (1996b).

Prol — *Prolegomena zu einer jeden künftigen Metaphysik, die als Wissenschaft wird auftreten können* [1783] [4: 255–383], trans. (Kant 2004).

Refl — *Reflexionen* [16]–[18], trans. in part in Kant (2005a).

Rel — *Die Religion innerhalb der Grenzen der bloßen Vernunft* [1793–4] [6: 1–202], trans. in Kant (2018).

RezHerder — "Rezension zu Johann Gottfried Herder, *Ideen zur Philosophie der Geschichte der Menschheit* (erster Teil)"; "Erinnerungen des Rezensenten der Herderschen *Ideen zur Philosophie der Geschichte der Menschheit* über ein in Februar des *Teutschen Merkur* gegen diese Rezension gerichtetes Schreiben"; "Rezension zu Johann Gottfried Herder, *Ideen zur Philosophie der Geschichte der Menschheit* (zweiter Teil)" [1785] [8: 43–66], trans. in Kant (2007).

SF — *Der Streit der Fakultäten in drei Abschnitten* [1798] [7: 5–116], trans. in Kant (1996b).

Tel — "Über den Gebrauch teleologischer Prinzipien in der Philosophie" [1788] [8: 157–84], trans. in Kant (2007).

TP — *Über den Gemeinspruch: Das mag in der Theorie richtig sein, taugt aber nicht für die Praxis* [1793] [8: 275–313], trans. in Kant (1996a).

UE — *Über eine Entdeckung, nach der alle neue Critik der reinen Vernunft durch eine ältere entbehrlich gemacht werden soll* [1790] [8: 187–251], trans. in Kant (2002).

Vigil — "Metaphysik der Sitten Vigilantius" [1793–4] [27: 479–732], trans. in Kant (1997b).

V-AnFried — "Anthropologie Friedländer" [1775–6] [25: 469–728], trans. in Kant (2012a).

V-AnPillau — "Anthropologie Pillau" [1777–8] [25: 733–847], trans. in Kant (2012a).

V-AnMrong — "Anthropologie Mronogovius" [1784–5] [25: 1207–429], trans. in Kant (2012a).

V-LoBlomberg — "Logic Blomberg" [early 1770s] [24: 9–301], trans. in Kant (2004c).

NOTE ON SOURCES AND KEY TO ABBREVIATIONS AND TRANSLATIONS   xiii

VorlM *Immanuel Kant: Vorlesung zu Moralphilosophie* [1770s], a newly edited version of MPC, using Kaehler's notes, Kant (2004b).

ZeF *Zum ewigen Frieden. Ein Philosophischer Entwurf* [1795, 1796] [8: 343–86], trans. in Kant (1996a).

List 2: Thomas Mann's Writings, Listed by Abbreviation

GR "On the German Republic [1922]," in *Reflections of a Nonpolitical Man*, ed. Mark Lilla, trans. Lawrence Rainey (New York: New York Review Books, 2021), 507–47.

N "Nietzsche in the Light of Modern Experience," *Commentary* 6 (1948): 17–26 and 149–56.

R "Reflections of a Nonpolitical Man [1918]," in *Reflections of a Nonpolitical Man*, ed. Mark Lilla, trans. Walter D. Morris (New York: New York Review Books, 2021), 1–489.

T "Thoughts in War Time [1914]," in *Reflections of a Nonpolitical Man*, ed. Mark Lilla, trans. Mark Lilla and Cosima Mattner (New York: New York Review Books, 2021), 491–506.

Introduction

On the Very Idea of Kantian Dignity

We ask ourselves, however, whether it might not be better to preserve respect for reason and truth among the masses and at the same time honor their demand for justice, rather than plant mass myths and let loose upon humanity mobs dominated by "mighty hallucinations."[1]

Difficulties with Dignity: Preliminary Considerations

In the twenty-first century, Immanuel Kant's midstream Enlightenment views continue to be assailed by those who espouse more radical positions. Some regard, and therefore reject, his work, in theoretical as well as practical domains, as hopelessly individualistic or subjectivist. Others praise him precisely because they imagine that he somehow meant that reality—descriptively and/or normatively—is largely a human construction, with everything meaningful in some sense made by us. In addition, even many philosophers who are not constructivists but are sympathetic to Kant's thought often present his philosophy as if it does not, or at least should not, have any metaphysical components.[2]

No doubt Kant's language is in part to blame. He wrote, for example, about offering a critique of reason and all ontology, and he insisted on characterizing his own Critical system as a kind of idealism. But he also composed something called a "Refutation of Idealism," and he continued to use the term "metaphysics" positively in the titles of a number of his works. Given these complications, one always has to read Kant's texts very closely, with full attention to context and the whole arc of his career, in order to begin to have a chance to work out a fair understanding of his ambiguous formulations and underlying positions. Kant definitely meant to criticize many of the dogmatic doctrines of his predecessors, rationalist as well as empiricist, but this was consistent with his continuing to hold on to the

---

[1] Thomas Mann, N 24.

[2] See, e.g., R. Lanier Anderson, "Transcendental Idealism as Formal Idealism: An Anti-Metaphysical Reading," in *Proceedings of the 13th International Kant Congress 'The Court of Reason' (Oslo, 6–9 August 2019)*, ed. Camilla Serck-Hanssen and Beatrix Himmelmann (Berlin and Boston: De Gruyter, 2021), 49–67. See Ch. 1, at note 79.

2 KANTIAN DIGNITY AND ITS DIFFICULTIES

truth of several strong claims of pure reason concerning the dignity, freedom, and equality of all finite persons. His emphasis on the doctrine that persons are subjects with a special status does not mean that he was ever a subjectivist in an individualist or simply psychological sense.

An extensive systematic defense of these broad interpretive and philosophical claims is not the project of this brief book. Nonetheless, some review of the basic features of his philosophy is necessary to give an indication of the kind of orientation that this study will be using in the chapters that follow. In earlier works, I have offered detailed interpretations of a "commonsense" Kant, that is, a defender of our "healthy understanding" as a proper intersubjective starting point for philosophy in general.[3] The task of his transcendental philosophy is to show how an investigation of this starting point reveals a set of basic human capacities. The use of these capacities turns out to require a priori forms of space and time governing sensibility, a priori forms of judgment governing understanding, regulative Ideas guiding the expansion of our empirical knowledge, and unconditioned Ideas underlying the postulates of pure practical reason and guiding our moral life and enhancing our aesthetic experience. In the full development of this position, Kant's system offers what, in our current terminology, can be regarded as a broadly objective view of theoretical, practical, and even aesthetic domains. His system avoids most of the "Cartesian" epistemological tendencies of classical modern philosophy even while going on to defend substantive a priori claims regarding all basic spheres of human life.

Unfortunately, the fundamentally rationalist and Enlightenment-oriented character of Kant's work has not prevented it from being repeatedly misunderstood by his successors, and in an especially egregious manner in regard to its normative implications. In particular, it has been forgotten how often influential right-wing writers twisted Kant's thoughts in a chauvinist direction in ways that had disastrous consequences for Germany into the twentieth century. An additional problem is that even in Kant's work, as with practically all

---

[3] See, e.g., the Introductions in Karl Ameriks, *Interpreting Kant's Critiques* (Oxford: Clarendon Press, 2003) and *Kant's Elliptical Path* (Oxford: Clarendon Press, 2012). The role of the term "common sense" as it appears in translations of Kant's work is a complicated one, and he is much more positive about the general notion than is usually understood. The way that the term *gemeiner Menschenverstand* (common human understanding) is used by the anti-systematic writers of the era is severely criticized by Kant (Prol [4: 259]), but *gesunder Menschenverstand* (healthy human understanding) is a term that has a positive meaning for him and corresponds to the most defensible uses of "common sense" in Anglophone philosophy. See Karl Ameriks, "A Commonsense Kant?", *Proceedings and Addresses of the American Philosophical Association* 79 (2005), 19–45. Matters are further complicated by the fact that Kant's term *Gemeinsinn*, which plays a major role in his *Critique of the Power of Judgment*, is also translated as "common sense," but might be better rendered as "common sensibility." In earlier work, I have argued that, despite an explicit interest in common sense right after Kant's Critical philosophy was introduced in Germany, serious misunderstandings, generated by figures such as Karl Reinhold, led to systematic confusions in the work of Kant's immediate successors. See Karl Ameriks, *Kant and the Fate of Autonomy: Problems in the Appropriation of the Critical Philosophy* (Cambridge: Cambridge University Press, 2000).

eighteenth-century figures, numerous disturbing prejudices appear, and some recent interpreters have therefore gone so far as to argue that they contaminate his entire philosophy.

No one study can aim to resolve all the problems with evaluating Kant's work, attitude, and impact. The aim of this volume is simply to add a new dimension to current discussions by exploring a few specific ways in which more attention needs to be given to the surprising *complexity*—both good and bad—of the influence (or lack of influence) of some of Kant's central concepts concerning issues such as race, religion, nationalism, colonialism, and cosmopolitanism. This still leaves out a lot of topics that merit discussion, such as Kant's relation to feminism, which fortunately has already received a considerable amount of sophisticated attention in recent years.[4] The main—but not exclusive—concern of the following chapters will be Kant's central concept of *human dignity* and how it has fared in relation to some highly influential writers whose connection with Kant has been considered rarely, if at all, in standard philosophical literature. Here the focus will be not on the likes of Karl Reinhold, J. G. Fichte, F. W. J. Schelling, or G. W. F. Hegel, let alone J. S. Mill or Henry Sidgwick, but on figures such as J. G. Herder, H. S. Chamberlain, Thomas Jefferson, Richard Price, and Thomas Mann. The figures in the latter group all had considerable influence in the political as well as intellectual world, but their relation to Kant's ideas is hardly well known, let alone adequately appreciated, by most contemporary philosophers.

Whatever the stance of their own views, contemporary philosophers are familiar with the fact that Kant's notion of human dignity, despite its many critics, still has a generally positive reputation and widespread influence. It is, after all, a notion that served as an inspiration for numerous leading Enlightenment thinkers within his own lifetime, and its insistence on absolute respect for human dignity directly influenced many post-World War II resolutions and constitutions. Nonetheless, there are contemporary scholars who, even apart from considerations of Kant's philosophy, resist the claim that universal human dignity is a fundamental and positive notion. Their opposition to the very idea takes several forms, many of which are rooted in fairly complicated philosophical beliefs that there are better concepts for guiding the improvement of individuals and modern societies.

Left-wing philosophers have tended to assume that any contemporary emphasis on dignity is typically tied to a policy of giving primacy to the notion of human

---

[4] See, e.g., essays in *Autonomy and Community: Readings in Contemporary Kantian Social Philosophy*, ed. Jane Kneller and Sidney Axinn (Albany: State University of New York Press, 1998); as well as Pauline Kleingeld, "On Dealing with Kant's Sexism and Racism," *SGIR Review* 2 (2019), 3–22; and Dilek Huseyinzadegan and Jordan Pascoe, "A Decolonial, Intersectional, and Materialist Feminist Re-appraisal of Kant's Notion of the Enlightenment: Complicity, Accountability, and Refusal," in *The Palgrave Handbook of German Idealism and Feminist Philosophy*, ed. Susanne Lettow and Tuija Pulkkinen (London: Palgrave Macmillan, 2023), 31–49.

4 KANTIAN DIGNITY AND ITS DIFFICULTIES

rights. In addition to objections concerning the vague, arbitrary, and self-interested nature of many rights claims, many leftists worry that the rhetoric of dignity tends to go hand in hand, not coincidentally, with merely providing legal protections for groups that are already relatively advantaged, while leaving unmet the urgent material needs and pressing structural demands of the exploited and ever-growing proletariat. Philosophers from a more traditional and broadly Aristotelian orientation can share these concerns and even combine them, as some of Alasdair MacIntyre's followers have, with traditional theological views that regard justice, in a deep ethical sense, as a more basic and useful notion.[5] This kind of position can also be espoused without reference to Thomistic ideas and can be based on a secular and communitarian critique of modern individualism. From this kind of perspective, a stress on Kant's notion of dignity can appear to threaten an appreciation of the primary need for society to be organized in a unified fashion around social structures, traditions, and progressive practices that have a real chance to achieve genuinely communal justice.

The critiques just described often presuppose that Kant's view must be tied to a narrow picture of moral life that is based primarily on contractual concerns, and on imagining how individuals characterized by little more than rational self-interest might construct an ideal society that they could at least visualize joining without fear of unfair treatment. In contrast to these kinds of criticisms, there are now many highly sophisticated expositions of Kant's philosophy that persuasively argue that his basic notion of value and dignity is the very opposite of possessive individualism and hyper-rationalist strategies that treat human life as a matter of constant market-like calculations.[6] Kant's system is not limited to claims about rights that should not be violated. It is very much about positive duties and all sorts of ways that people ought to be developing themselves and helping others, including through the cooperative construction of progressive social institutions. The Critical system culminates in the claim that we all should be oriented toward the highest good. Kant's version of this ideal involves a commitment to bringing about widespread happiness and flourishing social conditions in a way that, in principle, can be combined with most of what is clearly attractive in contemporary social theories of a neo-Aristotelian or even socialist kind.[7] Much more can

---

[5] See, e.g., Alasdair Macintyre, "Human Dignity: A Puzzling and Possibly Dangerous Idea" (lecture at the University of Notre Dame, November 2021). On the relation of the concept of dignity to claims about rights, see John Tasioulas, "Human Dignity and the Foundations of Human Rights," in *Understanding Human Dignity*, ed. Christopher McCrudden (Oxford: Oxford University Press, 2013), 293–314.

[6] See, e.g., the works of Marcia Baron, Barbara Herman, Thomas E. Hill, Jr., Onora O'Neill, and Allen W. Wood.

[7] Regarding the highest good, see Stephen Engstrom, "The Determination of the Concept of the Highest Good in Kant's Philosophy," in *The Highest Good in Kant's Philosophy*, ed. Thomas Höwing (Berlin: De Gruyter, 2016), 89–108. Regarding socialism, see Harry van der Linden, *Kantian Ethics and Socialism* (Indianapolis: Hackett, 1988); and Allen W. Wood, "Harry van der Linden, *Kantian Ethics and Socialism* (review)," *Idealistic Studies* 19 (1989), 271–3.

be said on all these issues but, in this study, the discussion of Kant's general philosophical concepts will be limited to matters that are most directly relevant to the notion of dignity and the specific historical contexts that will be examined in the following chapters.

Preview of Chapters: A Tale of Six Cities

The purpose of Chapter 1 is to provide a systematic background for the chapters that follow by characterizing and evaluating some of the main options in recent literature concerning how to define dignity in a way that fits Kant's texts and also has a chance of being intrinsically satisfactory. The chapter begins by quoting a number of key passages from Kant's main works to provide the framework for defining Kantian dignity in a manner that fits an approach to Kant's ethics that can be called the "mainline interpretation." Before positively elaborating the concept of a pure moral capacity, which is argued to be central to Kant's distinctive definition of dignity, critical attention is given to the tendency, in many treatments of Kant, to feature only simpler components of human nature, such as rationality, consistency, and the general capacity to set ends. In addition, a contemporary challenge to the mainline interpretation is examined in detail. To meet the objection that the mainline definition is not decisively supported by the texts, a detailed exegesis is offered of several key passages in Kant's works. Arguments are then presented against an objection to the very idea of grounding dignity on a person's possession of a capacity rather than on actual commitments and achievements. It is also argued that even some contemporary defenses of the mainline interpretation fall prey to unnecessary complications when they tie Kant's ethics to a version of constructivism that would wrongly deny dignity to a large class of human beings.

Even a successful completion of all the objectives of Chapter 1 would leave a lot undone. The chapter does not claim that there is a way to rigorously prove that human beings actually have dignity in Kant's strict sense, or even that his notion *by itself* points to clear norms that can be easily applied with sensible results. Other philosophies face similar limitations. With all theories that aim to offer something like the "groundwork" of a doctrine of morals, the road from the foundations of a moral theory to determining particular acts and policies requires empirical considerations that need to be context sensitive and are far from clear and certain in their implications. In addition, it must be admitted that several of Kant's own inferences and concrete proposals create special problems for contemporary readers. It will not be assumed that there is a convincing connection, for example, between Kant's basic notion of dignity and his defense of practices such as capital punishment. The following discussions are also not meant to imply that Kant's work is beyond criticism even if one goes so far as to have a sympathetic reaction to his philosophy in general and his notion of universal human dignity in particular. On the contrary, it will be argued that Kant himself, as well as some important figures who took themselves to be giving his system the highest respect, often betrayed the very principles that his basic notion of dignity was meant to protect.

Despite all these complications, there remain many points that count in Kant's favor, such as his influence on the fact that, in typical truly modern societies, certain procedures, such as public harassment or punishment of the innocent in order to threaten others for some distant end, are (at least in principle) clearly ruled out *from the start*. In what follows, a kind of innocent until proven guilty approach to Kant's system itself will be assumed so that, once the most relevant Kantian notion of dignity has been clarified, one can focus not on the minutiae of casuistry but on the following kinds of big questions: How well did Kant himself live up to the *most basic* principles that are explicitly tied to his notion of dignity? How well did various leading figures, who may be relatively neglected by philosophers today but who had considerable historical influence, *understand* Kant's notion? How significant were the *consequences* of their understanding, lack of understanding, or misunderstanding?

In addressing these questions, the chapters that come after Chapter 1 have a different kind of orientation, for their main focus is not directly on contemporary disputes but on the historical issues involved with the reception of Kant's philosophy. These chapters discuss a number of significant ways in which the concept of Kantian dignity has been seriously misunderstood, and in which opportunities to further elaborate, defend, or apply the concept have been neglected—often, by Kant himself. Instead of attempting to offer a continuous and exhaustive reception history, the chapters will attend to philosophical developments in five different historical and geographical contexts. The topics of these chapters have been selected because that they involve especially important international issues and happen to be interconnected in multiple striking ways that are still highly relevant to contemporary controversies. They bear on matters such as diversity, colonialism, racism, religion, and politics, as well as on metaphilosophical considerations about history and the role of philosophy in modernity. The chapters are not organized in strict chronological order because in some cases it helps to see, first, how certain problems in reacting to Kant became acute in the twentieth century and then, afterwards, one has a better sense of what to look for in re-examining events and ideas within Kant's own era.

Rather than returning to the considerable complexities of Kant's fundamental epistemological and metaphysical arguments, most of this book focuses on a number of little-known but highly significant aspects of the *cultural impact* of Kant's work. Given the numerous serious crises of our new millennium, it is only appropriate that the practical aspects of Kant's work and impact receive extra attention now. More specifically, the following chapters will consider Kant's relevance to a series of epochal events occurring in the revolutionary span from the eighteenth to the twentieth century. Special attention will be given, in order, to noteworthy developments centering in (2) the Baltics (*Königsberg*, *Riga*, and Prussia's relation to lands to its east), (3) *Berlin* (the rise of Fascism), (4) *Philadelphia* (the founding of the United States), (5) *London* (reactions to the French Revolution), and (6) *Washington* (reactions to World War I and World War II, discussed in three chapters concerning Thomas Mann's relation to Kant).

Chapter 2 concerns Kant's own Baltic area and argues that the very last work that Kant himself published, a Postscript for a German–Lithuanian dictionary, has a surprisingly important and close connection to some of his earliest philosophical efforts. In his first years as a lecturer, Kant's innovative and detailed treatment of empirical anthropological themes had a widespread influence and a long-term effect on his most famous student, Johann Gottfried Herder (1744–1803). Herder was a quick learner, and he soon left Königsberg (originally the seat of Prussia's king) and used his literary talents to write about his instructive time in Riga (where Kant's brother lived and Kant's most famous writings were published) and then his travel to other lands. He promptly developed his own kind of influential and pluralistic account of history and nationalities, one that many readers have assumed was in sharp contrast to Kant's insistence on a priori doctrines and largely rationalist views. The fact is, Kant and Herder always had much in common, although there were also some genuine differences. Just as Herder's approach needs to be qualified at certain points by a more rigorous Kantian treatment of epistemological and metaphysical issues, Kant's approach needs to be supplemented by the kind of extra attention that Herder gave to specific historical developments and local cultures. At the very end of his career, however, Kant made a little-known attempt to bridge some of these differences by acknowledging the special importance of a "friendly" respect for the diversity of cultures in smaller communities and, in particular, for the threatened Baltic languages with which he and Herder were directly acquainted. If only this side of Kant's thought had been developed further and more widely appreciated, there might have been fewer misguided attempts to appropriate Kant as a chauvinist—or to completely dismiss to him as one.

Chapter 3 focuses primarily on later developments within Germany in the era when it was led by autocrats (at first monarchists and then Fascists) in Berlin. Here the main question is *how* deeply Kant's philosophy can be linked to racism and anti-Semitism. Kant's long-term influence on Germany—albeit in a manner that often rested on shocking misinterpretations—was entangled with the most disastrous developments in German politics in many more ways than has generally been realized. Kant was not directly responsible for these developments, but he can be faulted for some unfortunate omissions as well as for still holding many of the worst prejudices of his time. Rather than attempting an exoneration or concluding with a blanket indictment, the chapter argues that, although serious

8 KANTIAN DIGNITY AND ITS DIFFICULTIES

charges can be leveled at some aspects of Kant's beliefs, it is important to distinguish the weaknesses in what was distinctive of Kant's own approach from the extreme errors of those who in some way may have been influenced by him but for the most part were guilty of distorting his ideas in an extraordinarily harmful manner.

The chapter compares and contrasts two recent critiques along this line: one by Michael Lackey, which discusses how Kant's terms were used by Houston Stewart Chamberlain and then the Fascists, and one by Paul W. Franks, who puts several of Kant's distressing comments in the context of German Idealism and anti-Judaism in general. The distinctive oddity of the prejudiced nature of some of Kant's views is that these views clearly contrast with the most fundamental orientation of his mature philosophy, and in particular his Critical doctrine that all human beings share basic capacities that give them a status of fundamental equality and dignity. The chapter concludes with a hypothesis that Kant's prejudices were not most deeply rooted specifically in racism but in a naïve elitist resistance to otherness as such (which is relevant to sexism as well), for this can explain why it appears to have concerned even racial and religious groups in North America that shared his own background in those respects but differed in other ways.

Chapter 4 develops this hypothesis in further detail by documenting the heretofore unappreciated fact that Kant was unusual, among leading Enlightenment figures, in not paying direct attention to the event of the July 1776 American Declaration of Independence in Philadelphia, let alone the enlightened doctrines and struggles of its philosophically astute leaders. This fact is all the more remarkable given the numerous close relations at the time between Germans and Americans, and the considerable attention that was given, within Germany, to the striking new form of American institutions, such as the outlawing of nobility and the official separation of church and state. This point has a broad and puzzling significance in view of the fact that Kant was, on the one hand, quite critical of England and colonialism in general and, on the other hand, he never took note of the fact that his own city, Königsberg, had a status that was the result of an eastward crusade that was itself a kind of colonizing project imposed by Germanic forces. An even more alarming fact is that later, when Hitler launched his monstrous eastward invasions, he modeled them on what he (like earlier European imperialists) thought was most significant about the United States, namely, that it seemed to owe its dramatic economic expansion to a ruthless treatment of native peoples and a willingness to enslave others and appropriate vast territory. Without denying the shameful side of American developments, it can be argued that, if only Kant had paid at least some direct attention to the uniquely progressive aspects of American developments, then—given his special stature—this might have helped to counter the kind of strictly chauvinist and unflattering picture of America that was developed by influential later writers and exploited by Fascist leaders. The chapter concludes with a brief discussion of arguments by

INTRODUCTION 9

Charles W. Mills and Lucy Allais, which point toward a diagnosis of the kind of "cognitive blindness" that Kant and others have exhibited on these issues.

Chapter 5 explores the surprising fact that, at the same time that Kant was developing his enlightened rationalist and broadly democratic normative philosophy in Germany, the renowned Welsh philosopher Richard Price was doing something quite similar but in an even more detailed and influential way in his London context—and yet these two major figures did not refer to each other and have very rarely been studied together. Unlike Kant, who was explicit only in his endorsement of the French Revolution, Price—in addition to having a distinguished career as a top scientist, liberal religious figure, and close advisor of numerous political leaders—waged a vigorous campaign in behalf of the American as well as the French struggle for independence. Price held that the direction of the English Glorious Revolution of 1688 pointed to a need for self-government elsewhere as well. Price's stirring support of the American independence movement had a major effect on developments in the colonies. This contrasts sharply with Kant's silence and his ignoring of parallel movements for freedom in Amsterdam that were inspired by what was happening in the United States in the early 1780s. (In his Enlightenment essay, he did not mention either government directly but they may well have been on his mind.[8]) The bold claim at the heart of the Declaration of Independence, that universal human equality is "self-evident," happens to fit a view that is central to Kant's philosophy as well as Price's. The claim is a radical one, however, and it understandably gives rise to the general philosophical question of what to make of a claim of self-evidence like this when it is presented in a revolutionary situation and in fact has not been stated anywhere else as forcefully in a political context.[9] This also leads to the contemporary philosophical question of in what sense Kant, or anyone who now subscribes to something like his view of basic moral doctrines, can defend the general notion of self-evident but still disputed principles. In discussing these points, the chapter draws on the work of contemporary scholars such as Danielle Allen, David Brink, Robert Audi, Sarah McGrath, and Thomas Kelly.

Chapters 6, 7, and 8 discuss Thomas Mann's life and work as a paradigmatic and multistage reaction to the whole tradition of German thought in Kant and after. The chapters present a detailed account of Mann's non-fictional writings and public activities as involving, at first, an especially striking example of yet another set of shocking set of misunderstandings about both Kant and the United States. Toward the end of World War I, Mann wrote a very lengthy and

---

[8] It is striking that, at one point in the 1780s (Auf [8: 41]), Kant uses the term *Freistaat* rather than *Republik*, which is the term that he usually uses. A *Freistaat*, or "free state," is a political entity that is independent in a sense but whose formal status and relation to other states is undefined—a status that can be said to fit developments right at that time in Amsterdam and the United States.

[9] On the general problem of introducing new ideas in a philosophical context, see Karl Ameriks, "The Very Idea of Innovation: From Descartes to Post-Kantianism," *Symphilosophie* 2 (2020), 247–71.

enthusiastic philosophical defense of the German cause and its authoritarian government in general. His defense had the bizarre feature of not only characterizing the Western powers as lacking in culture but also assuming that Kant's philosophy was in line with German chauvinism. In a Berlin lecture of 1922, however, Mann dramatically reversed course by explicitly endorsing the new German republic and urging the younger generation to reject all forms of extremism and support the nation's first democratic government. The most remarkable feature of this endorsement was that it was rooted in a newfound cosmopolitan attitude, a sudden appreciation by Mann of the fact that there was a common democratic link between his longtime favorites, the Early German Romantics (especially Novalis) and the writings and activities of Walt Whitman, whose *Democratic Vistas* (which had just appeared in a new German edition put together by one of Mann's best friends) is an especially powerful expression of the international significance of what is best in the fundamental principles of the post-Civil War United States.

Mann's belated appreciation of the American experiment in democracy was the crucial catalyst that allowed him to complete an elliptical path back to a proper understanding of what was truly best in his own German philosophical tradition. He also began to understand that the creative writers of the first Romantic generation had given the most appropriate and "lively" form to the enlightened practical principles of Kant's philosophy. In turning to the United States and eventually even emigrating there, Mann reversed his earlier errors. He developed many contacts with leaders in Washington and soon was vigorously campaigning, before the American entry into World War II, on behalf of engagement against the Fascists and in defense of democratic freedom. Mann's campaign overcame the provincialism that Kant had manifested in his worst moments and that Mann himself had exhibited, in a much more extreme form, in his World War I writings. Mann thereby accomplished a genuinely effective return to what was best about Kant and his closeness *in principle* (given the genuine meaning of his concept of dignity) to what is especially valuable about the new principles governing the United States.

The example of Mann is worth attending to in special detail not only because of the fact that he was regarded as the most significant German writer in the first half of the twentieth century but also because his career was not merely literary but expressed, most dramatically, a general tendency in German philosophical developments throughout the nineteenth century and after. Mann was reacting to two main waves of earlier German thought. There was, first, the Critical revolution in philosophy that was inaugurated by Kant and then made concrete by the enlightened and creatively pluralistic work of the Early Romantics of the Jena Circle, which flourished for a brief period right at the end of the eighteenth century. The second wave of philosophy that influenced Mann and most of his contemporaries was the late Romantic movement, which, in a broad sense, included Schopenhauer, Wagner, and especially Nietzsche. Although these authors, in line with a tendency that was shared by Hegel and Kierkegaard, declined to characterize themselves in Romantic terms—because they associated this word with chaotic or right-wing religious tendencies that developed mainly toward the mid-century— Mann understood them as part of an overarching Romantic orientation that always appealed to him.

The distinctive feature of this orientation in general was the emphasis it put on art and the role of the artist (especially literary figures). Most German philosophers, after the rise of modern science and the interminable conflicts that arose among the systematic Idealists that followed Kant, were unable to find any clearly positive role for late modern philosophy. Rather than giving in to the growing tendency to treat philosophy as just an incidental clarification of the methodology of modern science, Nietzsche and his allies held that, henceforth, philosophy should serve the purpose of helping to build a new aesthetic culture, that is, a late modern "tragic" culture that was beyond the belief that science, religion, materialism, or even anything like Kantian ethics could provide adequate guidelines for late modern agents.

Although there were, of course, numerous less radical German philosophers in this period, most of them were easily forgotten (one need only consider the list of insignificant figures who, unlike Nietzsche, had been able then to obtain a chair in philosophy in Germany), and none had an influence on early twentieth-century European culture that was comparable to Nietzsche's. In this context, Mann's philosophical reflections are worth unearthing in detail because he had an unusually accurate understanding, from early on, of both the powerful appeal and the significant dangers of the developments that led to Nietzsche and his pre-eminence in so many circles. Mann had a rare grasp of both the strengths and weaknesses of complex leading figures such as Hegel, Kierkegaard, Schopenhauer, and Wagner. Even when, in his early work, Mann was closest to Nietzsche's broadly aesthetic attitude, he had an awareness of its all too close connection to decadence and death, despite its enthusiastic rhetoric. The surprising fact is that it was only in his relation to Kant that Mann's philosophical beliefs were naive and had to undergo dramatic change later. Before 1922, Mann did not possess a truly Kantian concept of duty and dignity, for he claimed that there was a way to understand his own pro-Reich stance against the West as compatible with Kant's practical philosophy. It took a recollection of the significance of Early Romanticism—a movement for which Mann always had a special appreciation— to jar him into the recognition that this movement, in its best international forms, was held together by democratic and cosmopolitan principles, and that these Kantian principles were precisely what Germany needed to respect above all. If only more Germans had reached a similar understanding by the time that Mann had, the world might have been saved from the worst horrors of the century.

There is a further reason for paying special attention to Mann's words now, and this is because he displayed unusual foresight in eventually recognizing some of

12 KANTIAN DIGNITY AND ITS DIFFICULTIES

the greatest dangers for democracy in our own times—and he incorporated his insights in his highly successful creative writing as well. In the present context, however, it is necessary to avoid extra complications and so direct references will be minimal to what Mann is best known for, his prize-winning stories and novels This is not at all to deny that these writings are relevant, for most of them are at least implicitly concerned with the same issues that arise in his non-fiction. The literary works, however, are not written directly from Mann's own perspective but employ all sorts of highly subtle and ironic techniques that would complicate their interpretation in the following chapters, where the aim is to do justice, as efficiently as possible, to the neglected and most basic philosophical features of Mann's own beliefs and actions. Nevertheless, it is helpful from the start to keep in mind some remarks that occur in Mann's late novel *Doctor Faustus*.

In Chapter 34 the narrator is trying to make retrospective sense of the advent of "barbarism" in the twentieth century, and especially the enthusiasm in Germany for the disastrous political movements of the 1930s and before. With reference to Sorel's *Réflexions sur la violence*,[10] the narrator considers the thesis that "popular myths, or better, myths trimmed for the masses, would be the vehicle of political action—fables, chimeras, phantasms that needed to have nothing to do with truth, reason, or science to be productive, nonetheless, to determine life and history."[11] He then recounts how this "vehicle" in fact overwhelmed the masses, creating a new kind of illiteracy with obvious political dangers: "and the look on its advocates' faces grew all the more sardonically arrogant the more diligently one attempted to refute them on a basis that for them was totally irrelevant, on the basis of science, of respectable objective truth."[12] Not so long ago, these words may have seemed irrelevant for American citizens, and especially for those celebrating, without feeling a need for adequate evidence, "the end of history" (after the Berlin wall came down) and claims about a "mission accomplished" (after the first phase of the invasions in the Near East). Those days are gone, and there is general confusion about how to effectively counter the barbaric forces that have gained power even in circles and regions that once supported the realization of democratic ideals.

The example of Thomas Mann is a sobering reminder of how it was that, once upon a time, a progressive literary figure, and even one with a foreign background, could have a widespread positive effect on the American public. As Mann himself recognized, his style was highly literary and somewhat old-fashioned, and yet he also tried hard—and with noteworthy success then—to connect with a large audience. The victory of the Allies generated optimism for a while, but when

---

[10] See Georges Sorel, *Reflections on Violence* [1908], trans. Thomas Ernest Hulme, ed. Jeremy Jennings (Cambridge: Cambridge University Press, 1999).

[11] Thomas Mann, *Doctor Faustus: The Life of the Composer Adrian Leverkühn as Told by a Friend* [1947], trans. John E. Woods (New York: Alfred A. Knopf, 1997), 385–6.

[12] Mann, *Doctor Faustus*, 388.

Mann was finishing *Doctor Faustus* in California in 1947 (before his eventual return to Europe in 1952), his mood was gloomy and prophetic. He foresaw a time when (again, in the words of the narrator) there would be a retreat to "the ideographs of primitives," and people might say, "why words at all, why writing, why language?... [why not] abolish words and speech and converse solely by displaying the things themselves—although for discourse to take place one had to carry about as many things as possible on one's back."[13] Of course, Mann knew nothing of emojis, manipulated computers, and communication reduced to tweeting or acronyms, but for those who are familiar with such things, the challenge must be faced of finding a way, under new conditions, to make "truth, reason, or science to be productive nonetheless" so that responsible political action based on appreciation for genuine information can again gain sufficient traction.[14]

This book offers no "real world" solution for meeting this difficult challenge for this is a task that requires, at the least, an overcoming of the pernicious monopolistic forces that keep growing and radically reducing effective access, for those who most need it, to truthful content, impartial journalism, and fair representation. Perhaps, however, even an academic book like this can begin to stir into action some members of the new generation and at least serve as a reminder of how much influence words and philosophical ideas have had—and of how important it is to develop them properly and keep them from being misunderstood and misused.

The Political as Personal

To illustrate how closely interconnected the fates of the United States and Europe can be, and how important the doctrine of respect for all persons has become after Kant's era, I conclude this Introduction with a brief account of some facts behind my own interest in the topics of this book. More than a half-century ago, I happened to notice, on one of the first visits to my father-in-law's house in Mexico, a book that he had edited as a young international journalist. The book bears the title *I am an American*, and it contains a collection of brief essays that were originally presented as national radio broadcasts from Washington, DC in 1940.[15] The contributors are well-known figures, such as Albert Einstein, Thomas Mann, Igor Sikorsky, and Claudette Colbert, who had emigrated to the United States to escape the Fascist movements in Europe.

---

[13] Mann, *Doctor Faustus*, 388. Here Mann is invoking one of Jonathan Swift's satirical proposals.

[14] See, e.g., Onora O'Neill, *A Philosopher Looks at Digital Communication* (Cambridge: Cambridge University Press, 2022).

[15] *I am an American: By Famous Naturalized Americans*, ed. Robert Spiers Benjamin, with an Introduction by Archibald MacLeish, Foreword by Francis Biddle (New York: Alliance Book Corporation, 1941).

I did not study the book closely then but made a mental note of it, not only because of the significance of its authors but also because, like many others, I too came from a family that, as refugees and "displaced persons," had emigrated to the United States from Europe (although, in our case, not until 1949). Our arrival in the United States was facilitated largely by the help of a midwestern American woman (Lula Jean Elliott, who became my godmother in Munich) working with the United Nations Relief and Rehabilitation Administration. This woman happened to employ and befriend my mother, because my mother could speak English (and even its American version) as the result of the fact that her parents had fled to the United States from the Baltic area during the early twentieth-century revolts in Russia. Documents show that my maternal grandfather was admitted to the United States in 1906 at Fishkill, New York, on the condition that he renounce any allegiance to the czar and swear not to practice polygamy. (I never met any of my grandparents but presume that they would not have found such a condition onerous.) Further political unrest kept the family in Brooklyn until 1914, when my mother was born as an American citizen and then World War I broke out. As a consequence, the family never made it back to Riga until the early 1920s, but by then my mother had learned enough English that she could eventually get a job as a language teacher back in the family's native land, which meanwhile had just gained independence and relative prosperity. Little did she know that her family's first experience with emigration would provide just what was needed when later, at the end of World War II, it was crucial, as refugees, to connect with Western troops.

The thought of these experiences has become ever more vivid with the awful developments of our new millennium, in which wars and inhumane practices have generated a huge third wave of refugees worldwide. The thought became especially vivid when, a couple years ago, I had the good fortune to hear an inspiring lecture that Frido Mann gave when he was on a cross-country tour. He was repeating, in his own way, his grandfather's famous pre-World War II "Democracy Will Win!" campaign, which had attracted sold-out audiences across the United States. This experience convinced me of the need to research Thomas Mann's career in earnest, and the project proceeded quickly once it became clear that Mann was, surprisingly, most deeply *philosophically* influenced by my own heroes, Immanuel Kant and the Early Romantics.[16]

At first, I did not realize that, like my own family, Mann experienced two key stages of personal transition in relation to Europe and America: a first stage, in the 1920s, when a positive intellectual bond between the two cultures was forged in his mind, and a second stage in the era of World War II, when flight to the West

[16] Another catalyst was a gathering in San Diego, where Wolfgang Ertl pointed out the significance of the new center for scholars that the German government had recently set up at the Thomas Mann house in Pacific Palisades.

became imperative. It was not until almost the final research on this topic was completed that I understood the significance of Mann's 1940 "I am an American" radio address, for that occasion gave him perhaps his largest audience ever, and at a pivotal moment in world history. The book containing the addresses was not only edited by my father-in-law, but the whole project happened to be largely the responsibility of his mother-in-law, who was in charge then of a division of the United States Immigration and Naturalization Service. I also learned that not only had a professor of German, right at Notre Dame, written extensively on Mann's wartime activities but, most recently, he had even completed an article specifically about Mann's 1940 radio address.[17] All this is just a reminder of how we live in a small world, and if only more citizens would bother to look around, they would probably find out that their own roots, and those of many of their acquaintances, also contain stories of similar international connections and of being indebted to the chance—which millions do not have—of being able, when necessary, to relocate from one country to another. It is worth keeping in mind that the value of these physical transitions is in large part dependent on there being at least some safe harbors in the world, countries where the most fundamental ideals that inspired the European Enlightenment and the founders of the United States are, at least to some extent, still put into practice.

Kantian Dignity and its Difficulties. Karl Ameriks, Oxford University Press. © Karl Ameriks 2024.
DOI: 10.1093/9780198917656.003.0001

---

[17] Tobias Boes, "'I'm an American': Thomas Manns Zusammenarbeit mit der amerikanischen Einwanderungsbehörde INS," *Thomas Mann Jahrbuch* 35 (2022), 73–85. On October 2, 2023, the Nanovic Institute for European Studies of the University of Notre Dame hosted an exhibit, created by the Thomas Mann house, on Mann's "Democracy Will Win!" campaign, with talks by Tobias Boes, Jan Vondráček, and Meike Werner.

1

The Distinctiveness of Kantian Dignity: Its Meaning and Relevance

> ...morality and humanity, insofar as it is *capable of morality* [emphasis added], is that which alone has dignity. Skill and diligence in work have a market price; wit, lively imagination and humor have a fancy price...(GMS [4: 435]).

This chapter defends a "mainline interpretation" of Kant's basic concept of dignity as an unconditional, all-or-nothing, and inviolable feature of all human beings, one that deserves universal respect. This contrasts with earlier notions of dignity that make it a matter of contingent rank or a certain degree of achievement that can be gained or lost by individuals. Kant's concept is explained as rooted in a universal human capacity of reason for morality, and specifically duty in a pure sense that is ultimately aimed at the highest good, and with a meaning that is compatible with a form of moral realism. Understandings of dignity in terms of achievement or mere rationality are criticized as inappropriate and not representative of Kant's own view. The contemporary interpretations of Paul Formosa, Richard Dean, and others are evaluated in this context.

1.1 Defining Kantian Dignity: The Textual Background

A natural way to organize a characterization of dignity in a Kantian context is to make use of his table of categories and the fourfold scheme of quantity, quality, relation, and modality (cf. KpV [5: 66]). There are two prime models of dignity in European history,[1] and they differ most fundamentally with respect to *modality*.

---

[1] See Michael Rosen, *Dignity: Its History and Meaning* (Cambridge, MA: Harvard University Press, 2012); and *Dignity: A History*, ed. Remy Debes (Oxford: Oxford University Press, 2017). Rosen's book gives a helpful contrast of Kant's unconditional notion of human dignity, as based in our pure moral capacity, with pre-Kantian views that refer to a basis in general values, social status, or graceful behavior. He also shows the tensions between the original Catholic attitude against a focus on dignity, because of its association with liberal movements, and the reversal that occurred with Jacques Maritain and his influence on the United Nations charter, and then the drafting of the constitution of the Federal Republic of Germany. Rosen rejects Kant's metaphysical approach, but he ends up agreeing that human dignity is connected with an important value because of the respect that is always proper even in regard to the deceased. The book edited by Debes discusses an even wider variety of conceptions of dignity. In "Respect: A History," in *Respect: Philosophical Essays*, ed. Richard Dean and

THE DISTINCTIVENESS OF KANTIAN DIGNITY   17

In contrast to centuries of using the term "dignity" primarily in contexts concerning persons who happen to have a *degree* of value, as a matter of fortune or accomplishment, Kant has been understood, by most philosophers, as having introduced a strong stress on dignity as an unconditional (in *modality*) and all-or-nothing (in *quality*) feature that distinguishes persons as a matter of *metaphysical necessity*.[2] Typical passages in line with this view are the following:

> ...reason, in the consciousness of its dignity, regards with contempt...a mixed doctrine of morals, composed of feelings and inclinations and at the same time with rational concepts...that can lead only very *contingently* [emphasis added] to what is good, but quite often also to what is evil (GMS [4: 411]).

> For duty is [understood] to be practical *unconditional* [emphasis added] necessity of action; it must thus hold for all rational beings (to which an imperative can at all apply), and *only in virtue of this* be a law also for every human will. By contrast, whatever is derived from the special natural disposition of humanity, from certain feelings and propensity, and indeed even, possibly, from a special tendency *peculiar to human* [emphasis added] reason, and would not have to hold *necessarily* [emphasis added] for the will of every rational being—that can indeed yield a maxim for us, but not a law...(GMS [4: 425]).

> In the realm of ends [*Reich der Zwecke*] everything has either a **price** or a **dignity**. What has a price can be replaced by something else, as its *equivalent*; whereas what is elevated above any price, and hence allows of no equivalent, has a dignity.

> What refers to general human inclinations and needs has a *market price*; what, without even presupposing a need, conforms with a certain taste, i.e. a delight in the mere purposeless play of the powers of our mind, has a *fancy price*; but what constitutes the *condition* [emphasis added] under which something *can* [emphasis added] be an end in itself does not merely have a relative worth, i.e. a price, but an inner worth, i.e. *dignity* (GMS [4: 434–5]).

> The *essence* [emphasis added] of things is not altered by their external relations; and it is according to what alone—without thinking of the latter—constitutes

---

Oliver Sensen (Oxford: Oxford University Press, 2022), 1–25, Debes documents how, throughout the nineteenth century in the Anglophone world, the Kantian concept of respect for dignity did not figure directly in discussions. The lack of continuous engagement with Kant's thought (which for a time was also overshadowed by other movements in Germany, as well as by the reactions to Napoleon's wars), in addition to Kant's own failure to connect more positively with other countries (as will be argued in the following chapters), is no doubt part of the explanation for the serious misunderstandings that occurred later.

[2] See Thomas E. Hill, Jr., *Dignity and Practical Reason in Kant's Moral Theory* (Ithaca, NY: Cornell University Press, 1992), 166–7: "one should note that the moral worth in question here [of specific actions] is not the same as the 'intrinsic value' or 'dignity' of persons. Kant ascribes to human personality a worth that is not diminished or increased by what the person does."

18 KANTIAN DIGNITY AND ITS DIFFICULTIES

the *absolute* [emphasis added] worth of a human being…(GMS [4: 439], "absolute" missing in the Cambridge translation).

The words given in italics with emphasis added—"contingently," "unconditional," "peculiar to human," "condition," "can," "capable of morality," "essence," "absolute"—are explicitly modal. They are the ones that are most important in the following considerations, although appreciating their significance requires some prior clarifications regarding some other concepts. The quoted passages are all from Kant's *Groundwork of the Metaphysics of Morals* of 1785, but the views expressed are a constant in Kant's mature philosophy and appear in his late works as well, such as *The Metaphysics of Morals* of 1797:

> But a human being regarded as a *person*, that is, as the subject of morally practical reason, is exalted above any price…as an end in himself, he possesses a dignity (an *absolute* [emphasis added] inner worth) by which he exacts respect for himself from all other rational beings in the world (MdS [6: 435]; cf. MdS [6: 462]).

Already in the early 1760s, Kant's private remarks reveal a life-changing commitment, inspired by reading Rousseau, to the notion that human beings are distinguished, above all, by a faculty of absolutely free choice. For Kant, this fact implies that personhood falls under the relational category of *substance*.[3] Duty therefore basically concerns a *normative* necessity governing the fundamental *relation*s of personal substances (including the relation of self-respect) and enjoining an acknowledgement of the status of all persons as equal and independent agents. This claim is repeated in many writings and is formulated perhaps most concisely in a note taken from a recently edited anthropology lecture from 1784–5: "A human being is free by nature, and all human beings are equal" (V-AnMrong [25: 1419]). Our basic duty is to use our own free regard to give equal respect to all persons—and not only immediately and individually but also as fellow participants in what Kant calls a *Reich der Zwecke*, that is, a realm of ends that, in a human context, is best thought of as ultimately taking the form of a cosmopolitan federation of republics and not an empire or "kingdom" (contrary to how the phrase is usually translated).[4] Ideally, this realm is a globally-oriented sphere of end-setting agents cooperating together to build, for everyone, an

---

[3] See Kant, KrV A 361 and B 408; and Karl Ameriks, *Kant's Theory of Mind: An Analysis of the 'Paralogisms of Pure Reason'* (Oxford: Clarendon Press, 1982; expanded edition 2000), ch. 4.

[4] See Otfried Höffe, *Kant's Cosmopolitan Theory of Law and Peace*, trans. Alexandra Newton (Cambridge: Cambridge University Press, 2006); and Pauline Kleingeld, *Kant and Cosmopolitanism: The Philosophical Ideal of World Citizenship* (Cambridge: Cambridge University Press, 2012). This is not to deny that, with an eye to a broader context, Kant also speaks of the *Reich der Zwecke* as headed by a supreme being, and in that sense a "kingdom."

all-encompassing moral community with myriad nested forms of interactive harmony that promote independent development as well as beneficent practices.[5] Hence, Kant treats dignity *quantitatively* as a doubly *universal* feature of human life, one according to which all are to work for all.

1.2 Interpretive Controversies

Even if it is accepted that dignity in its basic sense applies to all persons, this fact, just by itself, does not tell us who, among all the beings that we may encounter, are actually persons, or precisely what it is about the faculty of free choice that gives them dignity and makes this feature so crucial. The response to this problem that will be defended in this book, for exegetical as well as general philosophical reasons, is one that rests on understanding Kantian freedom as part of a "thick" notion of the *basic capacities* of persons, one involving a primary definition of freedom in positive rather than neutral terms.[6] Such a characterization is a

---

[5] See Barbara Herman, *The Moral Habitat* (Oxford: Oxford University Press, 2021); and Karl Ameriks, "Barbara Herman, *The Moral Habitat* (review)," *Notre Dame Philosophical Reviews*, 2022.08.05.

[6] Kant clarified this best in his final published exchange with Karl Reinhold. See Karl Ameriks, "Ambiguities in the Will: Reinhold and Kant, *Briefe 2*," in *Studia Reinholdiana: Tagungsband der Reinhold-Tagung in Siegen 2010*, ed. Martin Bondeli and Marion Heinz (Berlin: De Gruyter, 2012), 71–90. Kant can easily defeat Reinhold's proposal—that freedom must be *defined* in terms of an option between accepting or resisting temptation—because this would mean that a being unlike us, such as God, could not be free. Kant has good reasons for saying that we should instead think at first in terms of positive freedom. Nonetheless, readers can be misled by the way he speaks at times about the positive (moral law) *conception* of freedom as "flowing" from the negative conception (GMS [4: 446], KpV [5: 33]), as if there is a reciprocal *logical* connection. Kant cannot mean that kind of connection, for as he writes in the Antinomies of the first *Critique* (A 445/B 473), one logically permissible way to understand, in general, the negative freedom of something is simply to describe it in terms of having an "absolute beginning" because it is not determined by anything. From that description nothing positive (let alone something specifically moral) can be deduced—and not even if one switches to speaking in non-phenomenal rather than phenomenal terms. It also does not help to claim that if, phenomenally speaking, things are governed by an external law, then speaking non-phenomenally requires something governed by an internal law. That does not immediately follow, and even if an internal law is granted, it could be a feature of an intellectual monadology that has no logical connection with morality. The way to begin to see what Kant likely has in mind is to appreciate what he says at GMS [4: 463] about how, just as speculative reason "leads to" an "absolute necessity of a supreme cause of the *world*," so too practical reason leads to an unconditional necessity of action. This is merely a description of how reason naturally *thinks* because it is defined as a faculty positing the unconditioned. This does not mean that Kant assumes all of reason's thoughts like this are true, let alone logically compelling. In the context of the second *Critique*, Kant's talk about the close relation of positive and negative freedom should be understood as a *consequence* of his crucial claim that for us the moral law is *the ratio cognoscendi* of freedom (KpV [5: 4, note]). What Kant is making clear here is that, on his view, it is through positive freedom (the law, as applying to us) that we "first become aware of freedom," including the absolute freedom of choice. This is worth repeating: we cannot justifiably affirm our freedom in the negative sense (our choice not being determined by anything outside, but absolutely by ourself) before we have affirmed our freedom in the positive, normatively informed, sense. Hence (contrary to what some interpreters have suggested), the affirmation of positive freedom arises *not* from an internal *entailment* from something simply negative to something positive but simply because an affirmation of positive freedom (in moral capacity) must already be our premise in this

20 KANTIAN DIGNITY AND ITS DIFFICULTIES

first step in understanding the claim that all beings equipped with the capacities essential for freedom deserve the status of dignity in a sense that has substantive normative consequences. There remain, however, many controversies, textual as well as systematic, about exactly what is meant by "basic capacities" in this context, and about whether the meanings that are relevant are (and should be) broad enough to include everyone with human parents.

These controversies concern the *qualitative* as well as quantitative characterization of dignity. Although most traditional Kantians stress the all-or-nothing version of the concept expressed in the passages that have been quoted (and which Kant believes can apply to higher spiritual beings as well), it must be conceded that there are also numerous occurrences of the term—especially in most discussions before Kant but also in some of Kant's own texts—in which dignity is spoken of in a way that involves *degrees* of goodness (for example, "a certain sublimity and *dignity* in the person who fulfills all his duties" (GMS [4: 439–40])). This should not be surprising, however, since it is quite understandable that on occasion Kant would make use of the familiar old meaning that his readers would easily understand. This kind of ambiguity is common with other philosophical terms, and it should not count against the focus of the arguments of this book, as well as of what I will call *mainline* interpretations in general,[7] which primarily concern the relatively new unconditional meaning that Kant employs in the famous passages that were quoted and have made his philosophy especially influential.

The ambiguities of "dignity" resemble those of several other key Kantian terms. For example, there are many passages, such as the one cited from *The Metaphysics of Morals*, in which Kant treats the concept of *respect* as a correlate of dignity and with a similar double meaning. In a Kantian context, respect is fundamentally directed to the moral law and the all-or-nothing capacity for appreciating the law, which is possessed by all beings with the status of dignity (see GMS [4: 401, note] and the quotation from MdS [6: 462] in section 1.7). There are, however, also contexts in which respect can understandably be said to be appropriate in various degrees in proportion to the value of the particular intentions and qualities that are assessed. (For example, "I respected her *a lot* for what she *did* in those circumstances.") Another term with this kind of ambiguity is "character." In ordinary contexts, this term can have a contingent meaning and thus Kant can speak, as

---

context. But it is true that *then* we are thinking of both kinds of freedom, and so in just that sense our thoughts of them are "reciprocal."

[7] Henry E. Allison gives a classic formulation of the mainline view when he defines dignity in terms of "the capacity to recognize and obey the categorical imperative." *Kant's Groundwork of the Metaphysics of Morals: A Commentary* (Oxford: Oxford University Press, 2011), 114. A similar position can be found in works by, e.g., Thomas E. Hill, Jr., Rae Langton, G. Felicitas Munzel, and Jens Timmermann. Paul Formosa, in *Kantian Ethics, Dignity and Perfection* (Cambridge: Cambridge University Press, 2017), 131, lists several other leading Kant scholars with a similar orientation on this issue: Reinhard Brandt, Volker Gerhardt, Otfried Höffe, Patrick Kain, and Ludwig Siep.

others do, of people as lacking character (that is, of not yet having a good character) or, at a certain point in life, as finally developing character for a first time. (Kant suggests that this point comes around the age of 40—which not everybody reaches.) But there is also a more relevant and unconditional meaning of the term in Kant's transcendental philosophy. Kant uses this meaning when he says that each person has an overall "empirical character" that is the phenomenal reflection of that person's underlying and timeless "intelligible character" (KrV A 539/B 567). One can never lack or gain character in this basic sense and, in that way, like dignity, it is a necessary and permanent feature of persons. The particular kind of moral character that an individual has, however, is constituted by the specifics of the basic attitude underlying all of that person's free choices and so, in this sense, intelligible character can vary from person to person.[8]

An additional complication arises when, in his late book on religion, Kant speaks of a possible "revolution" in one's commitment to morality (in a positive direction, in contrast to one's earlier priorities) that can seem to entail a complete division of character within what appears to be one person over time (Rel [6: 47]). This idea admittedly puts a strain on the view that each person has one and only one intelligible character. There may be a way, however, to understand the metaphysics underlying this talk of revolution as still consistent with Kant's system and as signifying what is, to be sure, a significant apparent discontinuity in one's empirical character but one that is rooted in a single timeless ground that has "not been earned in time" (Rel [6: 25]). This underlying character does not itself change even when it is expressed in a dramatically shifting fashion, just as a major change in attitude by a character in a novel can still be rooted all along in the author's single underlying conception of that character.[9] For Kant, the conversion to moral commitment that occurs in a revolution is not to be understood as a miracle, let alone a form of schizophrenia. It depends on a capacity that was in the person all along but one that, like an underground germ, could develop only after the person has reacted to its having been covered over by an "immature" attitude that was "self-incurred" (Auf [8: 35]). In this sense, even the best individual revolution will involve a unity in complexity that expresses a far from holy character overall, one afflicted by what Kant calls the "radical evil" in all of us (Rel [6: 19]).

Another basic term that has a central role and multiple meanings in Kant's system is "worth." Kant speaks not only of the absolute worth of persons as such, but also of the special moral worthiness of the virtuous, as well as of the moral worth

---

[8] On the significance of the notion of character for understanding the ambiguities in Kant's conception of good will, see Karl Ameriks, "Kant on the Good Will," in *Grundlegung zur Metaphysik der Sitten: Ein kooperativer Kommentar*, ed. Otfried Höffe (Frankfurt: Klostermann, 1989), 45–65.

[9] For a discussion of the relation between Kant's "revolutionary" and "gradualist" accounts of moral development, see, e.g., Formosa, *Dignity*, 187; and Karl Ameriks, *Kant and the Fate of Autonomy* (Cambridge: Cambridge University Press, 2000), ch. 7, and "Once Again: The End of All Things," in *Kant on Persons and Agency*, ed. Eric Watkins (Cambridge: Cambridge University Press, 2018), 213–30.

22 KANTIAN DIGNITY AND ITS DIFFICULTIES

of particular (properly motivated) actions and numerous act-types. These meanings are necessarily connected, because the absolute worth of persons implies a capacity to do deeds that are individually worthy and that instantiate worthy act-types that are prescribed by our fundamental duties. Confusion can arise if one mistakenly believes that the Kantian view implies that if a person only does deeds that are individually unworthy, one thereby loses all moral worth and dignity (see the discussion of MdS [6: 463] in section 1.7, note 72). It is important to keep in mind that, despite Kant's doctrine of an original propensity for evil in all human beings, this is a matter of free will and not of fate or a doom predestined for us by anything external, such as the sin of ancestors.[10]

1.3 Recent Interpretations

The ambiguities in Kant's terminology can lead some philosophers to speak in terms that can suggest Kant has two completely different notions of dignity. One might get this impression by quickly scanning, for example, Paul Formosa's *Kantian Ethics, Dignity and Perfection* (2017). Formosa's study is worth considering at length because its interpretive and philosophical positions are developed in impressive detail. Except for a few differences that will be discussed, its views on Kant and dignity are also quite similar to the ones that will be defended in this book. In contrast to the "status dignity" that persons have from early on, Formosa introduces a basic notion of "achievement dignity," which applies to persons only after, and on the basis of, significant moral accomplishments.[11] There are admittedly several passages in Kant that speak of instances of dignity in something like these terms (although he does not use the word "achievement"), and in general some distinction between a person's fundamental status and particular actions is certainly warranted. Nonetheless, it would be misleading to speak simply in terms of two species of dignity and not immediately emphasize that they are closely connected by a necessary relation of positive dependence. On Formosa's own analysis, situations of achievement dignity can also be described simply as examples of what Kant means by virtue.[12] Virtuous instances of achievement dignity are nothing other than the appropriate development of the basic capacity that defines a person as a being with status dignity, whereas status dignity itself is not an achievement but comes with the very constitution of a person.[13]

---

[10] See, e.g., Paul Formosa, "Kant on the Radical Evil in Human Nature," *Philosophical Forum* 38 (2007), 221–45.

[11] Formosa, *Dignity*, 70, and 125, 168.   [12] Formosa, *Dignity*, 168.

[13] See Onora O'Neill, *Constructions of Reason: Explorations of Kant's Practical Philosophy* (Cambridge: Cambridge University Press, 1989), 76; and Karl Ameriks, "Vindicating Autonomy: Kant, Sartre, and O'Neill," in *Kant on Moral Autonomy*, ed. Oliver Sensen (Cambridge: Cambridge University Press, 2013), 53–70.

THE DISTINCTIVENESS OF KANTIAN DIGNITY   23

All these points are in accord with mainline interpretations, which typically stress linking Kantian dignity all at once with necessity, universality, all-or-nothingness, and a fundamental insusceptibility to loss throughout life. There remain complications, however, because there are alternative readings according to which the quantitative and qualitative options need not be in alignment with each other. On these readings, one can hold that only some human beings have dignity, and their dignity is fundamentally a matter of degree and need not be permanent. There are also *historical* complications. As has been noted, dignity was regarded for a long time as just a matter of degree and/or rank, that is, as tied to the concept of sublimity and the quality of being *above others* in some respect (such as noble birth, talent, achievement) that distinguishes one's self from "lower" human beings and/or other animals. As will be discussed, this is a conception that a few interpreters have even taken to determine Kant's primary understanding of the term.[14] On a rank conception, dignity *can* be (although it does not have to be) regarded as a feature that in the past only a limited group of human beings *have held* (and in that case either as a matter of degree or of being simply "in" or "out"), and also as such that *now*, after the onset of modernity, practically all human beings can be said to have been elevated, by society, to a fully equal status of rank as citizens. At that point, dignity has become no longer a distinguishing factor within our species even if it is one with respect to other ("lower") species.[15]

There are additional complications with the notion of dignity in regard to its *epistemological* status. Various versions of dignity have seemed manifestly evident to some people and yet, even in the same era, manifestly non-evident or even dubious to others.[16] The institution of nobility, for example, went unquestioned for centuries. Now, however, in much of the modern world after the revolutions of the late eighteenth century, any substantive notion of nobility is widely— although not yet universally—regarded as superstitious and even insulting to the dignity of humanity in general. This is a complex issue because there are also numerous theoretical propositions that were at one time regarded as *evidently*

---

[14] See Section 1.7 for a discussion of an interpretation of Kant by Richard Dean that emphasizes a non-universal notion of human dignity that requires some degree of moral commitment. In *Kant on Human Dignity* (New York and Berlin: De Gruyter, 2010), Oliver Sensen presents a view that has some similarities with Dean's, and he documents the fact that in Kant's writings most uses of the *term* "dignity" involve a notion of comparative rank. This point is consistent, however, with still holding that Kant's *distinctive* emphasis on the philosophical concept of dignity concerns an unconditional all-or-nothing meaning, one that can also give all persons a status of rank that is at a whole other level than that of other beings. Sensen's approach is critically discussed in Dieter Schönecker and Elke Elisabeth Schmidt, "Kant's Ground-Thesis: On Dignity and Value in the Groundwork," *Journal of Value Inquiry* 52 (2018), 81–95. See also Patrick Kain, "Dignity and the Paradox of Method," in *Realism and Antirealism in Kant's Moral Philosophy: New Essays*, ed. Elke Elisabeth Schmidt and Robinson dos Santos (Berlin: De Gruyter, 2017), 67–90.

[15] See Jeremy Waldron, *One Another's Equals: The Basis of Human Equality* (Cambridge, MA: Harvard University Press, 2017).

[16] See Ch. 5.

24 KANTIAN DIGNITY AND ITS DIFFICULTIES

true even by the best scientists and logicians (for example, the universal applicability of Euclidean geometry), and yet at a later time it became clear that these seemingly noncontroversial propositions are not even true. Such changes should not, however, be taken to show by themselves that the notion of evident truth needs to be jettisoned (for even the refutation of earlier claims often relies on the general notion of something being evident) rather than simply qualified by a form of fallibilism.[17] Similarly, the fact that generations of educated people thought it evident that the institution of slavery is morally acceptable, and that countless Fascists believed that their extermination-oriented versions of racism were evidently correct, does not by itself undercut the view that now we can properly claim to know some evident truths about these matters.[18] Whether or not the specific term "evident" is used, it is hard to construct any epistemology that does not rely on accepting the general reliability of our faculties and of their access to some immediately recognized truths, such as, for example, that subjects, objects, other minds, and common faculties for space, time, and language exist.

For all these reasons, there is no ground for dismissing from the start, as simply "dogmatic,"[19] the widespread practice of taking it to be evident that human beings have a kind of unconditional dignity—although a lot depends on the context and manner in which this practice takes place.[20] The fact that many others have held directly opposite beliefs does not matter if there are all sorts of not very complicated ways to explain how it is that they came to their mistaken beliefs. We can, after all, understand the psychological pressures and misleading factual claims that converted millions of people into fanatical Fascists, and we can also understand how, once they were given a chance to see matters in a broader context, it was no surprise that there was an almost immediate and universal renunciation of earlier claims taken to be evident. Similarly, *if* we actually knew—which we do not—that there is a convincing "brainwashing" explanation, for example, of a Nietzschean or pseudo-Freudian kind, that has demonstrated that the unconditional notion of personal dignity is nothing more than a sick illusion, then, and only then, could we *immediately* rule it out of court as a relevant candidate for evident status. In the meantime, it remains evidently worthwhile to try to clarify this notion further, in order better to understand its historical role and compare it with alternatives.

These issues are also connected with a difficult *methodological* question, namely, whether the status of human dignity is best understood as requiring, for its appreciation, complex philosophical reflection or whether, instead, it is

---

[17] See Robert Audi, *The Good in the Right: A Theory of Intuition and Intrinsic Value* (Princeton: Princeton University Press, 2004).

[18] Formosa, *Dignity*, 46, suggests that the example of Nazis undermines claims of "immediate recognition" of dignity. The example does, of course, create a challenge, but there are ways that the intuitionist can reply.

[19] Formosa, *Dignity*, 51, n. 47.   [20] See Ch. 5.

basically rooted in the implicit presumptions of unconfused "common sense." Given all these complexities and varied opinions, it is important to have a clear notion, from the start, about the feature, or set of features, *most plausibly* regarded as necessary and sufficient for holding that a person has dignity in the basic sense that is most relevant for understanding Kant's own philosophy as well as his significance for our contemporary situation.

1.4 Problems with a Common Line of Interpretation

So far, the mainline view of Kantian dignity has been characterized as one that emphasizes the features of necessity over contingency, all-or-nothing status over rank and degree, and thoroughgoing universality over particularity, with respect to the agents themselves as well as the scope of their proper concerns. What still needs to be explained is how this emphasis is understandably rooted in a particular feature that, in the most relevant way, involves what Kant goes on to call the "keystone" of his system, namely, freedom (KpV [5: 3]). Formosa discusses a number of options, and he eventually develops a "thick" conception of the most relevant capacity of persons, a capacity that will also be argued for here as most appropriate. Nonetheless, there are also some thinner formulations, even in his work, that can be somewhat misleading *if* taken simply by themselves. It is instructive to examine these formulations first because they are similar to troublesome proposals that are found elsewhere in discussions of Kant. A lot hangs on these matters, because a major point in the chapters that follow is that different ways of responding to Kant's notion of dignity have had a huge, still underappreciated, and sometimes disastrous impact—not only on Kant exegesis but also on major developments in German culture and history, and then on all that Germany has had an effect on in recent centuries.

Formosa's account begins with a typical, but rather rough, expression of what he intends to present as the Kantian position. He formulates this position at first in terms that presumably are meant to express not only Kant's own view but also Kant's view of the implicit position of all modern agents insofar as they can overcome (as he believes that, in principle, they all can) the confusions of their self-incurred immaturity: "...dignity is something we each have despite the many imperfections of our rational capacities and which we retain even as our rational capacities grow, develop, fluctuate and even decline."[21] The two crucial notions in

---

[21] Formosa, *Dignity*, 1. Although we often speak of capacities that "grow," in this context it seems best to say that the *capacities* themselves do not literally grow. They stay the same, but various catalysts make it possible for (what I prefer to call) one's *capabilities*, and then one's *talents*, to develop on their basis, and these in turn can lead to various kinds of growth in one's *achievements*. And, of course, there may well be reasons for distinguishing even more than these four levels. One complication is that we often casually say that people are "incapable" of certain things, where we can mean either that

26   KANTIAN DIGNITY AND ITS DIFFICULTIES

this statement are "rational" and "capacity." For a long time, and in many different contexts, Anglophone discussions of Kant's ethics have often assumed that Kant's distinctive concern is with rationality that may take a fairly minimal form, one sometimes involving the mere notion of formal consistency. In another introductory passage in which even Formosa *might seem* to be concerned mostly with this minimal concept, he says "the core idea" of the Kantian approach is that we should "interact with each other first and foremost (but not exclusively) as rational beings who can choose how we will act on the basis of reasoned deliberation."[22] This passage reflects the fact that Kant, like many philosophers, believes that human beings are in fact distinctive already in their mere capacity to act on the basis of *any* reasons at all, that is, to deliberate about reasons and decide to choose in light of that deliberation. (Kant holds that other animals can choose, in the sense of selecting, for example, one kind of food rather than another, but he distinguishes that ability from any capacity for *rational* choice.[23]) Furthermore, this passage also fits the fact that there are aspects of Kant's own mode of argumentation, in his feverishly composed *Groundwork*, that can give the impression that substantive moral principles can be determined by a "categorical imperative procedure" that simply uses a "Formula of Universal Law." By exposing contradictions in common maxims when universalized, Kant's discussion of this formula can appear to suggest that neutral considerations, that is, with a minimal conception of rationality as a matter of mere consistency (of thought and will) and universality, can generally be sufficient to determine what kinds of actions are morally proper (GMS [4: 421]).

Fortunately, most recent interpreters have come to appreciate how much even the arguments of the *Groundwork* turn out to rely not merely on the Formula of Universal Law but also on its "Formula of Humanity" (GMS [4: 428–31]) and its

---

they have not developed the relevant talent yet or, instead, that they have absolutely no capacity for it. "Capability" is a useful term if understood more strictly as a property between these extremes. Thus we may say that people who are severely discriminated against, and are unlikely ever to get adequate housing or a decent education, will lack several valuable capabilities, because of contingent problems such as a lack of technical training and real chances to a get good job. Such persons are not so lacking in capacity that they could not overcome these problems if given a chance, for then they could develop significant talents and thereby produce achievements on the basis of improved capabilities. For a concise account of the significance of attending to "basic capabilities," see Amartya Sen, "Equality of What?" in *Equal Freedom*, ed. Stephen Darwall (Ann Arbor: The University of Michigan Press, 1995), 307–30. (Sen uses the notion of capacity, however, in a common meaning that is contingent and individual and therefore contrasts with the universal Kantian sense that is relevant to dignity.) See also at note 36.

[22] Formosa, *Dignity*, 1; see also 55.

[23] Much more can be said on this topic. See *Kant and Animals*, ed. Lucy Allais and John J. Callanan (Oxford: Oxford University Press, 2020); and Barbara Herman "We are Not Alone: A Place for Animals in Kant's Ethics," in *Kant on Persons and Agency*, ed. Eric Watkins (Cambridge: Cambridge University Press, 2018), 174–91. Regarding Kant's conception of human faculties and how it compares to his notion of the *liberum brutum* of animals, see Katerina Deligiorgi, "Interest and Agency," in *German Idealism Today*, ed. Markus Gabriel and Anders Roe Rasmussen (Berlin: De Gruyter, 2017), 3–25.

substantive presumptions about our having to treat all persons harmoniously as ends in themselves rather than neglecting them, treating them as mere means, or worse.[24] Even the mere notion of persons as ends in themselves, however, *if not given an adequately thick formulation*, can be insufficient for providing a conception of our basic capacities that would account for ascribing dignity in an unconditional sense to persons. A highly minimal—and inadequate—conception of persons as ends in themselves is one defined merely by the idea—the supposedly "core idea" quoted earlier[25]—that we are rational deliberators and thus can set ends ourselves, rather than being always pushed and pulled by nature or used simply as an instrument for ends set by other persons.

Formosa proposes an approach along this line that does not begin from a "normatively neutral starting point" but attempts "to derive the 'ought' of morality from the 'ought' of practical rationality."[26] The main idea here is that, if one grants that others have practical rationality at all, then one must think of them not as mere machines but as agents pursuing ends through their own rationality. Formosa then argues that to regard them as beings who set ends is to fulfill the Formula of Humanity, because one is then not treating them as a *mere* means.[27] In one sense this last claim is true—for they are recognized then as more than mere instruments—but it need not be in a sense that matters in a positive sense. As Kant notes already in his remarks concerning Rousseau (Bem [20: 92]), there is a kind of especially evil way of treating people that does not directly physically harm them, and in that way use them as a mere means, but exploits the tendencies of their *own rationality* to get them to set ends and do things that they would not otherwise do if they were given better options and not led astray by powerful influences.

A typical instance of this kind of situation commonly occurs in societies focused on luxury, the kind of society that was especially of great concern for both Rousseau and Kant. Now, even more than then (due to the "hidden persuaders" of advertising and contemporary media), businesses make use of their savvy sense of the egoism of people who can be lured into feeling a need, above all, to keep up with fashion (to have, in general, the appearance of being "in"), and thus can be enticed into using all their free end-setting capacities to load up with goods for themselves rather than ever consulting their moral conscience. The success of these business enterprises rests on their presumption that they are dealing with end-setting agents who, in one sense, are definitely understood as using their "practical rationality" and a kind of "normative" thinking (although often for projects that, in ways they do not appreciate, go against even their own

---

[24] See Formosa, *Dignity*, 8; Allen W. Wood, *Kant's Ethical Thought* (Cambridge: Cambridge University Press, 2019); and Thomas E. Hill, Jr., "The Dignity of Persons: Kant, Problems and a Proposal," in *Virtue, Rules, and Justice: Kantian Aspirations* (Oxford: Oxford University Press, 2012), 185–202.

[25] Formosa, *Dignity*, 1.　　　[26] Formosa, *Dignity*, 55.　　　[27] Formosa, *Dignity*, 58.

interest)—and yet this might not involve even one thought (by either the buyers or sellers) of "the 'ought' of morality."

The main problem, therefore, with a minimal and merely rational conception of personal agency and normativity is that it does not begin to do explicit justice to the positive orientation of Kant's *moral* philosophy, which goes beyond merely prudential considerations.[28] This orientation is defined by the thought that persons are not mere end-setters but have, among their basic capacities, a power of reason to *appreciate unconditional* ends of action (see again the passage from GMS [4: 411]). If one stays focused only on the idea of beings who have some rationality and can set some ends but have absolutely *no capacity* to set ends that are anything other than conditional, and perhaps are even entirely egoistic, it remains mysterious why they should be given the special moral status of dignity. As Kant repeatedly makes clear, a life like this, governed by the mere pursuit of immediate conditional ends, "purposeless play" (see again the passage quoted from GMS [4: 434]), or even a rational plan that transcends immediate inclination and can involve considerable prudential deliberation (the "rational concepts" of GMS [4: 411]), would be a mere "game" (*Spiel*) (Idee [8: 28]). Agents who have *no capacity* to do more than this, who are *nothing but* gamers, would be without what Kant means by being an agent with a basic capacity specifically for morality (see again the key phrase quoted from GMS [4: 435]), that is, for properly developing themselves and helping others.[29]

It is true that, for Kant, our capacity for morality requires capacities for selectivity, free choice, rationality, and deliberation, but it is essentially more than all that because it must also include some *positive* principles of its own, principles that are action-guiding in a fully moral, that is, unconditional, sense. This is not to say that, according to Kant, matters that are conditional are without value, or that we should not seek to assist beings who have no capacity beyond an appreciation of conditional matters. The goal of bringing about happiness and preventing pain is affirmed throughout Kant's philosophy, but its moral status is conditional and depends on this goal being pursued always in a manner that is permissible

---

[28] This objection is not like that of some critics, e.g. Suzy Killmister, "Paul Formosa, *Kantian Ethics, Dignity and Perfection* (review)," *Ethics* 133 (2023), 420–4, who argue that we should give primacy not to rationality but to what a person most cares about. The problem with that proposal is that often what people most care about are some terrible things, such as devoting oneself to a fanatical dictator. Rejecting giving primacy to contingent cares does not mean that Kantianism is just all about rationality. A problem with presupposing that Kant's ethics is a matter of trying to deduce substantive conclusions from the notion of rationality is that the mistaken impression can arise—as is apparent from Killmister's reading of Formosa—that Kantian dignity is supposed to be understood as relative to the possession of high intelligence, which is quite contrary to Kant's view.

[29] See Sections 1.6 and 1.7. The imagined scenario of totally non-moral agents is not meant to imply that there can be *human* beings with a capacity for prudence but not for morality. In addition to invaluable help on numerous other issues, Janelle DeWitt has pointed out to me that Kant suggests that nature has entangled our faculties too closely for the imagined scenario to be a real possibility for human beings. See MdS [6: 400].

because of adequate appreciation of the *distinctive moral capacity of persons*: the capacity of all free and equal agents to mutually respect and support each other as agents with that capacity, and hence to engage in the difficult work of creating conditions in which widespread (and eventually universal, in an international political sense) and decent human development that is intersubjectively oriented for its own sake can occur and flourish.

Efforts persist, nonetheless, to present an alternative position that does not accept, as a *starting* point, the notion of an underlying moral orientation involving status dignity as just defined. An especially prominent alternative approach is to be found in Christine Korsgaard's highly lucid and influential work.[30] Without disputing its merits within the debates of contemporary ethical theory, Formosa, like many others, ultimately questions the status of Korsgaard's position as a reflection of Kant's basic view. Like other critics, Formosa objects to her attempt to ground unconditional worth simply on the idea that the value of contingent ends depends on "our rational choice, as the source and condition of the worth of those ends," and this in turn on our positing "our own unconditional worth as rational agents."[31] The objection is that this approach does not disclose either a clearly unconditional value or one that can ground intersubjective moral claims as easily as alternative accounts can.[32] In the present context, it thus can be regarded as one more questionable attempt to develop a strategy inspired by trying to reconstruct Kant's system from a minimal starting point: the mere idea of

---

[30] Formosa (*Dignity*, 51) calls Korsgaard's approach a "standard reading of Kant," but it does not represent his own view or that of what I call the mainline interpretation. Nonetheless, constructivism continues to dominate the way many contemporary philosophers think about Kant—even some who might become allies of Kant if they did not presume the relevance of constructivism. Consider this observation in a review of a recent book on ethics: "The elephant in the room is Kantian constructivism. Kant himself gets one mention in a footnote, and there is no discussion of modern Kantianism. Since this is such a striking omission, it is worth asking where Kantian theories would fit in Huemer's taxonomy. I suspect that he would classify them as subjectivist, which is a fairly broad category for him. Subjectivists 'think that for an object to be good is for some person or group to have (or be disposed to have) some psychological attitude or reaction towards it' (p. 48)." David McNaughton, "Michael Huemer, *Moral Intuitionism* (book review)," *Notre Dame Philosophical Reviews*, 2006.09.10.

[31] Formosa, *Dignity*, 52. See Christine M. Korsgaard, *Creating the Kingdom of Ends* (Cambridge: Cambridge University Press, 2016), 123. See the critiques of her interpretation of Kant in Christine M. Korsgaard with G. M. Cohen et al., *The Sources of Normativity*, ed. Onora O'Neill (Cambridge: Cambridge University Press, 1996). See also Karl Ameriks, "Is Practical Justification in Kant Ultimately Dogmatic?", in *Kant on Practical Justification*, ed. Sorin Baiasu and Mark Timmons (Oxford: Oxford University Press (2013), 153–75; and "*Aufklärung über die Sittlichkeit. Zu Kants Grundlegung einer Metaphysik der Sitten*, by Bernd Ludwig" (review), *Archiv für Geschichte der Philosophie* 104 (2022), 786–90; and cf. Henry E. Allison, *Kant's Conception of Freedom: A Developmental and Critical Analysis* (Cambridge: Cambridge University Press, 2020).

[32] Formosa, *Dignity*, 53. Cf. Eric Watkins and William Fitzpatrick, "O'Neill and Korsgaard on the Construction of Normativity," *The Journal of Value Inquiry* 36 (2002), 349–67. The underlying objection here is that the valuing of one's own particular choices and capacity for choice is not truly unconditional if it is regarded as dependent on a project of maintaining one's "practical identity," a project that might well be understood in merely prudential terms (which is not the same thing as a promotion of harmful egoism). The inward-directed, contingent project of identity maintenance may not be of immediate concern to ordinary moral agents who can directly appreciate the moral law and its necessary intersubjective values.

30   KANTIAN DIGNITY AND ITS DIFFICULTIES

making rational choices, being a rational agent, and valuing oneself unconditionally, as an individual with a practical identity, simply on that basis. Such an ambitious strategy may be inspired by the ever-re-occurring interest in being able to philosophically defeat a moral skeptic from a basis within a particular self, but this project does not appear to map on to a necessarily moral position, let alone one that is truly close to Kant's own procedure. Kant calls his own work "dogmatic-critical" (Fort [20: 297, 305, 309, 311]), and although it certainly contains several notions that can seem overly dogmatic in our era (such as his impatience in his Critical period with any form of compatibilism or monism), there is still something to be said for his embrace of the notion of a *Faktum der Vernunft* (KpV [5: 42]). This amounts to a recognition, *from the start*, of our having a capacity to acknowledge the claims on us of pure practical reason, rather than at first insisting on finding an Archimedean point from which pure moral normativity can be deduced from a mere consideration of our more elementary capacities.

1.5 In Defense of a Mainline Interpretation

The pure moral orientation of Kant's practical philosophy fortunately becomes clear in most of the rest of Formosa's exposition, which goes on to endorse the key point that our "status dignity refers to the special respect worthy status of the *capacity* [emphasis added] for *moral* [emphasis added] agency,"[33] and "Kant makes it clear that it is our personality, our capacity to act for the sake of the moral law, and not our sheer *humanity* (when understood as a merely prudential capacity to set any ends whatsoever) that grounds our dignity."[34] Nonetheless, more detail is needed when Formosa, like other interpreters, sometimes speaks simply of "rational capacities for morality" and "latent potential to develop moral capacities."[35] The limitation of the first phrase is that by itself it does not specifically characterize our "capacity for morality." A shortcoming of the second phrase is that it adds an idea that conflicts with a more clearly absolutist terminology that is worth considering as preferable. The phrase speaks of a capacity as something that can be developed later, rather than as being a fundamental structure of our species, a structure that is present from the start and, in proper conditions, naturally allows for the development of various capabilities and talents. For example, unless babies had a general language *capacity* to begin with, they would never be able to develop linguistic *capabilities* in a particular natural language and then

---

[33] Formosa, *Dignity*, 5.

[34] Formosa, *Dignity*, 129; see also 122 and 50: "the rational moral capacity that makes them capable for autonomy."

[35] Formosa, *Dignity*, 10.

THE DISTINCTIVENESS OF KANTIAN DIGNITY   31

eventually a *talented* fluency and numerous particular *achievements*.[36] Similarly, with respect to what matters for dignity, what is crucial is a particular practical orientation, namely, one that is not merely instrumental or prudential[37] but involves a distinctive moral capacity. This capacity is like linguistic competence insofar as it is not dependent on a particular language or technical intelligence (GMS [4: 385]), and it allows us to appreciate categorical obligations that transcend all contingent interests, whether prudential or even outward-oriented but in a wholly contingent way.

This point is needed, once again, to correct the common characterization of Kant as a philosopher who holds that morality follows from rationality. This characterization is misleading because, in English, the term "rational" is used in all sorts of casual ways, often implying merely that an action has some reason or other behind it. This can obscure the fact that Kant's ethics is based precisely on the fundamental contrast between what is merely rational, in this minimal sense, and what requires the special faculty of *pure* practical reason, which for him is the only form of reason that can achieve reason's distinctive goal of making determinate unconditional claims that are consistent and warranted. This point can be easily missed because Kant often expresses his moral arguments as depending on what follows from one's "rational nature" (*vernünftige Natur*). Here the English term "rational" unfortunately obscures the important fact that the German phrase contains a reference specifically to *reason* (*Vernunft*), a higher faculty that, for Kant, is not to be identified with just any form of rationality.

A similar complication arises with understanding the culminating component of Kant's system, his claim that belief in the real possibility of the success of the moral community needs to be grounded in what he calls *Vernunftglaube*. This is a unique Kantian term that is generally translated as "rational faith," but this is a vague, minimal, and highly ambiguous phrase that can be misleading because it leaves out any indication of what specifically is meant by Kant's introduction of the term. *Vernunft-glaube* is best understood in terms of its components, that is, as a kind of faith *in* (and by) *reason*. This must be understood as commitment to the substantive validity of reason, in Kant's special sense, as determined by the unconditional moral principles of pure *practical* reason. In addition, although our mere dignity, as a capacity, can survive no matter how human beings act (as long as one's personal existence is not extinguished), Kant argues, in his "Postulates of Pure Practical Reason" (KpV [5: 132]), that it cannot be reasonably expected that, in the long run, full justice can be done to this dignity unless agents commit to *Vernunftglaube*.[38] This faith (by itself) is not a sectarian belief but is a matter of

---

[36] See note 21, and see also Patrick Kain, "Kant's Defense of Human Moral Status," *The Journal of the History of Philosophy* 47 (2009), 59–102.

[37] Formosa, *Dignity*, 75.

[38] See Allen W. Wood, *Kant's Moral Religion* (Ithaca, NY: Cornell University Press, 1970), and *Kant and Religion* (Cambridge: Cambridge University Press, 2020); John E. Hare, *The Moral Gap: Kantian Ethics, Human Limits, and God's Assistance* (Oxford: Clarendon Press, 1996); and Andrew Chignell,

32 KANTIAN DIGNITY AND ITS DIFFICULTIES

maintaining a hope that Kant takes to be a common rational feature of human life, one not needing to be introduced by philosophers or sects: the hope that, *if* we keep working toward reason's final end, the highest good—satisfaction proportionate to virtue throughout humanity *in general*—then some supreme power, with an appropriate providential orientation beyond all our theoretical knowledge, will make this really possible (KpV [5: 125–32]).[39]

Whatever one's attitude to religion, and to Kant's arguments for his Postulates in particular, Kant's discussion of the highest good remains relevant because it shows that he obviously takes very seriously a close connection between the moral capacity that is fundamental to dignity and the specific kinds of obligation that immediately come along with it, namely, the calling to use one's powers to forbear neglecting or disrespecting any persons and to develop one's own talents while, in a cooperative effort, helping others achieve their own ends insofar as this appears morally permissible.[40] Common worries that Kantian dignity is an empty concept can be met by pointing out, along this line, that the *term* dignity is not meant to supply content all by itself. The term needs to be understood, from the start, not as signifying a neutral sphere of mere possibility but as a reminder that we all begin with a most important specific kind of positive orientation, namely, a *vocation for* morality.[41] This vocation needs to be spelled out, as it is by Kant, in a full matrix of basic negative and positive duties concerning ourselves and others who share equal status with us as free, finite, and dependent agents in an interconnected world.[42] Exactly how one goes about best fulfilling that

"Religious Hope and Divine Action," in *The Cambridge Critical Guide to Religion within the Boundaries of Mere Reason*, ed. Gordon Michalson (Cambridge: Cambridge University Press, 2016), 98–117.

[39] Rather than being a form of dogmatic faith, what *Vernunftglaube* basically requires is *sincere*, consistent, and resilient commitment to the unconditional duties owed to *all* of humanity, including to oneself as a self-respecting but not egoistic agent. Cf. Barbara Herman, "Religion and the Highest Good: Speaking to the Heart of Even the Best of Us," in *Kant on Freedom and Spontaneity*, ed. Kate A. Moran (Cambridge: Cambridge University Press, 2018), 214–30. This implies—contrary to common unsympathetic readings of the Kantian (and traditional Christian) position by, e.g., Hegel, Murdoch, and Arendt—that any hypocrisy (or interest merely in one's own fate) on the agent's part would be directly self-defeating. Kantian "religion within the boundaries of mere reason" is anything other than a reprehensible self-serving project, let alone, as Goethe feared, a relapse to superstitious dogmatism. It is a matter of working toward a situation where *all* persons would be treated justly, which, for Kant, also implies a commitment to a project that could bring unhappiness to oneself.

[40] Kant does not make these obligations themselves dependent on *Vernunftglaube*. He simply argues that, without faith in some ground that can make the highest good other than a merely fantastic idea, one's *resolute* commitment to long-term moral projects risks being undermined—as it often has been in our time—by an understandable kind of practical despair. See the detailed argument in Hare, *The Moral Gap*.

[41] It was therefore fitting that many other writers, in the era before and after Kant (such as Fichte), wrote books concerning "the vocation of man," i.e., humanity.

[42] See GMS [4: 421–4], and Thomas E. Hill, Jr., "Dignity of Persons," 199: "The cluster of ideas encapsulated in Kant's idea of human dignity includes most of the different values we find in appeals to dignity in everyday moral discussions." Hill helpfully spells out six specific injunctions in this cluster: (1) "treat persons only in ways that we could justify to them;" (2) [do] "not proceed as if the dignity of persons can be compared and weighed against the dignity of others;" (3) "treat persons as beings with moral rights that restrict how we may treat them;" (4) [assume] "the existence of each

vocation, given one's actual individual situation, is an extra and difficult matter, one that should not be expected to be addressed in detail, let alone resolved, in a work like the *Groundwork*. The *Groundwork* is appropriately titled because it is primarily intended just to remind us of our basic moral orientation, given originally by a "compass" (GMS [4: 404]; cf. "common reason," KpV [5: 91]) that we already possess, and especially to ward off (in its clarification of the idea of a proper "metaphysics of morals") the confusions that repeatedly have arisen from improper philosophical perspectives on morality.

One common worry about treating Kant's ethics as focused in this way on an unconditional sense of dignity is that this may seem to conflict with his emphasis on autonomy and involve an unacceptable form of moral realism. This problem can be resolved by getting clear on what should be the most relevant meaning of "realism" in this practical context, and by making sure one has appropriate notion of what Kant actually means by "autonomy." Kant's use of the term contrasts sharply with common English usage now, where it can mean any kind of self-direction, and thus can even take the form of arbitrary choices. The most common stumbling block with respect to autonomy is the tendency to read too much into Kant's remark that the moral law not only holds for persons but is "self-legislated" (GMS [4: 431]). Here it is crucial that one not take Kant's talk about a "self" in contexts like this as a reference to the contingencies of human nature, let alone a mere individual project. Kant repeatedly makes clear that the moral law is a matter of eternal and essential truth that is rooted in the faculty of reason common to all higher rational beings (see again GMS [4: 425] and cf. MPC [27: 282] and Vigil [29: 633]).[43] Given the necessity of the basic truths of morality, he cannot mean by "legislation" any literal process, let alone an act of imposition in any kind of contingent and perhaps even arbitrary sense. He is instead pointing out (in analogy with a common threefold political division) that truly autonomous morality is not a matter of *executive* edict or *juridical* whimsy but is essentially constituted by *lawfulness*. This lawfulness is rooted in the strictly necessary "dictates" of the faculty of pure reason rather than in "an implanted sense or who knows what tutelary nature whispers" (GMS [4: 426])—let alone in something created by individuals, traditions, or governments, no matter how unanimous.[44]

At the same time, it remains true that all *instances* of moral conduct are a matter of particular persons actually using their own reason to construct specific intentions—but intentions that must be understood to accord with principles that

---

person is an objective end and so something to be valued by all rational persons;" (5) [assume] "dignity calls for *expressions* of respect and honor for persons, not for their social position, education, or achievements;" (6) [recognize that] "we fully respect human dignity only if we count the personal ends of others as worthy of our attention and aid."

[43] See Karl Ameriks, "On the Many Senses of Self-Determination," in *Kantian Subjects: Critical Philosophy and Late Modernity* (Oxford: Oxford University Press, 2019), 14–35.

[44] See Eric Watkins, *Kant on Laws* (Cambridge: Cambridge University Press, 2019); and Karl Ameriks, "Universality, Necessity, and Law in General in Kant," in *Kantian Subjects*, 103–19.

34 KANTIAN DIGNITY AND ITS DIFFICULTIES

have an a priori normative necessity. It is this psychological and methodological context that is relevant when Kant himself uses the term "impose" (GMS [4: 435]). Persons are supposed to impose the general deliverances of reason upon themselves in conceiving and acting on their life-plans, rather than sinking to the level of trying to "coax" (GMS [4: 435]) their use of reason into following moral principles for the sake of sensory incentives. This is a point that in no way implies that human beings, as contingent individuals or a group, are themselves the source of the normative necessity of the law. Kant speaks of the "unconditional necessitation," and "majesty of the law (like the law on Sinai)" (Rel [6: 23, note]). One can still speak of the importance of one's "legislating" one's own life in *affirming* a basic normative orientation, but according to Kant this can be done properly only if it is a matter of *reconstructing* the uncreated principles that are inherent in pure practical reason itself, as they apply to the human context of a multiplicity of finite and interdependent sensible beings.

In sum, Kant's statement that morality is self-legislated is not a matter of Luciferian caprice[45] but basically amounts to the idea that the moral law is correlative with reason in a pure practical sense. As the second part of the term indicates, *auto-nomy* requires an orientation to *lawfulness*, which is rooted in a universal *faculty* of reason that does not allow itself to be determined (either normatively or causally) from an external and contingent source, that is, by some *other faculty*, such as the will of an arbitrary theological power or the sensory force of the mere givens of experience, be they crude or ever so imaginatively refined. Without violating autonomy, Kant can also believe, as he does, that basic moral norms are totally in line with what a supremely powerful and reasonable being would necessarily endorse, command, and practice in its own existence. Any form of radically voluntaristic theological realism is therefore incompatible with Kant's ethics, as is the global realism of any kind of naturalism that regards the crucial components of human morality as fundamentally determined (normatively as well as causally) by mere forces from *outside reason*—whether by overarching quasi-Aristotelian teleological structures or all-inclusive quasi-Darwinian non-teleological factors.

These points are presumably appreciated by Formosa when he characterizes the Kantian view of the "value or dignity of rational agents" as something that cannot "be given independently of, and prior to, setting out the rational requirements of practical *reason* [emphasis added] itself."[46] Of course, *if* one were to insist that a Kantian realist practical philosophy has to be one that takes moral value and dignity to be something "in the world"[47] *apart* from practical reason altogether (and not simply from the actual thoughts of human agents), then one

---

[45] Iris Murdoch famously connected Kant's ethics with Lucifer. See Onora O'Neill's critique in *Constructions of Reason*, 75.
[46] Formosa, *Dignity*, 44. [47] Formosa, *Dignity*, 66.

could say that Kant is not a moral realist. This kind of way of talking has had considerable influence ever since the surprising claim by John Rawls that "the...order of values...is constituted by the activity, actual or ideal of practical (*human*) [emphasis added] reason itself. Kant's constructivism...goes to the very existence and constitution of the order of values. This is part of his transcendental idealism."[48] This is a controversial and all too quick move because Kant's arguments for transcendental idealism are always dependent on considerations of space and time, and Kant repeatedly stresses that the moral law should not be thought as depending on space, time, or humanity (see, e.g., KrV A 552/B 580, GMS [4: 414], KpV [5: 99–102]).[49] It is not clear why Rawls neglected this key point. Perhaps his thinking, from early on, was preoccupied with the tendencies of his era, almost a century ago. Because early Anglophone forms of moral realism were often presented in terms that appear to rely on questionable appeals to brute private intuitions, it is understandable that philosophers interested in something like an intersubjective "decision procedure" in ethics would want to stay away from anything looking like that kind of realism. But contemporary understandings of realism and intuitionism are more varied and sophisticated than in the era when Rawls was starting as a philosopher.[50] Furthermore, it is not clear why a substantive theory that takes moral values to be necessarily correlative with the disclosures of practical reason cannot still be called a realist theory in a perfectly understandable and non-mysterious sense—especially if one recalls that even a typical full-fledged realist such as Frege said he could make no sense of speaking of truths that would be independent of reason altogether.[51]

Nonetheless, even now there are skilled interpreters, such as Formosa, who want to combine a strongly objectivist and cognitivist reading of Kant's ethics with language that speaks of moral value as "projected" or "conferred" by "adoption," albeit not in a way that is dependent on the actual intentions of human agents.[52] Insistence on this way of speaking appears to involve a conflation of epistemological or methodological issues with ontological ones. A Kantian realist can agree that our *procedure for deciding* which principles and maxims to live by is something that, of course, *we* cannot carry out without our adopting certain

---

[48] John Rawls, *Political Liberalism* (New York: Columbia University Press, 1993), 99. Rawls's resuscitation of sympathetic interest in Kant and systematic practical philosophy in general remains, of course, one of the most important philosophical developments of the twentieth century.

[49] This is not to deny Kant's point, in the second edition Preface of *Critique of Pure Reason* (B xxix), that transcendental idealism is a *necessary theoretical precondition* for his pure practical philosophy because, without it, it would appear (especially after Newton) that transcendental freedom is impossible. There remains in any case a close connection between Kant and Rawls's primary view, which is that ethics needs to rests on a demanding conception of the person.

[50] See, e.g., Audi, *The Good in the Right*.

[51] Gottlob Frege, "By objectivity I understand an independence from our sensation, intuition, ideation...but not independence from reason." *The Foundations of Arithmetic* [1884], trans. J. L. Austin (Evanston: Northwestern University Press, 1968), second revised edition, section 26, 36.

[52] Formosa, *Dignity*, 41.

36 KANTIAN DIGNITY AND ITS DIFFICULTIES

propositions as reasonable. But to believe that these principles are reasonable is also naturally to believe—as Kant does—that this is because we *recognize* that they allow human beings to fulfill their full rational nature, which includes pure practical reason: "what is necessarily an end for everyone...constitutes an *objective* principle of the will and hence can serve as a universal practical law...the ground of this principle is: *a rational nature exists as an end in itself*" (GMS [4: 428–9]).[53]

What is fundamental, therefore, is our "rational nature," which is hardly something that can be constructed by us, for what else could we use in that construction but the nature that is already given with our *basic* capacities? It is understandable, nevertheless, that one might still choose to back off from the terminology of realism *if* one simply means thereby to make clear that Kant's views of moral value are to be distinguished from global versions of Aristotelian or contemporary reductionist naturalism, of an old-fashioned teleological or anti-teleological kind, as well as from mere appeals to theological visions or mystical intuitions. A similar issue arises with discussions of perfectionism, where one can cite Kant's critique of specific dogmatic conceptions of perfection (found in the Wolffian tradition and in others that rest on dogmatic notions of metaphysical perfection), while one can also say that there remains a form of *normative* perfectionism that is compatible with Kant's pure practical doctrines and can be defended in contemporary terms.[54]

1.6 Some Controversial Implications

With respect to the issue of how best to understand human dignity in this context, these kinds of general philosophical debates may not seem to matter as much as getting clear on exactly how, especially in a Kantian spirit, we should now treat human beings. Formosa, however, links the issues of realism, dignity, and treatment when he adopts a position called "not all the way down constructivism." For "all the way down constructivism," the status of dignity is dependent on the presence of a moral capacity that must be clear from either *past* accomplishment or

---

[53] See, e.g., Allison, *Commentary*, 207–28: "It is not that being human or having a rational nature has an independent value...it is rather that the categorical imperative bestows this value upon them." This is to be understood as meaning just that our nature is to be understood as having within it the capacity for morality. See also Facundo Rodriguez, "Reconstructing Kant: Kant's Teleological Moral Realism," *Kant Yearbook* 14 (2022), 71–95. Rodriquez argues that Kant "takes the value of rational nature to be objective and not 'constructed'" (p. 71), and that this nature is "teleological" just insofar as Kant stresses that our practical reason has the necessary ends of cultivating the self's powers and becoming virtuous (see MdS [6: 386]).

[54] See Paul Guyer, "Kantian Perfectionism," in *Virtues of Freedom: Selected Essays on Kant* (Oxford: Oxford University Press, 2016), 70–86; and David O. Brink, "Normative Perfectionism and the Kantian Tradition," *Philosophers' Imprint* 19 (2019), 1–28.

present potential. Formosa's version of constructivism, in contrast, extends the status of dignity to human beings that he considers to have *future* potential to exhibit a moral capacity.[55] On this ground, however, Formosa rules out giving status dignity to some very young human beings, such as anencephalic newborns, and also many older impaired people, such as those with "very advanced dementia."[56]

Against at least a part of Formosa's view it can be argued, on a charitable but concrete understanding of "potential," that the condition of "future potential" can still be satisfied in the case of elderly people with serious medical problems. We now know that even severely injured people in seemingly irreversible comas can sometimes regain many of their previous powers. Moreover, our limitations in treating such people appear to be just a matter of contingent developments in medical technology. In numerous ways, this technology has already developed helpful techniques that were not even imagined before. The most important fact here is just that, if such techniques ever do manage to significantly reverse a seemingly permanent loss of faculties, the result could appear, both from the outside and the inside, to be a matter of a person just returning to a relevant use of basic human capacities that it possessed all along. This situation need not be considered to be a matter of having entirely lost one's personal identity, let alone one's identity as a member of the human species. There is therefore good reason to hold that the status of dignity, throughout that person's whole life, should not be withheld, and that a similar future potential (however slim) for recovery, and dignity status, should be granted to others in that situation, even prior to any successful treatment. (This is not to claim, of course, that the best way to respect dignity in that situation is to increase suffering and wait forever on the development of stunning but very far off technological breakthroughs.) In its implications for deciding how to humanely *regard* those who have medical issues that appear reversible only after some truly extraordinary developments, a more charitable position than Formosa's not all the way down constructivism seems called for, one that fits most naturally with Kantian realism about universal human dignity.

Another way to see this point is to consider Formosa's discussion of "psychopaths," that is, beings *initially* described, perhaps by stipulation, as "agents who are capable of instrumental and prudential but not moral rationality."[57] It is easiest to accept his discussion here if psychopaths are understood this way in a *stipulated* sense, for then such beings would correspond to individuals in the thought experiment that was discussed, concerning an imagined species *defined* as totally without any moral capacity but otherwise equipped with rationality. Note, however,

---

[55] Formosa, *Dignity*, 120, 132.

[56] Formosa, *Dignity*, 145. Anencephalic newborns usually survive for only a very brief time and never have a complete brain.

[57] Formosa, *Dignity*, 141.

38 KANTIAN DIGNITY AND ITS DIFFICULTIES

that considering beings in this stipulated condition is not the same thing as suggesting anything about how, given current practices, to regard *current patients* that happen to be *called* psychopaths. Formosa's position becomes questionable when he begins to draw conclusions for how to treat psychopaths in this sense, that is, *actual human beings*. He goes on to remark that the "moral responsibility of psychopaths is often questioned," and then he goes so far as to assert that "it doesn't seem unreasonable to question their possession of dignity as well."[58] This looks like an all too quick and dangerous jump.

There certainly are reasons for regarding human beings with obvious pathological tendencies as in need of a very different kind of treatment (medical, legal, and social) than what one would give to agents with whom one could expect to be able to carry out a truly reasonable discussion about matters concerning what is right and what is very wrong. They can seem to totally lack an orientation toward morality, but that does not prove that they have absolutely no capacity for it. The temptation to hastily deny the protections of dignity in such cases is a chilling reminder of why the writers of the postwar German constitution made a point of rejecting the attitude of the numerous German doctors, lawyers, and politicians who went along with brutal Nazi methods (which in some ways were like those of many eugenicists elsewhere) of dealing with many kinds of people they considered undesirable and as if they were less than human. Fortunately, the new constitution explicitly insisted on outlawing any violation of human dignity and thereby also discouraged any attempt to quickly deny the status of dignity to those who have special needs or problems (and might be called "psychopaths," as political opponents have sometimes also been called) but are unquestionably human beings.

1.7 On a Challenge to the Mainline Interpretation

A perspective that goes far beyond Formosa's in denying dignity to some human beings can be found in a series of works by Richard Dean. Near the very end of his recent essay, "The Peculiar Idea of Respect for a Capacity," Dean continues to argue in the spirit of his book, *The Value of Humanity in Kant's Moral Theory*, which in its penultimate paragraph concluded, "dignity is not inalienable."[59] He inveighs against "dogmatically relying on an idea that any legitimate moral or political theory must begin by assuming all persons are equally worthy of respect."[60] He also contends, "it is not unreasonable to feel some pull toward

---

[58] Formosa, *Dignity*, 141.

[59] Richard Dean, *The Value of Humanity in Kant's Moral Theory* (Oxford: Clarendon Press, 2016), 260.

[60] Richard Dean, "The Peculiar Idea of Respect for a Capacity," in *Respect: Philosophical Essays*, 154.

THE DISTINCTIVENESS OF KANTIAN DIGNITY 39

thinking that merely possessing a profoundly important potential while doing little or nothing to fulfill it does not seem like an adequate ground for respect," and "an unrealized capacity for morality is as likely to be an obstacle as an asset."[61] Dean holds to the line that, upon close examination, the claim that there is an obligation to respect the dignity of all persons simply because of their capacity for morality is so peculiar that it is best not to ascribe it even to Kant's ethics. This is, of course, in direct contrast to the mainline interpretation that has been stressed so far, which to a large extent rests on interpreting and defending Kant precisely by emphasizing the notion of a basic capacity for morality as necessary and sufficient for ascriptions of dignity.

Dean admits there is evidence for the mainline interpretation, but he asserts that the evidence is equivocal and "not overwhelming."[62] In addition to the evidence that has already been given at the outset of this chapter, however, there is much more that can be cited in favor of the mainline view. In another essay, Dean argues against ascribing to Kant the position of "attributing an incomparable dignity and special status as an end in itself to some trait that all minimally rational adult humans already possess."[63] To say the least, this is hard to reconcile with material from throughout Kant's career, all the way, from private remarks of the 1760s and notes taken from lectures of the 1770s,[64] to this sequence of

---

[61] Dean, "Peculiar Idea," 144.   [62] Dean, *Value of Humanity*, 76.

[63] Richard Dean, "Humanity as an Idea, as an Ideal, and as an End in Itself," *Kantian Review* 18 (2013), 187. In this article, Dean quotes, as apparent evidence for the mainline view from *Metaphysics of Morals* §§ 38 and 39, only the first sentence of the first passage quoted from [6: 462], and he goes on to claim it is "undermined" (p. 188) by other passages. But one of these passages is discussed, and interpreted as not really counterevidence, in note 65, and the same reaction is appropriate for the only other passage offered to back the undermining claim: "for examples of respect we give others can arouse their striving to deserve it" (MdS § 43 [6: 466]). Dean reads this passage as implying that the person who is being encouraged to strive is someone who deserves *no* respect beforehand. Here there is a misunderstanding of the context. The overall concern of § 43 is not with a destruction or lack of dignity in someone but just the *effect* that one person's actions can have on another person, through expressions of defamation or encouraging examples. Kant begins by noting that an effect of a malicious rumor can be that it "diminishes respect for humanity as such, so as finally to cast a shadow of worthlessness over our race itself." Kant's point, obviously, is not that defamation makes defamed persons worthless, literally diminishing their humanity and their deserving of respect; all it can diminish is the amount of (achievement) respect that is in fact *shown* to these persons because of a misrepresentation (a "shadow") caused by the defamer. Something similar is going on in the passage about the person who is being encouraged to strive. Kant is not saying that for now the person deserves no respect. His point is just that the person can be motivated, by presumably proper and stirring examples of virtue and a corresponding practice of showing respect, to work to receive for himself an *equivalent degree* (*gleichmäßig*) of respect from others, one that would be like that which paradigms of virtue can expect from others for their good works. Unfortunately, the key German term is left untranslated in the Cambridge edition that Dean cites.

[64] "Well-wishing love can be enjoined upon everyone...even in the worst of villains there is still a kernel of good will" (MPC [27: 418]). A portion of this passage, as quoted by another scholar from an English edition of 1930, is cited by Dean (*Value of Humanity*, 73). The quotation given here is from the standard Cambridge edition version of 1997, for which there is now a corresponding and more recently edited German version of the notes: VorlM (2004). Dean also cites (*Value of Humanity*, 74) one sentence from the *Metaphysics of Morals* MdS [6: 441], about the "noble predisposition to the good," but he does not give weight to Kant's highly relevant *multi-page* repetition of the claim of universal dignity in the quotations that have been given, or even Kant's speaking, elsewhere right at MdS

40 KANTIAN DIGNITY AND ITS DIFFICULTIES

straightforward assertions in his final major work, *The Metaphysics of Morals*, Doctrine of Virtue, § 38 and § 39 [6: 462–4] (cf. MdS [6: 435]):

> *Every human being* [emphasis added] has a legitimate claim to respect from his fellow human beings and is *in turn* bound to respect every other. Humanity itself is a dignity, for it cannot be used merely as a means...It is just in this that his dignity (personality) consists, by which he raises himself above all other beings in the world that are not human beings. He is under obligation to acknowledge, in a practical way, the *dignity* [emphasis added] of humanity in every other human being. Hence there rests upon him a duty regarding the dignity of respect that must be shown to every other human being.

> To be *contemptuous* of others (*contemnere*), that is, to deny them the respect owed to human beings *in general* [emphasis added], is in every case contrary to duty...What is *dangerous* is no object of contempt, and so neither is a *vicious man*...I cannot deny all respect to *even a vicious man* [emphasis added] as a human being...[65]

> On this is based a duty to respect a human being even in the logical use of his reason, a duty not to censor his errors by calling them absurdities...The same thing applies to the censure of vice, which must never break out into complete contempt and denial of any moral worth to a vicious human being; for on this supposition he could never be improved, and this is not consistent with the idea of a *human being*, who as such (as a moral being) can never lose entirely his *predisposition* [emphasis added] to the good.

All these passages fit perfectly with, and only with, the view that Kant's position is that there is a most basic sense in which we should start with the thought that dignity is something that applies to every human being and grounds a universal duty of respect on account of a capacity for morality that we all have, independently of any specific degree of accomplishment, moral or otherwise.

[6: 441], of "the original predisposition to a good will within him, which can *never* [emphasis added] be lost." For other criticisms of Dean's book, see Patrick R. Frierson, "Richard Dean, *The Value of Humanity in Kant's Moral Theory* (review)," *Notre Dame Philosophical Reviews*, 2007.04.17.

[65] In the continuation of this passage (after "vicious man as a human being") Kant goes on to say: "I cannot withdraw at least the respect that belongs to him [the vicious person] in his quality as a human being, even though by his deeds [*Tat*] he makes himself unworthy [*unwürdig*] of it" (MdS [6: 463]). Dean regards passages like this as revealing a fundamental equivocation in Kant's theory, and thus as leaving open the possibility of regarding a stress on achievement dignity as the fundamental view to ascribe to Kant. But when one reads this sentence in its full context (the whole sections of the passages quoted from §§ 38 and 39), it is clear that what Kant is repeatedly emphasizing is the primacy and *permanence* of status dignity for all human beings. The point is that we "cannot withdraw" it *even* in this case. Kant's use of "unworthy" here needs to be understood in terms of this context, as indicating what one would say *if* one knew nothing more about this agent than the nature of the deeds and *disregarded* the man's fundamental status as a human being who, despite his actions, is said to *still* have a "predisposition to the good" (and the dignity that goes along with it).

THE DISTINCTIVENESS OF KANTIAN DIGNITY   41

In direct contrast to these kinds of statements by Kant, Dean's own position is well captured in this passage: "we must treat them [persons with dignity] as ends in themselves...not because the power of choice, or the power to act on overall plans of life, or the mere unrealized *capacity* [emphasis added] for morality confers on every human the highest possible worth."[66] In the website abstract for his book, Dean fills out what he takes to be Kant's position by saying, in similar but more positive terms, that the

'rational nature' that must be treated as an end in itself is not a minimally rational nature consisting of the power to set ends or the unrealized capacity to act morally, but instead is the more properly rational nature possessed by someone who *gives priority* [emphasis added] to moral principles over any contrary impulses.[67]

Although it is hard to see any way to reconcile Dean's reading with the position that Kant reiterates at length, there is value in much of Dean's discussion, especially in its drawing attention to Kant's primary concern specifically with morality and to the fact that others have focused on the notion of a capacity. Dean's account shares some important features with the mainline approach, insofar as they both object to a focus on the mere "power to set ends," that is, "the power of choice," or even what Dean refers to as the more complex "power to act on overall plans of life." This objection can also be applied to contemporary quasi-Kantian philosophical positions that may imply a willingness to ascribe dignity to agents simply on the basis of their proceeding in a *so-called* autonomous fashion by governing themselves in line with their highest individual values or deepest second-order desires, cares, or loves,[68] *whatever* they may be.

As has been noted, the problem with mentioning only minimal capacities like these is that, without any further characterization of an agent, we cannot say that the agent has even the *slightest capacity to attempt* to do anything moral. One can imagine, for example, a world with agents that can actualize their robust power of choice only by caring about and reflectively planning a life of bullying in a variety of brutal ways while having *no capacity* to think in terms of anything other than the exercise of this power. This may seem to be a far-fetched scenario (for we need not assume that any actual human beings are in this situation) but, as has been noted, there are even broadly mainline interpreters, such as Formosa, who

---

[66] Dean, *Value of Humanity*, 260. Cf. "*commitment* [emphasis added] to moral principles," *Value of Humanity*, 41.

[67] See Dean, "Abstract for *Value of Humanity*": https://academic.oup.com/book/11513 https://global.oup.com/academic/product/the-value-of-humanity-in-kants-moral-theory-9780199285723?cc=us&lang=en&

[68] For a criticism of the views of Gary Watson and Harry Frankfurt in this context, see Jada Twedt Stebbing, "Attributability, Weakness of Will, and the Importance of Just Having the Capacity," *Philosophical Studies* 173 (2016), 289–307.

propose a somewhat similar idea when speaking of the actual situation of people called psychopaths, who are indisputably human, as (on his suggestion) supposedly lacking moral capacity and dignity.

One way to characterize the problem that remains with an approach such as Dean's is that it appears to be a matter of leaping away from one extreme only to settle on an opposite and equally unsatisfactory extreme. Instead of characterizing dignity in terms of a minimal condition that may involve no capacity to set moral ends at all, Dean insists on a kind of maximal condition, a state of *actually* prioritizing moral ends and to some extent coming at least close to fulfilling morality's ideals. The underlying problem here may be that achievement-oriented philosophers like Dean are presuming that one has to dismiss the middle position[69] here—of explicitly stressing morality but requiring only a capacity for it—because this seems to them to be an option that is completely empty, no more than a "dogmatic" reference to mere potential. This is to forget that Kant does not conceive of our moral capacity as just a logical possibility or a bare and neutral state.

The most basic distinctive quality of human beings is that they are never an empty potential but have a concrete and ever-present power of oriented free choice, prior to any possible external effects. Because of his fundamentally positive theory of human freedom and will (*Wille*) as practical reason (GMS [4: 412, 458, and 459]), Kant always connects our free moral capacity with a substantive normative orientation, made possible by our original "predisposition for the good" (Rel [6: 28 and 6: 43]).[70] Furthermore, Kant's position is hardly a naïve, complacent, and overly optimistic view of human nature. It is combined with a complex theory of human beings as all struggling with radical evil, and in this context the notion of a good predisposition plays an essential and realistic role. To stress this predisposition is not at all to ignore the importance of valuing actual fulfillments of duties. The point is simply to acknowledge the fundamental condition of these fulfillments, the fact that they cannot arise out of thin air, without a substantial basis within each person. More generally, Kant's presumption is that all of our capacities are to be understood as positive powers, with specific norms of what would constitute proper functioning and an ideal of full realization built into them.[71]

---

[69] In his book, Dean dismisses a "middle ground" (*Value of Humanity*, 86) because he believes it implies an inconsistent ascription of "highest possible value" (p, 87) to both a capacity for morality and an achievement of morality. But Kant's key claim is about incomparable value, and many things can have an absolute and incomparable value. Furthermore, for Kant, neither our capacity for morality nor our achievement of it is literally the very highest value, since what he calls the highest good (morality with the addition of appropriate happiness) and God must be of greater value.

[70] The exact point at which this capacity should be said to be present after conception is a highly complicated issue that Kant does not resolve and it will not be addressed here. A discussion of a biological basis for dignity within human beings is found in Kain, "Kant's Defense of Human Moral Status."

[71] See, e.g., Karl Schafer, "Kant: Constitutivism as Capacities-First Philosophy," *Philosophical Explorations* 2 (2019), 177–93; and "Transcendental Philosophy as Capacities-First Philosophy," *Philosophy and Phenomenological Research* 103 (2020), 661–86.

THE DISTINCTIVENESS OF KANTIAN DIGNITY   43

Precisely because the level of our moral achievement is far from what it can and should be, Dean is still correct in stressing, as he does, the significant role that the *idea* of humanity plays as an *ideal* throughout Kant's work. But those who hold that a capacity is worthy of respect would also emphasize the importance of an idea of what it would mean to act in a way that amounts to a move toward a fulfillment of the capacity. For Kant, there obviously is such an idea, and it is there from the very start in what he calls each person's predisposition to the good. But even after recognizing that we can truly understand and appreciate the capacity for morality only in view of this idea, we need not say that the value of the capacity lies only in its actualization. We can have it both ways: without a good capacity, a good realization would be impossible, and without an orientation toward realization, a capacity cannot even be understood for what it specifically is, let alone in a way that makes its relevance clear.

Dean regards Kantians as caught in a vitiating ambiguity when they speak of both capacity and realization, but—as Kant's comments about how we should treat the vicious and ignorant show—the distinction and gap between real capacity and later realization (just like that between an intention and an external actualization) is something they understand well, and they can regard it not as an "obstacle" but as a spur. Others deserve respect rather than contempt because we can presume that they are still human beings and in engaging with them there is always something positive to build on within them. This situation is precisely what makes life a moral project, a process of persons learning to mutually respect and assist each other precisely because they all are starting with both a predisposition for the good and a situation of "red ink," where help is always needed, and has a real chance to be effective, in the transition from early ignorance and improper priorities.

In addition, the most basic distinctive quality of human beings is free choice itself, and to say it has no value prior to actualization, or outside of actualization, leaves no clear room for even saying that anything would be lost if persons were executed prior to having a chance to act. It is therefore not surprising that, even apart from any reference to Kant, Stephen Darwall and other contemporary ethicists have argued that there are good reasons for saying that what we ordinarily call respect for persons is not just a matter of "appraisal respect," which is tied to reflecting how much persons have accomplished. What matters, first and necessarily, is "recognition respect," which is a matter of just acknowledging the status dignity of persons whenever they exist.[72] To say that something is in our nature as

---

[72] See, e.g., Stephen Darwall, "On a Kantian Form of Respect: 'Before a Humble Common Man...my Spirit Bows,'" in *Respect: Philosophical Essays*, 192–203. Here "humble common" (KpV [5: 77]) is the translation of *niedrigen bürgerlich-gemeinen*, and this means that Kant is saying that even if a person has a low socio-economic status, this is irrelevant to the basic respect that a person deserves simply on account of having the dignity status of a human being. Dean refers to Darwall's view, but maintains there is no universal feature that "grounds universal recognition respect" ("Peculiar Idea," 144).

persons is not to say that this full nature is already, or ever will be, in *act*. Many people have a life that is cut short very early, or are born with serious disabilities that they eventually manage to overcome. When they do succeed, we can say the person is simply functioning properly, living like other human beings are naturally set up to do as members of a distinctive species,[73] and we would not say that the person was subhuman before then and could be treated as a mere thing.[74]

1.8 Other Challenges

A serious problem also remains for non-mainline views even if they adopt a more liberal position that may not be exactly like Dean's, that is, one that falls back on the less demanding idea that having merely a single significant accomplishment is enough to warrant ascribing dignity to an agent. Since the world appears to be filled, as Kant well knew, with villains who do not appear to fulfill their capacity for morality even to this minimal degree, the consequence could be that we would be morally permitted, supposedly as Kantians, to merely instrumentalize numerous human beings. Kant's doctrine that even villains and the vicious always have some sense of the moral law within them and always deserve to be treated in a positive manner, no matter what their past is like, not only is basic to his ethical system but has been much more than a philosophical theory. It has major legal implications and, for good reason, its implications concerning treatment have had an effect on common practice in non-authoritarian governments ever since at least the Enlightenment.

At the same time, a Kantian can hold on to the importance of the commonsensical assessments of achievement that positions such as Dean's emphasize. Although Kant insists that we should not claim to be able to judge with certainty about the moral worth of our actions or those of others, he does not discourage us from holding on, with a keen sense of fallibility, to the kind of commonsensical moral assessments that we regularly make about agents. It seems clear—especially with respect to what Kant calls the imperfect duties of helping others and improving oneself—that mainline Kantians can easily recognize that some actions are especially unworthy and others are morally much more worthy because they are more demanding or more beneficial than others. They can also accept Kant's

---

[73] There have been, of course, many developments in science since Kant's time that challenge the notion of sharp and unchangeable boundaries between species, but Kant is not tied to a narrow view that the notion of a rational nature has to be restricted to human beings. He is also not tied to any specific claim about exactly when, biologically speaking, life as a person begins.

[74] Kant speaks of the "law in us" as having dignity (MdS [6: 397]) as well as of persons having dignity. Concerning the different kinds of items that can be the object of Kantian respect, see, e.g., Apaar Kumar, "Kant on the Ground of Human Dignity," *Kantian Review* 26 (2021), 435–53; and Adam Cureton, "Treating Disabled Adults as Children: An Application of Kant's Conception of Respect," in *Respect: Philosophical Essays*, 273.

commonsense presumption that, although some acts are much more unworthy than others, people do not lose their standing as human even after vicious acts.[75] Moreover, they can stress, as Kant does, that a maximization of good is not an appropriate goal for us (in part because, as Kant insists, although happiness is an essential good, it is one that does not lend itself to a determinate system), and the notion of being thoroughly moral can serve as an ideal but should not make one obsessive. Kant was well aware of the drawbacks of a situation where those who are concerned with "fantastic virtue" are frenetically trying to outdo others in their goodness.[76]

Against Kant's position, it has been argued that Kantian dignity turns out to be a mysterious bare "transcendental kernel,"[77] an allegedly unconditional ground that has no phenomenal location because it cannot be identified with any merely natural tendencies, and thus supposedly could be present, behind the scenes, everywhere or nowhere. This worry is understandable, and the problem may seem to be exacerbated by Kant's constant insistence on cutting off any transparent access to the "intelligible character" of the self that must be the ultimate ground of a person's dignity. But the opacity of Kant's ultimate conception of the person can also be regarded as part of a properly modest critical attitude. There is nothing in his philosophy that would suggest that it is appropriate to locate the "kernel" anywhere other than as just another feature of the persons that we know ("one and the same will," KrV B xxvii–xviii), albeit as a feature not known by theory or sensory observation but affirmed as part of our common modern and distinctively moral attitude toward our self and others.

Kant's insistence on strong claims about non-phenomenal truth may at first seem otherworldly in a bad, mystical sense, but his basic theoretical notion (although not his argument for it) of a non-phenomenal dimension is just that whatever has intrinsic grounds, beyond what it appears we could ever sense or theoretically determine, is something that needs to be admitted to be not literally a phenomenon. Modern science now appears to need to admit something like this as well, even if its guesses about the specific nature of this extra dimension may not be like Kant's (although there is some surprising similarity insofar as physics now appears to see a need to posit something not fully knowable but even more fundamental than space and time).[78] It should be kept in mind, however, that although, like other commentators, I have often stressed Kant's non-phenomenal metaphysics, one thing that my general metaphysical interpretation of Kant has never advocated (contrary to what appears to be implied by some

---

[75] Cf. the quotation from Hill in note 42.

[76] See Kant, MdS [6: 409] and Formosa, *Dignity*, 184.

[77] Michael Rosen, who accepts a strongly metaphysical reading as an accurate representation of Kant's system, presses this point in *Dignity*, 143–55.

[78] See Brian Greene, *Until the End of Time: Mind, Matter, and Our Search for Meaning in an Evolving Universe* (New York: Alfred A. Knopf, 2020).

reactions to this kind of interpretation[79]) is that there is any claim in his Critical philosophy of *noumenal insight* into this dimension that would allow us to theoretically determine individual natures. In theoretical contexts, one can combine substantive metaphysical thoughts and beliefs with modest epistemological claims.

There are, of course, numerous determinist and compatibilist projects in contemporary philosophy that exhibit little patience with Kant's metaphysical libertarianism, although these projects no longer seem as clearly required by science as was previously believed. *Revisionist* reductions of all our common modern concepts of *ultimate* personal responsibility, and hence culpability and praise for moral evil and virtue, are repeatedly attempted, and their ever more sophisticated forms deserve continued attention. (Nietzsche remains interesting in this respect because he at least recognized that modern alternatives can be grim.[80]) In the meantime, however, Kantians who feel the strong pull of "unsettling obligations"[81] cannot help but ask themselves whether they can, right now, coherently shuffle off their own sense of deep responsibility to a series of merely empirical forces. Kant's own position here appears to have followed the sensible path of moving, from a dogmatic "Cartesian" claim of a certainty of absolute freedom backed by a theoretical proof, to a Critical appreciation of what is best in the attitude of Rousseau's Savoyard Vicar, who uses as his guide the consideration of what one "cannot honestly refuse to believe."[82]

Another kind of reductionism is the common attempt to explain dignity as grounded in fundamental relational practices of respect, rather than the reverse, and then to explain these practices in turn as a matter of attitudes developed in a particular social context. A detailed attempt along this line, with a focus on

[79] See R. Lanier Anderson, "Transcendental Idealism as Formal Idealism: An Anti-Metaphysical Reading," in *Proceedings of the 13th International Kant Congress 'The Court of Reason' (Oslo, 6–9 August 2019)*, ed. Camilla Serck-Hanssen and Beatrix Himmelmann (Berlin and Boston: De Gruyter, 2021), 49–67.

[80] In an era that on the whole chooses to condemn as monstrous ancient doctrines such as predestination, it is striking that there are many popular philosophers ("naturalists") who seem to find little problem with accepting modern forms of thoroughgoing determination by forces that are also ultimately outside individual agents and humanity altogether, and whose source and direction remains as theoretically unknown and threatening as any "transcendental kernel."

[81] See Allen W. Wood, *Unsettling Obligations: Essays on Reason, Reality, and the Ethics of Belief* (Stanford, CA: CSLI Publications, 2002).

[82] Jean-Jacques Rousseau, *Emile, on Education* § 960 [1762], trans. Barbara Foxley (London: J. M. Dent and Sons [1911], repr. 1974); and Karl Ameriks, "Kant, Human Nature, and History after Rousseau," in *Kant's 'Observations' and 'Remarks': A Critical Guide*, ed. Susan Shell and Richard Velkley (Cambridge: Cambridge University Press, 2012), 247–65. Rousseau is often cited as a source of Kant's distinction between dignity in a universal sense and ascriptions of dignity that rest on mere social status. Although Rousseau's influence was significant, Kant came to insist that the ground of dignity in the unconditional sense lies in reason, and that speaking of it as if rooted in feeling can be misleading even though there is a feeling of respect that is necessarily connected to dignity. "Though respect is a feeling, it is not one *received* by means of influence; it is, instead, a feeling *self-wrought* by means of a rational concept and therefore specifically different from all feelings of the first kind, which can be reduced to inclination or fear" (GMS [4: 401, note]).

THE DISTINCTIVENESS OF KANTIAN DIGNITY   47

politics, has been developed impressively in a recent book by Colin Bird.[83] His philosophical objections to the basic Kantian notion of dignity, however, can be countered in ways that are similar to those that can be used in meeting other arguments against fundamental normative necessities. As Ariel Zylberman points out in his otherwise sympathetic review, Bird ultimately needs to answer the question of what justifies a society's focusing the attitude of respect in a particular direction, and there his argument ultimately appears to rest on an appeal to a notion of the *value* of persons.[84] It would be simpler, therefore, just to acknowledge, from the start, the fundamental dignity status of persons (a status that has numerous political implications since it is defined as a capacity relevant to all relational obligations of persons), and then it becomes understandable why they all have value and deserve the respect of all. Kant's position has the advantage of reminding us from the start that dignity is connected with a positive capacity, for it immediately comes with the notion of a realm of ends that need to be pursued for the sake of beings with freedom and reason. Dignity in this sense is not subject to the constant changes of human emotions and social conventions, although its relevance can, of course, disappear if all human beings become all-destroying monsters or massive natural calamities arise.

Another reason why Kant's position on our free moral capacity may be said to be commonsensical is that it parallels other non-neutral claims that we make about basic human powers. We believe, for example, that it is not enough to say that we simply aim, symmetrically, at either what is true or at what is false. What we all really believe is that truth is the basic notion, and in principle it is within our grasp and reflects our most basic and positive epistemic capacity (even if someone is too lazy to use the capacity very much), whereas falsehood is not a mere absence but has to be understood as a derivative and negative notion. Similarly, we believe that human beings do not just *miraculously* start to exhibit their language and mathematical capacity. We believe that, unless there is direct evidence that we are dealing with something like a scarecrow, we can assume that a being that appears to be human just like us has a distinctive nature, one that involves some reflective moral features that make it unlike, as far as we know, all other species on this planet. It is only sensible to assume that this nature is

---

[83] Colin Bird, *Human Dignity and Political Criticism* (Cambridge: Cambridge University Press, 2021). Bird faults Kantians for focusing on individual responsibility and blame despite the fact that many offenses against dignity have their source in structures whose origin is not primarily a matter of individual intentions. Although Kant does not focus on this problem as much as later thinkers do, his discussions of history show that he was quite aware that hugely important social and political developments, which can be either harmful or beneficial (as with the results of "unsociable sociability" (Idee [8: 18–21])), have an influence on individual agents. The blind "cunning of reason" was Hegel's notion, but the idea was not foreign to Kant's thinking.

[84] Ariel Zylberman, "*Human Dignity and Political Criticism*, by Colin Bird (review)," *Notre Dame Philosophical Reviews*, 2022.08.03. Zylberman refers especially to Bird, *Human Dignity*, 208, 218, 229, and 232. Like many political scientists, Bird gives in too quickly to the thought that there is no point in going along with the metaphysical dimension in Kant's ethics.

attached to an inborn and interconnected linguistic/mathematical capacity of the species, one that is normally brought into action after a period of natural human growth, maturation, and education. If we encounter a human being who does not speak or react as others do when they are presented with language and instructions, we still presume that, as long as there is not the slightest evidence that we are dealing with a member of another species, we are in the presence of someone who, like Helen Keller, might someday actualize many capacities that at first seemed to be totally slumbering.

It is true that the attitude just described as commonsensical does not correspond to the practices of all human societies. There are numerous societies, including many with considerable physical and social power, that have treated many kinds of human beings—women, children, foreigners, slaves, the widowed, elderly, ill, or disabled—as practically subhuman beings that can be done away with like trash or exploited as one might use a farm animal.[85] But such practices are just as evidently repulsive to any normal modern agent as would be as any recourse to witchcraft, astrology, and other superstitions as a way of guiding modern technology and medicine (even though such irrational tendencies have unfortunately been making a comeback recently). Nevertheless, the struggle against superstition, prejudice, and mistreatment of human beings has a complex history. As Kant noted, and as is still true now, even though something called an "age of enlightenment" has begun, we have not yet arrived at an "enlightened age" (Auf [8: 40]). Some of the huge and surprising difficulties that have arisen on the rocky road of attempts to arrive at such an age are discussed in the chapters that follow.

Kantian Dignity and its Difficulties. Karl Ameriks, Oxford University Press. © Karl Ameriks 2024.
DOI: 10.1093/9780198917656.003.0002

---

[85] As even critics of Kant acknowledge, when respect for human dignity as an inviolable principle in his sense became part of the constitution of the Federal Republic of Germany, it certainly was at least a welcome change from the practices of the Nazi regime. That regime acquired power in 1933 in a manner that was in accord with the constitution in place then, and its standing was reaffirmed in popular referendums. Before as well as during World War II, the German government drew on an immense amount of support for its murderous actions within Germany itself and then in the vast occupied territories. These are familiar facts, and somewhat similar outrages have occurred in other places too, but how it became possible specifically in the context of Kant's own Germany, and areas under its control, is a mystery that still deserves further study—and many similar mysteries are occurring now. Hence the chapters that follow.

2
Dignity as Universal: Herder, Diversity, and Development

> One can never undo the effect of Jena and its influence.
> Countess Christine[1]

This chapter compares and contrasts the careers of Kant and his student, J. G. Herder, and their positions on issues such as dignity, diversity, history, and cosmopolitanism. Kant and Herder have a lot in common, although Kant was especially interested in necessity and universal duties, whereas Herder deserves respect for having introduced a stress on respect for contingency, diversity, and historical developments that are not a matter of linear and completely rational progress. The basic cosmopolitanism of their philosophies is defended against non-progressive interpretations of their work. A special emphasis is placed on Herder's early time in Riga and Kant's late Postscript in a German–Lithuanian dictionary. The Postscript exhibits an underlying philosophical friendship between them, based on a common respect for local cultures that are vulnerable to the harmful actions of powerful nations.

2.1 Dignity and Diversity

The original German version of the epigraph, which comes from the middle of a novel by Theodor Fontane entitled *Unwiederbringlich*, is: *Das Jenasche mit seinen Einflüssen ist nie ganz wieder zu tilgen*. The term *wieder* ("again") in this passage repeats a key portion of the novel's title, and this is a giveaway that the remark is meant by Fontane to have a central significance. As the title suggests, once big changes have occurred, we cannot exist again as we were before. The novel as a whole is built around a conflict of competing traditions. The old Halle Pietism that still dominates Countess Christine's thinking contrasts in numerous ways with the new liberalism of the spirit of Jena,[2] which infects other characters in the

---

[1] Theodore Fontane, *No Way Back* [1891], trans. Hugh Rorrison and Helen Chambers (New York: Penguin, 2013), 129. Other English translations have used other titles: *Irretrievable, Beyond Recall*.

[2] The reputation of Jena is well depicted in these recent overviews (although, as often happens, the Kantian backbone of the Early Romantic movement is neglected): Peter Neumann, *Jena 1800: The Republic of Free Spirits* [2017], trans. Shelley Frisch (New York: Farrar, Straus and Giroux, 2022); and Andrea Wulf, *Magnificent Rebels: The First Romantics and the Invention of the Self* (New York: Knopf Doubleday, 2022).

50 KANTIAN DIGNITY AND ITS DIFFICULTIES

book in a naïve way. The novel can be read as suggesting, more generally that, precisely because there is no way back (*nie ganz*) after Jena (that is, modernity), a nondogmatic—and also less naïve—reaction to this fact needs to be developed.

This theme is common in works by Fontane, whose familiarity with the conflict of traditions in late nineteenth-century Prussia gave him an ideal vantage point for observing the stressful pressures that late modern life was putting on age-old customs throughout Europe. Strict Germanic traditions concerning the duties of family, military, and religious life still placed an enormous weight on respect for dignity in a hierarchical sense, and in relatively local rather than cosmopolitan terms. As the nineteenth century developed, however, a cosmopolitan perspective was gaining ever more influence. This perspective owed its strength in part to ever-growing international developments in commerce and science, but it also had deep intellectual roots because of the influence of Kant and the bevy of German philosophers who started their careers in Jena (until Napoleon's victory there in 1807) and were inspired by Jean-Jacques Rousseau's ideals and the original aims of the French Revolution.

The Enlightenment's triple ideal of liberty, equality, and fraternity clearly fits best with an unconditional and universal conception of human dignity. There were strong reactions in Europe, however, to the chaotic developments in the radical French attempt to immediately realize those ideals, and they came from a variety of directions. Challenges to letting the French model monopolize European thinking arose not only from conservative defenders of emphasizing differences in social status and levels of success. The writings of Johann Gottfried Herder (1744–1803) featured a new kind of *enlightened* respect for particularity and local achievement of even a modest kind. Like his teacher, Kant, Herder came from a poor background, so it is not surprising that, when he brought attention to a need to value local traditions, he nonetheless held to a form of cosmopolitanism that, just as in Kant's philosophy, acknowledged basic dignity and a capacity for morality in all human beings. It was typical of Herder to ask, in his first essay on history, "Is not the good *dispersed* all over the earth? Because it could not be encompassed by one face of mankind it was dispersed in a thousand faces, ever changing—an eternal Proteus—through all continents and centuries..."[3] Decades later, he would make the point in an even stronger normative form: "Least of all, therefore, can our *European culture* be the measure of universal goodness and human value."[4] But he was not a relativist, for he also added that, when we read accounts by travel writers (an extremely popular genre in his time),

---

[3] Johann Gottfried Herder, "This, too, a Philosophy of History" [1774], in *Herder: On World History: An Anthology*, ed. Hans Adler and Ernest A. Menze (Armonk, NY and London: M. E. Sharpe, 1997), trans. Ernest A. Menze with Michael Palma, 41.

[4] Herder, *Letters for the Advancement of Humanity* [1793–7], Tenth Collection, in *Herder: Philosophical Writings*, ed. Michael N. Forster (Cambridge: Cambridge University Press, 2002), 396.

we must ask, "to what extent they had a pure eye and in their breast *universal natural* and *human sensitivity.*"[5]

Herder's prime interests and original gifts, like Rousseau's, were largely of a literary nature. His roots were in the far north, but he settled eventually in the center of Germany. He was hired by his friend, Johann Wolfgang von Goethe, to serve as the liberal religious leader of Weimar, the capital at that time of the area around Jena. Earlier, in Strasbourg, the young Goethe had spent some time with Herder, who by then had already traveled around much of Europe. Herder advised Goethe not to follow fashion by imitating traditions established elsewhere but to develop his unusually good ear for the nuances of his native language, which at that time was largely ignored in Europe and deserved also to have a place in world literature.[6] Herder similarly championed Shakespeare—against criticisms from classicist perspectives as well as praise from a narrow nationalist perspective—as an exemplary genius with a special gift for displaying all levels of human life and an "ability to express," as Kristin Gjesdal has noted, "a diversity that is constitutive of the modern world."[7]

A consideration of Herder's distinctive perspective, in combination with a reassessment of his relation to Kant, is relevant to an understanding of both thinkers. At the end of his career, Kant came up with a surprising formulation of a position somewhat like Herder's, an orientation that explicitly combines universalism with respect for honoring neglected talents beyond the centers of European power.[8] If only more could have been done along this line, it could well have helped to save German philosophy and society from the disastrous error of presuming that, just because there is something missing in merely universal conceptions of duty and dignity, the only alternative is to turn chauvinist and measure the worth of human beings entirely by the degree to which they merely serve the power-oriented duties of one's own nation. Unfortunately, the thought of Herder and even Kant eventually became linked, unfairly, to movements that were reactionary in an extremist manner and that even had an influence on the early thinking of later talents such as Thomas Mann.[9] This development not only brought disaster and shame to Germany but also blocked, within the

---

[5] Herder, *Advancement of Humanity*, 397.

[6] See Nicholas Boyle, *Goethe: The Poet and the Age, Vol. I: The Poetry of Desire* (Oxford and New York: Oxford University Press, 1992), 94–125.

[7] Kristin Gjesdal, *Herder's Hermeneutics: History, Poetry and Enlightenment* (Cambridge: Cambridge University Press), 141. Gjesdal notes that Herder's discussion of Shakespeare anticipates Kant's notion of "exemplary genius," that is, someone with a "capacity to expand the prevalent symbolic tradition," but in a way that is "both individual and expressive of a shared culture and tradition" (p. 135).

[8] See Onora O'Neill's insightful contemporary account of "modernity, universalists, and particularists: an alternative story," in *Towards Justice and Virtue: A Constructive Account of Practical Reasoning* (Cambridge: Cambridge University Press, 1996), 31–7.

[9] See Chs. 6–8.

52 KANTIAN DIGNITY AND ITS DIFFICULTIES

non-German world, a realization of the progressive potential inherent in the possibility of combining what is best in Herder's and Kant's views.

The fundamental idea here is fairly simple, namely that, especially after the upheavals of modern philosophy, science, and the French Revolution, it makes sense to supplement the newly popular doctrine of universal human dignity with attention to the rich diversity of the world's traditions and their distinctive role as a treasure of value relevant to humanity on the whole. Herder and the Early Romantics of Jena understood this point especially well and were famous for their translation work and openness to non-European cultural accomplishments, as well as for their bringing back into view neglected earlier aspects of their own culture, such as medieval art. In contrast to chauvinist relapses, such as Johann Gottlieb Fichte's argument in 1808 that genuine philosophic thought is possible only in the Germanic languages,[10] they saw that a fully developed Enlightenment philosophy should be inclusive and yet go beyond focusing only on the doctrine that human beings are fundamentally alike insofar as they deserve unconditional respect.

A similar idea can also be found in Kant's system. The reason human dignity deserves respect is that it is based on a recognition of all human beings as capable of morality and, therefore, as obliged not only to perfect their own powers but also to protect and enhance the development and moral agency of *all others*. As a consequence, it is only appropriate for Kantians also to believe that respect for persons needs to be universal in a local manner and engage in protecting, for all of us, the diverse values of small cultures that are in danger of being overrun by the levelling tendencies of modern life. The remainder of this chapter will illustrate this point by taking note of Kant's coming to express this position in a surprisingly direct way in a long-neglected publication from near the very end of his career. To understand the significance of this development, however, it is necessary first to review the contours of Kant's complex relationship with Herder.

2.2 Kant and Herder: A Backward Glance

A close linking of the notions of human nature, diversity, and progress, especially in a normative and secular context, became intense only in the eighteenth century. A complicating feature of this development within the German tradition is the pivotal role Herder played as a founding father of late modern philosophy of history.[11] Alongside his own peculiar brand of naturalistic religious optimism,

---

[10] See Richard Velkley, "Language, Embodiment, and the Supersensuous in *Fichte's Addresses to the German Nation*," in *Kant and the Possibility of Progress: From Modern Hopes to Postmodern Anxieties*, ed. Samuel A. Stoner and Paul T. Wilford (Philadelphia: University of Pennsylvania Press, 2021), 153–64.

[11] This development was, of course, heavily influenced as well as by Rousseau, Kant, and others such as Gotthold Ephraim Lessing. See Henry E. Allison, *Lessing and the Enlightenment: His Philosophy of Religion and its Relation to Eighteenth-century Thought* (Ann Arbor: University of Michigan Press, 1966).

Herder introduced the highly influential anti-Whiggish notions of the "spirit of an age" (*Zeitgeist*) and the "spirit of a people" (*Volksgeist*). These terms are a major source of the now common view that each culture needs to be respectfully understood on its own terms rather than through anachronistic, homogenizing, and progress-obsessed lenses. Herder insightfully connected these notions while also emphasizing the general philosophical significance of the perplexing phenomenon of change of taste, which is a fundamental kind of cultural development that is not easily understandable as progress, although it still involves going beyond the past even while learning from it.[12] Ever since, history generally has been conceived in terms of a basic contrast between relatively nonlinear Herderian conceptions and the more linear and less diversity-oriented conceptions that dominated European thought up through Kant's time and, for quite a while afterwards, in the work of Fichte, G. W. F. Hegel, Ludwig Feuerbach, Auguste Comte, Karl Marx, and their innumerable allies.[13]

While this familiar contrast is understandable, a closer look immediately reveals a need for numerous qualifications. Hence, this section will provide a brief three-part reappraisal of the relationship between Herder and Kant: first, a review of complexities in Kant's and Herder's own historical situation; second, a reassessment of the exaggerated contrast that is often made in discussions of their highly influential views; and third, an analysis of some especially valuable ideas in Kant's last publication that points toward a compromise with Herder and a foreshadowing of later movements. (After 1796, Kant's health was failing and most of the works published with Kant's name in this period—unlike the *Nachschrift*—come from much earlier lectures that it is not clear that Kant himself closely edited.) The compromise consists in Kant's coming to explicitly acknowledge the value to the world at large of even little-known local identities and thus arriving, at the very end of his career, on the brink of a third and fully cosmopolitan view of history. This view, which can be schematized in terms of an ellipse or spiral, was developed in a variety of fruitful ways by the Early Romantic successors of Kant, and it has become widely appreciated again in our own time. It invokes what is best in linear and nonlinear, as well as global and local, considerations of history in a manner that is especially appropriate for understanding how, in the hybrid culture of our late modern era, justice can still be done to endangered, diverse, and local interests even while respecting the universal status dignity of human beings.

Respect for local cultures need not be a matter of uncritical provincialism. Although Kant and Herder have often been taken to be archetypical heroes—or

---

[12] See Kristin Gjesdal, "Aesthetic Value and Historical Understanding," in *Herder's Hermeneutics*, 73–101; Karl Ameriks, "On Herder's Hermeneutics," *SGIR Review* 1 (2018), 1–12; and Rachel Zuckert, *Herder's Naturalist Aesthetics* (Cambridge: Cambridge University Press, 2019).

[13] See the classic discussion of the progressive tradition in Karl Löwith, *Meaning in History: The Theological Implications of the Philosophy of History* (Chicago: University of Chicago Press, 1949).

54 KANTIAN DIGNITY AND ITS DIFFICULTIES

villains—representing something called "the Prussian spirit" or "the German soul,"[14] the fact is each one of these leading figures of their era represents a complex variety of identities. In a sense, neither of them can simply be called "German," for Germany did not even exist as such in their era (the closest it had come to existing as a unity was in the form of a *Reich* that was "Roman"), and when it did come into being in 1870, the world had changed dramatically. In the Anglophone world, Kant is often taken to be arch-Prussian in a noncomplimentary sense, but in fact his relations with Prussian customs and authorities were often tense, and it is no accident that some of his best friends were connected more with Great Britain, Russia, or the Baltic peoples. In Kant's time, his hometown of Königsberg (often misleadingly characterized as "provincial") was one of Germany's largest and most internationally oriented cities, even though it had just lost its position as the political center of Prussia. In our own time, it has long borne a Stalinist name and a peripheral status entirely outside of Germany. Because of Königsberg's marginalized *later* situation, its most famous citizen suffered the strange fate of not even having a local organization that can appropriately support his status as a world-class figure in the way that Hegel and Goethe, for example, have been celebrated by their compatriots.

The bizarre fact of the lack of a fitting institution honoring Kant within the German nation was accompanied by the much more tragic event of the eventual philosophical reversal, within his own homeland, of the nineteenth-century call for a turn "back to Kant." A shocking eclipse of reason occurred when influential extremists on both the right and the left overreacted to the crises at the turn of the century[15] and the post-Versailles era, and then, by the 1930s, encouraged a widespread dismissal of Germany's most promising perspective on history, human dignity, and democratic development in general. They thereby turned their backs on the greatest philosopher in their own heritage—an Enlightenment writer who offered a path-breaking cosmopolitan view of history based on a respect for self-determination within a framework of free republics, and with an anti-chauvinist plan for an effective league of nations committed to seeking perpetual peace. The sad irony of history is that the special value of Kant's work was brought back to the center of attention in our time not by the most famous of twentieth-century German-speaking philosophers, such as Martin Heidegger, Ludwig Wittgenstein, György Lukács, and Hans-Georg Gadamer, but in large part through the eventual influence of refugees and non-German writers—such as Ernst Cassirer, Hannah Arendt, P. F. Strawson, Wilfrid Sellars, John Rawls, Onora O'Neill, and Michael Friedman—in the Allied countries that, twice, had to fight off millions of German invaders.

---

[14] A later maverick author went beyond a mere contrast of Kant and Herder to a general contrast of bad "spirit" and good "soul." See Ludwig Klages, *Der Geist als Widersacher der Seele* (Leipzig: Johann Ambrosius Barth, 1929–32).

[15] For a vivid sketch of the confused mood of the era, see Florian Illies, *1913: The Year before the Storm*, trans. Shaun Whiteside and Jamie Lee Searle (New York: Melville House, 2013). See also Chs. 6–8.

Even though Kant's background is more cosmopolitan than is generally realized, he was not an angel whose presumptions escaped the limits of his age and context. Looking back, current scholars continue to unearth disturbing layers of anti-Semitism, and racism, such as a marginal, anti-Slavic note that says, "Russians and Poles are not capable of any autonomy" (Anth [7: 315]).[16] The fact that passages such as this have only recently become central in academic discussions also reflects negatively on the work of later generations of scholars (including myself) who, for decades, gave little or no attention to the skeletons in Kant's closets. Kant's writings include many harsh statements like this, although sometimes they can be interpreted not as an indictment of particular individuals but as a mere repetition, as was the style then, of popular cultural stereotypes, or a remark basically about a contemporary political situation—for example, the fact that for a time Poland went to the extreme of allowing countless nobles to have a veto on any government action, whereas the Russians and Turks went to the opposite extreme of dictatorial power.

It should also be kept in mind that Kant's frequent negative characterizations of the intelligence and talents of non-Europeans was a consequence not of direct experience but of the perennial mistake of granting too much to the cultural beliefs of the celebrated scientists of one's era, such as, in Kant's case, Carl Linnaeus (1707–78).[17] Kant's insulting characterizations of other peoples are troublesome in numerous ways, but they are not *direct moral* critiques. They are still compatible with the basic doctrine that all human beings are equal in original dignity. Kant repeatedly distinguished moral worth from talent or achievement and, following Rousseau, he directed his moral criticism at the distinctive and especially blameworthy vices of "advanced" cultures. All the same, there remain serious moral issues concerning the *indirect* effects of the prejudiced characterizations, offered by Kant and practically everyone else in his era, of allegedly less culturally advanced groups.

One surprising sign of the limitations in Kant's cosmopolitanism—and one that is all the more striking because it is independent of issues such as racism, religion, and gender—is the fact that, right in the heart of his career in the mid-1780s and at the very time that he was most interested in political events and the idea of democratic and anticolonial government with a separation of church, state, and academy, he made no statement on the world-changing event of the creation of the United States (1776) and the revolutionary state constitutions that replaced British imperial rule in America. This is surprising because, as is well known to historians, "The progress of the war was watched with great interest, and even suspense, in Germany, and its events became known there with

---

[16] See Ch. 3, for more discussion of the problem of prejudice.
[17] On the influence of Linnaeus and his prejudices, see Kathryn Schulz, "You Name it: Carl Linnaeus and the Effort to Label all Life," *The New Yorker*, August 21, 2023, 50–4.

56 KANTIAN DIGNITY AND ITS DIFFICULTIES

surprising promptness and accuracy."[18] Unlike Kant, leading German writers such as Christoph Martin Wieland, Georg Forster, and Johann Benjamin Erhard went out of their way to champion the Americans, as did many others elsewhere.

A story about a discussion Kant had when he first met Joseph Green, a British businessman in Königsberg, used to be considered proof of Kant's enthusiasm for the American war of independence, but it is now clear that the date of the discussion was in the mid-1760s and could not have concerned later events.[19] In the 1790 *Critique of the Power of Judgment*, Kant offered a vague remark about a "recently undertaken fundamental transformation" (KU [5: 375n.]). Some readers (for example, George Bancroft and Hannah Arendt) have assumed this referred to America, but Kant's wording shows he was referring to France and the radically new "organization" of government that Sieyès had just proposed there.[20] Other parties were, however, clearly expressing their reaction to the monumental changes overseas.

At this very time, a significant revolt occurred in Amsterdam that was inspired by events in America and dominated by a party crying for "freedom"—a revolt that was eventually stifled by Prussian troops and met with no sign of protest from Kant. "Patriots" in the Dutch Republic went so far as to threaten to join a league of armed neutrality in order to trade with the American colonies in revolt. Even though Britain then declared war on the Dutch, the American position was so popular in Holland that the United States was recognized by the Dutch States General in 1782. Large democratic military groups were formed by 1783 to challenge the oligarchy in Amsterdam, and these were eventually put down only with the help of outside force in September 1787. On the excuse of an offense of lèse-majesté to a traveling princess, Frederick II offered the troops of Carl of Braunschweig to stifle the democratic movement in Holland.[21] At the same time, and unlike Kant, Prussian officials were showing an intense interest in the new American government, which was then represented in Amsterdam by no less than John Adams.[22] The ultimate aim of Prussian policy was to lessen the power

---

[18] James Taft Hatfield and Elfrieda Hochbaum, "The Influence of the American Revolution upon German Literature," *Americana Germanica* 3 (1900), 345. See also Horst Dippel, *Germany and the American Revolution 1770–1800*, trans. Bernhard A. Uhlendorf (Chapel Hill: University of North Carolina Press, 1977); David Armitage, *The Declaration of Independence: A Global History* (Cambridge, MA: Harvard University Press, 2007); and Jonathan Israel, *The Expanding Blaze: How the American Revolution Ignited the World, 1775–1848* (Princeton: Princeton University Press, 2017).

[19] See Manfred Kuehn, *Kant: A Biography* (Cambridge: Cambridge University Press, 2001), 154–5. See Ch. 4, for further discussion of Kant and American independence.

[20] See the helpful comparison of the situations in France and the United States in David Runciman's review of *Emmanuel Sieyès: Political Writings*, ed. Michael Sonenscher (Indianapolis: Hackett, 2003), in "Schockingly Worldly," *London Review of Books* 25 (October 2003), 7–10. Sieyès successfully advocated a reorganization of the French government by a leveling of the estates.

[21] See Simon Schama, *Patriots and Liberators—Revolution in the Netherlands, 1780–1813* (New York: Alfred A. Knopf, 1977), 60 and 127.

[22] On the enthusiasm for democracy that American independence generated at that time throughout Europe, see Ch. 4, and the reaction of John Adams as recounted in Page Smith, *John Adams, Vol. 1, 1735–1784* (Garden City, NY: Doubleday, 1962), 503.

of England, not to help the United States as such. Nonetheless, the Prussians were the first, after independence, to sign an international treaty with the new United States, a recognition of the rights of civilians on the open seas. The Treaty of Amity and Commerce between the Kingdom of Prussia and the United States of America, September 10, 1785, was negotiated by Thomas Jefferson as ambassador in France and signed by George Washington and Frederick II.[23]

There is no reason to assume that Kant neglected mentioning, let alone praising, the bold American experiment out of a fear of censorship. It is striking that even in his abundant private remarks there is no clear sign of direct interest in, or sympathy with, the United States as such, although he surely realized, from his British friends and the French press, that the American situation was a matter of constant discussion.[24] The final sentences of Kant's famous essay on "What Is Enlightenment?" (1784) discuss the dangers of encouraging too much "civil freedom" at once and reveal a clue about his overall attitude, although they never specify what countries he has in mind. The essay warns about chaotic attacks on authority that can arise from a too hasty public endorsement of change before the habit of "thinking freely" has been adequately developed, and for the meantime it praises the fact that in Prussia there is a "well-disciplined and numerous army to keep the public peace" (Auf [8: 41]). It should be noted, however, that in this essay Kant also expressed his theoretical independence by insisting that a "monarch's authority rests on his unification of a people's collective will" (Auf [8: 40]), and that it would be a "crime against human nature" to disrespect "the criterion of everything that can [presumably normatively] be agreed upon as law by a people" (Auf [8: 39]). He also went out of his way to make a reference to some of "the Dutch" for providing an example of an attempt at democratic church practices, and perhaps this was a subtle message that he was in accord with some developments in Holland although he did not want to make a direct political statement (Auf [8: 38]).

It is striking, above all, that although Kant was renowned for his detailed lectures about the far reaches of the world, his remarks about Americans ignore the new country's remarkable leaders and institutions and instead highlight what he calls savage Indians (Beo [2: 438], Rel [6: 33]) and lazy blacks (RezHerd [8: 62], PhysGeo [9: 316]). Kant took these characterizations from what was regarded as the most advanced anthropological research of his time, although he also warned that, so far, such work has been a mere "risky attempt" (Anth [7: 312]).[25]

---

[23] See Henry Mason Adams, *Prussian–American Relations, 1775–1871* (Cleveland: Press of Western Reserve University, 1960).

[24] See Henry Steele Commager, *The Empire of Reason: How Europe Imagined and America Realized the Enlightenment* (Garden City, NY: Anchor/Doubleday, 1977).

[25] On Kant's late and more liberal comments on race, see Pauline Kleingeld, "Kant's Second Thoughts on Race," *Philosophical Quarterly* 57 (2007), 573–92, and *Kant and Cosmopolitanism: The Philosophical Ideal of World Citizenship* (Cambridge: Cambridge University Press, 2012). See also Ch. 3, and Lucy Allais, "Kant's Racism," *Philosophical Papers* 45 (2016), 1–36; Georg Cavallar, *Kant's*

58 KANTIAN DIGNITY AND ITS DIFFICULTIES

In retrospect, it is impossible to deny that, even though Kant was by no means a reactionary, his remarks are another reminder that he exhibited a strange and quite non-cosmopolitan blindness about distant peoples—including those of his own ethnic background ("WASPs"), many of whom even shared his liberal religious views and progressive principles.

Given all these facts, it is not surprising that the work of Herder, Kant's closest and most famous student, has long been favored by non-Kantians precisely because it appears to be a corrective to what they find lacking in Kant.[26] Whereas Kant's work has been taken to be abstract, ahistorical, and overly rationalist, Herder has been regarded as a prime inaugurator of a radically different view of history and identity, one that is open to the whole world and appealingly stresses the values of concreteness, feeling, contingency, and diversity.[27] For a long time, Herder was also characterized, and then praised or castigated, as a "Counter-Enlightenment" figure whose work served not merely to supplement Kant's philosophy but to encourage reactionary religious and political sentiments. This reading, which goes back in large part to the work of the Riga expatriate Isaiah Berlin, has fortunately been sharply rejected by most recent specialists.[28] Here it is essential to keep in mind the enormous difference between *antirationalism* and *irrationalism* and to praise Herder insofar as, like many philosophers, he was simply an antirationalist, that is, unsympathetic to a priori *systematic* claims. On the whole, he was more open-minded and humanistic than Kant although, of course, not entirely without some biases of his own that can lend themselves to misuse. While both Herder and Kant deserve credit for introducing a stress on the key term *Humanität*, Herder belonged to the vanguard of a later generation that was generally more respectful of the actual variety of persons and societies throughout the world, and of the value of difference throughout history.

Because of his special interest in the notion of a *Volk*, or people, Herder is often stereotyped (or approved by reactionary writers) as a nationalist, but this term is ambiguous and can be highly misleading. At the least, it is necessary to distinguish *defensive* nationalism (aimed at the protection of relatively weak and often stateless groups, such as the Irish, Poles, and Lithuanians) and *offensive* nationalism (the chauvinism of expansionist powers), as well as the phenomenon of

---

Embedded Cosmopolitanism: History, Philosophy, and Education for World Citizens (Berlin: De Gruyter, 2015); Dilek Huseyinzadegan, *Kant's Nonideal Theory of Politics* (Evanston: Northwestern University Press, 2019).

[26] On Herder's interest in the American cause, see John Wall, "The American Revolution and German Literature," *Modern Language Notes* 16 (1961), 163–76.

[27] See, e.g., Charles Taylor, "The Importance of Herder," in *Isaiah Berlin: A Celebration*, ed. Edna and Avishai Margalit (Chicago and London: University of Chicago Press and Hogarth Press, 1991), 40–64; John H. Zammito, *Kant, Herder, and the Birth of Anthropology* (Chicago: University of Chicago Press, 2002); and Michael N. Forster, *Herder's Philosophy* (Oxford: Oxford University Press, 2018).

[28] See Robert E. Norton, "The Myth of the Counter-Enlightenment," *Journal of the History of Ideas* 68 (2007), 635–58, and "Isaiah Berlin's 'Expressionism,' or: 'Ha! Du bist das Blökende!'," *Journal of the History of Ideas* 69 (2008), 339–47.

paranoid nationalism, when the masses in the super powers are indoctrinated to believe that they are being seriously threatened by foreigners of all kinds and hence have to launch aggressive actions allegedly in the defense of freedom. The term "patriotism" can also cause many problems. There is, however, an excellent treatment of the phenomenon in Richard Price's essay "A Discourse on the Love of our Country" (1789), which eloquently argues that true patriotism requires an understanding of the *genuine* values of one's country and thus is compatible with a positive attitude toward autonomous government and respect for dignity elsewhere. Herder and Kant would certainly agree, although they were not international activists for this cause in the exceptional manner that Price was.[29]

One might at first suppose that the main divide between Kant and Herder is due to little more than a difference in their natural abilities and occupations. Herder was from the start at home in aesthetics, and he quickly made a name for himself through an impressive range of literary achievements—in creative as well as critical writing, and in translating and promoting local poetry, such as the folksongs of Riga's Baltic natives and other relatively unknown peoples. Kant might seem to be the very opposite kind of scholar, an academic who was at first most interested in the stunning revolution of modern physics and its metaphysical presuppositions. However, Kant had broader concerns that became evident once he was established in his early career, which began to flourish right in the early 1760s. At that time he was suddenly "turned around" by reading Rousseau,[30] and he also went out of his way to help support Herder, who was an impoverished young student. Kant was a highly popular lecturer, in large part because of his creation of the academic field of "geo-anthropology," that is, a detailed account of the variety of human cultures and their relation to their natural and historical context—an account that clearly was a huge influence on Herder.[31] Initially, Kant was even offered a chair in poetics in view of the fact that he had become best known because of a popular essay on aesthetics (which was for a long time his best-selling volume) in which, in the fashionable style of that day, he offered witty—but now often quite off-putting—sketches of contrasting temperaments and European national characters.

The fact of the matter is that Kant had a deep aesthetic and not merely rationalist side, and Herder was not merely an aesthetic writer but was, not coincidentally,

---

[29] See Ch. 5, for an account of Price's significance. For a helpful contemporary discussion, see C. Stephen Evans, "Patriotism and Love of the Neighbor: A Kierkegaardian View of a Contested Virtue," *Religions* 14 (forthcoming).

[30] See Karl Ameriks, "Kant, Human Nature, and History after Rousseau," in *Kant's 'Observations' and 'Remarks': A Critical Guide*, ed. Susan Meld Shell and Richard Velkley (Cambridge: Cambridge University Press, 2012), 247–65.

[31] See Günter Zöller, "Genesis und Klima. Naturgeschichte und Geo-Anthropologie bei Kant und Herder," in *Proceedings of the XI International Kant-Congress 2010*, ed. Claudio LaRocca and Margit Ruffing (Berlin: De Gruyter, 2013), 551–64.

60 KANTIAN DIGNITY AND ITS DIFFICULTIES

very concerned with nature, science, and rational development.[32] Herder also was well known—and looked down upon by the likes of Schiller—for being more direct than Kant in his rejection of aristocratic privilege.[33] It is therefore very unfair to both Kant and Herder to characterize them, as is still often done (and as they later even came to do to each other) in terms of a contrast between a rigid unfeeling rationalism and a soft tendency to reactionary irrationalism. And yet, despite all the ways in which a fair reading of Kant and Herder must be attentive to their complex commonalities,[34] there remains an undeniable *methodological* difference between their approaches. Kant always had a special interest in first seeking out the universal and necessary even in the particular, whereas Herder loved to express and linger over the particular and contingent for its own sake, without denying the basic value of humanity in general.

The final task of this section is therefore to explain how, despite this contrast, there can be an appropriate way to positively combine the insights of Kant and Herder in relation to issues of history, progress, and properly understanding human dignity. A striking document that bears right on this topic is Kant's unusual late publication of 1800, a "Postscript of a Friend" for a German–Lithuanian dictionary (Nachschrift [8: 445]). Fortunately, one can now rely heavily on an excellent recent analysis of the text by another Kant scholar with a Riga background: Susan Meld Shell.[35] As Shell demonstrates, this concise and long-ignored piece is a carefully crafted culmination of Kant's career-long agonizing over the issues of national character, friendship, and progress in a cosmopolitan context. It also bears—and this is my own extra claim—on his strained relation-

---

[32] See the judicious overviews by Daniel Dahlstrom, "The Aesthetic Holism of Hamann, Herder, and Schiller," in *The Cambridge Companion to German Idealism*, 2nd edn, ed. Karl Ameriks (Cambridge: Cambridge University Press, 2017), 106–27; and Allen W. Wood, "Kant and Herder: Their Enlightenment Faith," in *Metaphysics and the Good: Themes from the Philosophy of Robert Merrihew Adams*, ed. Samuel Newlands and Larry M. Jorgensen (Oxford: Oxford University Press, 2009), 313–42.

[33] As Michael N. Forster explains, "Herder is also committed to republicanism and democracy (advocating a much broader franchise than Kant, for example). He has several reasons for this position, each deriving from an egalitarian concern for the interests of all the members of society." Forster, "Introduction," *Herder: Philosophical Writings*, xxxi.

[34] See the argument that Herder's works are committed "to a set of general, albeit 'thin,' universal principles," in Vicki C. Spencer, "Unity and Diversity: Herder, Relativism, and Pluralism," in *The Emergence of Relativism: German Thought from the Enlightenment to National Socialism*, ed. Martin Kusch et al. (London: Routledge, 2019), 201.

[35] Susan Meld Shell, "*Nachschrift eines Freundes*: Kant on Language, Friendship, and the Concept of a People," *Kantian Review* 15 (2010), 88–117. In quoting from the *Nachschrift*, I cite several passages that are also discussed by Shell. See also J. D. Miniger, "*Nachschrift eines Freundes*: Kant, Lithuania, and the Praxis of Enlightenment," *Studies in East European Thought* 57 (2005), 1–25. "While Hamann and Herder are famous for their support of the Baltic peoples, the *Nachschrift* shows convincingly and proudly that Kant too belongs to this constellation" (Miniger, 24). More specifically, "Kant announces his politics not by linking the teaching of Lithuanian to some broader Prussian motive, but to the lives of the Lithuanian people" (Miniger, 12). The dictionary clearly had a political purpose and effect, for it was aimed, in part, at counterbalancing the force of what the dictionary editor called the "German colonists" (Miniger, 7).

ship with Herder. It does so in a manner that reveals a bridge toward Herder's views and also to related ideas about the relation of philosophy to history that were developed in the next generation in the writings of the Early Romantics.

Very soon after Herder left Königsberg for Riga in 1764, Kant admonished him to pay more heed to the philosophical virtue of conceptual clarity and not to lose himself in vivid but vague metaphors. Kant repeated this plea in his three (!) 1785 writings on the first volumes of Herder's massive *Ideas toward a Philosophy of History of Humanity* (*Ideen zur Philosophie der Geschichte der Menschheit*, 1784–91)—a book that intentionally starts with a plural term in its title. Kant could not help but regard this work as a competitor to his own just-published *Idea of a Universal History with a Cosmopolitan Aim* (*Idee zu einer allgemeinen Geschichte in weltbürglicher Absicht*, 1784)—a brief tract that, by no accident, starts with a singular term in its title.[36] Herder had also published even earlier works on history, and so his writings on the topic were widely known to have preceded that of his teacher—a fact that was perhaps an extra sore point between them. Herder took offense at Kant's schoolmasterly comments, and he forever resented being reminded about the need to be more rigorous in a philosophical way. What began as an ideal teacher–student relationship degenerated into a bitter misunderstanding, one that could never be entirely overcome, in part because it did involve a genuine difference in methodologies. Kant—in line with what he himself called the "characteristic German mania for method" (Anth [7: 319])— generally favored a systematic and ahistorical presentation of necessary structures of reason, whereas Herder favored a narrative approach with a colorful presentation of a varied series of phenomena in a rich historical setting.

Nonetheless, in his late work, the "Postscript," Kant came to focus on the obviously Herderian theme of the importance of the preservation of minority languages. Throughout the eighteenth century in Kant's hometown—which was also Herder's student home—Lithuanian had been a regular part of the scene, with even a royally established Lithuanian seminar at the university. Königsberg's Protestant Prussian–Lithuanian community included Kant's billiard partners and closest early friends, C. F. Heilsberg (who, along with Daniel Jenisch, also contributed supportive statements to the dictionary) and J. H. Wlömer. Kant was no doubt thinking back on these exemplary friendships when he agreed to contribute to the dictionary and to praise the Lithuanian "tone of equality and trusting openheartedness... willing to go along with all that is fair"—and, he added, with proper "pride," "courage," and "loyalty" (Nachschrift [8: 445]). Elsewhere Kant remarked that Germans, in contrast, mainly lack "originality" and a "principled

---

[36] See Karl Ameriks, "Kant's Fateful Reviews of Herder's *Ideas*," in *Kant's Elliptical Path* (Oxford: Clarendon Press, 2012), 221–37; and Rachel Zuckert, "History, Biology, and Philosophical Anthropology in Kant and Herder," *Internationales Jahrbuch des Deutschen Idealismus/International Yearbook of German Idealism* 8 (2010), 38–59.

62 KANTIAN DIGNITY AND ITS DIFFICULTIES

awareness of equality" (Anth [7: 318]). These are not at all casual terms for Kant, for they go right to the heart of his conception of dignity. Moreover, Kant's plea for supporting the Lithuanian language, even in the absence of a Lithuanian state, is rooted, as Shell notes, in a general argument for protecting the "peculiarity" of any "still unmixed language that is ancient and confined to a narrow region" (Nachschrift [8: 445]). This all fits in with a broader hypothesis that Kant had expressed very briefly in his third *Critique*, namely, that an ideal "enduring commonwealth" needs a combination of "highest culture" (found in dominant nations) and the "simplicity and originality" of more marginalized peoples that nonetheless have "a *free* [emphasis added] nature that feels its *own* [emphasis added] value" (KU [5: 356]). That Kant, unlike Herder, did not make a similar statement directly about Hebrew texts is, to say the least, quite unfortunate—although it is also striking that Kant did not appear concerned with the extinction of the Sambian or "Old Prussian" language that had its home right in the Königsberg area.

All this shows that, although Kant could not repair his personal relationship with Herder, he did eventually see the need indirectly to meet Herder's thought at least halfway, and to make explicit that our identity needs to be not only expressed in the spirit of the universal principles of pure reason but also revivified in the concrete letter of long-standing but marginalized and threatened languages and traditions. Thus, instead of having to choose sharply between preferring the universal or the particular, there is a way to see progress in respecting individual dignity as resting on a mutually supportive relationship between them. Philosophers, and modern educational institutions in general—including dictionaries—bring the particulars of archaic natural languages to explicit concepts, and these languages in turn add, at the very least, an original "measure of wit" to humanity in general.[37] One can also see the more concrete treatment of history by Herder (and his many post-Kantian fans) as complementing the first *Critique*'s notion of regulative Ideas of reason and the third *Critique*'s notion of reflective judgment, for these each imply a significant role for the self-correction of human rationality over time, often for aesthetic reasons.[38] Unfortunately, Kant gave these notions a relatively abstract treatment, and it was left to his successors to develop this inclusive attitude in more detail. Moreover, although in his final publication Kant moved toward a surprising "open door" attitude with regard to the little-known cultures to his immediate East, he unfortunately did not display a similar openness toward his far West by reversing his earlier indifference and making an effort to learn from the new leaders of the "new world."[39]

---

[37] These are Jenisch's terms; see Shell, "Nachschrift eines Freundes," 92, 108.

[38] For an account of the third *Critique*'s contribution to Kant's thinking on human history, see Naomi Fisher, "Kant's Organic Religion: God, Teleology and Progress in the Third *Critique*," in *Kant and the Possibility of Progress*, 77–93.

[39] See Ch. 8, for an argument that—like Herder and the Early Romantics—Walt Whitman and, eventually, Thomas Mann overcame Kant's error of a limited cosmopolitanism.

2.3 Later Developments

The key insights in Kant's late "Postscript" continue, nonetheless, to have philosophical relevance. They are a reminder that even the most rational and universalist of outlooks can and should be combined with the concrete encouragement that is needed, from those who come from the greater powers, to preserve endangered instruments of identity and autonomous development on a relatively small scale. Precisely because of their vulnerable "peculiarity," respect for these instruments serves a critical role in furthering the ideal of enriching truly enlightened and not simply homogeneous national and personal identities. This is crucial not only for national contexts that—like most actual societies—involve a rich mix of diverse peoples, but also in the cosmopolitan context of promoting human self-determination on the whole through historical rehabilitations taking place on an international scale.

An especially valuable version of a mixed and inclusive Kantian–Herderian approach to history and philosophy was developed in the "historical turn" initiated in the writings of Kant's immediate successors. At first, this approach was carried out in a highly abstract and systematic manner in narrative arguments in the Jena school, from Reinhold to Hegel, which incorporated a sequential critique of their immediate predecessors, along with a productive appreciation of foreign influences such as the ancients, Locke (for Reinhold), and Spinoza (for Hegel).[40] The historical approach in Jena was also developed, however, in a more creative and open-ended way in the project of "progressive universal poesy," a famous three-part phrase from a fragment (#116) in the jointly edited *Athenaeum* (1798). The three parts of this phrase capture much of what is best in the work of the geniuses of the Early Romantic era, such as Friedrich Schlegel, August Wilhelm Schlegel, Friedrich von Hardenberg (Novalis), F. D. E. Schleiermacher, Friedrich Hölderlin, and eventually, F. W. J. Schelling.[41] This new style of writing, which

---

[40] See Karl Ameriks, "Reinhold on Systematicity, Popularity, and the Historical Turn," in *System and Context. Early Romantic and Early Idealistic Constellations/System und Kontext. Frühromantische und Frühidealistische Konstellationen*, ed. Rolf Ahlers, *The New Athenaeum* 7 (2004), 109–38. Reinhold was himself a foreigner, a fleeing Austrian with a priestly Catholic background. He arrived as a converted Protestant radical in Weimar but kept with him the appreciation for clear writing that he had learned in Vienna. Soon thereafter, Herder officiated at the wedding of Reinhold and the daughter of Wieland. Reinhold's *Letters on the Kantian Philosophy* (1786–7) were originally published in a journal Wieland edited and were largely responsible for making the Enlightenment orientation of Kant's system widely appreciated in Germany. His popular lectures then established the university of Jena as a philosophical center that attracted practically all the top talents of the next generation.

[41] Friedrich Schlegel, "Athenaeum Fragments," in *Theory as Practice: A Critical Anthology of Early German Romantic Writings*, ed. Joachim Schulte-Sasse (Minneapolis: University of Minnesota Press, 1997), 320. See Karl Ameriks, "History, Idealism, and Schelling," in *Internationales Jahrbuch des Deutschen Idealismus/International Yearbook of German Idealism* 10 (2012), 123–42; "History, Succession, and German Romanticism," in *The Relevance of Romanticism: Essays on German Romantic Philosophy*, ed. Dalia Nassar (Oxford: Oxford University Press, 2014), 47–67; and "The Historical Turn and Late Modernity," in *Hegel on Philosophy in History*, ed. Rachel Zuckert and James Kreines (Cambridge: Cambridge University Press, 2017), 139–56.

64 KANTIAN DIGNITY AND ITS DIFFICULTIES

continues in our own time, involves a syncretic philosophical approach that can be characterized as not only a historical turn but also an aesthetic, subjective, and interpretive turn—and, at the same time, a rejection of the extremes of historicism, aestheticism, subjectivism, and relativism.[42]

All these writers recognized that philosophy's task in late modernity is primarily a matter of building on what is properly rational and cosmopolitan in Enlightenment thought. Yet they also recognized, like Herder, that the mathematical methods of the exact sciences, as well as the inductive methods in the empirical sciences, can no longer be imitated by philosophy or adequately complemented merely by the project of a transcendental grounding. This recognition defines the break from classical or early modern philosophy to what, in a broad sense, can be called romantic or *late modern* philosophy. The latter, as a kind of progressive universal poetry, is a distinctive style of critical and historical writing that all at once relies, at least implicitly, on broad moral ideals—hence is *progressive* in content[43]—and on argument—hence is in principle *universal* in intent—while regularly expressing itself in any one of the large variety of relatively nonabstract styles that Germans call *Dichtung*—and so, in that broad sense, is also *poetic* in form. In its reaction to modern philosophy's overly systematic pretensions and encouragement of scientism, this kind of writing naturally tends to be highly aesthetic, interpretive, and expressive of subjectivity and yet it remains respectful of rationality, although in an ironic, literary and non-Cartesian style.

Kant, of course, was not a literary figure, although his shorter essays are impressive rhetorical accomplishments. Because of their role as a catalyst, however, his writings can be taken to be positively linked to the Early Romantic conception of history and of philosophy's task in late modernity, a conception that effectively combines the notions of progress and autonomy with a more open-minded perspective than in traditional linear accounts. Even if Kant himself did not already make the historical turn, in the sense of completing a philosophical account that incorporates the kind of *detailed* historical procedure favored by later writers, his work played at least a crucial occasioning role.[44] The best way to explain how philosophical writing in this ongoing era can be understood as a form of progressive universal poetry is not to attempt a Procrustean definition but to be open to simply perceiving the stylistic family resemblances that connect

[42] See also Rüdiger Bubner, *Innovations of Idealism*, trans. Nicholas Walker (Cambridge: Cambridge University Press, 2003), 186, for a discussion of an "aesthetic turn with regard to the problem of modernity." Cf. Richard Rorty, *Philosophy as Poetry* (Charlottesville: University of Virginia Press, 2016).

[43] The explicitly moral meaning of this progress is filled out by Schlegel in his review of Kant's essay on perpetual peace. Friedrich Schlegel, "Versuch über den Republikanismus" [1796], in *Kritische Schriften und Fragmente [1794–7]*, ed. Ernst Behler and Hans Eichner (Paderborn: Ferdinand Schöningh, 1988), 52.

[44] Cf. Pavel Reichl, "Kant's A Priori History of Metaphysics: Systematicity, Progress, and the Ends of Reason," *European Journal of Philosophy* 29 (2020), 811–26.

the seemingly very different writings of Kant's most interesting successors. Consider not only the Early Romantics already mentioned but also the many later major philosophers whose work is marked by an intensely historical orientation and the offering of a creative new genealogy of Western thought that is meant to have a broad cultural impact: Friedrich Nietzsche, Martin Heidegger, Thomas Kuhn, Michel Foucault, Bernard Williams, Charles Taylor, and Alasdair MacIntyre.

In the secondary literature, Ernst Behler, Manfred Frank, Frederick C. Beiser, Jane Kneller, Fred Rush, Elizabeth Brusslan, and others have already shown in detail how the first Critical "symphilosophers"—Novalis and the young Friedrich Schlegel—very effectively used a medley of diverse genres to promote the Early Romantic philosophical program. It can also be argued that it was Hölderlin who, in his profound history-oriented poetry as well as in his deeply philosophical fiction, essays, and letters, carried out this program in the most surprisingly close adherence to the enlightened religious themes of Kant's moral writings. Hölderlin is sometimes dismissed as a merely poetic figure lost in nostalgic reveries concerning nature and the ancients, but there is a growing awareness of his significance as a serious philosopher with Enlightenment sympathies. His nonfiction offers a consideration of Germany's historical and political relation to the ancients and the French that is even more sophisticated than that of contemporaries such as Schiller and Reinhold.[45] In particular, Hölderlin, like Kant (Rel [6: 623, note]), argued that Schiller's famous contrast of "dignity and grace" was much overdone because the natural development of the moral capacity that is intrinsic to dignity naturally brings with it a kind of grace that is most relevant.

Hölderlin's main goal was to write as an educator of his own people, but for the purpose of universal enlightenment as well, rather than any appeal to what he sharply criticized, in his novel, *Hyperion* (1797, 1799), as the philistine attitude of most Germans in his time. His magnificent poem *Patmos* (1802) ends with an instruction to them that "the solid letter | Be given scrupulous care, and the existing | Be well interpreted."[46] Hölderlin's talk of seeking to awaken the "seeds" of good predisposition in his contemporaries, and of educating them for the sake of a future "revolution in dispositions," is a clear echo of his close reading of the Critical philosophy and his agreement with Kant's basic notion of *Vernunftglaube* and its foundation in the doctrine of universal human dignity.[47]

---

[45] See Karl Ameriks, "On the Extension of Kant's Elliptical Path in Hölderlin and Novalis," in *Kant's Elliptical Path* (Oxford: Clarendon Press, 2012), 281–302; and "Hölderlin's Kantian Path," in *Kantian Subjects: Critical Philosophy and Late Modernity* (Oxford: Oxford University Press, 2019), 189–206. Cf. Anthony Curtis Adler, *Politics and Truth in Hölderlin: "Hyperion" and the Choreographic Project of Modernity* (Rochester, NY: Camden House, 2020).

[46] "...daß geflegt werde | der veste Buchstab, und bestehendes gut | Gedeutet..." Hölderlin, *Patmos*, trans. Michael Hamburger, in *Friedrich Hölderlin, Hyperion and Selected Poems*, ed. Eric L. Santner (New York: Continuum, 1990), 257.

[47] See Ch. 1.5, as well as Ameriks, "Hölderlin's Kantian Path," 202, which cites Hölderlin's letters of 1793 to his brother, and January 10, 1797 to his friend Ebel. A similar admiration for Kant's philosophy can be found at this time also in the music and words of Beethoven, which explicitly stress respect

66 KANTIAN DIGNITY AND ITS DIFFICULTIES

The Early Romantics were admittedly not aware of Kant's Postscript for the Lithuanians, and they did not linger long over the purely transcendental features of Critical theoretical philosophy. They did, however, energetically espouse the Enlightenment goals of Kant's writings, and they were all deeply affected by Kant's *Critique of the Power of Judgment* (1790). This work emphasizes the notion of genius, the need for a sequence of exemplary figures to lead culture in general creatively forward, and the importance of using aesthetic Ideas, precisely as Kant noted that Milton did, to help actualize, and not merely thematize, the practical goals of a modern culture that respects human beings as such.[48] A close look at Kant's work on religion reveals that he gave considerable thought—in a way that clearly had a direct effect on all the main Jena writers—to understanding our history as basically distinguished by a series of extraordinary figures who were, all at once, aesthetic-moral-religious-philosophical leaders, democratic revolutionaries whose long-term influence continues to raise humanity step by step toward autonomous fulfillment.[49] Kant singled out the epochal changes initiated by the outsiders Job, Jesus, and Rousseau, and no doubt he also thought that Luther, Milton, and the full effect of his own Critical philosophy had special significance.[50] He also argued that not only can a moral culture be of assistance in helping art achieve a "determinate form" (KU [5: 356]) but, in addition, the exercise of the power of judgment in taste (which is oriented toward "disinterested" universal validity) can help make us more receptive to moral feeling (KU [5: 197]).

Like Schelling, Hegel, and other later thinkers, Kant understood that Herder's temporal notion of the "spirit of an age" has more importance than a merely spatial understanding of the notion of a "spirit of a people." A multiplicity of peoples can be understood geographically without considerations of significant causal influence, as in the early contrast of Europe and the Pacific Islands. Insofar as a sequence of spirits of an age comes to our attention, however, this implies not a mere disconnected variety of taste but the likelihood of an underlying causal connection and a succession of influential exemplary figures. This fact was recognized toward the end of the eighteenth century when, instead of a mere notional

---

for dignity in precisely Kant's basic sense. See Karl Ameriks, "Kant, Schiller, and Beethoven: Enlightened Connections of Aesthetics, Revolution, and Religion," *SGIR Review* (forthcoming).

[48] On the relevance of Milton to Kant as an advocate of anti-monarchic principles, see Sanford Budick, *Kant and Milton* (Cambridge, MA: Harvard University Press, 2010), and Ameriks, *Kant's Elliptical Path*, 22–3.

[49] See also Samuel A. Stoner and Paul T. Wilford, "Realizing the Ethical Community: Kant's *Religion* and the Reformation of Culture," in *Kant and the Possibility of Progress*, 94–114.

[50] On Kant's multistage history of our development, see Karl Ameriks, "Kant and the End of Theodicy," in *Kant's Elliptical Path*, 260–77. Kant does not completely subscribe to Lutheran orthodoxy, but it is striking how much he was influenced by two of the three main changes that Luther made in returning to, but also departing from, Augustine: a stress on an "invisible church" and a rejection of the idea that baptism removes radical evil. Kant moves toward late modernity in his rejection of Luther's third innovation, an insistence on absolute certainty of grace in the peace of conscience. See Richard Rex, *The Making of Martin Luther* (Princeton: Princeton University Press, 2017), 23 and 179.

contrasting of ancients and moderns, as if these are mere timeless models on isolated islands, there arose a reaction to the simultaneous revolution of modern science and the experience of the vivid contrast of modern Europe with the rich diversity of the cultural world of the ancients, as expressed in the writings of Johann Joachim Winckelmann (1717–68) and others. The underlying contrast in this context is not a matter of space as opposed to time, but of mere space (that is, isolated and history-deaf provincialism) as opposed to the developing web of cultural space-time.

In an era of such dramatic change, the past became of special interest the more it was realized that it is quite different but still part of our own undeniable heritage. In place of a mere juxtaposing of an ancient and a merely modern sphere, there arose a process of generating a third world, a *late modern world*. This world understands itself not only as distinct from its prior contrasting eras but also as a self-conscious successor culture that incorporates and reconfigures the lasting values of both its immediate and distant predecessors. Thus, Hölderlin, like many other eighteenth-century writers, looked back to Milton,[51] just as Milton looked back to Dante, who looked back to Vergil, who looked back to Homer. Somewhat similarly, Kant eventually looked beyond his immediate Wolffian surroundings to Leibniz, who remained worthy of a "true apology" (UE [8: 250]), and also way back to Augustine and Plato,[52] in order to work out his new Critical doctrine of "nature" and "grace" (KrV A 820/B 841). This is why intellectual history can be philosophically schematized better as an ellipse or spiral, rather than either a mere line or circle, for it involves a complex circling back that is also a moving forward onto an "eccentric," retrospectively revolutionized and higher path, as in what Kant also called, in a letter to Kästner, August 5, 1790 (Br [11: 186]) his own "roundabout route" (*durch einen Umweg*).

The Early Romantic development of the historical turn is in general more flexible and Herderian than the more systematic versions of post-Kantianism found in Fichte, Schelling, and especially Hegel, but it does not go so far as to fall back into a form of hyperflexible pragmatic holism.[53] The orthodox Hegelian

---

[51] Milton was everywhere in mid-eighteenth-century continental literature. Even if there is no proof of direct influence on Hölderlin, there are deep similarities and numerous indirect influences through Herder and Klopstock. See Michael Hamburger, "The Sublime Art: Notes on Milton and Hölderlin," in *Contraries: Studies in German Literature* (Boston: E. P. Dutton, 1970), 43–65.

[52] On the turn to Plato by Kant and others in this era, see Rüdiger Bubner, *Innovations of Idealism*; Michael Franz, *Tübinger Platonismus. Die gemeinsamen philosophischen Anfangsgründe von Hölderlin, Schelling und Hegel* (Tübingen: Francke, 2012); Lara Ostaric, "Absolute Freedom and Creative Agency in Early Schelling," *Philosophisches Jahrbuch* 119 (2012), 69–93; and Naomi Fisher and Jeffrey Fisher, "Schelling and the *Philebus*: Limit and the Unlimited in Schelling's Philosophy of Nature," *Epoché* 26 (2022), 347–67.

[53] For a contrast of the concept of the Historical Turn, as presented here, with pragmatic readings of Hegel, such as that offered by Robert Brandom, see Karl Ameriks, "Beyond the Living and the Dead: On Post-Kantian Philosophy as Historical Appropriation," *Graduate Faculty Philosophy Journal* 40 (2019), 33–61.

68   KANTIAN DIGNITY AND ITS DIFFICULTIES

version of the historical turn, even in successors such as Marx, holds to what can be called a *rigid modular* model of historical development in society and philosophy.[54] It is "modular" in holding not only that we change as we develop significantly over time, but also that this change is not continuous but involves discrete stages defined by a relatively short list of interconnected but radically new frameworks. In addition, this systematic model is "rigid" in that it claims not merely that a demarcation of stages of thought is helpful, but also that very specific necessary stages and sharp breaks, corresponding to fundamental metaphysical or economic categories, can be identified (for example, pre-feudal, feudal, capitalist, and socialist). The Romantics are also attracted to the thought of a series of key stages—the ancient, medieval, modern, and later modern worlds—but for them the borders of these stages are highly permeable, with cross-currents of contingent influence from faraway times and places, and with room for numerous significant transitions that are more like deep changes in taste that are compelling but are not (even retrospectively) demonstrable necessities.

A final point about this conception is that it can be progressive without being Whiggish, for it can concede that it has sensed something lacking in itself and has turned to the past (as well as foreign lands and neglected cultures in its own sphere) as something intrinsically valuable, and as providing a stimulus for new forms of expression rather than imitation. This conception also is not to be confused with the historicist notion, suggested occasionally in Herder's writings (and their Gadamerian interpretation), that other works and ages are simply different. It is true, as Herder deserves credit for arguing, that Shakespeare should not be criticized just because he is not "classical" in style; but neither should we concede, for example, that ancient views of slavery are beyond criticism just because we are outsiders to that culture. Insofar as there is an underlying *philosophical* strand in the succession of civilizations, we can still claim that there are some later positions that are argumentative improvements on their predecessors. That is precisely why we are attached to these later, more complex notions, as when we now hold that humanity involves not only the favor of nature or supernature, in talent or perhaps grace, but above all some kind of basic equality and dignity of human beings—and, eventually, in a concretely recognized and not merely abstract, inward sense.

These points can be used to characterize an attractively balanced and broadly Herderian position. Despite Herder's own tendency at times to suggest backing off altogether from comparing cultures, or even to seem simultaneously to be endorsing cultural relativism and the presumption of some specifically European

---

[54] See Mark Alznauer, "Hegel on the Conceptual Form of Philosophical History," in *Kant and the Possibility of Progress*, 165–84.

ideas as universally valid standards,[55] his main concern appears to be simply to warn his contemporaries against assuming that in *all* respects our own modern society is superior to cultures of other times and places. He properly stresses that weaknesses elsewhere that were in fact unavoidable can hardly be morally blamed, that condemnation of others is unfair without something close to a full contextual understanding of their situation (which modern critics rarely made the effort to achieve), that partial aspects of another culture that are admittedly negative in themselves can nonetheless be an inescapable part of a valuable total social structure that corresponds in many ways to our own mixed situation, and that even very negative characteristics of a particular culture can have an indirect value in leading to improvements in other cultures and in giving the eventual course of humanity a progressive form. Kant could agree with all these points while at the same time adding that, except as a regulative ideal, much more caution than Herder himself exhibited is called for in regard to claims of an evident teleological pattern in history on the whole.

In addition to all these qualifications, any late modern conception of history and progress has a shadow side to it for, precisely as post-Kantian, it comes with a sense of belatedness and of the limitations of any purely rationalist model. Philosophy in the late modern age has learned that in large part it is neither a deductive nor decisively empirical enterprise, let alone a clearly convincing transcendental "metaphysics as a science."[56] By induction, it should concede that, since it has repeatedly found ways—as Kant discovered when he read Rousseau and reconsidered Plato—in which it has needed to correct itself radically by means of returning to obscured notions in its own past, it is only sensible to leave room in its future for similar progressive reversals. This implies that autonomy in philosophy, culture, and personal life can consist not in finding oneself totally independent by means of positing an Archimedean point (for example, the "I") from which a full system can be deduced. Instead, it can be a matter of realizing more and more how the corrections that we make are the ongoing, and in part backward-looking, self-corrections of embedded human rationality—in other words, the implications of what we have at first neglectfully inherited, not created. This also implies that, for all that we can foresee, we will never be able to construct, even in approximation, a unified all-inclusive system, although parts of our current way of thinking, in morality as well as science, can nevertheless be regarded as having achieved an irreversible status.

This kind of progression can be taken to be consistent, in a Schlegelian manner, with a variety of competing "research programs." This need not be relativism,

---

[55] See, e.g., Kurt Mertel, "Historicism and Critique in Herder's *Another Philosophy of History*: Some Hermeneutic Reflections," *European Journal of Philosophy* 24 (2014), 397–416.

[56] For a contemporary argument that even science as metaphysics is not convergent, see Anjan Chakravartty, *Scientific Ontology: Integrating Naturalized Metaphysics and Voluntarist Epistemology* (Oxford: Oxford University Press, 2017).

for even if this process is not be to be thought of as all converging toward a limit (as in Kant's language), there can be evident progress within each program, and the sophisticated development of competing rational outlooks can amount to a clear advance in human self-understanding on the whole. In this way, post-Kantian writing in a broadly Herderian style can also be distinguished from proposals of more anarchic positions, such as those suggested sometimes by Richard Rorty and Raymond Guess, who speak of "changing the subject" rather than of moving forward.[57] Examples of this kind of fruitful multitrack development may also be found in numerous scientific controversies (such as in metamathematics) as well as in philosophy, the humanities in general, and even the wayward evolution in our conception of political institutions.

In conclusion, it is appropriate to recall a brief old story (a variation of La Fontaine's "The Golden Pitcher") about philosophical indebtedness, alluded to by the young Kant in the context of his looking back at Leibniz's denial of causal influence. It is worth retelling here to indicate, poetically as it were, how the argumentative dynamics of history can function as part of philosophy itself. The story is about a dying father who tells his sons that he has buried gold in the fields that are to be left to them. And the point is, the statement in this story, although not literally true, turns out to be metaphorically correct. Although the successors were at first disappointed, their relentless digging in search of gold sufficed to turn up the earth and thereby made the fields more fertile than ever before. In Kant's own words: "If this science [of traditional philosophy] be thus carefully cultivated, its soil will be found to be not so barren. The objection of futile and obscure subtlety, raised against it by those who scorn it, will be refuted by an ample harvest of more remarkable knowledge" (Nova [1: 390]).[58]

Kantian Dignity and its Difficulties. Karl Ameriks, Oxford University Press. © Karl Ameriks 2024.
DOI: 10.1093/9780198917656.003.0003

---

[57] See Richard Rorty, *Philosophy and the Mirror of Nature* (Princeton: Princeton University Press, 1979); and Raymond Geuss, *Changing the Subject: Philosophy from Socrates to Adorno* (Cambridge, MA: Harvard University Press, 2017).

[58] This reference corrects a mistake in the earlier version of this essay. I am indebted to audiences at Boston College and Simon Fraser University and owe special thanks to Susan Meld Shell, Allen Speight, and Sam Stoner, as well as to an anonymous reviewer's comments. For the original impetus for work on this topic, I am especially indebted to Elvira Simfa and her colleagues at the University of Riga.

3

Dignity as Unconditioned:
Race, Religion, and Fascism

> ...the idea of a *human being*, who as such (as a moral being) can never lose entirely his predisposition to the good. (MdS [6: 463–4])

This chapter evaluates serious accusations against Kant and his philosophy as being tied to racism, religious prejudice, and even the horrors of Fascism. The criticisms of Kant by Charles W. Mills, Michael Lackey, and Paul W. Franks are distinguished and assessed. A distinction is made between Lackey's more radical critique of Kant and Christianity in general as playing a major role in the rise of Fascism, and the critique by Franks, which focuses on specific aspects of the anti-Judaic tradition in German philosophy. Lackey is commended for his detailed documentation of the little-known but significant influence on Fascism of Houston Stewart Chamberlain's nationalist and racist interpretation of Kant. It is argued, however, that Chamberlain and the Fascists horribly distorted both Christianity and Kant's real views on duty and dignity. Franks's criticism of anti-Semitism in Kant and others, however, is argued to be well-founded.

3.1 A Beclouded Fate

Despite the growing positive interest in Kant's work, many philosophers continue to decry his appeal to the notion of human dignity because of a variety of what can be called relatively moderate objections. This notion, like many of the other staples of Kant's Critical philosophy, such as equal rights, absolute freedom, and idealism, is often criticized, even by partially sympathetic readers, for its vague generality[1] as well as its stress on purity, which can seem to distort the highly complex nature of human development and action.[2] Important as these

---

[1] See Introduction, and James Griffin, *On Human Rights* (Oxford: Oxford University Press, 2008); Charles R. Beitz, "Human Dignity in the Theory of Human Rights: Nothing but a Phrase?" *Philosophy & Public Affairs* 41 (2013), 259–90; and Jeremy Waldron, *One Another's Equals: The Basis of Human Equality* (Cambridge, MA: Harvard University Press 2017).

[2] See Michael Rosen, *Dignity: Its History and Meaning* (Cambridge, MA: Harvard University Press, 2012); and Peter Bieri, *Human Dignity: A Way of Living* (Cambridge: Polity, 2017). Bieri's volume is an elegantly written account of the difficulties of treating human beings in a dignified manner, but it does not enter into foundational ethical or metaphysical issues.

72 KANTIAN DIGNITY AND ITS DIFFICULTIES

frequently voiced (but, I believe, also manageable) worries are, now is the time to face a more radical kind of objection, one that has only grown in significance ever since it was forcefully expressed in Charles W. Mills's bold accusation of 1997: "Kant is also the foundational theorist in the modern period of the division between the *Herrenvolk* [master race] and *Untermenschen*, persons and subpersons, upon which Nazi history would later dwell."[3] Mills does not himself explore in detail the historical issue of how much of a direct impact Kant's thoughts actually had and, unlike some theorists, he is clear that any categorizing of human beings as in fact "subpersons" would be incompatible with the categorical imperative and Kant's basic conception of dignity.[4]

One especially provocative discussion that does enter into historical issues is by a professor of literature, Michael Lackey, in a chapter of his *The Modernist God State: A Literary Study of the Nazis' Christian Reich*.[5] His remarks are philosophically controversial and highly polemical but nevertheless worthy of scrutiny by all Kant scholars, for they draw attention to the thorny issue of how Kant's ideas may have had a pernicious impact on later developments within his own country. Lackey presents a detailed and eye-opening account concerning the dire "philosophical influence" on German Fascism that the English Germanophile and Aryan supremacist Houston Stewart Chamberlain (1855–1927) appears to have exerted because of his extensive discussions of Kant. Whether this is a case of the genuine effect of Kant's *philosophy*, however, is an issue that needs to be examined carefully.

Chamberlain was a major influence on Kaiser Wilhelm II, eventually married Richard Wagner's daughter, and wrote admiringly to Hitler, who in turn was flattered by the chance to meet the aged author and the Wagner family and claim their blessing. Chamberlain's discussion of what he calls Kant's "idealistic" conception of the person is undeniably central to his turn-of-the-century huge best-seller, *The Foundations of the Nineteenth Century* (which eventually went through 24 editions), as well as to its two-volume follow-up work on Kant in 1905, which

---

[3] Charles W. Mills, *The Racial Contract* (Ithaca, NY: Cornell University Press, 1997), 56. Cf. Mills, "Dark Ontologies: Whites, Jews, and Black Supremacy," in *Autonomy and Community: Readings in Contemporary Kantian Social Philosophy*, ed. Jane Kneller and Sidney Axinn (Albany: State University of New York Press, 1998), 131–68; and Mills, *Black Rights/White Wrongs: The Critique of Racial Liberalism* (Oxford: Oxford University Press, 2017). For an evaluation of these kinds of charges, see also Ch. 4; Pauline Kleingeld "Kant's Second Thoughts on Colonialism," in *Kant and Colonialism*, ed. Katrin Flikschuh and Lea Ypi (Oxford: Oxford University Press, 2014), 43–67; and Lucy Allais, "Kant's Racism," in *Philosophical Papers* 45 (2016), 1–36.

[4] Charles W. Mills, "Reflection: A Time for Dignity," in *Dignity: A History*, ed. Remy Debes (Oxford: Oxford University, Press, 2017), 264. In this article, however, Mills accepts the questionable charge that Kant "supported European colonialism," 263.

[5] Michael Lackey, "The Making of Hitler and the Nazis: A Tale of Modern Secularization or Christian Idealism?", in *The Modernist God State: A Literary Study of the Nazis' Christian Reich* (New York and London: Continuum, 2012), 225–79; at 239, Lackey cites the passage about *Herrenvölker* quoted from Mills.

was edited by a major figure in British politics.[6] Chamberlain's writings received worldwide attention at the highest level, scholarly (for example, from Hans Vaihinger and Paul Natorp) as well as from the general public—even occasioning a witty critical review by none other than the former US President, Theodore Roosevelt.[7] Because of its references to the surprisingly frequent mention of Kant by Chamberlain—and the fact that Kant is also mentioned even by Hitler as well as other leading Fascists, such as Alfred Rosenberg and Joseph Goebbels[8]— Lackey's discussion raises issues that are of general philosophical relevance. This is not only on account of its citation of several disturbing and relatively little-known passages, but also because of how it dramatically interweaves these quotations with a variety of harsh allegations—for example, that Kant's rationalist ethics and race theory rule out respect for disadvantaged or supposedly inferior groups—that are familiar from discussions elsewhere and are independent of claims concerning Fascism.[9] The level of distortion by the Fascist writers themselves can be gathered from Goebbels's fabrication: "Kant once said: 'Act as if the principle of your life could be the principle for your entire nation.'"[10] Kant's statements of the moral law were, of course, never limited by reference to any nation or restricted group.

In this context, it is necessary to reiterate that any kind of non-universal position regarding human dignity and duty is inconsistent with what Kant had in mind in speaking of the seeds that in part constitute the distinctive and essential identity of all members of our species. In particular, this includes an "original" capacity for the good that is possessed by all human beings as a fundamental feature of "personality" (Basedow [2: 451], Rel [6: 26] and [6: 44]), despite their also

---

[6] Houston Stewart Chamberlain, *The Foundations of the Nineteenth Century*, with an Introduction by Lord Redesdale [1899], 2 vols., trans. John Lees (London: John Lane, 1911); and *Immanuel Kant: A Study and a Comparison with Goethe, Leonardo da Vinci, Bruno, Plato and Descartes* [1905], trans. with an Introduction by Lord Redesdale, 2 vols. (London: John Lane, 1914). "No great writer ever had a more devoted disciple than Chamberlain to Kant" (Lord Redesdale, "Introduction" (1914), ix).

[7] Theodore Roosevelt, "The Foundations of the Nineteenth Century," in *History as Literature* (New York: Charles Scribner's Sons, 2013), 233–43. It should not be forgotten that beliefs in some version of white supremacy can also be found in the attitude, at some point in their life, of countless renowned figures, even after Kant's time, such as Abraham Lincoln, Woodrow Wilson, Harry Truman, and the English theologian Hastings Rashdall.

[8] See, e.g., Alfred Rosenberg, *Race and Race History and Other Essays by Alfred Rosenberg*, ed. Robert Pois (New York: Harper & Row, 1970), 187. Cf. Rosenberg, *Houston Stewart Chamberlain als Verkünder und Begründer einer deutschen Zukunft* (Munich: H. Bruckmann, 1927), and *Der Mythos des 20. Jahrhunderts. Eine Wertung der seelisch-geistigen Gestaltkämpfe unserer Zeit* (Munich: Hoheneichen, 1930).

[9] See, e.g., the (critical) discussion of Kant in Nicholas Wolterstorff, *Justice: Rights and Wrongs* (Princeton: Princeton University Press, 2008), 325–33, which on some interpretive points parallels Richard Dean's view that Kant was committed to restricting dignity to human beings that have a certain degree of ability or accomplishment. See Ch. 1.7, and see also, Jordan Wessling, "A Dilemma for Wolterstorff's Theistic Grounding of Human Dignity and Rights," *International Journal for Philosophy of Religion* 76 (2009), 277–95.

[10] Speech of January 9, 1928. Joseph Goebbels, "Erkenntnis und Propaganda," in *Signale der neuen Zeit. 25 ausgewählte Reden von Dr. Joseph Goebbels* (Munich: Zentralverlag der NSDAP, 1934), 29.

being "radically evil" in predisposition.[11] For Kant, this capacity of the will involves more than mere choice, rationality, or inherent language ability; it involves the presence of the *positive* faculty of pure practical reason, which gives everyone the real capacity to appreciate the moral law as such. This capacity is part of the original nature of even impaired or not yet developed human beings, since from the start they are unlike members of other species—which is why all human beings always deserve respect. This means that there is a fundamental distinction in Kant's moral theory between status dignity, which attaches to every being that has a capacity for morality as part of what Kant calls our innate *Anlagen*, and developed talents and achievements, which are contingent and can vary widely.[12] Basic capacities in this essentialist sense are also to be distinguished from what some philosophers speak of as capabilities, which are higher-order powers, such as good health, that are needed for persons to have a chance to have a "normal" life in various rather elementary ways, but are not necessary for having dignity in Kant's basic sense.[13]

On the basis of this clarification of Kant's basic stance on dignity, the concern of this chapter is a general *hermeneutical* point rather than a review of the full range of literature on the topic of racism, philosophy, and prejudice in general. The main aim is simply to illustrate how important it is, especially in controversial matters like this, to work carefully with the technical terminology and full systematic context of complex writers such as Kant, so as to focus attention on what is truly most relevant and to discourage repetitions of unfortunate misconceptions. This kind of hermeneutical investigation is a relatively small step to take, one that can hardly resolve the larger social issues that are involved, but it is a first step that deserves the effort of philosophers in particular. Looking closely at a few test cases of interpretation can help create an awareness of the difference between overly harsh charges that overlook key distinctions and carefully articulated objections that warrant further serious reflection. Keeping this difference clearly in mind can then encourage progressive social developments all the more effectively in the long run.

---

[11] See Ch. 1.7, and Kant, MdS [6: 464].

[12] This point is stressed in Onora O'Neill, *Constructions of Reason: Explorations of Kant's Practical Philosophy* (Cambridge: Cambridge University Press, 1989), 76; Thomas E. Hill, Jr., *Dignity and Practical Reason in Kant's Moral Theory* (Ithaca, NY: Cornell University Press, 1992), 166–7; and Jean Hampton, *The Intrinsic Worth of Persons: Contractarianism in Moral and Political Philosophy*, ed. Daniel Farnham (Cambridge: Cambridge University Press, 2007), 122. Cf. Karl Ameriks, "Vindicating Autonomy: Kant, Sartre, and O'Neill," in *Kant on Moral Autonomy*, ed. Oliver Sensen (Cambridge: Cambridge University Press, 2013), 53–70. This distinction is overlooked in criticisms that falsely presume that Kantian dignity is something one needs to "achieve" over time. See Ch. 1, and (as another example of the mistaken belief that Kant gives primacy to achievement) Timothy L. Jackson, "The Image of God and the Soul of Humanity: Reflections on Dignity, Sanctity, and Humanity," in *Religion in the Liberal Polity*, ed. Terence Cuneo (Notre Dame, IN: University of Notre Dame Press, 2005), 44.

[13] See Ch. 2.5, and cf. Beitz, "Human Dignity in the Theory of Human Rights," 9.

The consideration of any popular attack such as Lackey's also indirectly raises the perplexing broader issue of what to make *in general* of highly influential readings that obscure crucial complications in the works of major philosophers.[14] This difficult problem can hardly be treated in its full range here, but the troublesome fate of Kant's work shows that the problem is not restricted to obviously inflammatory philosophers such as Marx and Nietzsche. Another complication is the fact that some of the more radical conclusions about Kant expressed by nonspecialists such as Lackey can appear to gain support from *seemingly similar* critiques by scholars such as Paul W. Franks, one of the top experts on German philosophy in general. Franks, like Lackey, makes the claim (discussed in Section 3.4) that several remarks by Kant fit a dangerous "idealist" pattern, but he backs his claim with a detailed scholarly analysis of exactly how Kant's work, "perhaps unwittingly," embodies a "long-standing" attitude of extreme "hostility" toward "Judaism."[15] This is an attitude that can understandably lead to cataclysmic consequences, especially when connected with more extreme expressions by other German Idealists as well.

There are, therefore, methodological as well as substantive reasons to compare Lackey's and Franks's stylistically quite different treatments of Kant, and to begin to assess the implications of these *kinds* of critiques in general for the Critical doctrine of human dignity. These matters are especially significant now because—unlike what one usually finds in Kant literature and much of contemporary philosophy in general—in this case there clearly appears to be a close connection between statements made by a highly systematic philosopher and concrete issues that still concern large numbers of people in their daily life. In earlier decades, it might have been tempting to focus simply on the technical details of Kant's Critical system and not worry so much about relatively popular readings of seemingly incidental passages that can appear highly improper to contemporary readers. Nonetheless, just as Rousseau, and English supporters, such as Richard Price, cannot fairly be blamed for the later excesses of the French Revolution, or Hegel for the later excesses of nationalism or totalitarianism, it seems wrong to judge Kant's philosophy now primarily on the basis of misleading references to it by

---

[14] This becomes an especially worrisome problem if one argues, as I have, that a distinguishing feature of late modern philosophy has been its tendency, in a kind of historical turn in methodology and along the lines of a suggestion in Kant's aesthetics, to rely on a sequence of creative "exemplary" interpreters who build directly on, but radically modify, the impact of masterworks of the past. See Ch. 2.3, and Karl Ameriks, "Interpretation After Kant," *Critical Horizons* 10 (2009), 31–53. Radical changes have been managed in good art and science as well, but philosophy is not quite art or science, and so it must find its own way in sorting out what is genuine over time. See the helpful observations in Thomas Grundmann, "Progress and Historical Reflection in Philosophy," in *Philosophy and the Historical Perspective*, ed. Marcel von Ackeran and Lee Klein (Oxford: Proceedings of the British Academy 214, 2018), 51–68.

[15] Paul W. Franks, "Inner Anti-Semitism or Kabbalistic Heresy? German Idealism's Relation to Judaism," *Internationales Jahrbuch des Deutschen Idealismus/International Yearbook for German Idealism* 7 (2009), 262.

76 KANTIAN DIGNITY AND ITS DIFFICULTIES

horribly irresponsible figures more than a century after his work. As John Stuart Mill once observed, any good idea can be made to look awful by the wrong kind of interpreter, especially when there is considerable complexity in the original idea. We now live in a time, however, when suddenly all sorts of powerful movements throughout the world employ highly effective expressions that are frighteningly similar to aggressively racist notions popular a century ago in the era that spawned Fascism. Therefore, if Kant's system—and even his central notion of dignity—is in fact to be understood in some ways that are *essentially* linked to highly offensive notions, this is a problem that must be confronted with great care. In addition, precisely because in so many ways it still seems, to many philosophers, that Kant's thought is one of the best bulwarks we have for supporting enlightened rather than regressive movements, it is important to give his critics a fair hearing and to see how he ultimately is to be best understood, that is, when his words are taken in their full context and without either hasty antipathy or unjustified defensiveness.

3.2 Lackey's Attack: Problems of Interpretation

The conclusion of Lackey's interpretation is a direct attack on the effects of Kant's discussion of dignity: "While Kant's philosophy of moral and intellectual autonomy is calculated to secure and affirm the *dignity* [my emphasis] of the human, it actually set the stage for one of the most dehumanizing systems to afflict the West"—and it did so because "Kant, via Chamberlain, was certainly one of the most important influences on National Socialism."[16] This "stage setting" remark is tied to a claim by Lackey that

> if it can be shown [as he implies that according to Kant it can] that a certain being 'by nature' cannot experience 'the autonomy of his freedom,' then it would follow that this being would not qualify as full-fledged human and therefore could be used as a means.[17]

Here Lackey is referring to a pre-Critical remark by Kant about blacks, who at one point (but not untypically) are characterized as "by nature" lacking "feeling that arises above the trifling" (Beo [2: 253]), and then Lackey adds, in his own words, that Kant regards non-European natives and Jews as "people *fundamentally incapable* [emphasis added] of behaving as autonomous moral agents."[18]

---

[16] Lackey, *Modernist God State*, 236 and 276.   [17] Lackey, *Modernist God State*, 239.
[18] The first passage uses the translation in Lackey, *Modernist God State*, 238. The second quotation, from p. 242, is connected with a reference, at p. 240, to Rel [6: 125], where Kant is tendentiously characterizing Judaism as a merely political organization. I take Lackey's conclusion about "fundamental" incapability to be unwarranted, given Kant's position on universal human moral capacities—which is

Lackey's statement about incapacity is a stunning accusation: that Kant, the philosopher best known for a doctrine of human autonomy and dignity under universal moral law, in fact systematically denied autonomy and dignity to huge portions of humanity. This claim conflicts with numerous texts, such as Kant's clear statement on our universal moral capacity, and therefore dignity, at MdS [6: 434–5], quoted as the epigraph of this chapter. Fortunately—although this does not settle the matter—the grounds given by Lackey turn out to rest in large part on a serious, although fairly common and understandable, confusion about Kant's anthropology and the development of his moral philosophy. Lackey cites passages from Kant's early *Observations on the Beautiful and Sublime*, a highly popular work composed in 1763 (the publication date of 1764 can be misleading), right before Kant's intense study of Rousseau led him to radically invert his philosophy by switching from a compatibilist metaphysics to a serious concern with ethics and a firm (although slowly developed, because of the need for new metaphysical foundations) advocacy of the doctrines of absolute free choice and universal human equality.[19] There is perhaps no passage more often cited now by Kant scholars than this famous remark added after the *Observations*:

> There was a time when I believed this alone [the search for knowledge] could constitute the honor of humankind, and I despised the rabble who knows nothing. *Rousseau* has set me right. This blinding prejudice vanishes, I learn to honor human beings, and I would feel by far less useful than the common laborer if I did not believe that this consideration could impart a value to *all others* [emphasis added] in order to establish the rights of humanity. (Bem [20: 33])

In reflecting on Rousseau, Kant realized that it is a serious mistake, one that even Rousseau's terminology can obscure, to speak of human beings primarily in terms of "nature." Kant became convinced that the most fundamental feature of human beings is precisely a capacity for absolutely free moral choice, which gives us *all* dignity and in a sense places us, in principle, above[20] mere nature in a way that is not endangered even by the universal predictive successes of modern science (which had at first preoccupied Kant). It is true that *defending* this very substantive point requires working through the tortuous complications of Kant's mature Critical system but, fortunately, Kant held that common people themselves never need to develop such a demonstration. Recourse to the system is required simply

---

not to deny that Kant believed human beings in different cultures tend to vary considerably in their *degree* of moral *development*.

[19] See Karl Ameriks, *Kant's Elliptical Path* (Oxford: Clarendon Press, 2012), chs. 1 and 2.

[20] Here "nature," in the phrase "above mere nature," is meant in the specific sense of sensible nature, rather than in the general sense that can refer to any kind of essence. See Oliver Sensen, "Dignity: Kant's Revolutionary Conception," in *Dignity: A History*, ed. Remy Debes (Oxford: Oxford University Press, 2017), 237–62, for an account of how central this "elevating" feature is to Kant's notion of human dignity at an individual as well as a species level.

78 KANTIAN DIGNITY AND ITS DIFFICULTIES

in academic contexts as a counterattack on the dogmatic schools and their authoritarian allies, which he believed an enlightened society will eventually learn to put in their place. Unlike traditional Cartesianism, Kant did not rest his libertarian view on claims to metaphysical, theological, or psychological insight but was instead persuaded by what he took to be a commonsense and universally valid moral stance, found even in the uncontaminated attitude of a "Savoyard vicar" or young child. In later work Kant even insisted that children as young as "eight or nine" can use this capacity to immediately distinguish right from wrong in some difficult contexts (TP [8: 286]). Kant came to presume (perhaps all too quickly) that this kind of reference to a universally available moral capacity is the only alternative to prevalent anti-egalitarian intellectualistic or sensualistic understandings of human capacities. The common problem of these kinds of views—which Kant, after Rousseau, saw as gaining increasingly unfortunate influence on account of the vanities and confusions of modern culture—is that they regard the work of all our capacities as simply a function of *predetermined natural* powers.

Similar considerations are relevant to the passage Lackey cites about blacks being given to "trifling" feelings "by nature." There are several passages like this in Kant and they definitely have an ugly character, but Lackey's treatment of them misses some very relevant points. Lackey takes the passage about a lack of fine feeling to concern the same issue that Kant writes about, decades later, in the second *Critique* when discussing "moral feeling" (KpV [5: 75]; cf. GMS [4: 404, note] and [4: 460]). This is to overlook the fact that the passage from the *Observations* occurs even before Kant has begun to think systematically about, let alone publish, his Critical moral theory. It is, in any case, a fundamental feature of all Kant's work that aesthetic and moral feeling need to be distinguished, and a lack of one does not entail a lack of the other. In addition, Kant holds that a preoccupation with fine taste can be a sign of an evil rather than a good disposition and that, in general, anything that is a result of what happens *merely* "by nature" is not even subject to moral evaluation, since it does not involve freedom, positive or negative. Furthermore, Lackey misconstrues a statement that he cites from Kant's later work (KpV [5: 61]), which he takes to mean that unless people use reason to "behave" morally (which Lackey falsely believes that Kant has said is impossible for black people), they remain "totally animalistic or more animal than human."[21]

---

[21] Lackey, *Modern God State*, 237 and 238. Later, Kant speaks more generally of four feelings relevant to "the mind's receptivity to the *concept* [emphasis added] of duty as such," namely, moral feeling, conscience, love of one's neighbor, and self-esteem (MdS [6: 399]). Feeling in this sense requires thought and freedom, and Kant believes this is part of everyone's "human nature"—which includes freedom, and is distinguished from what one regards as that which happens by mere nature, that is, without absolute freedom and reason. Unfortunately, "feeling" is an awkward term for Kant to use in a moral context, because he uses it in other quite different senses. In addition to the specific aesthetic notion of "trifling" feelings, Kant's original general conception of the term "feeling" refers to mere

Kant's statement is entirely hypothetical. Kant is just repeating an old point, namely, *if* we did not have freedom and reason at all, then, all of us would always be behaving exactly like animals because our action would be a matter of mere instinct. In this context, Kant's prior sentence, which Lackey does *not* quote, makes a huge difference: "But he [the human being] is nevertheless *not* [emphasis added] so completely an animal as to be indifferent to all that reason says on its own." In other words, what KpV [5: 61] is actually saying is that *no* human beings are mere animals.

Kant does hold, however—and this may be what misled Lackey—that when human beings *choose* ends that are not moral, then their acts do not have a higher "worth," and in that respect, although they really would never be mere animals (because they always have free choice), their choice in *that* instance would be *somewhat like* animal behavior *just insofar* as these human choices, like all animal behavior, would lack the special merit of moral worth. The reasons for the lack of worth would be quite different, though, since in one case it is a matter of a free misuse of a higher faculty, and in the other case it is a matter of completely determined nature. Nothing in Kant's text amounts to a suggestion that any human beings are, for a moment, actually just animals, or more animal than human, let alone that they always must behave just like animals. In addition, the whole point, for example, of Kant's later work on religion and his doctrine of the *universality* of "radical evil" is to emphasize that *all* human beings are free even when they choose to aim (as they can at any moment, and often do) at something evil rather than moral—and this choice by itself is subject to blame (or merit, if the intention is instead for the good, which is always possible) even if it does not issue in behavior.

Clarifying these fundamental points does not remove the fact that Kant definitely makes negative and unsupported claims, typical of his era, about the *talents* of people of other races. Kant's prejudiced remark in the *Observations* is followed merely by a reference to claims by Hume regarding a lack of "demonstrated talents" in black people. The factual claim about blacks is inexcusable, especially given other evidence at that time (it was, for example, well known in Germany that a black man from Ghana was an instructor at the university in Halle in 1724–47), but the claim does not bear on the moral issue, in Kant's philosophy, of the status dignity of all human beings, given what has already been noted about the basic distinction that Kant repeatedly makes between that issue and evaluations of talent.

---

inward affective states that are even more primitive than sensations because they do not play a role in generating cognitions (KrV A 29, note and A 801/B 829). Another meaning of the term concerns "moral feeling" (GMS [4: 442]) as used by *other* philosophers that he disagrees with, and that he characterizes as implying that there is a way to rely on empirical feelings *without* thought to somehow directly *sense* moral truths. For Kant, this is absurd, since such feelings would be contingent and blind.

80 KANTIAN DIGNITY AND ITS DIFFICULTIES

One reason why readers have misunderstood Kant's Critical position—in addition to their being overly influenced by his pre-Rousseauian or casual remarks in unpublished or merely popular statements—is that, alongside his system, Kant simultaneously developed a highly questionable descriptive theory of race. This theory affirms a common origin for humanity but identifies four distinct races that are ranked on the basis of supposedly significant differences not only in color but also in natural talent and cultural abilities.[22] Several passages in lectures and incidental works repeat harsh stereotypes, culled from biologists and travel reports by white Europeans, about how various groups are inferior to Europeans in achievement and commonly misuse, or do not get to effectively use, their basic capacities (Tel [8: 174–6], V-AnFried [25: 655], V-AnPillau [25: 843], MK [25: 1187]). Nonetheless, the fundamental normative doctrine of Kant's Critical system, made explicit in his first major publication on ethics, is that human beings are *all* autonomous persons with dignity in the basic sense of having the capacity to act with free and fair motivation (GMS [4: 435]).

This doctrine about a universal basic capacity is consistent with his view that we also all have self-inflicted and socially reinforced strong *tendencies* that— especially in extreme or highly unjust circumstances—in fact go against our duties to properly exercise and develop our moral capacity.[23] In addition, it cannot be denied that Kant is blameworthy for having gone along with the common thought then that so-called "primitive" societies, in either overly indolent or chaotic conditions, are naturally characterized by practices that can strongly inhibit the higher feelings typical of a flourishing moral life.[24] However, as was noted in the previous chapter, in his late work Kant went so far as to characterize even his own German people, in contrast to their eastern neighbors, as lacking in a "principled awareness of equality" (Anth [7: 318])—and yet he surely did not mean thereby that this presumed fact about how a group actually behaves shows that they lack the fundamental predisposition for the good that everyone else has.

---

[22] See Phillip Sloan, "The Essence of Race: Kant and Late Enlightenment Reflections," *Studies in the History of Biological and Biomedical Sciences* 47 (2013), 191–5. Review of *Kant and the Concept of Race*, ed. Jon M. Mikkelsen (Albany: State University of New York Press, 2013). Kant was part of a significant shift, which took place in the biology of his era, to classifying species and races by means of a causal account (*Naturgeschichte*) rather than on the basis of appearance characteristics (*Naturbeschreibung*), although he still put an emphasis on (inherited) differences in skin color. Sloan notes that Kant did not take racial distinctions to be constitutive of the very identity of persons, but he was among the many theorists who thought that the mixing of races can lead to degeneration of cultural abilities—a point that Chamberlain picks up on. See Chamberlain, *Foundations*, 258.

[23] On the problem of the "radical evil" in these "strong tendencies," see Allen W. Wood, *Kant's Ethical Thought* (Cambridge: Cambridge University Press, 1999); and Lucy Allais, "Evil and Practical Reason," in *Kant on Persons and Agency*, ed. Eric Watkins (Cambridge: Cambridge University Press, 2017), 83–101.

[24] In Kant's popular works, such as Beo and Anth, there are numerous offensive passages about stereotypes in European societies as well, which Kant probably took to be harmless play in the popular style of his day. One shudders to think how future generations will look upon our attempts to keep up with the latest styles.

It is precisely because of his interest in the difficulties of moral development that Kant became clearly concerned, as scholars such as Pauline Kleingeld have shown,[25] with hastening the day when aggressive European colonial powers would avoid exploiting "primitive" societies and would make way for a turn toward democratic governments and just institutions for all. Here it is especially important to note that the critique Kant made against slavery and imposed treaty "contracts" (MdS [6: 353]), even involving tribes with allegedly "indolent" or "savage" behavior that he (like the authors of the United States *Declaration of Independence*) harshly criticized, presupposes that he still regarded the members of such groups as persons with an inviolable dignity and capacity for free moral choice that prohibits their being treated as a mere means. Right after his reading of Rousseau, Kant remarked, "Now, there can be nothing more horrendous than that the action of a human being shall stand under the will of another. Hence no antipathy can be more natural than that which a human being has toward slavery" (Bem [20: 88]). As has been noted, a similar position is expressed in notes from a late lecture, "the human being is free by nature, and all human beings are by nature equal" (V-AnMron [25: 1419]; cf. [25: 1300]), as well as in notes from the 1770s: "Still, about the misuse of freedom: for example, one must not always infer that a former slave would misuse it and for this reason give him no freedom at all. He will surely learn to avail himself well of it" (V-AnFried [25: 582]). In his published work, slavery is ruled out from the start by Kant's principle of freedom as "our only one innate right" (MdS [6: 237]), and by his remark on the relation of a master of a household to his servants: "he can never behave as if he owned them" (MdS [6: 283]).

Here again, what must be kept in mind above all is that Kant's theory is grounded in a metaphysical view about our *basic capacities*, as beings that all from the start possess a universal moral "compass" (KpV [5: 162]) that is somewhat similar to our all sharing categories of the understanding and essentially the same kind of spatiotemporal forms of intuition and underlying language capacities.[26] This is not a point argued for on the basis of induction, and it is not at all a matter of needing to be especially intelligent, mature, or reflective. Contrary to many caricatures, Kantian autonomy in its most basic sense, as a general inner capacity in principle to be sensitive to the moral law, is also not a matter of an individual or group's particular talents, choices, or constructions.

Misunderstandings can arise on this point because Kant does hold that, at an overall social level, if a *society* is to become morally flourishing in what it

---

[25] Pauline Kleingeld, "Kant's Second Thoughts on Colonialism." Some of the lesser-known limits in Kant's cosmopolitanism are criticized in Ch. 4. Thanks to Alix Cohen for pressing me to say more on these issues.

[26] For a discussion of possible parallels of innate structures for language and morality, see Susan Dwyer, "How Good is the Linguistic Analogy?", in *The Innate Mind: Structure and Contents*, ed. Peter Carruthers, Stephen Laurence, and Stephen P. Stich (Oxford: Oxford University Press, 2006), 145–67.

accomplishes (effectively helping the needy and so on), a first stage of technical, educational, and legal progress is crucial—but this does not mean that a *proper individual* attitude is not possible until one gets into an advanced society. Ordinary people have been moral for centuries even though social life has been mostly brutish, and even when there are developments in social structures and technology, the power of evil leaders can make use of them to create so many problems (as Rousseau suggested) that "advanced" cultures can encourage more immorality than before. On Kant's view, a moral capacity does not *require* any special level of intelligence, familiarity with abstract concepts, or experience with a "work ethic." The capacity does not even have to be something that is in fact naturally exercisable in a healthy life. A severely impaired child or a person in a deep coma still has this original capacity, like the rest of its distinctively human equipment, and is worthy of respect on this account, quite unlike any other animal (or so Kant held; if additional species have this gift, this would only extend the notion and not undermine his point about human beings). This is why, if some kind of remarkable medical reversal were to occur with seriously disabled or undeveloped human beings, we would say that these persons are being restored to what they have been, or would naturally be when properly functioning, and not that a different being has been created.[27] Moreover, although Kant limits *moral* praise to acts and persons exemplifying the feature of a character with proper motivations, this hardly means that this is the only value he recognizes; pleasure, pain, or even unexperienced indignities and death still matter enormously in his system, as in common life.[28]

3.3 The Genuine Problem That Lackey's Research Reveals

The complications just discussed, concerning the exact meaning of the pivotal notion of freedom presumed to underlie the capacity for morality, are crucial in evaluating Lackey's discussion of Chamberlain's relation to Kant, and in characterizing the later evil figures that the *Foundations of the Nineteenth Century* may have inspired. Chamberlain agreed, in *letter*, with one idea that truly is central to Kant's Critical view, namely, that however important the achievements of modern science are, science does not exhaust our access to truth because it cannot reveal what Chamberlain also *called* the human capacity for freedom.[29] The key

[27] See Ch. 1.6, and Patrick Kain, "Kant's Defense of Human Moral Status," *Journal of the History of Philosophy* 47 (2009), 59–102.

[28] This point meets some of the concerns raised in Rosen, *Dignity*, and John Tasioulas, "Human Dignity and the Foundations of Human Rights," in *Understanding Human Dignity*, ed. Christopher McCrudden (Oxford: Oxford University Press, 2013), 293–314, that our notion of dignity should include respect for the deceased; and in Griffin, *Human Rights*, that avoiding pain is an important part of well-being. An appreciation of these values is presupposed in Kant's conception of the highest good.

[29] Lackey, *Modernist God State*, 243.

complication here is that this *verbal* agreement does not at all amount to an agreement in *substance*. This is because Chamberlain did not rely on Kant's Critical notion of absolute libertarian freedom. Instead, he (like many other writers) used the term in a determinist sense, and connected it to the kinds of special talents and contingent liberties that his racist doctrines reserved for elite *Herrenvölker*—not a term that Kant himself used or would have ever condoned.[30] Thus, one finds that, as Lackey points out, Chamberlain accepted and even stressed the idea that "peoples and countries are mechanistically determined by their environment."[31] Jews in particular were then singled out for being "materialists [who] never exercise negative or positive freedom."[32] For Chamberlain, this means not only that, like *all* parts of nature, they supposedly lack the freedom asserted in traditional libertarianism. According to Chamberlain's additional racial theory, Jews are further characterized as being "materialistic" in the doubly bad sense of lacking what he calls the "positive freedom" of "creative force" and the "negative freedom" of a capacity to transcend egoism. These are powers of freedom that, supposedly, nature has bestowed only on the "idealistic" and higher Aryan peoples, who alone have a heroic "love of the fatherland" of the kind eventually stressed in "Hitler's political vision,"[33] that is, fanatical racist German chauvinism.

Lackey's reference to Hitler is highly perceptive and based on notes from 1919 in which, in a discussion that clearly appears to reflect terms taken from reading Chamberlain, Hitler stressed a fundamental conflict between positions he called "idealism" and "materialism."[34] The misleading fact, however—which Lackey does not mention—is that, just like Chamberlain, these notes employ these "isms" simply in a popular *political/psychological* sense that contrasts crude selfishness, which it identifies with "materialism," with the power of "creative force" for the *Volk*, which it identifies with "idealism." This kind of popular meaning for the term "materialism" can be found in casual English as well, but it has nothing to do

---

[30] Mills takes the term from elsewhere: "I take this term from the sociologist Pierre van den Berghe's description of white settler states such as the United States, Australia, and South Africa as 'Herrenvolk democracies,' polities that are democratic for the master race, the *Herrenvolk*, but not for the subordinate race(s)." "Dark Ontologies," 135.

[31] Lackey, *Modernist God State*, 246.

[32] Lackey, *Modernist God State*, 251 and 324; cf. 253: "Jews are materialists who lack freedom." Chamberlain praises Kant's notion of human dignity in contrast to theological doctrines of inherited sin, but on his understanding of original Christianity, dignity is a matter of "true nobility," and it thus falls under the general (and not genuinely Kantian) heading of a contingent achievement. See Chamberlain, *Foundations*, vol. 1, 175, and *Die Grundlagen des XIX Jahrhunderts*, vol. 2 (Bruckmann: Munich, 1919), 13th edn, 1120.

[33] Lackey, *Modernist God State*, 253.

[34] Lackey, *Modernist God State*, 254, which refers to Werner Maser, *Hitler's Lectures and Notes*, trans. Arnold Pomerans (Evanston: Northwestern University Press, 1974), 283. Similar remarks were made by Paul de Lagarde, an influential anti-Semitic, anti-Christian, and anti-Slavic Orientalist whose work was studied by the young Hitler. See Peter Watson, *The German Genius: Europe's Third Renaissance, The Second Scientific Revolution and the Twentieth Century* (New York: HarperCollins, 2010), 673.

84 KANTIAN DIGNITY AND ITS DIFFICULTIES

with the core *metaphysical* and *epistemological* meanings that are standard in philosophy, including in Kant's usage, where "materialism" signifies the view that physical matter alone exists, or at least that its elementary structure entirely determines our thinking. Like Hitler, Chamberlain insisted, furthermore, on the absurd and evil assumption that this naturalistic and psychological contrast of "idealism" and "materialism" maps onto a distinction between races that are Aryan and good, and races that are non-Aryan and bad, the former alone supposedly understanding that "the German conception of duty means serving the community rather than the self."[35] Lackey himself does not challenge the practice of calling such a socially defined notion of duty "moral autonomy"[36]—as if the mere teamwork of a group of gangsters could make them moral or autonomous in a Kantian sense. This practice was exhibited by figures such as Goebbels, in a passage cited by Lackey from the novel *Michael*, where the "Godly virtues" are defined as "honor, work, the flag,"[37] and "honor" is understood in terms of the fanatical soldierly duties of German nationalism, in contrast to the moderate virtues of classical or Christian thought.[38]

It should be painfully obvious that by this point any *genuine* relation to Kant's *philosophy* has been long lost. To count as a Kantian, it is hardly enough to merely invoke *words* such as "idealism," "duty," and "creative anti-selfishness." Kant did indeed speak positively when using terms like these, but with a meaning that implies (as important successors such as Hermann Cohen and Ernst Cassirer well understood) absolute freedom, categorical moral obligation, and hence an anti-selfishness that is defined by egalitarian justice and *universal* benevolence rather than aggressive nationalism or any kind of absolute devotion to a local community or race simply as such—in other words, the very opposite of what Chamberlain and his ilk had in mind.

Similar seriously misleading uses of terminology also infect the claims that Lackey and others make when they attempt to connect Kant and Fascism by reference to *religious* notions. Lackey is correct in noting that Hitler often played the religious card (like cynical American politicians) and invoked the term "God" in his tactical efforts to gain support from all sorts of conservative factions.[39]

---

[35] Lackey, *Modernist God State*, 255.

[36] The "most defining feature of humanness is not intellectual capacity but moral autonomy, which is why Aryans, Hitler claims, rank so high on the hierarchical scale of being... the German is superior insofar as he puts 'all his abilities in the service of a community'" (Lackey, *Modernist God State*, 256). The quotation about community service is from Adolf Hitler, *Mein Kampf* [1925–6], trans. Ralph Manheim (Boston: Houghton Mifflin, 1971), 297.

[37] Lackey, *Modernist God State*, 273–4. Cf. Claudia Koonz, *The Nazi Conscience* (Cambridge, MA: Harvard University Press, 2003).

[38] According to Lawrence Rees, *Hitler's Charisma: Leading Millions into the Abyss* (New York: Penguin Random House, 2012), 103, Goebbels held that Christian virtues "crippled all that is noble in humanity." Cf. Ian Kershaw, *Hitler: A Biography* (New York: Norton, 1998), 661.

[39] See Richard Steigmann-Gall, *The Holy Reich: Nazi Conceptions of Christianity, 1919–1945* (Cambridge: Cambridge University Press, 2003), 61, on Hitler's cynical admiration for how some Viennese politicians knew better than others how to exploit Catholic voters. A similar view of phony Nazi religious appeals is repeatedly confirmed in Klemperer's trenchant on-site observations of party

DIGNITY AS UNCONDITIONED   85

Issues here become especially complicated, however, because of what can *seem* to be a strikingly *parallel* way that Kant referred to Jews, religion, and God. It is true—although sometimes forgotten—that Kant held both the negative thesis that "original" Judaism, because of an improper (supposedly merely "statutory") sense of duty, was not a genuine religion with a proper God concept (Rel [6: 125–6]),[40] and also the positive thesis that a different kind of religion, with a proper God concept, is still needed. Similarly, the Nazis proclaimed (though in viciously harsh action) both the negative thesis that Jews lack a proper notion of duty, religion, and God, and also—at least some of the time—the positive thesis that some kind of God concept is still needed.

Despite the truly disturbing initial similarities in appearance, the *meaning* of Kant's statements, negative as well as positive, is directly *opposed* to that of the Nazi statements. Kant's negative attitude toward what he understood as defining "original" Judaism was part of his general opposition to *any* kind of tradition— hence centuries of Christendom as well—with norms and practices that appear to be based *heteronomously*, as for instance solely on allegiance to mere institutional or allegedly supernaturally dictated commands in contrast to the autonomous self-legislation of the categorical imperative of pure practical *reason* (Rel [6: 115]).[41] Similarly, when Kant went on to endorse a positive concept of God and religion in line with his moralistic reading of the New Testament, he argued for a pure form of religious life that would lead to an *eventual* dissolution of *any* heteronomous reliance on traditional church practices and institutions, and especially on any kind tied to the whims of political authorities. He called this the religion of "the teacher of the Gospel," but in so doing he was just approving an internal moral ideal inspired by, but not limited to, the Lutheran and Pietist notion of the "priesthood of all believers," and he by no means meant thereby to endorse any permanently established Christian church or traditional Trinitarian beliefs about a supernatural messiah.

In sum, in direct contrast to the meaning that Kant's statements have because of their ground in a *pure, rational,* and *universal* notion of duty, the Nazi statements regarding Jews, God, and religion have their ground in a *naturalist, racist,* and German *chauvinist* understanding of duty, one defined in terms of an absolute commitment to a local and contingent community led by the Führer's unchallengeable will. Hence, in insisting, *negatively*, that the Jews lack a proper sense of God and religion, the Nazis were contending (in a way that, ironically,

---

statements during the Nazi era. See Victor Klemperer, *I Will Bear Witness: A Diary of the Nazi Years 1933–1941*, trans. Martin Chalmers (London: Weidenfeld and Nicolson, 1998).

[40] Cited in Lackey, *Modernist God State*, 240, and Franks, "Inner Anti-Semitism," 263.

[41] The historical inaccuracy of Kant's understanding of Judaism is of course another issue, for Kant appears to have been all too accepting of the harshly anti-Judaic treatments of the "Old Testament" by Protestant theologians in his era. I have seen this point documented best in Ursula Goldenbaum, "The Shift from Leibniz's Theodicy toward Protestant Philosophy of History as a Decrease in Religious Tolerance and Increase of Anti-Judaism," Templeton Conference talk, Lisbon, 2012. https://www. youtube.com/watch?v=VDyyLx06Qmk

86 KANTIAN DIGNITY AND ITS DIFFICULTIES

can be understood as a significant kind of unintended compliment) that they could not be counted on to be devoted to the absolutist Nazi state (a self-fulfilling belief, since the Nazis' antecedent terrorization of Jews would make any such devotion from them especially irrational). In other words, whereas Kant's worry, in his critique of what he understood as original "Judaism," concerned an apparent heteronomy of being *too closely tied* to contingent social institutions, the Nazi worry was just the opposite, for it concerned a *failure* to be closely tied to (what Kant would call) the heteronomous duty of worshipping the tightly unified but contingent social complex of a particular state, race, and dictator.

The *positive* Nazi call for commitment to a Fascist and Erastian sense of religion and "God" was also in sharp contrast to Kant's positive call for understanding "religion within the bounds of pure reason alone." There is, to be sure, a residual negative similarity here, because Kant, like the Nazis, did not want to grant lasting authority to any traditional churches as such, and (in this case like most Enlightenment thinkers) especially not to the church of Rome. But Hitler's positive notion of religion itself, if it can be called that, was simply an acknowledgement of omnipotent "providence," in the crude sense of a feeling of awe in the face of the global battle between warring species and races, with an outcome entirely determined by the most powerful amoral and supraindividual forces of nature.[42] In a speech to party leaders in 1941, Hitler's main assistant, Martin Bormann, stated this view clearly:

> National Socialist and Christian conceptions are incompatible. The Christian churches build upon men's ignorance; by contrast [National Socialism] rests upon *scientific* foundations. When we speak of belief in God, we do not mean, like the naïve Christians and their spiritual exploiters, a man-like being sitting around somewhere in the universe. The force governed by natural law by which all these countless planets move in the universe, we call omnipotence or God.[43]

This is the very opposite of Kant's ideal of an eventual condition of "perpetual peace," supported through the growth of an "ethical commonwealth," with free agents holding to charity to all as well as postulates about a divinely grounded path toward the highest good—a path that would build on, but go beyond, the legal stability achieved by a plurality of genuinely democratic and just states. Given all these clarifications, it should be obvious how misleading it can be to

---

[42] Hence what Hitler admired was not soft Christian love but a merciless combination of what he called the "idealist" (!) forces of "brutal fist" and "genius." Hitler, *Mein Kampf*, 299, cited in Lackey, *Modernist God State*, 257.

[43] Quoted in Joachim C. Fest, *The Face of the Third Reich: Portraits of the Nazi Leadership*, trans. Michael Bullock (London: Weidenfeld and Nicolson, 1970), 132–3. Sharp rejection of the traditional biblical doctrine of a creator God was a common feature of Nazi thinking. See Chamberlain, *Foundations*, 218, and Rosenberg, *Race*, 116.

directly link the rise of Fascism to Kant's philosophy rather than to contrary movements, such as nihilism or the wholly anti-religious and crude versions of Darwinism and Nietzscheanism that became so popular by the end of the nineteenth century.

Insofar as Hitler directly commented on Christianity in this context, his most revealing attitudes may have been his early decision to avoid "wasting time" by thinking through what "religious reformation" might involve,[44] and his statement, near the end of *Mein Kampf*, that he agreed with what he took to be "Kant's complete refutation... of the dogmatic philosophy of the church."[45] It is significant that these remarks indicate no more than a naïve impression that, supposedly, it was shown by Kant, in his critique of traditional *theoretical* arguments, that there is no strictly rational ground for Catholicism, and also that there is no point in even trying, as Kant did, to work out a pure new form of Protestantism. All this is consistent with also saying Hitler believed politics needs a "religious" basis, in the vague sense of some kind of global rather than traditional "party" vision, but it is crucial that this requires the immediate qualification that, as Lackey admits, what Hitler took to be "God's law" for human beings is simply the power of race.[46]

Similar qualifications must be made concerning Lackey's scathing claim, against what he goes so far as to call the attitude of "profoundly dishonest... or totally blinded readers" who fail to acknowledge that Fascism was not a result of "modern secularization" but instead a form of specifically "Christian idealism."[47] We have already seen what the Nazis' odd "idealism" actually signifies—namely, the belief that human beings are all determined by natural forces aiming at power—and Lackey's attempt to connect that belief conceptually with Christianity collapses similarly on the evidence of even his own quotations. He cites Rosenberg, for example, as espousing a view that is to be held "in spite of all churches,"[48] just as he cites Chamberlain as endorsing "reproaching the churches."[49] Furthermore, the Nazi leaders (and their academic followers) were well known for going so far as to treat Jesus himself, as Chamberlain had, as Aryan, and to reject Paul and Augustine.[50] But what could a "Christianity" be that is independent of *all* churches, of all its original leaders, and of all its centuries of self-understanding (as having roots going back to Abraham and Moses), while also being, as was just noted, opposed to "pure" rather than naturalist and nationalist and racist morality?

---

[44] Watson, *German Genius*, 673.

[45] Hitler, *Mein Kampf*, 1971, 720, cited in Yvonne Sherratt, *Hitler's Philosophers* (New Haven, CT: Yale University Press, 2013), 20.

[46] Lackey, *Modernist God State*, 232; cf. Steigmann-Gall, *Holy Reich*, 29.

[47] Lackey, *Modernist God State*, 242.   [48] Lackey, *Modernist God State*, 229.

[49] Lackey, *Modernist God State*, 252.

[50] Cf. Geoffrey Field, *Evangelist of Race: The Germanic Vision of Houston Stewart Chamberlain* (New York: Columbia University Press, 1981), 307; and Steigmann-Gall, *Holy Reich*, 117.

88 KANTIAN DIGNITY AND ITS DIFFICULTIES

Lackey's final strategy is to rely on the Nazis' own words, the mere fact that many of them *said* they were "Christians," and even said they were following Jesus, albeit an invented and not-at-all-Jewish Jesus. But words are pointless without a specified meaning, and any honest look at what the Party really meant in its actions, at all that its leading ideologues truly held, and at all the evidence Lackey offers does not amount to even the beginnings of a plausible argument for a *warranted* philosophical or theological connection to a recognizable form of either genuine Christianity or Critical philosophy. One might, after all, mount a similar argument against morality, by noting that the Nazis—and many other evil groups—have repeatedly *said* they were acting precisely as "moral" people. (It would be absurd to conclude that just because the term "moral" has been misused in this way, we should give up the notion of morality altogether.) This complication is, to be sure, a disturbing problem, for the fact is that there was such a thing as what the title of an informative recent book has called the "The Nazi Conscience."[51] The perpetrators of great evil, including many kinds of racist fanatics, can be evil precisely because they do not understand themselves as evil but rather, in a kind of (at least occasionally) sincere but condemnable delusion, clothe themselves in popular terms such as "morality," "religion," "science," "patriotism," or "socialism." But this just means that these perpetrators are very confused and wicked, and not at all that we must regard the genuine referents of these terms as evil.

Nonetheless, there is at least one obvious way in which the Nazis' superficial references to religion, and to Christianity in particular, were essential in an especially nefarious way. This is because in simply requiring, in the way that they did for a long time (but not toward the end), some kind of public confessional identification, they were insisting on a move that they knew that Jews in particular could not make, given the Nazis' purely racist restriction on what was allowed to count as "Christian" (or at least non-Jewish). Of course, their revolutionary way of doing this in practice, their insistence on making a particular kind of *racial* background a necessary condition for even the possibility of public religious recognition and social acceptance, flies in the face of the history of Christian doctrine, which, as such (in contrast, admittedly, to the actual practice of innumerable political actors that have *called* themselves "Christian"), has stressed being open

---

[51] Koonz, *The Nazi Conscience*. This is not to deny that there were renegade theologians who supported the party. Every religion has its heretics but, by definition, they are not what define it. There were also prominent party leaders who regularly attended church (see Steigmann-Gall, *Holy Reich*, 6)—but the same might be said about the ritual of mafia members attending church funerals, without proving any coherent overlap in ideology. This is also not to deny that all too many Germans (unlike those who resisted the official "German Christians") went along with being encouraged to take occasional inflammatory statements from long ago by genuine church leaders, such as Augustine or Luther, to license aggressive discrimination and worse in the current age. See Doris Bergen, *Twisted Cross: The German Christian Movement in the Third Reich* (Chapel Hill: University of North Carolina Press, 1996).

DIGNITY AS UNCONDITIONED 89

to persons of all races and nations (and, at least originally on its own part, to keeping some distance between church and state).

And yet: despite the limitations of Lackey's account, there still might be senses in which, especially in the German context, there are significant interconnections after all between *strands* of Kantian or Christian thought that can be understood as encouraging Fascism and anti-Judaism in particular. For a further consideration of this serious issue, there is no better place to look than Paul Franks's essay.

3.4 Franks's Foresight

Paul Franks's discussion exhibits a deep knowledge of the Jewish philosophical and theological tradition as well as a specialist's insight into the technicalities of all the main German Idealist systems and the Critical philosophy. His overall assessment is that these Idealists went astray not because of devotion to traditional church doctrines but because of "prejudice and ignorance" concerning Jewish traditions in general.[52] One could add that none of these philosophers had the inside experience of their own culture being marginalized and worse for centuries by mainstream German society, and in general they did not show appreciation for how anything less than a truly sensitive treatment of any minority could have ugly repercussions. It is, after all, one thing for someone from a background connected with an established church to point out flaws within the establishment system; it is something else for someone with the power of that background to allege flaws in a culture lacking that status. Hence, it should be added that although it is true that Kant, like many Idealists, was very critical of *all* kinds of traditional religious *institutions*—as were also several Jewish writers by his time—it still matters that any critical remarks he made of minority cultures would have an extra bite and could easily have unfortunate consequences, especially in reinforcing bad tendencies already within the broader public.

This point is especially relevant in regard to the offensive passages Franks cites that look forward to a "euthanasia" of Judaism (SF [7: 53])[53] and encourage an overthrow of anything in its practice that goes beyond its "sublime" reverence for law (KU [5: 274]).[54] It is true, of course, that Kant's philosophical opposition to all sorts of traditional "isms" was different from intending disrespect for any particular persons, and he was well known for showing special public respect for individual Jews—in particular, his student Markus Herz, as well as Moses Mendelssohn upon a visit to Königsberg. Kant repeatedly stressed that one should not rush to

---

[52] Franks, "Inner Anti-Semitism," 276.

[53] Cited at Franks, "Inner Anti-Semitism," 263. Compare Kant's disparaging remarks about contemporary Jews in Poland as an "entire nation of nothing but merchants" (Anth [7: 206]).

[54] Cited in Franks, "Inner Anti-Semitism," 261.

90 KANTIAN DIGNITY AND ITS DIFFICULTIES

make judgments about the inner worth of other persons, and that the respect owed to their human dignity is in any case independent of agreement with their ideas or actions. Nonetheless, even if in general one can make a philosophical distinction between presenting a critique of various *cultural practices* and encouraging attacks on *individual persons*, that would be a quite inappropriate point to stress here because, in the relevant historical context, all persons within the minority, whatever their own attitude and individual situation, would remain vulnerable to the threats of whatever culturally destructive attitudes the powerful majority might support. So, even if some features of Kant's thought amount to a similar position on non-Jewish religious institutions and traditional practices in general (he goes so far as also to call anything *like* traditional Christian church services, or *Gottesdienst*—which he stayed away from as an adult—an *Afterdienst*, which is a vulgar way of describing a kind of counterfeit service), it could only be expected that, in the violent context of European history, his ominous choice of words might eventually be followed by especially harmful consequences for Jews in particular.

One can therefore only agree with Franks's foresight in observing that "Judaism may not be Kant's primary target, but it all too easily becomes the focal point of the criterion of autonomy, whether in his or others' hands."[55] This worry is especially understandable given that Kant's *Religion*, despite its many anti-traditional features, repeats a fairly common story (found also, by no accident, in Hegel's early *Life of Jesus*) about Jesus coming to *replace* a *dogmatic* view of the moral law (as arbitrarily commanded from on high, and being like the burden of an imposed force) as presented in what has been called the Old Testament. Although Kant also placed emphasis on some parts of the Old Testament, such as the story of Job, praising it for proto-Critically combining genuine faith with humility about human powers of comprehension (Rel [6: 265–7]), he still appeared to be far from aligning himself with those who were open, for example, to understanding Jesus as coming more to try to *fulfill* than to replace the law of the earlier Jewish community.[56]

At the same time, looking at the *Religion* alone, it seems fair to note a point that Franks does not stress, namely, that Kant's critiques there are directed largely against what he took to be the Jewish faith as "originally" established (Rel [6: 128]), and so this *by itself* does not imply that he needed to have been against those who follow modern rationalist versions of that tradition as inspired, for example, by Philo and many others.[57] Moreover, given the serious respect that Kant showed for Mendelssohn's work, especially in the *Orientation* essay, where

---

[55] Franks, "Inner Anti-Semitism," 262.

[56] Cf. Franks, "Inner Anti-Semitism," 261, which distinguishes (relatively moderate) "prefigurationism" and (hostile) "preconditionalism." Chamberlain sharply rejects speaking of Christianity as any kind of development incorporating values in Judaism. See Chamberlain, *Foundations*, 213.

[57] On "Judaism as a philosophical religion," see Carlos Fraenkel, *Philosophical Religions from Plato to Spinoza: Religion, Reason and Autonomy* (Cambridge: Cambridge University Press, 2012), 108–22.

his position was definitely favored over F. H. Jacobi's, one could argue (as have Hermann Cohen and others) that overall Kant's Critical position is *philosophically* sympathetic to (even if he did not show much positive interest in) the rationalist and reform Jewish thinkers of his time.

All this makes it all the more surprising, therefore, that at one point Kant suggested that Jews should be granted citizenship—something of a revolutionary idea in his country—*if* they accepted "the religion of Jesus" (SF [7: 53]). It seems clear that Kant did not mean this proposal in a sectarian confessional spirit but rather meant, by this "religion," basically his own anti-establishmentarian notion of a pure moral attitude (the term "religion" originally signifies a manner of personal being, not an institution). All the same, it is obviously offensive, to say the least, to single out a particular minority group upon which to oppose an explicit *political* requirement like this, especially one that conflicts with that group's understandable traditions of maintaining useful customs of its own, and especially since Kant seems to have understood the requirement as bringing along with it a total elimination of the "garment" of those particular traditions and therefore of their cultural group identity altogether. Moreover, if Kant simply meant his condition to be taken as basically an internal requirement, this was hardly a matter that, on Kant's own view, could ever be appropriately monitored. Kant was adamant, for example, in criticism of setting theological loyalty tests in the training of Protestant ministers, or in general of making special moral tests a condition of legal status.

3.5 Final Evaluation

If we now look in an evaluative way at the full record, at all the obviously prejudiced and injurious remarks already cited as well as those in Kant's *Anthropology* and other places,[58] it becomes impossible even to begin to "save the man," in contrast to the core of his system, with respect to the foreseeable effects of his words on later German readers. In addition, even though it is true that almost all other well-known thinkers in that era held views that we now regard as equally offensive, it is significant that Kant sometimes expressed, or implied, surprisingly negative attitudes about the actual talents and tendencies of an unusually large *variety* of peoples and not just typical minority groups. This can make Kant's prejudices look at the same time both a little better and a lot worse. That is, one can see that Kant was not locked in a particular fanatical racist obsession in a way that amounts, as with typical supremacists, to a direct disrespect of the dignity of one group of other human beings. But then one also has to admit that Kant's problem

---

[58] See also Rudolf Malter, *Immanuel Kant in Rede und Gespräch* (Hamburg: Meiner, 1990), 446–7. A broad review (and more critical treatment) of relevant material can now be found in Huaping Lu-Adler, *Kant, Race, and Racism: Views from Somewhere* (Oxford: Oxford University Press, 2023).

92 KANTIAN DIGNITY AND ITS DIFFICULTIES

becomes not "mere" anti-Semitism but a host of worrisome prejudices, and although these prejudices do not *aim* at denying dignity, in practice their mere expression can certainly *lead* to serious disrespect and damage. Although, *by themselves*, insulting expressions and actions cannot kill people or diminish their status of dignity, they can involve an a serious "appearance of degradation" that can have horrible consequences.[59]

The extent of Kant's prejudices has still not been fully appreciated. It is surprising that the few remarks he bothered to make about North Americans in general are strongly negative.[60] As has been noted, Kant totally passed over commenting on the remarkable generation of American citizens that was constructing an Enlightenment-inspired government, with a sophisticated republican constitution worked out right during the heart of his Critical period. Like many European intellectuals then, Kant may have had reservations about a country that still accepted the practice of slavery. Nevertheless, given the general European awareness of the achievements of international figures such as Benjamin Franklin, Thomas Paine, George Washington, John Adams, and Thomas Jefferson, as well as the closeness of their basic ideals—especially anti-colonialism—to that of the Critical philosophy, Kant's lifelong silence seems very odd. He regularly discussed current events with close friends who had very good connections with the English-speaking world, and yet for decades he lectured in exhaustive detail on exotic traveler's accounts of the rest of the world while ignoring the trailblazing principles and founders of the United States. Kant's surprising neglect in this instance is worth keeping in mind because it shows that even philosophers who are very concerned with trying to be cosmopolitan may still have all kinds of serious blind spots—apart even from race, religion, and gender—that keep them much too closed up against not only traditional outsiders but also even very similar parties elsewhere that they should have easily appreciated as natural allies.[61] In other words, Kant's errors are not simply a matter of racism but should be understood as rooted in a broader blindness about cultures (even ones that he takes to be of the same race) outside his particular northern European background.

Given all these complications, whatever might be said in the way of personal apologetics for Kant can only go so far. It is true that we should not forget the long self-critical trajectory of Kant's work, his dramatic Rousseauian movement away from intellectual elitism, his late taking back of some racist views concerning

---

[59] See Hampton, *Intrinsic Worth*, 122.   [60] For more detail, see Chs. 2, 4, and 5.

[61] More than a century later, Rainer Maria Rilke (like Martin Heidegger) famously worried that even an American apple could not be as earthy as a European one. German militarists, in two wars, made a similar but much more destructive underestimation of the bountiful power of the United States, a mistake that also seems to have rested on bizarrely stubborn cultural provincialism rather than racial prejudice. The United States, of course, is capable of practicing its own kind of harmful provincialism.

blacks,[62] and his short but surprising publication, near the very end of his career, in which he went out of his way to make an eloquent quasi-Herderian brief for the value of small and endangered cultures and languages (Nachschrift [8: 445]).[63] His focus there—which he presented as only one possible example—was on the attitude of some local Lithuanian friends that he contrasted favorably with the character of Germans. Nonetheless, even this piece is a reminder that, unlike his student Herder, Kant did not go on to say anything similar concerning the Hebrew language and nearby Jewish culture, which was newly flourishing but still also constantly endangered.[64] This is an odd failing because Kant's own subtle understanding, in his discussions of morality and religion, of the complex psychological structure of self-deception, should have made him sensitive to the phenomenon that contemporary scholars, such as Lucy Allais, have discussed as a kind of nefarious cognitive blindness that arises with prejudice and provincialism.[65]

In sum, although it is highly inappropriate to propose, in the same way that Lackey suggested, anything like a near-identity of Kant's system with that of the writings of Chamberlain and the Fascists, even a sympathetic perspective on Kant's entire career cannot exculpate the way he expressed his attitudes toward Jews and other groups. When one adds that, on Kant's own view, all human beings are riddled by radical evil, there is all the less reason to expect him, as a person, to be without significant fault. Ironically then, in concluding with an acknowledgement of the seriousness of the problem of his prejudiced expressions, we are in a sense also endorsing all the more strongly the relevance of his own principle of categorical respect for universal human dignity, as well as his insight that all human beings, especially in a world still filled with unjust and corrupting structures, are evil enough to have a deeply entrenched tendency to encourage violations of that principle. Even if Kant's philosophical doctrines can be said to have been fundamentally misunderstood and misused by the horribly powerful racist politicians of later Germany, it is a feature of the unfortunate *Weltgeschichte* that turned out to be twentieth-century Germany's *Weltgericht*, that Kant's now well-documented prejudiced expressions stand in the way of concluding that he was entirely blameless in regard to what the worst of his later countrymen chose to make out of him.[66]

Kantian Dignity and its Difficulties. Karl Ameriks, Oxford University Press. © Karl Ameriks 2024.
DOI: 10.1093/9780198917656.003.0004

[62] Cf. Kleingeld, "Second Thoughts," and Allais, "Kant's Racism."

[63] See Ch. 2.2, and Susan Shell, "*Nachschrift eines Freundes*: Kant on Language, Friendship, and the Concept of a People," *Kantian Review* 15 (2010), 88–117.

[64] See Kristin Gjesdal, *Herder's Hermeneutics: History, Poetry, Enlightenment* (Cambridge: Cambridge University Press, 2017), on the broader cosmopolitanism of Herder and its limitations as well.

[65] See Ch. 4.3, and Allais, "Kant's Racism," and "Evil and Practical Reason."

[66] My thanks to the editors of *Kant's Concept of Dignity*, and also to participants at a NAKS workshop at the University of California-San Diego.

4

Dignity and Democracy: Missed Connections with the United States

> Now the *republican* constitution is the only one that is completely compatible with the right of human beings, but it is also the most difficult one to establish, and even more to maintain... (ZeF [8: 466])

This chapter argues that, surprisingly, there is no evidence that Kant endorsed the *Declaration of Independence* or the widely known ideas of figures such as Thomas Jefferson and John Adams.[1] At the same time that Kant was ignoring the Americans, philosophers such as Richard Price and Jeremy Bentham were vigorously debating and influencing American developments. At that time Kant also did not show an interest in the problems caused by the effects of aggressive German expansion in the Baltic area where Kant himself lived. In his double lack of interest in the progressive side of American politics and the repressive side of Germany's expansion, Kant's entrenched elitist attitude resembled, in some ways, the later position of Fascism. Kant's odd attitude in this case was not a matter of racism, however, and it was inconsistent with his doctrine of universal human dignity and his critique of colonialism.

4.1 A Surprising Problem

A rising wave of recent literature challenges Kant's reputation as a defender of human dignity by sharply criticizing his connection with distressing historical phenomena such as racism, anti-Semitism, sexism, and colonialism. In contrast to traditional praise of Kant as an advocate of Enlightenment values, contributions in this vein attack Kant for having dangerously encouraged anti-progressive

---

[1] Leading philosophers have overlooked this point. For example, Jürgen Habermas has remarked that "[Kant was] an archer who aims his arrow at the most actual [i.e., relevant] features of the present and so opens the discourse of modernity." "Taking Aim at the Heart of the Present," in *Foucault: A Critical Reader*, ed. David Couzens Hoy (Oxford and New York: Basil Blackwell, 1986), 105, seconding Michel Foucault, as quoted in Alice Kuzniar, "Kant and Herder on the French Revolution," in *The French Revolution in the Age of Goethe*, ed. Gerhart Hoffmeister (Hildesheim: Georg Olms, 1989), 27, n. 20. This remark, praising Kant, expresses a rare moment of agreement between Habermas and Foucault. Unfortunately, the remark misses the fact that although Kant was very concerned with the epoch-defining events of his time, he underestimated some that were "most actual" in 1776.

positions on all these issues.[2] These are huge and interrelated topics and there are some special complexities concerning colonialism that have not yet been appreciated.

Traditional analytic criticisms of Kant have mostly limited themselves to a relatively mild philosophical rebuke of Kant's notion of dignity for being too vague and general or, conversely, too restrictive and overly harsh on our natural interests. There are many new cultural criticisms, however, that go much further and often declare Kant guilty in a world-historical sense, sometimes even condemning him for being, at least in part, indirectly responsible for the horrors of the rise of Fascism. There is more behind these criticisms than one might expect, even though much can still be said in defense of the generally progressive tendency of Kant's principles.[3]

Some new light can be shed on the issue of colonialism by concentrating on one topic that has remained oddly underthematized in Germany as well as the United States, namely, Kant's relation—that is, lack of a relation—at the very peak of his career, to the remarkable event of the founding of the United States. In this context, for those who stress broad cultural criticisms of Kant, it can be useful to have a reminder of the argumentative complexity and most basic doctrines of his main texts, and especially of his radical, American-sounding principle—insisted upon explicitly also in the postwar German constitution and now reiterated in numerous other ones—that *all* human beings have a basic dignity which *all* human beings have a *categorical* duty to respect.[4] At the same time, for those who have focused on narrowly philosophical aspects of Kant's work, it should be a revelation to learn what an at times distressing impact his thought—or at least popular refashionings of it, channeled by the astoundingly influential Houston Stewart Chamberlain (1855–1927)[5]—had on society at large. It is still not well known that, during the turn to Fascism, Kant and the United States were in fact very closely linked by prominent German writers and politicians, who spoke of dignity as a fundamental concept but—like many Americans—interpreted it in racist

---

[2] On Fascism, racism, and anti-Semitism, see Ch. 3. On sexism, see, e.g., *Feminist Interpretations of Kant*, ed. Robin May Schott (University Park, PA: Penn State University Press, 1997); Jane Kneller, "Kant on Sex and Marriage Right," in *The Cambridge Companion to Kant and Modern Philosophy*, ed. Paul Guyer (Cambridge: Cambridge University Press, 2006), 447–76; and Dilek Huseyinzadegan, "For What Can the Kantian Feminist Hope? Constructive Complicity in Appropriations of the Canon," *Feminist Philosophy Quarterly* 4 (2018), (1), Article 3, doi:10.5206/fpq/2018.1.3.

[3] See Chs. 1–3.

[4] Michael Rosen, *Dignity: Its History and Meaning* (Cambridge, MA: Harvard University Press, 2012), and Jeremy Waldron, *One Another's Equals: The Basis of Human Equality* (Cambridge, MA: Harvard University Press, 2017) trace the historical-political development of this principle, but they do not connect Kant's work directly with the founding of the United States.

[5] Houston Stewart Chamberlain, *The Foundations of the Nineteenth Century*, trans. John Lees with an Introduction by Lord Redesdale [1899], 2 vols. (London: John Lane, 1911), was a worldwide bestseller, influencing Hitler and many others, and Chamberlain considered his lengthy sequel, *Immanuel Kant: A Study and a Comparison with Goethe, Leonardo da Vinci, Bruno, Plato and Descartes*, trans. Lord Redesdale [1905], 2 vols. (London: John Lane, 1914) to be even more important.

96 KANTIAN DIGNITY AND ITS DIFFICULTIES

terms and denied its application to numerous "unhealthy" and "non-Aryan" groups.[6] This disturbing phenomenon still deserves much more attention than it can be given here, but it also should motivate philosophers to consider what kind of more positive connections between Kant and the United States might be defended, and how it is that, on both sides, these connections have been ignored.

A special motivation for carrying out this project in a more complex way than usual is that Kant is not alone in manifesting a bizarre double tendency on these topics: a well-known primary orientation of progressive broad-mindedness, along with a long-forgotten secondary orientation of regressive narrow-mindedness. Kant's narrow-mindedness has some similarities to limitations found even in outstanding recent scholarship, and this fact can provide one more lesson of how even philosophers generally oriented in a laudable cosmopolitan direction can still fall prey to surprising instances of "self-incurred" blindness in the form of a tendency to focus on relatively distant issues while overlooking serious problems closer at hand. Awareness of striking examples of this phenomenon in our own time may make it somewhat easier to understand, at least by analogy, how even an extraordinarily wide-ranging and enlightened philosopher such as Kant could sometimes be so strangely blind about his own situation.

Consider, for example, an impressive recent volume of essays called *Kant and Colonialism*.[7] The essays in this collection are excellent with respect to what they directly discuss, and the co-editors deserve high praise for their own contributions as well as for simply having the idea of putting together such a volume. Nonetheless, despite the wide range of topics addressed in the collection, readers will find—as is still typical of work on Kant[8]—no reference in it to either of the two major scenes of colonization that are arguably the most directly relevant for Kant. These are the *Western* phenomenon of the unprecedented *American* secession from British colonial rule in 1776, and the equally large-scale phenomenon of the *German* drive to the east (*Drang nach Osten*), which goes back to the era of

---

[6] See *Race and the Enlightenment: A Reader*, ed. Emmanuel Chukwudi Eze (Oxford: Blackwell, 1997); Bernard Boxill, "Kant and Race," in *Race and Racism*, ed. Bernard Boxill and Thomas E. Hill, Jr. (Oxford: Oxford University Press, 2001), 448–71; *The German Invention of Race*, ed. Sara Eigen and Mark Larrimore (Albany: State University of New York Press, 2006); Thomas McCarthy, *Race, Empire, and the Idea of Human Development* (Cambridge: Cambridge University Press, 2009); Michael Hardimon, *Rethinking Race* (Cambridge, MA: Harvard University Press, 2017); and, still valuable, Jacques Barzun, *Race: A Study in Modern Superstition* (New York: Harcourt Brace and Co., 1937).

[7] See *Kant and Colonialism: Historical and Critical Perspectives*, ed. Katrin Flikschuh and Lea Ypi (Oxford: Oxford University Press, 2014). See also Raidar Maliks, *Kant's Politics in Context* (Oxford: Oxford University Press, 2014), which provides valuable details about Kant's thought after 1789, but does not discuss significant earlier developments in America.

[8] There is also blindness in the other direction, as is noted by Flikschuh and Ypi, *Kant and Colonialism*, 4: "Russell Berman's probing and unjustly neglected book, *Enlightenment or Empire: Colonial Discourse in German Culture* [Lincoln: University of Nebraska Press, 1998], makes no mention of Kant at all." It is also striking that the topic of colonialism and Kant's critical discussion of contracts with native peoples (MdS, Doctrine of Justice § 62) is neglected in Sharon Byrd and Joachim Hruska, *Kant's 'Doctrine of Right': A Commentary* (Cambridge: Cambridge University Press, 2010).

the Teutonic Knights' invasion of the area around what became known as Königsberg (1254).[9] The first phenomenon involved a path-breaking philosophical as well as political rejection of overseas colonization, although accompanied by a growing invasion by United States citizens of vast North American territories; the second established an aggressive German presence (twice obliterating Poland) in the whole Baltic region, one that culminated in Hitler's surprise assault all the way to the Volga.[10]

In the context of reconsidering Kant's notion of dignity, it is by no means inappropriate to assign extraordinary importance to these two scenes and to link them. The American revolt, praised on the continent as an unprecedented liberation from the strongest of colonial powers then, was explicitly oriented toward a first realization of the Enlightenment idea of human rights combined with a precedent-setting full independence from political control by nobility and clergy. As a recent volume on the United States Declaration of Independence has amply documented, the success of this particular kind of struggle for independence was an event with a "global history" that inspired numerous imitations.[11] It occurred precisely during the central part of Kant's Critical period, and it obviously involved a philosophical orientation very close to Kant's own—and yet, Kant himself astonishingly offered no discussion of it, just as American experts on the event have ignored directly linking it with Kant's contemporaneous thought.

Morton White, in his classic *The Philosophy of the American Revolution*, refers in passing to Kant's critical remark, in the 1784 (that is, right between the Declaration and the Constitutional Convention) essay on Enlightenment, that one hears on all sides, "do not argue!" (Auf [8: 37]), but White does not bother to explicate the main point of Kant's subtle essay.[12] That essay's point is that an obedient attitude toward conditional authorities in standard contexts (legal/military, medical, and theological) is understandably important as a default practice, but this fact can never override the unconditional authority of "the *public use* of one's reason in all matters" (Auf [8: 36]), which alone vouchsafes "the sacred right of humanity" (Auf [8: 39]), the "collective will of the people" (Auf [8: 40]), and, in

---

[9] See Neil McGregor, "Lost Capitals," in *Germany: Memories of a Nation* (London: Penguin Books, 2016), 38–58. The connection between Hitler and the Teutonic knights is highlighted in Klaus Fischer, *Hitler & America* (Philadelphia: University of Pennsylvania Press, 2011), 282.

[10] See Timothy Snyder, *Bloodlands: Europe Between Hitler and Stalin* (New York: Basic Books, 2010).

[11] See David Armitage, *The Declaration of Independence: A Global History* (Cambridge, MA: Harvard University Press, 2007). Armitage stresses that the Declaration has two different sides, emphasized by readers differently at different times, namely, as the announcement of a new and recognition-worthy nation (with a unity that was to be settled only later), and as a general proclamation insisting on universal human rights. I am indebted to John McGreevy for this and other historical references.

[12] Morton G. White, *The Philosophy of the American Revolution* (Oxford: Oxford University Press, 1981), 14.

the very last words of the essay, can lead "finally even to principles of *government*...
in accordance with [human] *dignity* [emphasis added]" (Auf [8: 42]).

White does not note Kant's remark about "sacred rights," but he observes that
the *Declaration's* bold claim about "certain inalienable rights" as "self-evident"
might seem authoritarian, an elitist appeal to the intuitive powers of higher intel-
lects. White then constructs an argument, which he takes to be implicit in both
Locke's and Jefferson's thought, that the *Declaration's* claim about rights is rooted
in more elementary truths about universal *duties* and is not meant dogmatically.[13]
That is, it is to be regarded as *derivable*, in a "moral rationalist" way, as "undeniable" from the more fundamental thought that we are created equal in our *basic
species capacities* as human beings with reason, irrespective of individual differences in talent, opportunity, and achievement.[14] White then argues that, just as in
Locke's view (and, I believe, also like what Kant held about dignity), the
Declaration's presumption about fundamental truths that all human beings *can*
recognize does not mean that these *first* truths generally need to be accessed by
complex *demonstrative* powers, that is, special intellectual talents that ordinary
"laborers" might not have.[15] It is sufficient that philosophers can defend and clarify them to each other,[16] and that they can be revealed to humanity at large by
popular means such as the moral lessons of deist biblical readings—as was
believed by John Adams, Kant, and many others as well as Jefferson.

The late eighteenth-century revolutions in philosophy and politics were
epochal but they also left much that needed to done. Precisely by ending his
Enlightenment essay with a reference to an eventual proper respect for dignity,
Kant was signaling that the absolute monarchy of Prussia in 1784, whatever its
advantage for the time being as a keeper of order and a force for freedom of
expression, was still far short of having brought into an ideal state the good "seed
concealed" (Auf [8: 41]) in the disposition of humanity. Similarly, it is obvious
that even the most generous reading of the enlightened founding characteristics
of the United States government cannot overlook that it had fundamental flaws,

---

[13] White, *American Revolution*, 187.

[14] White, *American Revolution*, 74 f.; cf. 164. Here again it is crucial to keep in mind the fundamental distinction in Kant's moral theory between dignity, which attaches to our basic capacities or
Anlagen, and particular talents or achievements. Onora O'Neill's work is helpful in this regard because
it stresses that Kant's philosophy, with its fundamental emphasis on basic duties (and hence the duty
to respect human dignity), is not vulnerable to common complaints about inflated contemporary
claims for numerous kinds of controversial rights. See Onora O'Neill, *Constructions of Reason:
Explorations of Kant's Practical Philosophy* (Cambridge: Cambridge University Press, 1989), 76; Patrick
Kain, "Kant's Defense of Human Moral Status," *Journal of the History of Philosophy* 47 (2009), 59–101;
Patrick Frierson, *What is the Human Being?* (Abingdon and New York: Routledge, 2013); and Karl
Ameriks, "Vindicating Autonomy: Kant, Sartre, and O'Neill," in *Kant on Moral Autonomy*, ed. Oliver
Sensen (Cambridge: Cambridge University Press, 2013), 53–70.

[15] White, *American Revolution*, 53. For more on the significance of this point, see Ch. 5.

[16] See White, *American Revolution*, 59 and 129.

most notably in its still allowing the practice of slavery and an expanding mistreatment of Native Americans.[17]

This unfortunate fact is also very relevant in a way that is now well-documented,[18] but still not widely enough appreciated, for understanding later manifestations of the German eastward colonial drive. Hitler's constant international project was precisely to reject the idea of universal human equality while imitating what he took to be the most remarkable feature of the rise of the United States, namely that, despite its liberal rhetoric, its dynamic economy was in large part based on long-standing racist laws and ruthless expansion on a continental scale, with a thoroughgoing exploitation of native and imported peoples—slaves even if not Slavs or serfs.[19] By planning invasive measures that, at least initially, were often modeled on what Americans had been doing for centuries, the Nazis aimed at what was called turning the Volga into their "Mississippi." They were far from the only ones with such thoughts. From 1870 to 1950, leaders throughout Europe argued that, precisely in imitation of what the United States had achieved in economically colonizing extensive territories on its continent throughout the nineteenth century, it was necessary for Europeans to take over vast lands to their south and east. These leaders spoke openly, for example, of controlling the riches of the "shores of the Congo" and beyond, and of treating Ethiopia as "our Far West."[20]

Despite Kant's exceptional perceptiveness about philosophy, science, and much of history, there is a sense in which his position on colonialism had a limited but mysterious and disturbing similarity to the wrong turn taken by the Nazis. The similarity concerns two multipart facts: first, the fact that both the Nazis and Kant seemed to miss what was especially positive about the United States in regard to colonialism, and, second, the fact that they also both went along with something quite negative about Germany in regard to colonialism. More specifically, on the first point—as will be documented in more detail in the next section—they missed the considerable positive significance of the success of the United States in first gaining independence from a leading colonial power by instituting a wholly

---

[17] See Jonathan Lear, *Radical Hope: Ethics in the Face of Cultural Devastation* (Cambridge, MA: Harvard University Press, 2006).

[18] See Fischer, *Hitler & America*; Carroll P. Kakel III, *The American West and the Nazi East: A Comparative and Interpretive Perspective* (New York: Palgrave Macmillan, 2011); James Q. Whitman, *Hitler's American Model: The United States and the Making of Nazi Race Law* (Princeton: Princeton University Press, 2017); and Alex Ross, "The Hitler Vortex: How American Racism Influenced Hitler," *The New Yorker*, April 30, 2018, 66–73.

[19] Problems were not limited to the southeastern parts of the United States. See, e.g., a front-page story in the February 16, 2018 *Brookline Tab* (Massachusetts). documenting that numerous slaves were held there by leading families into the nineteenth century. Similar issues haunt many New England sites, such as Brown University in Rhode Island's Providence Plantations, with its connections to the Brown family's slave trade.

[20] Sven Beckert, "American Danger: United States Empire, Eurafrica, and the Territorialization of Industrial Capitalism, 1870–1950," *The American Historical Review* 122 (2017), 1162 and 1166.

100 KANTIAN DIGNITY AND ITS DIFFICULTIES

new and truly modern form of government. It is easy, of course, to understand how the Nazis missed the significance of this fact, because they were hardly interested in, let alone enthused about, the founding of a liberal state. But it is all the more perplexing to see how little, if any, interest Kant also expressed in this founding, even though he presumably shared its general Enlightenment principles.

With respect to the second disturbing fact, it is also easy to understand how, given their murderous ideology, the Nazis easily went along with, and took to a new level, all that was negative in Germany's eastward colonial drive. Kant's relation to that colonialism was much milder, more a matter of neglect than malevolence, although it was combined with a form of racism that was deplorable even though it can hardly be compared to the horror of the Nazis. Altogether then, it is not difficult to see why fanatical Nazis would miss what was good in America's relation to colonialism while holding to an evil position regarding their own colonial drive. Kant's position, in contrast, generates genuine philosophical perplexity even though it was considerably more moderate, for it would seem that he, of all people, should have been able to pick up on what was best in his own time while also more clearly warning about what was immoral, although—contrary to what most of us have believed—this is precisely what he did not do.

4.2 Surprising Facts

Although Kant eventually became a sharp critic of the overseas colonialism of the European naval powers[21] and highlighted the need to acknowledge the right of hospitality (*Besuchsrecht*) for persons in business outside of their own homeland,[22] he seemed insensitive to the specific implications of the long-standing German imperialist drive to the east. He did have good personal relations with Russians and Lithuanians, whose communities were well established in his area, and, in the end, he even contrasted flaws in German character with the virtues of peoples from small nationalities, such as his Baltic friends.[23] Nonetheless, it appears that he was not particularly interested in his own colonial situation, for the city that he inhabited all his life was, of course, not always called "Königsberg," that is, "the [German] king's mountain." For centuries, the area around the "mountain" belonged instead to the Sambian people, who inhabited the Samland peninsula that extends from Königsberg north to the exceptionally amber-rich

---

[21] See Pauline Kleingeld, "Kant's Second Thoughts on Colonialism," in *Kant and Colonialism*, 43–67.
[22] See Onora O'Neill, *Constructing Authorities: Reason, Politics and Interpretation in Kant's Philosophy* (Cambridge: Cambridge University Press, 2015), 207.
[23] See Ch. 2.

Baltic shoreline.[24] These people have also been called "old Prussians," but this is a misleading term. The so-called "old Prussian" language and culture does not belong to what we are familiar with as Prussia or Germany but is instead, along with Lithuanian and Latvian, one of the three distinct Baltic cultures (not Germanic, Slavic, or Finno-Ungaric).

Within this group, what is special about the Sambians is that, shortly before Kant's birth, their independence and language disappeared altogether. The main cause for this was probably their relatively small population, along with their greater proximity to the German lands and the effects of invasion and disease. Unlike what happened in later colonialism, it appears that the Sambians, who attempted occasional uprisings, were at least not immediately exterminated or exiled but were made serfs and lost their distinctive culture as they melted into the population of their invaders through intermarriage. In view of the fact that these conquered natives would have likely resided originally in the poorer section of Königsberg, which was also where Kant's family lived, it would not be surprising if Kant himself was in part Sambian (just as many Midwesterners of German origin may be in part Cherokee). For all we know, Kant never realized this possibility and did not explore the issue. But if he had considered it, he should have cared. Since colonialism can be said to make people refugees in their own country,[25] it could even be the case that some of Kant's own ancestors (or at least those of his close neighbors) were, in this sense, refugees, and that he was blind to their plight even though it may have been part of his own identity. To the extent that, in a popular sense, autonomy can be said to involve being able to own (and own up to) one's identity, it can be said that, through this apparent lack of interest in his own situation, Kant himself may have suffered a self-incurred loss of cultural autonomy—one that was no less serious for its remaining unknown, especially because it may have prevented him from being a more effective critic of colonialism.

Our initial considerations thus turn out to disclose a number of related instances of blindness: the blindness, to hugely relevant American and German phenomena, exhibited by even excellent contemporary researchers on colonialism, as well as Kant's own surprising neglect of details of the American and

---

[24] In a late discussion recounted by Abegg, Kant showed considerable knowledge about the scientific significance of the amber found at the coast near him. See *Immanuel Kant in Rede und Gespräch*, ed. Rudolf Malter (Hamburg: Meiner, 1990), 449–50. There is some evidence that the family of Kant's father came from a coastal region northeast of Königsberg where the native language was a Latvian dialect. In a nearby village (now in Lithuania) along the coast, Thomas Mann built a summer home in 1930 in what was then still East Prussia. The family had to abandon it in 1932 and for a while it was taken over by Hermann Göring.

[25] It should be noted, however, that unlike many victims of imperialist rulers the American colonists were not vanquished by outsiders, and they did not turn the native areas that they invaded into settlements with the official privileges of colonies. Thanks to discussions with Arthur Ripstein and Karl Martin Adam on this point.

102 KANTIAN DIGNITY AND ITS DIFFICULTIES

German colonial situations despite the fact that he was extraordinarily well-informed about international geographical and political phenomena. Kant's discussions of Americans are generally limited to very negative remarks about Native Americans and blacks, with no reference to the young country's many remarkable leaders, who were widely regarded as impressive intellectuals as well as gifted politicians. A passing reference to Franklin concerning swimming (Ped [9: 466]) is the main exception to this surprising pattern.[26]

A striking repetition of this kind of blindness can be found in a comment by Hannah Arendt, who was not only a distinguished Kantian native of Königsberg but also a keen student of international affairs and eventually an American immigrant. She asserted: "The sad truth of the matter is that the French Revolution, which ended in disaster, has made world history while the American Revolution, so triumphantly successful, has remained an event of little more than local importance."[27] This misperception has been appropriately corrected by the leading current historian on this topic, David Armitage (an Australian): "On the contrary, the American Revolution, so triumphantly successful, was an event of truly global importance. Its contagious consequences came to encompass the entire world of states we all now inhabit."[28] Armitage's remark is backed not only by the arguments and numerous documents contained in his *The Declaration of*

---

[26] There is no mention of the distinctive economy of North America, which was well-known from works such as J. Hector St. John de Crèvecœur's widely discussed and translated *Letters from an American Farmer* (1782). Already at that time there were, of course, large numbers of French, Dutch, and German immigrants. There are some references to Franklin's work in charting ocean currents, and also a late reference to a very early British religious group in Connecticut (Rel [6: 176]). Most striking is Kant's 1756 reference (which influenced Mary Wollstonecraft Shelley's *Frankenstein* (1818), and thus may also have an indirect connection to the influence of Price) to Franklin as a "Prometheus" figure whose famous discovery regarding lightning might lead to the dangerous hubris of making too much of scientific progress: "From the Prometheus of modern times, Herr Franklin, who sought to disarm the thunder, to that man who sought to extinguish the fire in Vulcan's workshop, all such endeavors are proofs of the boldness of man, allied with a capacity, which stands in a very modest relation to it, and ultimately they lead him to a humbling reminder, which is where he ought properly to start, that he never can be anything more than a human being" (Earthquakes [1: 472]).

[27] Hannah Arendt, *On Revolution* (Harmondsworth: Penguin, 1973), 56, cited in Armitage, *Declaration of Independence*, 138. Later, Arendt took Kant to be a public supporter of the American Revolution, but on the mistaken basis of presuming that § 65 of the *Critique of the Power of Judgment* (1790) is about the American rather than French Revolution. See Arendt, *Lectures on Kant's Political Philosophy*, ed. Ronald Beiner (Chicago: University of Chicago Press, 1992), 16. Kant's focus there on the "recent" use of the term "organization" surely refers to Emmanuel-Joseph Sieyès's epochal 1789 Paris pamphlet, *What is the Third Estate?* (Thanks to Michael Morris for a reminder on this point.) From her twentieth-century perspective, Arendt was, to be sure, positive about aspects of the US constitution (see Richard J. Bernstein, *Why Read Hannah Arendt Now?* (Medford, MA and Cambridge: Polity, 2018)) but, like Kant, she exhibited a blindness toward the considerable impact of the American process on many Europeans in the 1780s. Similarly, although Hegel endorsed American independence, his overall attitude can be summed up this way: "He thought it to be rather unimportant for European history since it was an event that took place far away in a not yet significant part of the world, as far as European affairs were concerned" (Terry Pinkard, *Does History Make Sense?* (Cambridge, MA: Harvard University Press, 2017), 224, n. 140).

[28] Armitage, *Declaration of Independence*, 138. Cf. Rosemary Zagarri, "Scholarship on the American Revolution since *The Birth of the Republic*," in Edmund S. Morgan, *The Birth of the Republic, 1763–1789*, 4th edn (Chicago: University of Chicago Press, 2012), 207: "[The American Revolution]

Independence: A Global History (2007) but also by contributions in his co-edited volume, *The Age of Revolutions in their Global Context, c. 1760–1840.*[29] Gary Nash's essay in that volume cites a point made earlier by the celebrated historian R. R. Palmer, namely, that the founding of the United States "dethroned England and set up America as a model," with a revolutionary doctrinal package of "freedom of religion" and a belief in "popular sovereignty, the rights of man as inalienable and universal, and that all government should flow from written constitutions constructed by the people themselves."[30] Kant's mature philosophy is obviously in close alignment with all these doctrines and developments—and yet, like Arendt, he had a strange blind spot and did not discuss them even after what we all know as the famous "shot heard around the world" in 1775, against the Redcoats in Massachusetts.

Claims like Armitage's have long been made by other leading historians, for example, Gordon Wood:

> Of course the American Revolution was very different from other revolutions. But it was no less radical and no less social for being different. In fact, it was one of the greatest revolutions that the world has ever known, a momentous upheaval that not only fundamentally altered the character of American society but decisively affected the course of subsequent history...[It] destroyed aristocracy as it had been understood in the Western world for at least two millennia. The Revolution brought respectability and even dominance to ordinary people long held in contempt and *dignity* [emphasis added] to their menial labor in a manner unprecedented in history.[31]

Despite all this evidence, it is surprising that the influential school of work generated by John Rawls's writings—which appear intended in part to provide philosophical grounding for the underlying principles of American government— never focuses on the issue of a *direct* connection between Kant's mature philosophical work and the Declaration, despite their close temporal and systematic relation. It is similarly striking that when Kant's doctrine of dignity was explicitly placed at the basis of the constitution of the Federal Republic of Germany, the

---

enabled the country to create a form of government—an extensive federal government—that had never before existed in the history of the world."

[29] See *The Age of Revolutions in their Global Context, c. 1760–1840*, ed. David Armitage and Sanjay Subrahmanyam (London: Palgrave Macmillan, 2010).

[30] Gary Nash, "Sparks from the Altar of '76: International Repercussions and Reconsiderations of the American Revolution," in Armitage and Subrahmanyam, *The Age of Revolutions*, 1, citing R. R. Palmer, *The Age of the Democratic Revolution: A Political History of Europe and America* (Princeton: Princeton University Press, 1959), vol. 1, 282. There is no reference to Kant in *The Age of Revolutions*.

[31] Gordon S. Wood, *The Radicalism of the American Revolution* (New York: Random House, 1991), 5 and 8.

104　KANTIAN DIGNITY AND ITS DIFFICULTIES

forging of this document was obviously influenced by the postwar American presence and an awareness of its founding documents, but this relationship generally remained an "elephant in the room." Several scholars have noted the influence of international sources such as Catholic social teachings and discussions at the United Nations,[32] and some have focused on the question of whether a stress on the notion of rights is part of a scheme that limits more radical social change, but this kind of focus can distract from the more fundamental question of how the mere notion of dignity may be the key common bond between the most significant philosophical and historical events of the 1770s through the mid-1780s.

The similarity of the "momentous upheaval" in America to the Rousseauian ideals that motivated Kant's ethics in the 1760s is too obvious to require further comment here.[33] The radicalism of the underlying ideas of the *Declaration of Independence* was immediately recognized by none other than Jeremy Bentham. Although some Englishmen, such as Richard Price,[34] recognized that the United States would become "a place of refuge for opprest men in every region of the world,"[35] Bentham immediately composed the unofficial British government response to the document and mockingly argued:

> '*all men*,' they tell us, 'are created equal.' This surely is a new discovery; now, for the first time, we learn that a child, at the moment of its birth, has the same *natural* power as the parent, the same quality of *political* power as the magistrate.[36]

Bentham's critique runs roughshod over the crucial distinction, noted earlier, between basic human *capacities* and individual *talents* or capabilities. This distinction has massive implications to this day for properly understanding Kant, and to overlook it is to exhibit the fundamental Fascist error[37] of presuming that

---

[32] See Rosen, *Dignity*; and Charles Beitz, "Human Dignity in the Theory of Human Rights: Nothing but a Phrase?" *Philosophy & Public Affairs* 41 (2013), 259–90.

[33] See Karl Ameriks, *Kant's Elliptical Path* (Oxford: Clarendon Press, 2012).

[34] See Ch. 5. Price was an enormously influential figure on many fronts, and his writing in support of the Americans in 1776 was "translated into German, French, and Dutch, and circulated widely on the continent." Bernard Peach, "Preface and Introduction," in *Richard Price and the Ethical Foundations of the American Revolution: Selections from his Pamphlets, with Appendices*, ed. Bernard Peach (Durham, NC: Duke University Press, 1979), 9.

[35] Richard Price, *Observations on the Importance of the American Revolution and the Means of Making it a Benefit to the World* [1784], in *Political Writings/Richard Price*, ed. D. O. Thomas (Cambridge: Cambridge University Press, 1991), 117, cited in Nash, "Sparks from the Altar," 5.

[36] Jeremy Bentham, "Short Review of the Declaration," in [John Lind and Jeremy Bentham] *An Answer to Declaration of the American Congress* (London, 1776), 119–32. Reprinted in Armitage, *Declaration of Independence*, 173–86, and quoted from Armitage 2007, 174. Cf. Jack Miles's recent claim: "Is it not empirically self-evident that *not* all men are created equal?" (*Religion As We Know It: An Origin Story* (New York: Norton), xxxiv). This is to overlook how the *Declaration's* claim holds as a *normative* truth about equal standing and therefore is not contradicted by the fact that "some are born beautiful and brilliant, others physically or mentally handicapped" (p. xxxiv).

[37] See, e.g., *Hitler's Second Book: The Unpublished Sequel to Mein Kampf*, ed. Gerhard Weinberg, trans. Krista Smith (New York: Enigma Books, 2003), based on a 1928 manuscript.

the fact of differences in human powers and talents undermines the very idea of fundamentally equal human capacities and hence duties to all humanity as such. The general notion that all human beings have an inviolable dignity, because of basic capacities (a universal potential for language and related moral capacities) that deserve constant respect, is quite independent of any idea that the actual development of these capacities will be similar around the globe or at different stages in one's life. All human beings have from the start a *capacity* for understanding English, but there has been only one person with Shakespeare's special powers, and no doubt even he lacked his distinctive talents at the edges of his life. This "all or nothing" capacity concept of human beings and their dignity is to be distinguished from older, more restrictive, and scalar notions of dignity, which are associated with living in an especially dignified manner or belonging to a group with relatively high status.[38]

All this shows that there are numerous basic misconceptions and underappreciated notions that are highly relevant to beginning to explain how it could have been that there has been such a shocking blindness, on both sides, to the close positive connection *in principle* between Kant's practical philosophy and the contemporaneous founding of the United States. It is true that, like Arendt later, many late eighteenth-century continental Europeans were fascinated by French developments, and this was especially understandable in the German lands that bordered on France and could anticipate being directly affected. But the unparalleled events of the American scene came considerably earlier, with numerous revolutionary state constitutions and political and religious innovations that, in addition to the Declaration, were well-known throughout the continent, thanks especially to the activities of renowned travelers such as Franklin, Paine, Adams, and Jefferson.[39]

The American struggle for liberty involved clearly stated radical principles that were widely understood as concerning basic human dignity, and they must have been familiar to anyone in Königsberg who, like Kant, was fascinated by politics, regularly read French commentaries, and talked with local Englishmen and visiting travelers. At a time when Kant was still actively publishing on political issues, one of his closest students, Friedrich Gentz, for example, was very well known for writing on Burke and the connection of American and French events.[40]

---

[38] For a thoughtful discussion of how, in different situations, to *treat* people with dignity, see Peter Bieri, *Human Dignity: A Way of Living* (Cambridge: Polity, 2017).

[39] Between 1787 and 1788 the *Berlinische Monatsschrift* devoted three issues to the recently enacted Virginia Statute for Religious Freedom. Thanks to James Schmidt on this point.

[40] Gentz was highly recommended by Kant to Mendelssohn and others. He eventually had a long diplomatic career at the highest levels of European politics. See *Kant-Gentz-Rehberg: Über Theorie und Praxis*, ed. Dieter Henrich (Frankfurt: Suhrkamp, 1967). In a letter to Kant on March 4, 1794 (Br [11: 490–2]), the editor J. E. Biester remarks that he assumes that Kant has read Gentz's contributions to his journal, the *Berlinische Monatsschrift*. Biester himself had already written on the American situation. See Johann Erich Biester, "Etwas über Benjamin Franklin," *Berlinische Monatsschrift* 2 (1783),

106   KANTIAN DIGNITY AND ITS DIFFICULTIES

Franklin and, to a lesser extent, Jefferson were influenced in the 1770s and 1780s by the anti-slavery writings of figures such as Condorcet,[41] which seem to have made no impact on Kant. One can also contrast Kant's lack of interest in figures such as Jefferson with the close relationship to Jefferson forged by contemporaneous Europeans such as the well-known revolutionary aristocrats Lafayette (who later boasted that he had become an American citizen before the concept of French citizenship even existed) and Tadeusz Kosciuszko.[42] Kosciuszko fought skillfully with the Continental Army in 1776 and returned to Polish lands in 1784, not all that far from Kant, to lead a futile fight for independence. Franklin was well known for invoking the example of a highly gifted former black slave in the Philadelphia area as a direct refutation of those (such as Hume and Kant) who claimed not to have heard of such a thing.

An accurate indication of the state of things in Europe in 1782 can be found in an observation by a future President, John Adams, who was in Amsterdam then negotiating with the Dutch for significant help for the American cause. The Adams biographer Page Smith describes the situation at that time in these terms: "the United Provinces were especially agitated by a pamphlet which had attacked the Stadtholder in bitter terms and advocated a 'democracy or regency of the people.'" Smith goes on: "To Adams the pamphlet indicated 'that there is a party here, and a very numerous one, too, who are proselytes to democratical principles.'" "Who and what," Adams asked, "has given rise to the assuming pride of the people, as it is called in Europe, in every part of which they have been so thoroughly abased?" The answer Adams gave was "The American Revolution." He added:

> The precepts, the reasoning of the example of the United States of America, disseminated by the press through *every* [emphasis added] part of the world, have convinced the understanding and have touched the heart.[43]

To the extent that scholars have focused on Kant's discussions of the politics of his time, they have, like Kant, passed over the events of 1776 and tended to make too much of the question of his attitude toward revolution as such. Kant, at one point in his career, stressed the somewhat trivial point that there is no "right" to revolution (MdS [6: 319]), which technically means that it cannot be a part of a *definition* of a genuinely sovereign power that this power licenses the *legal* right of

11–38. No less than John Quincy Adams, who served as ambassador in Berlin, translated and prefaced Friedrich Gentz, *The Origins and Principles of the American Revolution, Compared with the Origin and Principles of the French Revolution* [1800], ed. Peter Koslowski (Indianapolis: Liberty Fund, 2009).

[41] See Nash, "Sparks from the Altar," 8–13.

[42] Jefferson befriended Kosciuszko but reneged on a promise to release slaves, although he did consider an interesting project of importing German farmers to work alongside his slaves—a proposal that at least shows that, unlike so many others later, he was not an opponent of mixing races. But Jefferson never acknowledged his fathering a child with one of his own slaves.

[43] Page Smith, *John Adams: 1735–1784*, vol. 1 (Garden City, NY: Doubleday, 1962), 503.

others to supplant it by violence.[44] But this is consistent with allowing that tyrannical governments can be disobeyed, and that a sovereign can be pressured to cede authority, as Kant believed that Louis XVI did upon the convening of the Estates-General (MdS [6: 321, 342] and Refl 8055 [19: 585]). In other words, Kant can simultaneously be called a critic in principle of a right to revolution and also a genuine supporter in fact of what is commonly called the "French Revolution."[45]

In sum, it is clearly improper to believe that Kant would not have wanted to discuss the American situation because he had to focus on the French situation alone or because he was against anything like revolution as such. Moreover, it can be argued that in a technical political sense the American revolt, despite what it is commonly called, was not even literally a revolution. It did not aim at replacing the British king in his basic position in London but simply sought to limit a relatively small part of his powers by making the American colonies independent of British rule.[46] This point is consistent with agreeing with Gordon Wood's important argument that, in a broadly popular sense, the American revolt can nonetheless be called a kind of revolution, and even a "radical revolution," because it involved the upending of a significant range of basic and long-standing institutions. After 1776, there arose a whole new form of life in the United States, one in which "commoners" were no longer distinguished from "gentlemen," let alone imperial nobility. It is an anachronism to say this was not a radical change just because it lacked the extreme aspirations of the later French and Soviet revolutions.[47]

---

[44] Kant expressed more radical views on this issue at other times. See Dieter Henrich, "On the Meaning of Rational Action in the State," in *Kant & Political Philosophy: The Contemporary Legacy*, ed. Ronald Beiner and William James Booth (New Haven: Yale University Press, 1993), 97–116. This is a translation of the Introduction in Henrich, *Kant-Gentz-Rehberg*. It has been argued that it was for pragmatic reasons, with the ascension of J. C. Wöllner, that Kant chose his later, more conservative expressions regarding revolution. See Frederick C. Beiser, *Enlightenment, Revolution, and Romanticism: The Genesis of Modern German Political Thought 1790–1800* (Cambridge, MA: Harvard University Press, 1992), 35–56.

[45] It has been argued that Kant was sympathetic to Milton's defense of the English regicide of Charles I, despite his recognition of how such acts, like the French terror, strike us with horror. See Sanford Budick, *Kant and Milton* (Cambridge, MA: Harvard University Press, 2010), and Kant, MdS [6: 321, note].

[46] Similarly, the so-called American "civil war," or "war between the states," was neither but, as Walt Whitman understood, was instead a war of attempted secession in a non-colonial context. A confederation of individual states rebelled with the limited aim of separating from an agreed-upon constitution that had given the federal government sovereignty over all US territories.

[47] Even a recent international scholar sympathetic to more radical later events asserts, "The American Revolution was a crucial inspiration for the French, Dutch, German and British democrats alike" (Jonathan Israel, *The Revolution of the Mind: Radical Enlightenment and the Intellectual Origins of Modern Democracy* (Princeton: Princeton University Press, 2010), 40). See also Israel, *The Expanding Blaze: How the American Revolution Ignited the World, 1775–1848* (Princeton: Princeton University Press. 2017); Dorinda Outram, *The Enlightenment*, 4th edn (Cambridge: Cambridge University Press, 2019), 50 and 147–50; and the detailed account in Horst Dippel, *Germany and the American Revolution 1770–1800*, trans. Bernhard A. Uhlendorf (Chapel Hill: University of North Carolina Press, 1977), 22–3: "By the end of 1774, at the latest, America had become the most important topic in German political newspapers."

108 KANTIAN DIGNITY AND ITS DIFFICULTIES

Because no other proof is given for the claim, it appears to be hasty presumptions about a conversation with the British businessman Joseph Green that lie behind the common belief expressed by scholars who speak of "Kant's attested enthusiasm for the American Revolution."[48] It is said that Kant criticized Green's defense of the British government's treatment of Americans, and that Green was so struck by the civility and intelligence of Kant's remarks that they soon became the best of friends, despite different opinions on some matters. We now know that this conversation must have taken place around 1765, long before the major events of the American war for independence,[49] and that Kant was *in general* critical of shortcomings in the British system, which he regarded as at that time a kind of sham democracy. The fact of his initial discussion with Green says nothing about what his attitude was specifically toward the events occurring at the founding of the United States. By 1765, however, Kant had already been deeply influenced by Rousseau. Consequently, even though Kant did not specifically address the American struggle, he was by then regularly lecturing about fundamental freedom-oriented principles in practical philosophy,[50] and so he certainly had reasons for specifically addressing the American situation—and yet, we lack evidence of what he actually thought about the Declaration, even long after its publication.[51]

The most noteworthy feature of Kant's attitude is that even in his *private* notes, as well as his numerous publications on social issues, that attitude was never spelled out, let alone emphasized—and hence one can also hardly explain matters by saying that fears of censorship were the cause of his silence. This silence is especially odd in view of a fact about Kant's fundamental principles (see MdS, Doctrine of Justice §§ 45f.) that Hans Reiss is correct in pointing out:

> Parliamentary democracy as practiced, for instance, in Britain or Canada, would not, according to Kant's conception, be as close an approximation to his ideal of the separation of powers as provided by the constitution and political practice of the United States.[52]

---

[48] Hans Reiss, "Postscript," in *Kant: Political Writings*, 2nd edn, ed. Hans Reiss (Cambridge: Cambridge University Press, 1991), 261; cf. 3.

[49] See Manfred Kuehn, *Kant: A Biography* (Cambridge: Cambridge University Press, 2001), 154–5. Some indirect evidence for Kant's continuing objections to British politics (especially against Pitt) can be found in reports by J. F. Abegg of discussions in 1798. See reports that Kant expressed support for Irish and Scottish independence, while not saying anything about the United States. See *Immanuel Kant in Rede und Gespräch*, ed. Rudolf Malter (Hamburg: Meiner, 1990), 393, 453, and 460.

[50] Here one can agree with Beiser, *Enlightenment, Revolution, and Romanticism*, 33: "By the late 1760s Kant had laid the foundation of his mature political theory: the doctrine of the social contract."

[51] In contrast, the influential German writer Christoph Martin Wieland, for example, had already in 1775 written in support of the Americans, with an attitude similar to what Georg Forster arrived at "by early 1777" (Beiser, *Enlightenment, Revolution, and Romanticism*, 163 and 349). See also Pauline Kleingeld, "Kant and Wieland on Moral Cosmopolitanism and Patriotism," in *Kant and Cosmopolitanism: The Philosophical Ideal of World Citizenship* (Cambridge: Cambridge University Press, 2012), 13–39.

[52] Reiss, "Postscript," 261, n. 2. Cf. Guenter Zoeller, "Law and Liberty: Immanuel Kant and James Madison on the Modern Polity," in *Revista de Estudios Kantianos* 3 (2018), 1–13.

This point is a reminder that in general Kant was fairly negative about the political practices of Britain because he took its parliament not to be representative of the people at large but instead a mere tool that the nobility used to continue extending its privileges for nefarious imperialist goals. There is one Reflection in which Kant makes this point in a highly compressed way, one that at first sight might seem to express some concern with Americans as such:

> In the history of England at the present time, its subjection of America leads cosmopolitan reflection on England back to the past. The English want the Americans to be subjects of subjects and the English want to pass the burden off to others. Good government is not crucial but good form of government. (Refl 1452 [15: 626])

The last sentence is a giveaway that Kant's main concern was not about a particular "revolutionary" movement but was just his long-standing thought that there was a fundamental problem in the very *form* of English government, insofar as it did not allow even its own subjects to be fairly represented. The prior sentence is presumably making the point that the military costs of preserving an empire (in particular, the French and Indian War) were so excessive that, rather than simply taxing once again the poor masses in England, the attempt was being made to pass these costs on to colonial peoples, who thereby became exploited to a second degree, as mere "subjects of subjects." (A similar point could be made, of course, about the contemporary situation.) This Reflection reveals nothing about what exact time frame and particular events Kant had in mind, and it instead reconfirms the impression that his basic concern was not with Americans in particular but with the general character of leading European states.

A similar impression is supported by a nearby Reflection: "The revolutions of Switzerland, Holland, England are the most important in recent times. Russia's transformation contributes nothing to the well-being of the world except in a distant way" (Refl 1438 [15: 628]). A likely explanation for the omission of a reference to the United States is that the passage may come from before the time of the Declaration of Independence. But even if this is true, it is all the more remarkable then that no similar passage mentioning the United States is to be found in Kant's papers even after the time of the Declaration. The development of modern English government, as well as the formation of the Swiss Confederation and the Dutch revolt against the Habsburgs were important events, but in none of these cases was there, as with the United States, the origination of a massive modern republic, fully independent of nobility and church control, and explicitly oriented toward universal human dignity rather than a restoration of traditional rights. It is, to be sure, an important fact that the United States soon manifested extraordinary shortcomings of its own, especially regarding slavery and racism, but this tragic fact does not undermine the special significance, in its time, of the American revolt and its original ideals.

110 KANTIAN DIGNITY AND ITS DIFFICULTIES

There is one late remark in Kant's published work that expresses a direct awareness of at least one basic fact about the new American government. The remark
gives no evaluation of the principles of that government but (with a point that,
whether he realized it or not, certainly was highly relevant to the future of the
United States), simply says:

> By a *congress* is here understood only a voluntary coalition of different states
> which can be dissolved at any time, not a *federation* (like that of the American
> states) which is based on a constitution and therefore cannot be dissolved. (MdS
> [6: 351])

The very next section then goes on to make a point that is evaluative and is obviously critical of the United States, albeit in a way that shows awareness that colonial problems are not limited to America. Here Kant raised the question, what
should be said about lands where there is settling [*accolatus*] in "possession in the
neighborhood of a people that had already settled in the region, even without its
consent?" His answer was:

> if these people are shepherds or hunters (like the Hottentots, the Tungusi, or
> most of the American Indian nations) who depend for their sustenance on great
> open regions, this settlement may not take place by force but only by contract,
> and indeed by a contract that does not take advantage of the ignorance of those
> inhabitants. (MdS [6: 353])

Kant then immediately went on to attack "the pretext" by which some try
"to excuse the bloody introduction of Christianity into Germany" (MdS [6: 353]).
If he had only explicitly made the same point about the original crusade *from*
Germany into the area of his own hometown, then it could be said that Kant did,
after all, appreciate a link between his own locality, the *Drang nach Osten*, and the
distant colonial activities he condemned.

Kant's silence about the founding principles of the United States is additionally
surprising given the fact that in 1785 Frederick II was engaged in significant
diplomacy with Thomas Jefferson and George Washington even though German
armies had recently helped crush the Amsterdam revolt by parties who were
explicitly inspired by America and agitating for "freedom."[53] The fact that the
Prussians cynically presumed that the American republic was immature, and
eventually might well need to have recourse to European royalty (such as
Friedrich II's brother), reveals what may be the most significant general fact
here—one that bears not only on Kant and Prussians but on elitist thinking in

---

[53] See Ch. 2, and Otfried Höffe, *Kant's Cosmopolitan Theory of Law and Peace*, trans. Alexandra
Newton (Cambridge: Cambridge University Press, 2006), 11.

general, and might simply be called the self-centered blindness of the *Establishment Attitude*.

4.3 Toward a Diagnosis

Rather than racism or German chauvinism, it is basically the narrow-mindedness of the *general* Establishment Attitude that I suspect is most relevant for understanding Kant's—and not only Kant's—peculiar blindness about liberating phenomena such as the actuality and potential of the new American republic.[54] Historically, older nations often underestimate the remarkable speed by which a new (in structure, if not in existence) and distant "upstart" culture may be developing. In technological and military matters, this hubris was a serious mistake, for example, for Russia (in 1905) and the United States (in 1941) with regard to Japan, as well as, obviously, for Wilhelm II and Hitler with regard to the United States. Similarly, philosophers may recall how, well into the twentieth century, there were still condescending attitudes in Germany in general toward non-European thought, just as in England toward America and, within America, among intellectuals in the north-east toward people further west. In the eighteenth century, the key fact that homebound European leaders tended to forget about the American colonies is that the inhabitants there had the singular advantage, from the very beginning, of drawing on the most adventurous part of the population from the most "advanced" of European cultures, and these settlers brought along many of the best institutions of those cultures, leaving behind much of what was worst. In addition, they were greeted by circumstances that offered opportunities that were suddenly open in an unparalleled way,[55] and with relatively unlimited prospects of growth for all ambitious types (or, more precisely—as was the case throughout the industrialized world—for male Caucasians).

Insofar as they amount to a *moral* failing, Kant's racist beliefs, as repeatedly displayed in insulting remarks about Poles, Russians, Chinese, blacks and other natives of non-European cultures, can thus often be understood more as an *effect*

---

[54] Cf. Thomas Bernhard, *Immanuel Kant: Komödie* (Frankfurt: Suhrkamp, 1978). In Bernhard's comedy, Kant is placed on an ocean voyage to New York and Columbia University, accompanied by a bizarre entourage of family, naïve admirers, and a parrot (his "best student"). This Kant has a very low opinion of America, but he harbors hopes that the specialists there can correct a serious eye problem (in fact, the doctors will take him to an insane asylum)—no doubt one that Bernhard might have diagnosed as involving lenses that were not only transcendentally ideal but also overly rose-colored about the relative prospects of the European establishment. Poking fun at provincialism, Bernhard has his traveling lead character reverse the common thought, "wherever Königsberg is, there is Kant," into the self-satisfied claim, "wherever Kant is, there is Königsberg." Thomas Mann made a somewhat similar comment about himself upon his arrival in the United States.

[55] See Henry Steele Commager, *The Empire of Reason: How Europe Imagined and America Realized the Enlightenment* (Garden City, NY: Anchor/Doubleday, 1977).

112 KANTIAN DIGNITY AND ITS DIFFICULTIES

than a *cause* of his Establishment Attitude.[56] The fact that Kant looked down on, or did not bother to appreciate *even* Americans with a WASP (white Anglo-Saxon Protestant) background is a clue that it need not be specifically racism that *ultimately* lies behind even such absurd remarks (in notes taken from 1775–6 lectures) as, for example, that "All Oriental nations are completely incapable of judgment in accordance with concepts" (V-AnFried [25: 655]). A partial (but only partial) excuse for this strange comment could be that Kant may have had a fairly strong notion of "concepts" in view here, just as he suggested elsewhere that a "dawdler, drunk, [or] gambler" should be characterized as "bad" rather than "evil" because for persons in such a situation the thought of the moral law supposedly does not even arise (V-AnMrong [25: 1386]). In other words, despite his general philosophical view that reason and all the pure categories implicitly structure all human minds from the beginning, Kant could grant that in actual life much of the potential of this structure was left unrealized and that, in certain contexts and cultures, strict principles in general could go entirely unappreciated *as* principles that are strict in his categorical sense. Similarly, although geometrical truths have always structured human experience, it was only late in human history that the exact (and still almost adequate in ordinary life) geometrical system of Euclid was developed, and for a long time it was used only by a small part of the human race.

Especially relevant here is another remark from the 1775–6 lecture notes:

> who has seen a savage Indian or Greenlander, should he believe that there is a germ [or "seed," *Keim*] innate to this same [being], to become just such a man in accordance with Parisian fashion, as another [would become]? He has, however, the same germs as a civilized human being, only they are not developed...(V-AnFried [25: 694])

This passage is just one more confirmation of the fact that Kant was ultimately open to the thought that all human beings are fundamentally equal in original capacity, in the "germs" needed to develop a proper theoretical and moral life, even though in fact all sorts of circumstances can severely inhibit this development.

Kant's frequent harsh claims about the apparent lack of development in others thus should not be understood, as they all too often are, as directly tantamount to a (nasty) *moral* judgment. On his post-Rousseauian philosophy, intellectual and cultural sophistication (or "perfection") do not at all run parallel to moral value, and Kant even stressed that "the greatest scoundrels are often people with the greatest talents" (V-AnFried [25: 651]). For similar reasons, he noted that the

---

[56] Anti-Semitism is a special case. See Ch. 3, and, e.g., the remark about Jews as "vampires," attributed by Abegg to Kant in a discussion of 1798 (Malter, *Kant in Gespräch*, 456–7).

sophisticated powers used by colonial enslavers were something that made them especially evil, rather than the slaves that they exploited (ZeF [8: 358–9]). It cannot be denied, however, that remarks like Kant's about "Oriental nations" indirectly reflect a grievous moral failing on his part because they are evidence of a typical Establishment Attitude's condemnable failure in humane open-mindedness. Kant should have known much better. Despite his stunningly wide range of reading, he should have known—after the era of Leibniz, Wolff, Forster, and others, who appreciated the wisdom, and not just the exotica, of faraway places—that there is much to be learned, aesthetically, politically, and morally, from cultures outside the establishment circle of European Protestants. His failure to pick up on this fact, along with his tendency to accept too much from questionable sources, can be said to have contributed to severely retarding a truly open cosmopolitanism among many of his significant successors. Given his influential powers, if Kant had in fact, from the 1770s on, clearly extolled the revolutionary principles of the American founders (while also working against Prussian militarism and northern European racism) and generated a closer connection, like the Dutch had, with the United States, this might well have significantly redirected the concerns of later German thinkers and politicians, and the later misuse of Kant's notion of dignity by the likes of Chamberlain might have been prevented.

Kant's remarks exhibit an attitude common to most—even if not all—northern European intellectuals at the time, but they are, in the end, especially disturbing in our context because of two features that apply specifically to him: their obvious tension with his own introduction of a fundamental principle of universal dignity, and the fact that at the same time he went so far as to even propose a "scientific" theory about a descriptive (even if not necessarily morally normative) hierarchy of races, a theory that was cited later by hugely influential nationalist writers and thus was indirectly instrumental in leading to the most horrendous of racial crimes. In addition, even though Kant's cultural criticisms of groups of "outsiders" does not, given his Rousseauian perspective, directly challenge their dignity, the insulting manner of the *expression* of his judgments can certainly encourage foreseeable harms to these groups, especially in situations where they are vulnerable to stronger, unsympathetic powers. In this context, however, simply knowing about the *in general* questionable character of Kant's Establishment Attitude can be helpful in considering how to react to the surprising fact of Kant's lack of a positive relation to the founding of the United States.[57] Recognizing the unfortunate narrow-mindedness of Kant's attitude on so many related issues can

---

[57] After I first drafted this essay, I came across the valuable work of Inés Valdez, who also argues that Kant's provincialism has roots beyond racism. She points out that Kant was so focused on the balance of powers within Europe that this led him to improperly discount developments elsewhere. See Inés Valdez, "It's Not about Race: Good Wars, Bad Wars, and the Origins of Kant's Anti-Colonialism," *American Political Science Review* 111 (2017): 819–34, and *Transitional Cosmopolitanism: Kant, DuBois, and Justice as a Political Craft* (New York: Cambridge University Press, 2019).

114 KANTIAN DIGNITY AND ITS DIFFICULTIES

at least go some way toward making it not totally mysterious that he would fail to take up the seemingly golden opportunity to explicitly connect his progressive principles with the revolutionary phenomenon of the American struggle. At the same time, facing up to even the worst things about Kant's attitude here still need not lead to jettisoning the core of his systematic philosophy but, on the contrary, can leave us with reasons to try to complete the work that Kant did not himself take on, namely, using his own progressive insights to help understand and work against the unfortunate effects of the Establishment Attitude found in his work and elsewhere.

An especially helpful treatment of the dynamics underlying Kant's general blindness can be found in recent work by Lucy Allais.[58] Allais carefully documents the extent of Kant's racist sins and judiciously evaluates current discussions of them. She then proceeds systematically by building on Charles Mills's insightful notion of "cognitive deficiency" and connecting this with Kant's own doctrine of radical evil. The aim here is not to excuse Kant's blindness but to understand it as an example of a much broader phenomenon, one that he was in part, but only in part, on the way toward appreciating himself. The general Kantian point that Allais begins with is that all human beings face the daunting task of overcoming their laziness and self-centeredness by developing an "ordered will" that does not deceive itself about the demands of morality. Kant showed sensitivity to this issue in one small way by writing, for example, about how one ought to choose a route in going around town such that one sees the plight of one's poorer neighbors and is thereby vividly reminded of one's broader duties (MdS [6: 457]).

Immediately after reading Rousseau, Kant came to emphasize that the luxury of modern society was mostly an obstacle for our moral life, and especially for those who are becoming more and more "well off." He argued, in terms that would resonate with the broader themes of the Critical philosophy, that the life of luxury leads naturally to an overvaluing of appearance, blindness to the unseen needs of others, and self-deception about the extent of one's own blindness. Calling upon Kant's late work on religion, Allais develops these ideas further this way. Given the increasing demands of morality, and of the extent to which we fall further short of meeting these demands

> an obviously tempting way of avoiding despair and holding onto a view of ourselves as basically good and ordered is to fail to pay attention to the ways in

---

[58] See Lucy Allais, "Kant's Racism," *Philosophical Papers*, 45 (2016), 1–36, and "Evil and Practical Reason," in *Kant on Persons and Agency*, ed. Eric Watkins (Cambridge: Cambridge University Press, 2018), 95–101. Some independent but somewhat similar considerations can be found at the end of Laura Papish, *Kant on Evil, Self-Deception, and Moral Reform* (Oxford: Oxford University Press, 2018), 235, which draws on work by Cynthia Stark on how the mechanics of failing to appreciate even one's own moral situation may be understood largely in terms of socio-cultural pressures rather than evil self-deception. See Cynthia Stark, "The Rationality of Valuing Oneself: A Critique of Kant on Self-Respect," *Journal of the History of Philosophy* 35 (1997), 65–82. See also Allen W. Wood, *Kant's Ethical Thought* (Cambridge: Cambridge University Press, 1999).

which we are implicated in the sufferings of others...we will have a psychological need to form attitudes, patterns of interpretation and moral salience that dehumanize those who our ways of life fail to respect.[59]

This is, admittedly, a somewhat indirect form of malevolence. The immediate concern here is not with direct and extreme evils such as sadism, violence, and expropriation, but with subtler and yet still quite destructive forms of dehumanizing attitudes that can arise even with outstanding intellectuals such as Kant—and philosophers like ourselves in more recent times—who can be blind, as he was, to blatant instances of dehumanization right in one's own backyard. Mills convincingly develops this thought by noting the way in which, for decades, the extensive evils of racist colonialism continued to multiply while not even becoming a matter of discussion in mainline ethics and analytic philosophy. In 1997 Mills wrote:

[In] a standard undergraduate philosophical course...though it covers more than two thousand years of Western political thought and runs the ostensible gamut of political systems, there will be no mention of the basic political system that has shaped the world for the past several hundred years. And this omission is not accidental. Rather, it reflects the fact that standard textbooks and courses have for the most part been written and designed for whites, who take their racial privilege so much for granted that they do not even see it as political, as a form of domination.[60]

The relevant general idea here, in Allais's words, is that "the ideology of white supremacy will typically involve white cognitive deficiencies,"[61] and that the dehumanizations arising from these deficiencies are to be understood not as matters of mere personal prejudice but as rooted in pressures generated by deeply embedded unjust structural relations, relations that distort the perception and attitude of even those who are "on top." This might seem to be an overly complicated thought to apply to Kant, but extra resources are clearly needed in trying to explain his cavalier attitude (and the long blindness of others toward that attitude—except for the Fascists who chose to appropriate and radicalize it) toward the colonial bounty of Prussian privilege that he was benefitting from, and

---

[59] Allais, "Kant's Racism," 30. In "Restorative Justice, Retributive Justice, and the South African Truth and Reconciliation Commission," *Philosophy and Public Affairs* 39 (2011), 331–63, Allais discusses how to deal with the consequences of dehumanization in the context of her homeland of South Africa. Cf. Barbara Herman, "Religion and the Highest Good: Speaking to the Heart of Even the Best of Us," in *Kant on Freedom and Spontaneity*, ed. Kate Moran (Cambridge: Cambridge University Press, 2018), 214–30.

[60] Charles W. Mills, *The Racial Contract* (Ithaca, NY: Cornell University Press, 1997), 1, cited in Allais, "Kant's Racism," 34, n. 64. See the updated discussion in Mills, *Black Rights/White Wrongs: The Critique of Racial Liberalism* (Oxford: Oxford University Press, 2017).

[61] Allais, "Kant's Racism," 30.

116 KANTIAN DIGNITY AND ITS DIFFICULTIES

that left even him blind to thinking intelligently, let alone fairly, about the immediate potential of American, Chinese, Jewish, or black people. Fortunately, as Allais goes on to argue, in the end one also has to keep in mind the radical potential of Kant's full practical philosophy. That philosophy was ahead of its time in, for the most part, not only recognizing but even emphasizing that we have a pervasive and ever more strongly reinforced tendency to deny the full respect that, in principle, is deserved by the dignity of each and every human being—a dignity possessed independently of differences in social status, rational and physical talent, and even moral achievement, positive or negative (MdS [6: 463]).[62]

Kantian Dignity and its Difficulties. Karl Ameriks, Oxford University Press. © Karl Ameriks 2024.
DOI: 10.1093/9780198917656.003.0005

[62] I am especially indebted to Camilla Serck-Hanssen, for her invitation to be a keynote speaker at the 13th International Kant Congress in Oslo. Thanks to her and Beatrix Himmelmann also for much help at the Congress itself, and to especially helpful discussions there with Gerold Prauss, Raidar Maliks, and Michael Friedman. In addition to those already noted, my work on this topic is very indebted to Noell Birondo, Patrick Frierson, Gary Gutting, Anja Jauernig, Markus Kohl, Steven Naragon, Susan Purviance, Susan Shell, Allen Speight, Clinton Tolley, Eric Watkins, and to audiences at Boston College, Simon Fraser University, University of California at San Diego, Wittenberg University, the University of North Carolina, and Oslo. The original stimulus for this work came from a gift, in the 1960s, of a book on John Adams by my brother, a reference long ago to the work of Charles W. Mills by Jane Kneller, and a recent query by my wife, Geraldine.

5

Dignity Beyond Price: Kant and His Revolutionary British Contemporary

> All these considerations, however, were below the transcendental dignity of the Revolution Society.[1]

This chapter provides a comparison of the philosophies of Richard Price and Immanuel Kant. They were almost exact contemporaries and equally important in their respective cultures but apparently did not know of each other. Price's outstanding achievements have been underappreciated ever since he was unfairly criticized by Edmund Burke. In their general moral theory, common respect for dignity, positive orientation to rationalism, and enlightened involvement in public issues, Price and Kant have a lot in common that is still relevant to contemporary philosophy. But whereas Price hailed the Glorious Revolution, the Declaration of Independence, and French Revolution, Kant only mentioned the French. Like Thomas Jefferson, they both asserted the self-evidence of human equality, and yet they did not explain how a doctrine could be presented both as revolutionary and self-evident. The chapter concludes with a discussion of self-evidence in the context of writings by Danielle Allen and other contemporary scholars.

5.1 A Common Background

The sharp sarcasm of Edmund Burke's highly influential rebuke of Richard Price's philosophical endorsement of the French Revolution has yet to receive an adequate reply.[2] Burke was responding to Price's widely circulated speech, on November 4, 1789, to the liberal British Revolution Society, which was celebrating the centennial of the agreements safeguarding the advantages gained by

---

[1] Edmund Burke, *Reflections on the Revolution in France* [1790], ed. T. H. D. Maloney (Indianapolis: Hackett, 1955), 10.
[2] Mary Wollstonecraft, *A vindication of the rights of men: In a letter to the right honourable Edmund Burke; occasioned by his reflections on the revolution in France* [1790]; *and A vindication of the rights of woman: with strictures on moral and political subjects* [1792], ed. D. L. MacDonald and Kathleen Sherff (Peterborough, ON and Orchard Park, NY: Broadview Press, 1997), provides a vigorous defense of Price, but it is a tribute to his inspiring character as a mentor rather than an exposition of his philosophy.

118   KANTIAN DIGNITY AND ITS DIFFICULTIES

Parliament in Britain's Glorious Revolution of 1688.[3] Price combined his praise of 1688 with a hearty endorsement of the momentous changes in his own time, when sovereignty had just been transferred to the National Assembly in France. Price's stirring speech, *A Discourse on the Love of our Country*, was an immediate sensation but no surprise, for his general position was well-known. He was already famous for his support of the claims of the American colonists, a cause that Burke had in part shared with him.

Price's activism followed naturally from his long-standing commitment, as a Dissenter, to liberal religious and political movements. It was also rooted in the philosophical doctrines of his 1758 treatise on moral principles, which carries on the rationalist tradition of Ralph Cudworth and Samuel Clarke.[4] In addition, as a world-class economist and probability theorist who was asked to serve as an editor of Thomas Bayes's works, Price was a distinguished member of the Royal Society. Among his closest friends were Joseph Priestley, Lord Shelburne (who served briefly as Prime Minister), and Benjamin Franklin. His writings gained the close attention of no less than John Adams (who frequented his sermons), Thomas Jefferson, George Washington, and leading French figures such as Anne-Robert-Jacques Turgot, Baron de l'Aulne, and Honoré Garbiel Riqueti, Count of Mirabeau. His reputation brought him invitations to take on important tasks in the United States as well as Britain and, although he declined official appointments, he had a considerable influence on major governmental policies. Rarely has a first-rate mind had such an eminent position in the world at large while also forcefully articulating a prescient philosophical plea in behalf of many of the most valuable progressive movements of the future.

Given Price's extensive worldly experience, it is shocking to see Burke attacking him for not appreciating the actual complexity of politics and being drawn to an out of touch philosophy contaminated by, of all things, a notion called "transcendental dignity." To our ears—although there is no evidence that this was its intent—Burke's memorable insult naturally appears to bring Price (1723–90), and

---

[3] Richard Price, *Political Writings/Richard Price*, ed. D. O. Thomas (Oxford: Oxford University Press, 1991), 176–96. Burke writes as if Price endorses the violence in later French developments, even though Price's speech is just about the initial events when Louis XVI himself accepted the authority of the National Assembly. Kant also notes this acceptance (MdS [6: 341]). Burke's account anticipates the violent chaos that quickly developed in France, but Price, *Political Writings*, 187, also warns that even egalitarians should maintain respect for figures in authoritative positions. And Burke errs, for example, in claiming France would soon become a negligible military power. See Alexis de Tocqueville, *The Ancien Régime and the Revolution* [1856], trans. and ed. Gerald Bevan (London: Penguin, 2008), 18. In *A Short History of Ethics* (New York: Macmillan, 1966), 228, Alasdair MacIntyre takes note of Burke's perception of non-revolutionary motives (to save monarchy) behind the events of 1688, but this does not invalidate Price's basic point that the Bill of Rights of 1689 changed British politics in a democratic direction. Kant mentions the 1688 Revolution at R 8043, R 8044 (Refl [19: 590–1]), and (TP [8: 303]).

[4] Richard Price, *A Review of the Principal Questions in Morals* [1758], ed. D. D. Raphael (Oxford: Oxford University Press, 1974). On the relation of this work to politics, see Susan Rae Peterson, "The Compatibility of Richard Price's Politics and Ethics," *Journal of the History of Ideas* 45 (1984), 537–47.

his revolutionary concern with the *self-evident dignity* of human beings as such, into connection with the most famous philosophical exponent of the notion of dignity then, namely, Immanuel Kant (1724–1804). There is, astonishingly, no evidence that either cosmopolitan philosopher took any note of his distinguished North Atlantic contemporary.[5]

The Critical Kant of the 1780s and 1790s was, just like Price, deeply concerned with political events as well as technical philosophy. He was well known as the founder of transcendental philosophy and a supporter of the regime change in France. Kant's theoretical philosophy is based on the metaphysical doctrine of transcendental idealism, and his mature practical philosophy is marked by a special emphasis on the inviolability of human dignity. It thus easily lends itself to talk of transcendental dignity, although Kant's writings stress these two words separately rather than explicitly conjoin them. As a rationalist like Price, what Kant holds, above all, is that the *capacity* to appreciate the strict moral demands of pure reason is what gives *every* human being a necessary and even *unconditional* value (unlike happiness), which he vividly characterizes as a *dignity beyond price*: "elevated above any price…an inner worth, that is, dignity [*über allen Preis erhaben…einen inneren Werth, d.i. Würde*]" (GMS [4: 434–5], cf. GMS [4: 426], Rel [6: 46]). This view contrasts with much of ordinary language and traditional practices going back to figures such as Cicero, according to which dignity is a matter of *degree* and is typically ascribed to particular agents in proportion to the contingent fact of their elevated social rank or inspiring manner.[6] For Kant, dignity is fundamentally an all or nothing feature, one that we human beings— and only beings like us—all have from birth, given our faculty of *Wille*. This is a technical term that he uses to signify practical reason, which is not mere rationality but necessarily includes the capacity for elevating oneself above conditioned goods by respecting the moral law and treating all others as ends in themselves.

This faculty is part of our unique transcendental—that is, necessary for experience rather than accidental—nature, and for this reason a Kantian can hold that we are all endowed with a kind of transcendental dignity. The notion of capacity is crucial here, and I take it to mean—contrary to interpretations by some astute

---

[5] Kant's first works are in the 1740s but he did not publish anything in his early days comparable to Price's 1758 treatise on morals. After reading Rousseau in 1762, Kant lectured regularly on practical philosophy but did not publish a systematic treatise on morals until the *Groundwork* (1785). Price was influenced by the British legal tradition rather than by Rousseau. "The first references to Kant appeared in the English periodical press in…1787" (Giuseppi Micheli, "The Early Reception of Kant's Thought in England 1785–1805," in *Kant and His Influence*, ed. George Macdonald Ross and Tony McWalter (Bristol: Thoemmes, 1990), 211).

[6] See Ch. 1, and Michael Rosen, *Dignity: Its History and Meaning* (Cambridge, MA: Harvard University Press, 2012); Jeremy Waldron, *One Another's Equals: The Basis of Human Equality* (Cambridge, MA: Harvard University Press, 2017).

120   KANTIAN DIGNITY AND ITS DIFFICULTIES

philosophers[7]—that Kant does not restrict moral status and dignity to persons who exercise their rationality to a high degree. Even a very disabled child can be said to retain its distinctive capacities (for example, to learn a language) because these are such that, since it is a human being, its disablement could in principle be removed without change in the child's species and underlying personal identity.[8]

Although this strictly universal notion of human dignity is a metaphysical notion, rooted in religious tradition, it also has a political meaning appreciated in secular contexts throughout the world and in large part because of Kant's writings. This notion is also behind Kant's calling attention to the striking phenomenon of the dismantling of aristocratic privileges in the French Revolution being widely welcomed not only by the oppressed but also by many of the privileged (SF [7: 85]). Kant takes this phenomenon to show that the claim of universal human dignity is becoming not only an accepted truth for rationalist philosophers but also a notion with broad popular significance and a sign that fundamental moral/political progress could be rationally hoped for after all. Just as Kant and Price would have wished, the notion has come to be enshrined in the German federal constitution and thereafter in numerous other charters throughout the world.

5.2 A Disappointing Disconnect

Even though Price, like Kant, was not a fundamentalist but a critic of enthusiastic religious movements, he offered an exceptionally optimistic reading of the political upheavals of the eighteenth century. He took the American as well as the French revolts to herald nothing less than a turning point in global history, one of millenarist significance.[9] There was in his time, as he concluded in his

---

[7] See Ch. 1.7. Many contemporary philosophers fail to see that Kant's concern is not with intelligence but with an original and universal moral capacity. See, e.g., Nicholas Wolterstorff, *Justice: Rights and Wrongs* (Princeton: Princeton University Press, 2008), 329: "[for Kant] what counts for the grounding of human rights [dignity] is one's sheer capacity for rational action... [but] some human beings...do not *have* it—infants and those suffering from dementia, for example;" and Hilary Putnam, *Jewish Philosophy as a Guide to Life: Rosenzweig, Buber, Levinas, Wittgenstein* (Indianapolis and Bloomington: Indiana University Press, 2008), 71: "Kant grounds ethics not in 'sympathy' but our common rationality. But then what becomes of our obligations to those whose rationality we can more or less plausibly deny?" However, given the basic genetic makeup of human babies (what Kant regards as the innate endowment of our *Anlagen* and *Keime*), the capacity for moral orientation is in *all* of us—just like our capacity for spatiotemporal orientation, language, and elementary mathematics, whatever differences there may be for now in capability and performance. Cf. Thomas Nagel, *Moral Feelings, Moral Reality, and Moral Progress* (New York: Oxford University Press, 2024), 52: "The cognitive and motivational capacities that are needed to understand specifically moral reasons seem to be present only in humans, and they are present in very young children, revealing an innate endowment."

[8] Cf. Ariel Zylberman, "The Relational Structure of Human Dignity," *Australasian Journal of Philosophy* 96 (2018), 749.

[9] Price's position is *millenarist* rather than *millenarian* in holding that a millennium of moral improvement has begun in his day, *followed* by *infinite* reward in heaven. See D. O. Thomas, "Introduction," in *Political Writings/Richard Price*, xi. Cf. Kant, End [8: 327–39], and Karl Ameriks,

speech—and as has been echoed recently in the title of a major book on the international impact of American independence—a "light [that] after setting America free, reflected to France, and there kindled into a blaze that lays despotism to ashes and warms and illuminates Europe!"[10] Despite these deep similarities in endorsing the revolutionary character of the age, Kant—even in what we have of his private writings and contrary to what many scholars have believed—never discussed, let alone defended or praised, either the American struggle for independence or the dignity-oriented writings of its well-known advocates.[11] Although Kant appears not to have studied works in English,[12] Price's writings, as well as those of his American acquaintances, were widely translated and discussed on the continent, and events in America at that time dominated publications throughout England, France, the Netherlands, and Germany. Price's February 1776 essay went into twenty editions. According to a recent editor, the essay

> circulated widely on the Continent almost as rapidly in the colonies where it was reprinted or published in Philadelphia, New York, Boston, and Charleston. It was widely recognized to be, and frequently referred to as 'the most famous British tract on the war with America.'[13]

Nonetheless, although Kant's famous 1784 essay on enlightenment makes direct reference to some church developments in the Netherlands, it passes over directly mentioning the political uprising in Amsterdam at that time, which was inspired by events in America.[14]

The preceding chapters have also discussed several of the long-standing ramifications of Kant's strange blindness to the political significance of the United States despite the considerable attention that other German writers, including some of his best students, paid to matters such as the burning issues of American independence and European colonialism.[15] In the present context, this unappreciated

---

"Once Again: The End of All Things," in *Kant on Persons and Agency*, ed. Eric Watkins (Cambridge: Cambridge University Press (2018), 213–30.

[10] Price, *Political Writings*, 196. Price's remark is the source of the title aptly chosen by Jonathan Israel, *The Expanding Blaze: How the American Revolution Ignited the World, 1775–1848* (Princeton: Princeton University Press, 2017).

[11] See Ch. 4.

[12] In a letter of November 1768 (Br [10: 77]), Herder recommends Burke's book on the beautiful and the sublime, and he adds for Kant's benefit that the book is now available in French.

[13] Bernard Peach, "Preface and Introduction," in *Richard Price and the Ethical Foundations of the American Revolution: Selections from his Pamphlets, with Appendices*, ed. Bernard Peach (Durham, NC: Duke University Publications, 1979), 9. On the widespread familiarity in Germany with American events at that time, see Horst Dippel, *Germany and the American Revolution*, trans. Bernhard A. Uhlendorf (Chapel Hill, NC: University of North Carolina Press, 1977).

[14] Kant (Auf [8: 38–9]) argues that the vote of a Dutch church council has no right to make a rule aiming to compel conscience by oath. Price certainly would agree.

[15] Most notably, Friedrich Gentz, who in 1794 translated Burke's book on the French Revolution. Gentz's *The Origin and Principles of the American Revolution. Compared with the Origin and Principles of the French Revolution* [1800], trans. John Quincy Adams and ed. Peter Koslowski

122 KANTIAN DIGNITY AND ITS DIFFICULTIES

historical complication is relevant as background for a consideration of some more straightforwardly philosophical aspects of a comparison of the thought of Price and Kant. Kant's status as a philosopher of the highest rank has remained fairly constant ever since the 1780s, but Price's reputation, especially after Burke's attack and then the general rise of anti-rationalism in British philosophy, has more often waned than waxed.[16] Despite the growing interest in the history of modern ethics, Price has received limited attention from leading philosophers, who have tended to do little more than briefly acknowledge that he deserves credit for expressing a kind of rationalist intuitionism that W. D. Ross and others eventually resurrected as one of the main options in contemporary ethics.[17] None of these experts focuses in full detail on Price on his own or on the international impact of his lifework. The considerable philosophical similarities and parallel practical agendas of Price and Kant certainly deserve further attention. An appreciation of the ideas of one author can help one to better understand the very similar, but differently expressed, ideas of the other. Right in the era of the most dramatic shifts from feudal to enlightened modes of political structure, they are the major defenders in their respective countries of the notion of human dignity.

In addition to the similarities between Kant and Price in the underlying rationalist *substance* of their general philosophy and the progressive themes of their conceptions of politics and history, an additional reason why they are highly relevant for our contemporary situation is that there is a significant *methodological* similarity in their view of the relation of philosophical treatises to the concrete contexts of practical life—a fact that is highly relevant as a model for our own time. This relation is a major issue throughout the Enlightenment era, and it is not surprising that a recent work on the era bears the title, *A Revolution of the Mind: Radical Enlightenment and the Intellectual Origins of Modern Democracy*.[18] Kant and Price each thematize the importance of the *relationship* between different

---

(Indianapolis: Liberty Fund, 2010), 73n., mentions Price briefly, and in an introductory remark Adams calls this book the "clearest account of the rise and progress" of the war in America (*Origin*, 3).

[16] However, Hastings Rashdall, *The Theory of Good and Evil* (Oxford: Oxford University Press, 1924), vol. 1, 80n., calls Price's *Review* "the best work published on ethics in recent times" and claims it "contains the gist of the Kantian doctrine without Kant's confusions."

[17] See Stephen Darwall, *The British Moralists and the Internal "Ought": 1640–1740* (Cambridge: Cambridge University Press, 1995), 10; David McNaughton, "British Moralists of the Eighteenth Century," in *British Philosophy and the Age of Enlightenment*, ed. Stuart Brown (London and New York: Routledge, 1996), 217–24; Jerome B. Schneewind, *The Invention of Autonomy: A History of Modern Moral Philosophy* (Cambridge: Cambridge University Press, 1998), 380–8; John Rawls, *Lectures on the History of Moral Philosophy*, ed. Barbara Herman (Cambridge, MA: Harvard University Press, 2000), 77; Terence Irwin, *The Development of Ethics: A Historical and Critical Study*, Vol. 3, *From Kant to Rawls* (Oxford: Oxford University Press, 2008), 719–53. For a systematic view compatible with Price but presented as a broadly Kantian contemporary defense of moral realism and intuitionism, see Robert Audi, *The Good in the Right: A Theory of Intuition and Intrinsic Value* (Princeton: Princeton University Press, 2004).

[18] Jonathan Israel, *A Revolution of the Mind: Radical Enlightenment and the Intellectual Origins of Modern Democracy* (Princeton: Princeton University Press, 2010).

levels of thought, the rise of the influence of abstract thought on radical change, and the need to address the nature of moral awareness at a pre-systematic level.

A direct concern with different levels of thought is evident, for example, in the transitions indicated by the titles Kant gives to the first two sections of his most widely read work, the *Groundwork of the Metaphysics of Morals*, namely, "Transition from Common to Philosophical Moral Rational Cognition" and "Transition from Popular Moral Philosophy to the Metaphysics of Morals." These titles distinguish a number of fundamental levels in moral thinking. There is, first, the level of *basic* common sense or *healthy understanding*, which Kant addresses by discussing reactions to a series of examples from ordinary experience, such as different ways of being motivated to give change to a customer. There is then a transition from this popular level to the recognition that some kind of more systematic and philosophical "rational cognition" of such cases is needed, one that connects them with a general view of moral principles. At this point, however, Kant argues that instead of going directly into a proper metaphysics of what is required for morals, there is a need to evaluate what he calls "popular moral philosophy," which is only a first level of "philosophical cognition." This philosophy, which is presented as expressed in four traditional alternatives (GMS [4: 442–3]) that Kant rejects, is treated as an unfortunate hybrid of popular thought and philosophy. As *heteronomous*, it is riddled by long-standing misconceptions— traditional versions of empiricism or broadly rationalist dogmatism—that not only corrupt it at a philosophical level but also reinforce bad attitudes at the level of ordinary life. Even though it at least has the merit of being expressed at a systematic level, this kind of philosophy needs to be replaced by an appropriate Critical metaphysics of morals, one based on the proper autonomous perspective that Kant believes underlies both true philosophy and a virtuous life.

Kant recognizes that the exposition of a philosophical system does not by itself generate virtuous citizens, but he holds that it can be a crucial factor, from the top down, in properly energizing citizens and protecting them from being seriously misled by dangerous abstract doctrines. At the same time, and from the bottom up, more informal writings and talks—such as Kant's political essays and Price's Revolution Society speech—can function as popular instruments for directly countering modern forms of superstition, relativism, skepticism, and extremism. For this reason, it can be said that the writings of Price as well as of Kant are especially relevant for political thought because of how well they exemplify a methodological feature analogous to a characteristic Wolfgang Amadeus Mozart nicely captured. He said his work contains "passages here and there that only connoisseurs can derive satisfaction from; but these passages are written in such a way that the less learned cannot fail to be pleased, though without knowing why."[19] Transposed into a philosophical key, this becomes the idea that an

---

[19] Wolfgang Amadeus Mozart, *Mozart's Letters: An Illustrated Selection*, trans. Emily Anderson (Boston: Little, Brown and Co, 1938), 182, in a letter to his father, December 28, 1782.

124 KANTIAN DIGNITY AND ITS DIFFICULTIES

exemplary philosopher is someone who not only can embed his main ideas in a system worthy of the highest level of professional recognition but also can succeed in presenting them in a way that gives them a direct and lasting effect at a popular level. Price and Kant are clearly both exemplary in this rare sense, and especially because of how the intended impact of their pamphlets and popular essays is appropriately connected to their systematic emphasis on the concept of human dignity and related notions such as liberty, equality, and self-evidence.

Kant was not as directly involved with heads of state as Price was, but in Germany many of his works were widely admired for their style. He was a popular teacher who influenced numerous students who went on to significant positions in public life. His essays on aesthetics, enlightenment, history, religion, and peace are carefully crafted works that immediately had a broad public impact. Kant's lecture hall and lunch table eventually became a pilgrimage destination for idealists and future politicians. Somewhat similarly, the Newington Green church and activist community that Price organized had a significant effect on later luminaries such as Mary Wollstonecraft and John Stuart Mill.[20] Henri Laboucheix, the leading French expert on Price's work, goes so far as to claim that, in comparison with Franklin, Adams, Paine, and Turgot, Price was the "best theoretician" of American independence from the moral and political points of view.[21] Laboucheix also argues that Price's writing deserves a place of honor in *literary* history comparable to John Milton (one of Kant's main heroes) because of its powerful rhetorical effect on a wide range of minds. He calls Price a "philosophical artist" who understood how to make the most effective use of philosophy's midway position between art and science.[22]

On the basis of this sketch of the common background of Kant and Price's era and their similar methodological orientation, Section 5.3 will offer a more detailed comparison of the substance of their moral philosophies. Sections 5.4 and 5.5 will focus on the notion of self-evidence and how a distinction between different levels of moral cognition relates to some contemporary discussions of moral knowledge that bear on evaluating the political philosophies of Price and Kant.

5.3 Overlapping Philosophical Positions

In even a brief comparison of Price and Kant, it is helpful to focus on four main components essential for understanding any practical philosophy, namely, its

---

[20] See Eileen Hunt Botting, *Wollstonecraft, Mill, and Women's Human Rights* (New Haven and London: Yale University Press, 2016).

[21] Henri Laboucheix, *Richard Price as Moral Philosopher and Political Theorist* [1970], trans. Silvia Raphael and David Raphael (Oxford: Oxford University Press, 1982), 111.

[22] Laboucheix, *Price*, 5, 11.

account of the *content, motivation,* conditions of *possibility* (which involve not only metaphysics but also religion, history, and politics), and mode of *knowledge* crucial to a proper life. The topic of moral knowledge is an especially important one, and its discussion will be deferred to later sections except for a few preliminary remarks here. Price and Kant are often contrasted by caricaturing Price as a dogmatic intuitionist and Kant as married to an abstract categorical imperative procedure—a procedure that continues to be bedeviled by disputes concerning alleged formal contradictions in universalizations of maxims. Rather than revisiting those issues, it is worthwhile to explore a different kind of perspective by noting that these dismissive approaches tend to overlook an important feature that Price and Kant share, namely, a "contextual" approach to morality,[23] that is, an appreciation for pre-philosophical healthy understanding, empirical factors relevant to the application of principles, and the contingent conditions favorable to developing what Barbara Herman calls "the practice of moral judgment" and "moral literacy."[24]

This is not at all to deny that Price focuses also on a priori aspects of the *content* of morality. His rationalism makes him a Kantian *avant la lettre*[25] in a way that builds on elements of the British tradition. He starts from Clarke's idea that the mind's self-motion makes it unlike matter, as well as Cudworth's earlier claim that self-determination is of primary importance and has a libertarian meaning that is essential for distinctively moral blame and praise. Above all, Price accepts John Locke's moral realism and the view that there are moral truths that are necessary and evident, even though, like Kant, he sharply rejects details of Locke's account and his theory of empirical knowledge.[26] Price also agrees with Bishop Butler's distinction between the power and the authority of feeling, and he accepts a basic distinction between conditional instrumental value and what is necessarily good in itself.[27] Necessary value is central to Price's concept of our inalienable human dignity, which he ties to the consciousness of equality that each person has through awareness of a capacity to choose what is right and condemn what is evidently unjust, such as the mistreatment of the innocent.[28] As a late child,

[23] This term comes from the title of Susan Purviance, "Richard Price's Contextual Rationalism," *Studies in the History of Ethics* 6 (2005), 1–21.

[24] See Barbara Herman, *The Practice of Moral Judgment* (Cambridge, MA: Harvard University Press, 1993), and *Moral Literacy* (Cambridge, MA: Harvard University Press, 2022); and Karl Ameriks, "*The Moral Habitat,* by Barbara Herman" (review), *Notre Dame Philosophical Reviews,* 2022.08.05, as well as work by Onora O'Neill and the flood of recent scholarship on Kant's anthropology. Price's career-long work as an influential educational reformer is also relevant in this context, as is Kant's extensive concern with pedagogy.

[25] Laboucheix (*Price,* 80) speaks of "the moral law, as it emerges from Price's work…before Kant."

[26] Terence Irwin, *Development of Ethics,* Vol. 3, 166–72, offers a valuable account of Kant as, like Price, not a constructivist about moral value. Sarah McGrath, *Moral Knowledge* (Oxford: Oxford University Press, 2019) unfortunately does not question the constructivist reading of Kant.

[27] See Price, *Review,* 43, and Laboucheix, *Price,* 47.

[28] See Price, *Political Writings,* 30, 66, 86. On regarding notions such as equality as "immediately accessible to all," see also Laboucheix, *Price,* 20, 49, 143.

126 KANTIAN DIGNITY AND ITS DIFFICULTIES

smarting from the experience of a strict father who favored a first son from an earlier marriage, Price likes to stress that the "superiority of a parent," and of what in general happens to be older or more powerful, is not the same thing as "true dignity."[29] Against the argument that the colonists owe continued allegiance to their "mother country," Price points out that children grow up and eventually deserve independence.[30]

There are obvious parallels here with Kant's insistence on our "innate equality" and his famous call for emergence from "self-incurred" immaturity (MdS [6: 237]; Auf [8: 35]). Also like Kant is Price's stress not on individual acts but the tendencies of one's character, its "temper" and "habits."[31] Although both philosophers closely link the values of individual and political independence (in international as well as domestic contexts), there is an odd disconnect in the fact that Price heralds the United States, with its rejection of aristocracy, as the first country with this kind of civil equality in its founding document,[32] whereas Kant ignores this crucial development. Price makes clear, however, that he is not tied to radical democracy. He regards the checks and balances system of common law constitutionalism as the best model for his own country,[33] even though he always stresses that it needs considerable reform so that Parliament can become truly representative. Kant agrees with this general orientation[34] but regards the actual working of the British system as too corrupt to serve as a model. At that time in Germany there was, in any case, no likely approximation to it and nothing like the tradition of 1688 and before in England.

What remains most important here is that both philosophers hold that political power ultimately derives from the consent of the governed.[35] Kant certainly would agree with Price's general stress on liberty and his basic distinctions between *physical, civil* (a voice in government), *religious* (freedom of conscience and worship), and *moral* liberty (free will as a precondition for virtue), with this last form being the most important but requiring for its full realization the protection of all the other kinds.[36] There is also an obvious overlap in their general conception of our duties. Price's list of basic headings consists of duties to self (prudence), God (and others with authority), beneficence, gratitude, veracity (honesty), and justice.[37] This is close to matching Kant's four basic headings:

---

[29] Price, *Political Writings*, 171, 182, 186.　　[30] Price, *Political Writings*, 39.

[31] Price, *Political Writings*, 82; Price, *Richard Price and the Ethical Foundations*, 278.

[32] See Price, *Political Writings*, 125, 146.

[33] See Price, *Political Writings*, 165, and Carl B. Cone, *Torchbearer of Freedom: The Influence of Richard Price on Eighteenth Century Thought* (Lexington, KY: University of Kentucky Press, 1952), 184. Price stresses freedom of conscience, jury trial, free press, elections, and a constitution where law is above royalty.

[34] See Guenter Zoeller, "Law and Liberty: Immanuel Kant and James Madison on the Modern Polity," in *Revista de Estudios Kantianos* 3 (2018), 1–13, for an excellent comparison of many similarities between Kant's views and James Madison's constitutional ideas.

[35] See Price, *Political Writings*, 16, 29, 88, and Kant (Auf [8: 39–40]).

[36] Cf. Price, *Political Writings*, 21–3.　　[37] Price, *Review*, 217 ff.

imperfect duties of self-development and practical love for others in the form of beneficence, and perfect duties involving self-respect and respect for others by treating them honestly and justly. Kant does not initially discuss gratitude but he eventually gives it a place as a distinctive kind of duty (MdS [6: 454–6]). He also discusses duty to God but prefers to speak of respect for the moral law in oneself and, like Price,[38] he takes this law to be central to the divine intellect, not a matter of arbitrary will (MdS [6: 443–4]).

Objections are often made to the rambling nature of Price's list and the non-systematicity of intuitionism, and yet, after all the problems that grand theories have had, it can be considered a realistic advantage now that Price does not claim to have a complete list of important duties. Similarly, and despite his overly systematic reputation, any close look at Kant's *Metaphysics of Morals* will reveal that he seems open to an indefinite extension of significant duties and hardly takes their disclosure to be a matter of linear deduction. Moreover, in addition to being willing to agree on the claim of self-evident human equality, Price and Kant can give a unifying substance to that claim, and also to their lists of duties, by connecting them all with the notion of dignity, as spelled out by the doctrines of moral liberty in Price and persons as ends in themselves in Kant.

When it comes to an account of moral *motivation*, Price's general view does not match caricatures of it as holding to a purely theoretical view of reason, where that signifies the odd belief that moral value for us can be understood independently of what is reasonable for persons to choose in a situation of a plurality of finite and dependent beings. This is not to say, however, that for him a deliberative *process* is essential to our most basic experiences of moral motivation. Price can appear to hold a simplistic form of rationalism when he states "the perception of right and wrong does *excite* to action and is alone a sufficient *principle* of action."[39] But matters are not so simple. Price goes on to call judgment the first "spring" of action, but he adds, it is "often not prevailing," and he frequently stresses a need for the assistance of inclination and feeling.[40]

Kant's account of motivation is similar but more complex. Although he is often characterized as someone who believes that rationality is sufficient all by itself to motivate right action, this does not do justice to his full view. What Kant actually holds is that, *if* rational agents *add* an orientation of *will* to their perception of what the moral law demands in a particular situation, this can lead to right action—but this does *not* mean that *mere* reason is sufficient by itself to motivate. In the *Groundwork* Kant declares that reason needs not only to work together with will but to do so by being supplemented (after the intellect's judgment) by a

---

[38] Price, *Review*, 138.   [39] Price, *Review*, 313.
[40] Price, *Review*, 318. See also Daniel Eggers (2019), "Moral Motivation in Early 18th Century Moral Rationalism," *European Journal of Philosophy* 27 (2019), 552–74.

unique *feeling* of respect for the moral law (GMS [4: 401, n.])[41] Only with a properly generated feeling of respect is there an active motivation (somewhat analogous to how a proper judgement of taste grounds the *feeling* of disinterested satisfaction that is essential in aesthetic appreciation) that can finally lead to right acts. In addition, at MdS [6: 399] Kant highlights four separate feelings essential to our "receptivity" to duty (moral feeling, conscience, love of one's neighbor, and self-esteem). Hence, even though for Kant an attempt at right action *ultimately* follows if all goes well with the direction of *pure* reason, it does not follow from our intellectual faculty all by itself. Kant realizes that persons who limit themselves to mere prudence, and may have some feeling of respect for the moral law but ignore it, are not without rationality. Something more radical holds for those who are much worse than even imprudent. Kant takes evil to be a corruption that goes beyond avarice, stupidity, or mere harm. It is always something for which *rational* agents themselves bear untransferable responsibility and is a matter of will rather than unclear intellect or dim feeling. The faculty of *reason*, which is more than mere understanding, is present even in "the most hardened scoundrel" (GMS [4: 454]). It provides a mode of access for wicked human beings to perceive the moral law within themselves—and this justifies their condemnation—even when they nonetheless choose self-conceit and, at least sometimes, need not actually be moved toward morality. (Unlike devils, though, they can be led, *after* reflection, to have *wishes* in a moral direction.)

Details like this are not found in Price's account and he falls back on some troublesome formulations. Sometimes when Price describes what happens when serious wrong occurs, he does not mention its being self-incurred by one's evil will but speaks simply of the "tyranny" of the passions and their overcoming one's understanding.[42] Even though at times Kant has been misunderstood as also holding something like this position, a moment's reflection should make it clear that this kind of deterministic language is directly counter to the fundamental libertarian orientation, and concern with strict blame, that characterizes Kant's philosophy and Price's most basic beliefs as well. This point is another indication that for these philosophers the primary condition of the *possibility* of our moral action is the transcendental, or *absolute*, freedom of the human will. It is crucial that they both understand this not as bare freedom of choice among just any alternatives but as choice in a context constantly governed, for human beings, by

---

[41] See Karl Ameriks, "Kant, Hume, and the Problem of Moral Motivation," in *Kant and the Historical Turn: Philosophy as Critical Interpretation* (Oxford: Clarendon Press, 2006), 89–107. A Kantian can say that the consciousness of the moral law is "sufficient" to move one to action, but that does mean that the consciousness in a mere intellectual sense is by itself sufficient. It can still be the case, as Kant indicates in the *Groundwork*, that when the consciousness of the moral law leads to proper motivation and action this is because it is accompanied by the feeling of respect, which depends on reason, unlike feelings that are mere contingent effects of sensibility.

[42] Price, *Political Writings*, 23.

the real options of acceptance or rejection of the demands of moral law.[43] Price's account is, to be sure, not as systematically developed as Kant's. The metaphysics of transcendental idealism is hardly part of Price's philosophy, and Price does not make use of the distinction between *Willkür* and *Wille* that Kant works out, let alone anything like Kant's complex account of different degrees of culpability in radical evil (Rel [6: 29–32]). Nonetheless, both philosophers take moral error very seriously, and yet—contrary to common criticisms—they also both affirm a basic human orientation toward happiness as such that is natural and good (GMS [4: 415]).[44] Problems arise only when one goes so far as to follow self-conceit and go against duty. Furthermore, Kant affirms a basic human orientation, and even a duty, in favor of self-development. For this reason, one could say, as David Brink has recently argued, that there is a sense in which Kant's ethics can be read as open to being understood in a "normative perfectionist" manner—"normative" because of its focus on rational agency rather than an order in mere external nature.[45] It is true that the Critical Kant, in a normative context, says only negative things about what he treats as "ontological" perfectionism (GMS [4: 443]),[46] but this is arguably because he focuses only on the inadequate forms of it in his day, construed as making moral value depend on a dogmatic teleology of nature or particular conditional forms of skill or happiness.

Given the above considerations, it is worth noting that there is, in many contemporary circles, a popular but questionable non-perfectionist way of reading Kant that attaches moral value to bare choice. Against this reading, imagine a world in which there are groups of beings consisting only of totally lethargic agents (members of a "Drones Club") who use their time for nothing more than playing childish video games. Imagine in addition that these indulgent goons go so far as to *choose* to sign on to a pact licensing their attitudes in a political manner. If confronted by such a thought experiment, *defined* in terms of agents whose *capacities* do not at all go beyond these silly practices, Kant—like Price—would, I believe, insist that something more, some kind of capacity for responding to broadly perfectionist duties is essential for being a moral agent, properly speaking.[47] Kant surely would not assign any *moral* value to beings defined by the bizarre attitudes just described if such crude intentions are all they can have, since they

---

[43] Price, *Political Writings*, 22.

[44] See Price, *Review*, 45, 70. In saying human beings necessarily have an interest in happiness, Kant does not mean they have to give it priority.

[45] David Brink, "Normative Perfectionism and the Kantian Tradition," *Philosophers' Imprint* 19 (2019), 1–28. Cf. Price, *Review*, 45, 70.

[46] Terence Irwin, *The Development of Ethics: A Historical and Critical Study. Vol. 2: From Suarez to Rousseau* (Oxford: Oxford University Press, 2008), 538, contends that "Kant...rejects...the harmony of self-love and conscience." Here one might defend Kant by considering his contrast between self-love and self-conceit and his view, like Price's, that being moral is a matter of heeding what ultimately serves one's *true self* (in which case there can be a "harmony").

[47] See Ch. 1.4, for a similar argument.

are limited by a minimal range of concerns in their power of free choice (which does mean they should be treated inhumanely). Kant regularly mocks the moral value of a life of *mere play*, and there is an understandable reason for that. He assumes that in fact *we* understand ourselves not as mere gamers, let alone brutes, for we are not totally neutral but all have from the start a "good seed" (Auf [8: 41]). This seed is part of our basic practical capacity, and it involves not only free causality but also a "compass" pointing toward morality—just as our basic epistemic capacity is not neutral but is truth-oriented.[48]

Price's largely similar positive understanding of our rational capacities is rooted not in scholastic teleology but in an orientation that begins, as Kant's does, in a fascination with the achievements of mathematical physics.[49] Price's view, however, is that modern physics is basically just a doctrine of matter in impelled motion and, therefore, it cannot by itself account for everything. He sees no way to avoid positing the existence of non-material self-propelled activity, as metaphysically required by considerations of the world in general and also as internally evident from the mind's awareness of its own nature: "Activity and self-determination are as essential to spirit as are the contrary to matter."[50] Unfortunately, although Price adds a spirited critique of determinism in a debate with the quite different kind of religious metaphysics espoused by his scientific materialist friend Joseph Priestley, Price's arguments still do not go beyond broadly Cartesian considerations of the kind that Kant is famous for criticizing. By the time of the second *Critique* Kant backs off from any suggestion that mere theoretical considerations entail the claim that we have absolute spontaneity, and he turns to the moral "fact of reason" as our "*only*" *ratio cognoscendi* for this claim (KpV [5: 4n.], [5: 32]). In this systematic way Kant goes significantly *beyond* Price—even though politically he unfortunately tends not to go as far as his British contemporary.

The philosophical debate concerning determinism remains unsettled. Contemporary compatibilists (like quasi-Kantian successors such as T. H. Green) would argue that whatever one thinks of absolute free choice, it may not make much difference to the *content* of one's ethics, political policies, or everyday practices. The most remarkable fact here is that nevertheless both Price and Kant—unlike most contemporary philosophers—continue to assume that libertarianism is *clearly* the constant—and proper—default position at the level of *popular* thinking. This assumption is another reason why it is important to try to get clear on how they understand the status of thought at a popular level and how this relates to moral knowledge relevant to politics.

Extra complications arise from the fact that both Price and Kant ultimately hold that much more than absolute freedom, pure reason, and respect are needed

---

[48] McGrath, *Moral Knowledge*, 12.
[49] See Price, *Political Writings*, 161; Laboucheix, *Price*, 79.   [50] Price, *Review*, 26.

for a full moral life. They both claim that agents can continue to proceed rationally in their moral commitment only if there is some sensible ground for hoping that their moral actions will eventually help lead to appropriate happiness. For this reason, and although he expresses it in the mode of confident assertion rather than mere rational hope, Price accepts all the conclusions of Kant's postulates of practical reason: our free acceptance of the moral law needs to be supplemented by the positing of a God who (with our free cooperation) can found a situation of thorough justice in the long run. On this view, anything less than belief in a real chance for progress toward this highest good—overall happiness in proportion to virtue and some kind of accompanying afterlife, which only a superhuman power can ground—would eventually undermine the rational motivation of any human being on the path of a life of serious moral effort.[51]

The ground for connecting this forward-looking view specifically with Christianity and history is a basically Arian belief that Jesus's life is the original long-range catalyst for radical moral change on a global scale. His teachings and treatment of all kinds of people as equals with each other are seen as the decisive model that inspires the passage from tribal customs and local political claims to an eventual observance, from pure free will, of what the moral law declares as appropriate for the respectful treatment of all human beings on account of their mere personhood.[52] Whatever one thinks of this theological interpretation of events, Price and Kant are hardly alone (Jefferson's views, for example, are quite similar) in the late eighteenth century in taking there to be a deep connection between these religious ideas and many of the epoch-making liberation movements of their revolutionary age. And yet—while for Kant the events of 1789 are the turning point of the age, for Price it is the struggle for American independence that already introduces a "new era" fundamentally unlike any other, the greatest event since the life of Jesus.[53]

In addition, both philosophers insist that the way to work toward the highest good is through forswearing absolute commitment to the ceremonies of any official church—an attitude that at that time only the United States fully protected. Instead, they advocate the development of a (presumably providentially enabled) liberal Christianity that takes the form of socially active cosmopolitanism, an

---

[51] Price, *Review*, 250: "happiness is the *end*...of God's providence...[God] pursues this end in subordination to rectitude." For a contemporary defense of the main idea of Kant's postulates, see John E. Hare, *The Moral Gap: Kantian Ethics, Human Limits, and God's Assistance* (Oxford: Oxford University Press, 1996). The Critical—but not the Pre-Critical—Kant would reject Price's *theoretical* arguments (*Review*, 86) for God's existence, e.g., from the need for something to support infinite "knowables."

[52] See Price, *Political Writings*, 90, 130, 150.

[53] Price, *Political Writings*, 119, 183; *Richard Price and the Ethical Foundations*, 173. On Kant's account of the main historical stages of our moral/religious development, which features Rousseau rather than the British or Americans, see Karl Ameriks, "Kant and the End of Theodicy," in *Kant's Elliptical Path* (Oxford: Clarendon Press, 2012), 260–77.

132   KANTIAN DIGNITY AND ITS DIFFICULTIES

"invisible church" that renounces all entanglement with nationalism and traditional power politics (Rel [6: 101]).[54] They take this to be a genuinely religious movement but one ultimately independent of any particular church organization. Instead of relying on traditional organizations, both Price and Kant see the Scientific Revolution as the crucial prerequisite for future progress,[55] although they recognize that a long incubation period is needed before the modern scientific attitude can stimulate a full moral/religious revolution with universal scope. The crucial initial step in this revolution's last phase, which occurs for Price in a kind of "Copernican turn," is the breakthrough that follows when people begin to *universally accept* that the testimony of past authorities (Aristotelian science, Scholasticism) and naïve sense experience has to be replaced by what our *reason* discerns—by which he means at first the pure theoretical accomplishments of fields such as modern physics.[56] Price emphasizes the need for a *deferred* process of continued education and improvement here, presumably also involving something like the economic–political progress outlined in Kant's *Idea of a Universal History with a Cosmopolitan Aim* (1784).

5.4 Declaring the Self-Evident

All these bold claims lead back to the epistemological issue of what kind of knowledge, in addition to science, Price and Kant take to be fundamental for a social revolution that would support a proper moral life in general. The famous events of the era provide an obvious clue here. There is perhaps no clearer statement of the relevant epistemic attitude than the opening words of the *Declaration of Independence*'s second paragraph: "We hold these truths to be self-evident, that all men are created equal..."[57] Obviously, the issue of what "self-evident" means here, and how it involves "all" of us and our innate equality, is central. Danielle Allen has recently provided a highly original analysis of the document and persuasively argued that the terms "we" and "hold" are also very significant.[58] Here the verb "hold" can be read as part of an autonomous and performative divorcing *act*, one not needing external permission, and roughly equivalent to: we *now take* these truths as authorizing us to *hereby* declare ourselves independent. The Declaration as a whole is an *official* speech act in which a new state is thereby

---

[54] Cf. Price, *Political Writings*, 162, 168.

[55] Hence, Price and Kant are not vulnerable to the worry of Sophia Rosenfeld, *Common Sense: A Political History* (Cambridge, MA: Harvard University Press, 2011), 256, about encouraging political appeals to common sense that take the form of crude populism and reject all learning.

[56] See Price, *Political Writings*, 158–61.

[57] Danielle S. Allen, *Our Declaration: A Reading of the Declaration of Independence in Defense of Equality* (New York: Liveright Publishing, 2014), 227. To mark the difference between the Declaration as an act and as a text, I italicize the term only in the latter context.

[58] See Allen, *Our Declaration*, 79–82, 146.

brought into existence—a state with historical uniqueness in its universal political import.[59] The term "we" is used not in an authoritarian figure's edict but simply by a new *group* of *elected representatives*, and it is a reminder of the fundamental phenomenon of political pluralism, creative teamwork, and solidarity. Furthermore, there is a way of understanding the term "we" so that it stands for not only the individuals assembled in Philadelphia then, or even the states they represent, but ultimately humanity in general and its self-legislative capacity. The *Declaration* speaks with a "universal voice" in a sense somewhat like that of the concept Kant uses in his *Critique of the Power of Judgment* (KU [5: 216]). What is expressed by "we" and "all" here is not simply *for* the benefit of all but concerns a perspective that in principle *all can and should take*—and, in this case, upon their own essence.

When Kant indirectly employs the notion of a universal voice in politics, this occurs not only in his characterization of the reaction to the French Revolution but already in his remarks in the Enlightenment essay (often misread as defending blind obedience) about the "public use" of reason (Auf [8: 37]). Like Price, he calls for proper respect for authorities under ordinary conditions, but he also makes clear that this is a matter of limited and conditional rather than categorical obedience. The genuine *public* use of reason, in contrast, is founded on a presumably a priori claim about how *a* "public should enlighten itself" (Auf [8: 36]) through representatives of "the society of *citizens* of the *world*" (Auf [8: 37], emphasis added). Given his situation in Germany, which is without significant representative government at that time, Kant is thinking of these representatives in the only way he can, as writers who use popular means to address, and try to speak for, the entire public, as he does in his own essay. The key point is that the "touchstone" of the principles advocated in public reason should be "whether a people could impose such a law upon itself" (Auf [8: 39]). This is not a matter of whatever might be simply imposed in fact. Rather, it concerns the reasonable "collective will of the people" in such a way that "the people" can work "eventually even upon the principles of *government*...keeping with his [a human being's] dignity" (Auf [8: 42]).

One cannot help but wonder how audacious claims like this, which were hardly universal at that time, let alone before then, could be connected with terms such as "self-evidence." The notion of evidence, and especially the strong form that is called "self-evidence," is often associated with the special capacities of scientists, experts, and dogmatic philosophers claiming certain insight. Such an intellectualist attitude is often ascribed to rationalists such as Price and Kant, but that does injustice to their general philosophy and it surely would not be fair to ascribe to the framers of the *Declaration* or their French successors. "Self-evident" happens

---

[59] See Price, *Political Writings*, 117.

to be a term that Price frequently uses and that Franklin was familiar with from his close friendship with Price. It is considered likely that it was Franklin who at the last moment suggested that Jefferson substitute the word "self-evident" for "sacred" at this point in the *Declaration*.[60] This substitution can be taken as a reminder that these Enlightenment figures were looking for terms that could most easily resonate then with all the public rather than any particular sect, party, or special authority.

For present purposes, it would be a mistake to take anything to depend philosophically on the specific *word* "self-evidence." Kant uses just the term *Evidenz*, and basically for mathematical intuitions: "mathematical propositions are evident. But we are certain of many things without their having evidence" (V-LoBlomberg [24: 150]). Price and others sometimes use the term "self-evident" not for something that requires a special extra look at, or sorting out, of evidence but as similar to how contemporary *"non-evidentialist"* epistemologies understand what they call "basic beliefs," which spontaneously arise as obvious, as in the deliverances of recent memory or simple math.[61]

Rather than having a dogmatic tone or presumption of expertise, the *Declaration's* use of the simple verb "hold" is a confession that what is being advanced is basically a claim, albeit a very strong one. That is, it is not presented as the conclusion of any argument and attempt at explicit justification, let alone a scholastic syllogism or appeal to expertise. Nonetheless, the confident use of the term "hold" here can be taken as an indication of being in a condition that is presumed to be manifestly *justified* even though its assertion itself is *not*[62] a result of an *activity* of justification. The Price scholar Bernard Peach connects the self-evidence referred to in the *Declaration* with Price's philosophy and concludes that for Price self-evidence is to be

> interpreted in terms of the occasions on which a process has culminated in the acceptance of a principle (or imperative) and become submerged through frequent acceptance and unexceptional use...there is a rationally justified acceptance but the process of eliciting, displaying, or considering the justification is unnecessary or irrelevant.[63]

This statement does not mean that what is said to be self-evident could never *also* be supported by some form of demonstration. For example, although Price takes the injustice of slavery to be self-evident, he also indicates that one *could argue* with a slaveholder. One could begin by pointing out that if the slaveholder

---

[60] Laboucheix, *Price*, 105.
[61] See Alvin Plantinga, *Warrant and Proper Function* (New York: Oxford University Press, 1993).
[62] This is a correction of a typo in the prior version of this chapter.
[63] Peach, "Preface and Introduction," 39.

insists that human beings can be treated as slaves, then it is only fair for other persons to claim, as a reductio, that he should admit that he too could be enslaved.[64]

This line of argument is not sufficient by itself, but it is a reminder that there are different levels in Price's constant opposition to slavery. Allen cites a dramatic remark by Locke[65] that compares one's subjection to a nonrepresentative and oppressive government with the situation of being shipped off to a slave auction—a passage that Price and Franklin likely would have known and seconded.[66] Price's abolitionist convictions come out clearly in his writings, although at one point they fall prey to wishful thinking in implying that Jefferson and others would move quickly toward the elimination of slavery in the United States.[67] Kant shows no sign of this kind of optimism. He does not comment on slavery in the States, but he harshly criticizes the treatment of the natives in North America and the colonial slave practices in the Caribbean. It is *possible*—although we have no evidence of this—that qualms about slavery in the United States are one reason for Kant's strange silence on the *Declaration* and related documents (and yet this did not keep other Germans from discussing American independence). He surely would have been, like Price, strongly in favor of the statutes instituting separation of church and state. There are, however, also the disturbing aspects of Kant's views that have already been discussed: his errors in regard to racism, anti-Semitism, colonialism, and northern European cultural chauvinism. In addition, even with respect to substantive issues where Kant's position seems admirable, such as his endorsement of the basic value of human equality, there remains a *general episte-mological* problem issue, one that also affects Price's similar rejection of divine right theories as a "stupid scheme" and "insult to common sense."[68] It is a problem relevant for all advocates of enlightenment who would rely on basing rejections like this on considerations appealing to notions such as self-evidence, especially in a world that still exhibits a large variety of attitudes on what is permissible.

The problem here is a deep one, and not only for Price and Kant. Their kind of appeal might seem simplistic, but issues like this are not at all easy to resolve given difficulties that afflict alternative approaches. Even stronger objections to utilitarianism, for example, can immediately be made here. It is no accident that the main government response to Price's defense of the *Declaration* lies in a very unappealing document composed by John Lind and Jeremy Bentham, which

---

[64] Cf. Price, *Political Writings*, 150.

[65] John Locke, *Second Treatise. An Essay Concerning the True Original, Extent and End of Civil Government* (London 1698, 3rd edn), section 20, paragraph 210.

[66] Allen, *Our Declaration*, 112.

[67] See Price, *Political Writings*, 56n.; Cone, *Torchbearer of Freedom*, 113.

[68] Price, *Political Writings*, 87, 129.

136   KANTIAN DIGNITY AND ITS DIFFICULTIES

haughtily mocks political uses of the notion of human equality.[69] In contrast, and in favor of rationalism, it is rarely appreciated how much Price's moral theory, like that of similar contemporary Kantian rationalists such as Robert Audi, balances appeals to pure reason and common sense with an explicit stress on defeasibility, the fallibility of conscience, and the consideration of consequences and contingent factors in difficult judgments about how to respect persons in specific cases. Price holds that although "*general duties* [regarding liberty]…are obligatory…[there is] perfect indifference with regard to the *particular action* in view;"[70] and "It is by attending to the different relations, circumstances, and qualifications of beings, and the natures and tendencies of objects…that we judge what *is* or *is not to be* done."[71]

This point is supported by the fact that an interest in consequences follows naturally from Price's assumption that human beings constantly have a rational concern with happiness, a matter on which Kant agrees. Hegel and others have claimed that Kant's argument for pursuit of the highest good involves an inconsistent or even hypocritical concern with happiness. This is to misunderstand Kant's argument and to overlook the fundamentally realistic nature of his anthropology. There are numerous ways in which Kant recognizes the significance of consequences and the value of happiness. Kant's basic duties of beneficence and self-perfection can only be understood in terms of the thought that bringing about an appropriate better natural condition in other persons is valuable in a way that goes beyond the moral worth of one's intentions in that direction. Furthermore, the moral hope for one's own happiness in the situation of the justice of the highest good is immediately undermined if one's ulterior motive is impure.

It is only rational, Kant and Price both believe, for agents committed to a life of moral activity to need to hope that the *general effects* of their efforts will not be fundamentally futile even though, on account of our finitude, there is no way for us to know that this will be the case. However much we try to help others, it is always quite possible that these efforts will actually cause more moral inequities than we could ever anticipate. Not only is it beyond our ken to *know* who in fact most deservedly needs our help, but the means for best bringing about overall help in the long run are ultimately just as uncertain for us as even medium-term forecasts of politics are unreliable.[72] Even the best-intentioned progressive movements and technological innovations can often result in harmful repercussions

---

[69] For a critique of Lind and Bentham for missing the point that the relevant notion of equality concerns fundamental human capacities, not talents or achievements, see Ch. 4.2.

[70] Price, *Review*, 122.

[71] Price, *Review*, 165. See also Peach, "Preface and Introduction," 19–20, 37–40; Purviance, "Contextual Rationalism," 13, 16; and Audi, *The Good in the Right*.

[72] This point is made in a way that applies to many kinds of moral theories in Robert Merrihew Adams, "Moral Faith," *The Journal of Philosophy* 92 (1995), 75–95.

and catastrophes of enormous proportions.[73] In hoping for an actual balance of moral efforts and proper happy results, a fully rational agent needs to think about a better *entire* future world, and then it is only natural, and not selfish, to include the hope that such a balance is connected with oneself as well. Kant holds that it is the eventual satisfaction of the human species, rather than of one generation or individual, that it is most appropriate to try to be hopeful about. Price, in contrast, goes beyond rational philosophy at this point by holding to the religiously influenced mathematical view that even the slightest possibility of a proper *infinite* gain (or loss) in an otherworldly hereafter for oneself can clearly outweigh all other considerations.[74]

Despite the fact that this is no longer such a widely shared view, most current philosophers should agree with the rarely noted contextualism that dominates most of Price's moral philosophy. He elaborates his position on judgments about particular situations with a valuable distinction between "practical virtue," which is a matter of acting on the basis of the best evidence that one has, and "absolute virtue," which corresponds to what one would do if one had, *per impossibile*, fully adequate evidence.[75] This distinction could be developed in a Kantian manner by using the notion of absolute virtue as something like a regulative idea to guide us in improving specific judgments. In addition, Price's recognition of our fundamental limitations, and our need to focus on rules of thumb, the details of particular situations, and basic common sense is similar to how Kant often proceeds, with his recognition that philosophy has significant limitations and agents constantly have to fall back on proper education, patient casuistry, and interpretive judgment. For both Price and Kant, the main aim of practical philosophy is not to insist on a new system for everybody to study; its aim is to publicly combat overly abstract schools and reductive dogmatic theories, which cloud the deliverances of sound human understanding by begging open questions, claiming naturalistic reductions of normativity, proposing only one kind of value, or encouraging extremism. Kant and Price both take sound understanding to be at least as immediately clear on *basic practical* issues, such as common moral decency, as in regard to manifest *non-practical* truths, such as the existence of an external world with a common spacetime framework.[76]

A similar perspective can be found in a classic study by Morton White, which argues persuasively that the *Declaration*'s appeal to the "self-evident" is meant as a *contrast* to the invoking of any authoritarian or demonstrative *process* of intuition that would be available only to experts rather than "laborers" using common

---

[73] See Toby Ord, *The Precipice: Existential Risk and the Future of Humanity* (New York: Hatchett, 2021).

[74] See Price, *Review*, 271–5.   [75] Price, *Review*, 177; cf. Laboucheix, *Price*, 64.

[76] Price, *Review*, 43 f., 253, 285, sometimes makes this point using the term "common sense," and sometimes by saying, e.g., "Tis self-evident that virtue *ought* to be happier than vice." McGrath, *Moral Knowledge*, 3, 79, notes contemporary philosophers making similar claims.

138   KANTIAN DIGNITY AND ITS DIFFICULTIES

sense.[77] It is precisely with regard to the advantages of a broadly commonsense approach that one can find some of the most valuable connections between the work of Price and Kant and insights in contemporary moral epistemology. These insights, as developed recently in important work by Sarah McGrath, are the focus of our brief concluding section.

5.5 Contemporary Considerations

The main relevance here of McGrath's recent book, *Moral Knowledge* (2019), concerns a problem that can be called the paradox of self-evidence. The paradox comes from the fact that after 1776 we may have reached a point where it appears very difficult to live *without* reliance on something like self-evidence, and yet— given problems that become apparent upon reconsideration of influential documents such as the *Declaration*—it seems not easy to live *with* it either. Many theories try to ignore invoking self-evidence and moral intuition and proceed at a reflective level. In earlier collaborative work, McGrath raises a fundamental objection to the most influential current methodology along this line, namely, John Rawls's reflective equilibrium procedure. The objection is that reflective equilibrium is inadequate *if* taken in an *ambitious* meaning that claims it can by itself provide necessary and sufficient conditions for *moral knowledge*.[78] Even though reflective equilibrium incorporates restrictions, such as starting with "considered judgments" and "non-interested" inputs, its procedure can only yield results indicating what positively coheres with its given data, and thus it cannot exclude manifestly odd results with agents who begin from deep attachments to bizarre initial judgments.[79] Reflective equilibrium also fails here as a necessary condition. McGrath argues that "substantial moral knowledge" often comes originally and *pre-reflectively* from the immediate social context in which one is brought up.[80] Although reflective equilibrium can be helpful at the theoretical level of ideal philosophical justification, it misses the fact that moral knowledge occurs already at the level of what Kant calls "ordinary understanding" (GMS [4: 404]).[81] Like Kant and Price, McGrath accepts that persons can be in a "justified state" of knowledge even when they are not engaged in "an activity of justifying"

---

[77] See Ch. 4.1, and Morton G. White, *The Philosophy of the American Revolution* (New York: Oxford University Press, 1978), 59, 114, 129. On positive connections between Kant, Reid, and common sense, see Karl Ameriks, "A Commonsense Kant?" *Proceedings and Addresses of the American Philosophical Association* 79 (2005), 19–45. Contemporary theorists often link Price's intuitionism with G. E. Moore's commonsense realism, e.g., Christine M. Korsgaard, *The Constitution of Agency: Essays on Practical Reason and Moral Psychology* (Oxford: Oxford University Press, 2008), 306. A general pre-reflective approach that draws on Moore is defended in McGrath, *Moral Knowledge*, and also in works (some co-authored) by Thomas Kelly.

[78] See Thomas Kelly and Sarah McGrath, "Is Reflective Equilibrium Enough?" *Philosophical Perspectives* 24 (2010), 325–59.

[79] See McGrath, *Moral Knowledge*, 34 ff.

[80] McGrath, *Moral Knowledge*, 59.   [81] Cf. McGrath, *Moral Knowledge*, 82.

and even when, as with children, they have not developed the skills for such reflective activity.[82] People can know something important is true without being at the level of knowing *why* it is true.

McGrath goes on to explore special difficulties with moral knowledge. One problem is diversity, the fact that moral knowledge claims do not seem to *converge* in the relatively easy way we find in other fields of knowledge. A second problem is fallibility, the fact that agents often feel a need to make significant corrections in what they seemed to know earlier. In particular, they often make revisions dependent on nonmoral empirical knowledge or defer to others who appear to know better on moral issues. McGrath notes that moral *deference* is understandable in many instances, but there also cases where this is not clearly appropriate in the way it is for non-moral claims, where independent calibrating of expertise is common. If adults allowed "full-blooded moral experts" to simply overrule their own *basic sense* of right and wrong, this would be tantamount to sacrificing autonomy.[83] To illustrate permissible deference, McGrath discusses common contemporary examples of correcting moral claims given new empirical evidence, such as when rationally changing one's views on sexual practices by paying attention to practices of friends one already esteems. Matters remain more complicated when one considers claims made at a *basic* a priori level. Should we now be open to correction of the *Declaration's* claim, which Price and many others support fighting for, that it is true and self-evident that all are created equal? McGrath adds a footnote against the assertion that it was *ever* "all things considered reasonable for anyone to believe slavery is morally acceptable."[84] Relying on mere social-empirical processes of knowledge alone, however, would not refute such an assertion in a society that converges on enforcing slavery. As McGrath notes, convergence does not guarantee truth, and lack of convergence alone does not undermine realism.[85] In general, truth can be evidence transcendent.

One reason to focus on the claim that *we* hold truths about equality to be self-evident is that this approach is *meant* to avoid deference and divergence because it is a matter of expressing some claims supposedly so elementary that *all* agents can in principle see them as such, no matter what their starting point. McGrath remarks, however, that in mathematics only the most elementary claims clearly have this status.[86] There are many claims that are said to be *evidently* true to those who have the skills to work through the proofs for them, but this requires training and does not correspond to what is meant by *self*-evidence in the sense most relevant for Price and Kant. They can concede that philosophical skill is needed to construct and evaluate their a priori accounts of specific headings of duties, and hence controversies and some lack of self-evidence can be expected there.

---

[82] McGrath, *Moral Knowledge*, 61 ff., 97.   [83] See McGrath, *Moral Knowledge*, 100.

[84] McGrath, *Moral Knowledge*, 133, n. 36.

[85] See McGrath, "Moral Realism without Convergence," *Philosophical Topics* 38 (2010), 59–90.

[86] McGrath, *Moral Knowledge*, 85–148.

140 KANTIAN DIGNITY AND ITS DIFFICULTIES

But Price and Kant would presumably add that, under unclouded conditions, most relevant *basic* duties—such as not to enslave people—can still be self-evidently known at a *common* level even though the account that organizes them all is at a less certain higher level (this point mirrors the division of levels noted earlier in Kant's *Groundwork*).[87]

McGrath emphasizes that many truths are learned from others early in life, and even with arithmetic the original source can be elementary school. With morality we begin even earlier and rely on the actions as well as the testimony of those closest to us from the start. McGrath defends this socially generated process as providing paradigm instances of moral knowledge taken up largely without reflection. If one considers the huge variety of moral views obtained this way in the course of "our" history, however, the problem of divergence can still appear severe. Unlike the truths of arithmetic, insistence on doctrines such as equality, universal dignity, freedom from slavery, and even free will, is largely absent in revered ancient cultures. Moreover, the addition of Judeo-Christian and liberal humanist views has resulted, according to Alasdair MacIntyre and others, in an anarchy of current values and value theories that can *seem* to undermine claims to knowledge at all concerning doctrines arrived at simply from one's upbringing or alleged common sense.

This is an especially serious problem for moral rationalists like Price, Kant, and Jefferson, who advance their basic claims in the context of what are explicitly presented as *revolutions*. Their bold belief in self-evident truth here may be appealing, but is it too naïve? There is, admittedly, cause for concern when one recalls that, even in the era of Händel ("Handel" in England) and Hanover ("Hannover" in Germany), these cosmopolitan thinkers—unlike the musicians of the era—take practically no note of each other's traditions. In such a situation, can Anglophone philosophers really say what is self-evident even to contemporary Germans or vice-versa? There remain, in the end, reasons for remaining critical in reaction to knowledge claims arising simply from what McGrath calls "*our* [emphasis added] moral inheritance."[88] The most "advanced" countries of the modern world have instituted horrible racial and eugenic practices in movements with huge public support, even from prize-winning scientists. Millions have been raised in twisted surroundings that deeply convinced practically their whole society that they were *obviously* doing the right thing. This issue of a sick inheritance is much too complex to begin to settle in this context. Nonetheless, it would be hasty to jump to skepticism. I conclude instead with two positive thoughts concerning the long arc of enlightenment.

---

[87] In one student transcript, Kant is reported as having said that "our obligation to moral action" is "more certain and solid" than "*any* science" (Pöl-Rel [28: 1011]), but perhaps one should not claim too much on the basis of one note from a lecture.

[88] McGrath, *Moral Knowledge*, 60–1.

One point is that the development and dissemination of science is a long-term but encouraging process. It has already led to irreversible moves in dismantling some superstitions that pushed people into morally monstrous beliefs they may have understandably treated as self-evidently proper. The witch-craze involved numerous eyewitness claims of demonic forces. But once demons were cleared away from the realm of plausibility by modern education, witch-hunts practically disappeared. If people are regularly led to believe that so-called witches—or people of a different religion or race—have ingrained devilish traits, then harsh treatment of them can become so popular it seems self-evidently correct. Fortunately, many cultures have learned over time from the better informed and come to change their ways about grievous errors in once prevalent causal attributions. Something similar has happened at the political level with the disappearance of the attribution of divine power to secular leaders, which now does seem self-evidently absurd. The test of time gives us something of a tool, after all, for calibrating normative judgments. Bad "scientific" claims behind racism, social Darwinism, and eugenics have largely been put into our past. Moreover, philosophical historians of science such as William Whewell have shown that modern science itself does not support the non-cognitivist/positivist denial of necessary moral truths but relies on intuitive Ideas of reason and can be regarded as a possible (although independent) partner for rationalist morality.

This point leads to a second Enlightenment thought, namely, that the diversity of fundamental views in our moral history can be reconceived as a *complex ascending spiral* rather than a plurality of disconnected cultures. Despite worrisome divergence and questionable deference, one can rationally postulate, between the most elementary and the abstruse, a realm of the *eventually* self-evident to all, made explicit in the course of genuine revolutionary progress. Looking back, one can appreciate history as a dialectical *self-correcting* process where, through asymmetric causal and intentional links that involve more than science alone, later societies come to understand themselves in political ways that incorporate the best of their traditions while leaving deep errors behind. Feudalism is not coming back, and all effective political movements feel obliged now to at least pay lip service to democratic values (even though, most recently, there have been powerful forces working again against these values). Much disagreement in higher-level practical thinking remains, but this is also ultimately true of parts of science to this day.

In Price's and Kant's historical remarks, there are illustrations of this ultimately progressive perspective, albeit in still relatively simple multistage accounts of the rationalization of Western religion and politics.[89] In our own era, it is worth keeping in mind that the United Nations has come into existence and been supported

---

[89] On more complex views of change in science and philosophy, see Karl Ameriks, "The Very Idea of Innovation: From Descartes to Post-Kantianism," *Symphilosophie* 2 (2021), 247–71.

in enforcing—even though in a limited way—many broadly recognized moral standards that reflect the language of the *Declaration* and Kant as well. None of this means that the millennium is here yet, or even near—and at least with *that* commonsense political thought, Kant goes one good bit beyond even Price.[90]

Kantian Dignity and its Difficulties. Karl Ameriks, Oxford University Press. © Karl Ameriks 2024.
DOI: 10.1093/9780198917656.003.0006

[90] For help on this essay, I am especially indebted to Robert Audi, John Davenport, Dietmar H. Heidemann, Markus Kohl, Thomas Kselman, Susan Purviance, and Fred Rush, as well as participants in the Cardiff 2023 Price Tercentenary Conference and in a conference at the University of North Carolina.

6
Dignity Lost and Regained: Thomas Mann's Elliptical Path, Part I: Background

We must define democracy as that form of government and of society which is inspired above every other with the feeling and the consciousness of the dignity of man.[1]

We hear so much defeatist talk in some countries about outworn forms of government, and young vigorous modern ideologies with which the enemies of Democracy have sought to trick us... Democracy can and will triumph![2]

This chapter discusses the career of Thomas Mann as an especially relevant illustration of the difficulties that have arisen in the reception of Kant's doctrine of universal human dignity and pure duty. Mann's positions vividly illustrate the tendencies of post-Kantian German thought. Mann's early work exhibits the common and deep misunderstanding of Kantian duty in contingent, achievement-oriented, and chauvinist terms. Mann's early career took place in an era of German culture that had been struggling to make a decision between religious, ethical, and aesthetic conceptions of humanity's vocation. At first Mann strongly endorsed an aesthetic orientation. In his later career, however, he began to appreciate what Kant really meant by dignity and duty, and, inspired by Walt Whitman, he turned to advocating democracy. Here it becomes essential to grasp exactly how Mann's eventual understanding of Kant, the Early Romantics, and Nietzsche contrasts with common and unappealing stereotypes of their philosophies.

---

[1] Thomas Mann, *The Coming Victory of Democracy*, trans. Agnes Meyer (New York: Alfred A. Knopf, 1938), 22.

[2] "[I Am an American] by D. [*sic*] Thomas Mann," in *I Am an American, by Famous Naturalized Americans*, with an Introduction by Archibald Macleish, Foreword by Francis Biddle, ed. Robert Spiers Benjamin (New York: Alliance Book Corporation, 1941), 31, 35. Mann had established a homestead in the US but he did not become an American citizen until 1944. Thomas Mann's favorite grandchild, Frido Mann, was recently back in the US on a tour repeating his grandfather's World War II message. He recounted spending many pleasant hours with his grandfather in California as well as the experience of going to elementary school there and pledging allegiance, along with other young Americans, not to a *Führer* but to a republic "with liberty and justice for all."

144 KANTIAN DIGNITY AND ITS DIFFICULTIES

6.1 Transitional Prologue

In the philosophical discussions that have been reviewed so far, concerning the meaning and reception of the doctrine of universal human dignity, the results have been mixed but with evidence that was relatively clear. On the one hand, there is the doctrine itself, with its strikingly progressive implications, in principle, for all human beings. On the other hand, there is the fact that many leading thinkers of the late eighteenth century and after (Richard Price again stands out as a hero by contrast), including Kant, often betrayed the revolutionary principles of the era in all sorts of ways—elitist, imperialist, racist, sexist—in their words and action as well as in inaction and inattention to supremely relevant developments. Nonetheless, hugely important distinctions remain. There were those, such as Herder, who at least introduced or furthered important progressive ideas, in his celebrations of the values of diversity, and also the advocates of American independence, with their commitment to new rights central to modern life. In contrast, there were those who directly campaigned against these ideas, such as Bentham and Burke in their extreme moments or, in addition, distorted them for ultimately monstrous purposes, such as Houston Stewart Chamberlain and his many powerful followers.

The final chapters in this book will turn to giving extensive attention to a more complicated case, the *philosophical* attitude of Thomas Mann. For most of his career, Mann was not only the leading writer in the German language but also a figure who attained worldwide recognition for his political as well as intellectual achievements. There are special complications in Mann's case because of his development, which underwent more major changes than the other figures that have been discussed, and also because of the fact that it is practically unprecedented to treat him as a philosopher at all. It has been recognized, of course, that there are numerous philosophical issues that underlie his fiction. In some of his major works, such as *The Magic Mountain*, discussions of these issues are a major feature and are essential to understanding the main characters involved. Nevertheless, it is rare to consider Mann to be more than a detached and ironic observer of intellectual developments. A close look at the full trajectory of Mann's thinking, however, reveals that, despite a shocking early lapse in regard to Kant (but one not unusual for the times), he had, on the whole, an impressive grasp of the thought of all the major philosophers in the German tradition from the immediate post-Kantian era up to his own era. He is therefore, surprisingly, one of the most relevant figures to study in order to gain a broad understanding of how Kant's fundamental notion of dignity was received, especially in settings affected by German philosophy.

In addition to the fact that he did not write argumentative treatises in a typical philosophical manner, there are a number of reasons why scholars have

overlooked the significance of Mann's perspective even though it is an exceptionally vivid expression of the most influential philosophical currents of the age,
from roughly 1850 to 1950. From an Anglophone perspective, the mere fact that
Mann's philosophical beliefs are largely channeled through aesthetic considerations is enough to keep them out of the center of mainline philosophical discussion. Ever since Hume, and outside of "the continent," aesthetics has ranked far
below logic, epistemology, philosophy of science, and metaphysics in prestige and
serious attention. There have been only a few temporary and limited exceptions,
such as the effect that Wordsworth and Coleridge had on broadening Mill's perspective in his midlife crisis, and the effect that changes in modern lifestyles (such
as the Bloomsbury circle exhibited) had on privileged and highly influential
groups such as the Cambridge Apostles. These effects, however, just basically
reinforced tendencies that were already developing in the general turn, taken
by leading philosophers, away from questions (emphasized repeatedly in English
by Milton, Shaftesbury, Pope, and many others) about how our aesthetic interests,
in a broad sense, relate to ethics as well as the traditional metaphysical issues of
immortality, God, and the hope for signs of a providential order.[3] On the continent itself, extreme philosophies such as positivism, communism, and nihilism,
as well as the excitement generated by modernist revolutions in art, captured so
much attention that the return to middle-of-the-road liberal views, of the kind
that Mann and others began to espouse in the Weimar years,[4] was somewhat of
an exception in avant-garde circles.

In the context of considering responses to the crises that arose in Mann's lifetime, an objection that has often been made to Kantian ethics is that it is too pure
and abstract, and that its central notion of dignity is hard to define non-
controversially and is difficult to apply. But similar objections can be made to the
basic concepts of all general philosophical theories (consider, for example, the
vagueness of "happiness," "flourishing," and "well-being"). The objection is also
often expressed in a way that presupposes a "non-continental" view that Kant did

---

[3] One sign of the changing of the times can be found in the fact that G. E. Moore, at one influential
point in his Cambridge career, simply announced that he was not talking about these topics at all.
More recently, leading analytic philosophers, such as John Martin Fischer, Mark Johnston, and Samuel
Scheffler, have turned to offering impressive treatments of the issue of immortality, and analytic philosophy of religion has experienced a notable resurgence that has again brought attention to Kant's
work in that area.

[4] A typical event of that all too brief era was the joint awarding of honorary degrees in Heidelberg
in 1928 to Gustav Stresemann (1878–1929) and Jacob Schurman (1854–1942). The former was postwar Germany's most successful liberal politician, and the latter was an ambassador to Germany and
an organizer of American funding for the rebuilding of the University of Heidelberg. He had been
President of Cornell University and a founder of *The Philosophical Review*, and his first book, *Kantian
Ethics and Evolution* (1881), defended the "back to Kant" view that he had learned from studying
abroad under Eduard Zeller (1844–1908). (Only decades after my in-laws had often talked fondly
about "grandpa Schurman" did I realize what a significant Kantian figure he had been in trying to
reestablish a bridge between the better aspects of German and American culture.)

146   KANTIAN DIGNITY AND ITS DIFFICULTIES

not accept, namely, that human life in general can and should be guided by a *grasp* of purely philosophical *theories*. Kant's own view—and it is similar to the common ground of left-wing as well as right-wing critiques of many versions of Anglophone liberalism—is that human beings live primarily in accord with given and deep *pre-theoretical* interests. (Kant often called them "interests of reason," but this has a much broader meaning than any form of mere intellectualism.[5]) These interests lead most people who are not totally adrift (not yet the estranged "outsiders" of modern literature) to implicitly guide their life by some kind of overriding meaning, something that usually fits in with traditional conceptions of a concrete aesthetic, ethical, or religious lifestyle and community.

Thomas Mann assumed this view when he began his extensive reading of German philosophers and, in particular when he regarded Kant, both early and later in his career, as the most substantive thinker of all. Unfortunately, Mann fell prey at first to some of the same basic misconceptions about Kantian ethics that have been discussed in previous chapters. The sophistication of his escape from these misconceptions can be properly appreciated only by reviewing the depth and range of Mann's comprehension of all the main figures in Germany after Kant. An evaluation of his basic understanding of these figures will therefore be the focus of the chapter that follows. For non-continental philosophical readers, an explanation of Mann's reading of these complicated figures may at first seem to be an all too detailed detour. The review is essential, however, for making clear the broad strengths of Mann's thinking and for establishing that, even with (and in part because of) his early mistakes, his career contains lessons that make him an especially worthy object of philosophical reflection for our own times. Before getting into details, however, it is appropriate to stand back and consider the *general* relevance of the *kind* of writing and career exhibited in Mann's life.

6.2 MacIntyrean Prelude

In a 1997 review of two works by Charles Larmore, *The Morals of Modernity* and *The Romantic Legacy*, Alasdair MacIntyre raised a historical worry about Larmore's broadly Platonic view that moral knowledge in general is "best understood as the reflective knowledge of reasons."[6] MacIntyre praised Larmore's books but charged that they showed a "singular lack of interest in the genesis of reasons and of beliefs about reasons," for "we know a good deal about how such beliefs are

---

[5] See Richard Velkley's general accounts of continental thought since the eighteenth century: *Freedom and the End of Reason* (Chicago: University of Chicago Press, 1989), and *Being After Rousseau: Philosophy and Culture in Question* (Chicago: University of Chicago Press, 2002).

[6] Alasdair MacIntyre, "Review of *The Morals of Modernity* and *The Romantic Legacy* by Charles Larmore," *The Journal of Philosophy* 94 (1997), 488, quoting *The Romantic Legacy* (New York: Columbia University Press, 1996), 96.

produced and on occasion manipulated."[7] Among the common modern beliefs that MacIntyre found suspicious, and that Larmore accepted, are the fundamental liberal principles that there is a "norm of rational dialogue" that governs "public debate," and that there is an "equality of respect for persons" such that "each is entitled to participation and a hearing in political dialogue."[8] After noting Larmore's own stress on the "complexity" of modernity—made explicit in the title of Larmore's first book, *Patterns of Moral Complexity* (1987)—as well as on the "incommensurability of standpoints" that Larmore argued is part of the "legacy" of Romanticism, MacIntyre ominously concluded by pointing out that "the outcomes of debate are in fact not determined by how the arguments go...but by solicitations of power and interest."[9]

Even if this last claim may appear true as an assertion of *fact*, does this mean that Larmore's liberal *philosophical* position is undermined by the complexities of corrupt tradition and cross-cultural incommensurability? This is a serious issue and it will be explored here by examining the impact of several positions central to the contested era usually called "modernity," but which I prefer to call "late modernity," that is, the era characterized, in the aftermath of Immanuel Kant's work, by a sense of the *limitations* and not only the achievements of modern science and philosophy.[10]

The main positions relevant in this context are associated with the terms Kantianism, Romanticism, and Nietzscheanism. These movements will be examined not for their own sake, however, but primarily for the purpose of clarifying the general philosophical significance of the career of Thomas Mann. Scholars have been hesitant to closely study this aspect of his work and yet, as the noted Germanist Stanley Corngold has observed, Mann "meant by the term 'culture,' to a degree remarkable for an imaginative writer, the German *philosophical* tradition."[11] Mann's early literary works made him a public figure with an international standing but, even apart from his renowned fiction, his startlingly lengthy and fiercely chauvinist tome of 1918, *Reflections of a Non-Political Man*,[12] along with numerous essays after his turn toward democracy in his 1922 address, "On the German Republic," merit special attention as a uniquely revealing expression of

---

[7] MacIntyre, "Review," 489. In several later works, Larmore has addressed historical considerations more directly.

[8] MacIntyre, "Review," 488, 490.   [9] MacIntyre, "Review," 490.

[10] See Karl Ameriks, *Kantian Subjects: Critical Philosophy and Late Modernity* (Oxford: Oxford University Press, 2019).

[11] Stanley Corngold, "Mann as a Reader of Nietzsche," *boundary 2* 9 (1980), 50.

[12] Thomas Mann, *Betrachtungen eines Unpolitischen* [1918] (Frankfurt: S. Fischer, 2009). This work, along with two others, has recently been reissued in English: *Reflections of a Nonpolitical Man*, ed. Mark Lilla, trans. Walter D. Morris (New York: New York Review Books, 2021). The reflections in Mann's book are "nonpolitical" in the Nietzschean sense that they express (with thousands of implicit references and quotations) the view of a person who takes not politics but something else to be most important—in this case a kind of metaphysical/aesthetic culture.

148   KANTIAN DIGNITY AND ITS DIFFICULTIES

many of the most influential beliefs underlying the cultural crises of his pivotal era.[13]

Mann's philosophical significance lies not in a discovery of *new* arguments that he offered that would convince contemporary theorists, but in the fact that the complicated combination of his life and work can be understood as an especially instructive reaction to the general intellectual resources and sicknesses of his tradition as well as of our own times. As Mann himself recognized: "...the writer (and the philosopher also) is a reporting instrument, seismograph, medium of sensitivity, though lacking clear knowledge of his organic function and therefore quite capable of making wrong judgments also."[14] A reconsideration of Mann's response to his tradition reveals, at first, a philosophical failure of the first magnitude, especially in its surprisingly crude confusion (but one occurring with many other figures then as well) in its early reaction to Kant. This confusion is *indirectly* connected to the problem, noted in previous chapters, of Kant's surprising lack of appreciation for the significance of the founding ideas of the United States, which may have influenced the unfortunate fact that liberal political theory lacked prestigious proponents in nineteenth-century Germany.[15]

6.3 Metaphilosophical Interlude

One of Mann's sharper insights was his recognition that philosophical writings, like literature, often influence readers in ways that are independent of an understanding of argumentative structure or agreement with the author's main beliefs. Mann admitted that he generally did not agree with many of the main doctrines that Arthur Schopenhauer and Friedrich Nietzsche espoused but, like countless other readers, he was struck by the appealing "tempo" of their writing.[16] A similar

---

[13] Erich Heller characterized the *Reflections* as offering "an invaluable record of a certain stage of European history" (*The Ironic German: A Study of Thomas Mann* (Chicago: Henry Regnery, 1979), 132). Others have not been so charitable. Mann himself admitted that its odd content and rushed form made it a kind of "non-book" (R 32)—and yet it is one that he reissued in a second edition in 1921 with only minor changes, cutting out only some of the more disturbing passages praising war in general. Much of the book is dominated by a thinly veiled and often shrill attack on his older brother Heinrich, a successful leftist writer who opposed the German war effort out of solidarity with the French Republic and international socialism.

[14] Thomas Mann, *The Story of a Novel: The Genesis of Doctor Faustus* [1949], trans. Richard and Clara Winston (New York: Alfred A. Knopf, 1961), 143.

[15] See Ch. 4. Richard Rorty was one of the few major philosophers recently who took note of the significance of the anti-aristocratic founding of the United States and of gifted writers such as Walt Whitman, who stressed presenting philosophical ideas in a style that can reach, educate, and inspire a broad public. See, e.g., Rorty, *Philosophy and Social Hope* (London: Penguin, 1999). Rorty combined this insight with the debatable contention that enlightened political views are most appropriately combined with a philosophical form of pragmatism that is anti-Platonist, anti-representationalist (substituting "justification" for truth), and nonreligious.

[16] See Paul Bishop, "The Intellectual World of Thomas Mann," in *The Cambridge Companion to Thomas Mann*, ed. Ritchie Robertson (Cambridge: Cambridge University Press, 2002), 23 and 27.

phenomenon complicates our times because, in an era in which "the medium is the message," it has become all too easy for the combination of oligarchic powers, corrupt media, and strangely charismatic charlatans to gain enormous influence and swamp rational options (see, for example, Mann's 1929 novella, *Mario and the Magician*). All this involves a kind of *aesthetic* phenomenon in the broadest sense, a danger warned about already in Plato's *Statesman* and reiterated in Max Weber's warning about the role of charisma in modern politics. In Mann's time and after, rhetorical magicians have confused millions who then fell into vigorously fighting for movements, such as imperialism, Fascism, "crusades," and insurrections that in the end severely harmed even their own interests.

Persuasive techniques can, however, be employed by progressive thinkers as well. With his goal of reaching the general public, Mann resembled figures such as John Locke, Jean-Jacques Rousseau, Immanuel Kant, Richard Price, Mary Wollstonecraft, Thomas Jefferson, Abraham Lincoln, Walt Whitman, the Roosevelts, Simone Weil, Simone de Beauvoir, and Martin Luther King Jr.[17]— authors whose lifework, like MacIntyre's, combines intellectual depth with a will and ability to reach a wide and varied audience. Inspired by Whitman and FDR as much as by German predecessors such as Kant, Mann was so distressed by the onset of World War II that he took up the challenge of addressing the public not only by sending regular radio broadcasts to Germany, to counter the lies of the Nazis, but also by speaking directly to the American people in a nationwide broadcast arranged by the United States government.

In the war-torn world of mid-nineteenth-century America, Whitman had expressed his view of democracy and universal dignity in these dramatic Kantian terms:

> What Christ appear'd for in the moral-spiritual field for human-kind, namely, that in respect to the absolute soul, there is in the possession of such by each single individual, something so transcendent, so incapable of gradations (like life,) that, to that extent, it places all beings on a common level, utterly regardless of the distinctions of intellect, virtue, station, or any height or lowliness whatever—is tallied, in like manner, in this other field, by democracy's rule...[18]

Mann's message, in the ominous times of mid-twentieth-century America, was the same in content but more straightforward in form. It explicitly invoked the notion of human dignity, which he regularly linked with democracy: "Not 'America

---

[17] King's father took on the German theologian's name after being inspired by a church convention in, of all places, 1930s Germany.

[18] Walt Whitman, *Democratic Vistas* [1871], in *The Works of Walt Whitman*, vol. 2, ed. Malcolm Cowley (New York: Minerva Press, 1969), 222.

First' but 'Democracy First' and 'Human Dignity First' are the slogans that will really lead America into first place in the world."[19]

In our own dim decades, the role of literacy has become ever more imperiled, and more investigative journalists have probably been eliminated by international monopolists in "first world" countries than even by authoritarian governments and gangster assassins elsewhere. It is beginning to look again as if "the lamps are going out,"[20] and it may be that articulate leaders such as Nelson Mandela and Barack Obama will lack effective successors. In this situation, the ideal result of a clarification of Mann's thought, and of its ultimately positive trajectory, would be for it to motivate others to attempt, as he did, to develop techniques that would *effectively* break away from the elitist rut of speaking only to people in situations like one's own, and that could once again reach the masses in ways in which they can feel their concerns are being properly addressed.[21]

It is worth pausing over the fact that, in the connected areas of modern aesthetics and politics, few writers have had as broad as well as deep an impact as Kant, Nietzsche, and Mann. Like the classics of Plato, Rousseau, and others, the well-crafted form and intellectual content of their works succeeded in influencing the general public as well as scholars of all kinds. There are several reasons why Mann was called "the greatest living man of letters"[22] in the first half of the twentieth century. In addition to writing legendary fiction, he was the German literary figure most extensively engaged in reacting to the first world war as well as to the lead up to the second and then its aftermath. He was among the very first, in his defense of the early Weimar Republic, to speak out vigorously against the temptations of extremism. He emigrated from Germany in 1938, settled in California in 1941, and eventually played nothing less than the most prominent role of all transplanted writers in opposing Hitler. Right after FDR's 1940 re-election, he joined with a number of scholars in publishing a volume called *The City of Man: A Declaration on World Democracy*, which presented itself explicitly as an anti-Fascist declaration inspired by the Declaration of Independence. Encouraged by numerous figures close to FDR, he traveled across the United States in 1941 on a grueling and highly popular lecture tour, promoting his inspiring view that

---

[19] Thomas Mann, lecture, as reported in the *Greensboro News*, Oct. 31, 1941. See also the epigraphs to this chapter, and Ch. 1.4; and Tobias Boes, *Thomas Mann's War: Literature, Politics, and the World Republic of Letters* (Ithaca, NY: Cornell University Press, 2019), ch. 4.

[20] British Foreign Secretary Sir Edward Grey made this comment on August 3, 1914. See his memoir, *Twenty-Five Years 1892–1916* (New York: Frederick A. Stokes Company, 1925), 20.

[21] See, e.g., Katherine J. Cramer, *The Politics of Resentment: Rural Consciousness in Wisconsin and the Rise of Scott Walker* (Chicago: University of Chicago Press, 2016); and Karl Ameriks, "In Graceland: Hope and History in Michael Collins' Fiction," *The Irish Times*, March 10, 2017: https://www.irishtimes.com/culture/books/in-graceland-hope-and-history-in-michael-collins-fiction-1.3005572.

[22] Boes, *Thomas Mann's War*, 1.

THOMAS MANN'S ELLIPTICAL PATH, PART I   151

"democracy will win" even before the tide had turned and the United States had officially joined in the fight against Fascism.

What is not so well known is that Mann's positive attitude toward the Western allies and democracy was a reversal of his extensive intellectual defense of Germany's militarism in World War I. This defense, which was presented near the very end of that war and not, as with many other writers, only at the beginning, was rooted in a position called a "conservative revolution."[23] Mann linked his early ideas not only to reactionary figures such as his close friend, the Nietzsche expert and later Nazi supporter, Ernst Bertram,[24] as well as the influential racist scholar, Paul LaGarde (R 125, 225), but also to what he argued was an appropriately anti-democratic tradition in Germany in general, as represented by the warrior monarch of Kant's era, Frederick II.[25] Mann's misunderstanding of Kant in this context is especially striking, for it is distressingly similar to that of other highly influential figures such as Houston Stewart Chamberlain (R 467), an Aryan supremacist whose multivolume classic, *The Foundations of the Nineteenth Century*, was an influential bestseller, at first in Germany in 1899, and then worldwide in an English edition in 1911. In addition to being a British aristocrat closely connected with the Kaiser, the Wagner family in Bayreuth, and Adolf Hitler, he was the author of a lengthy study of Kant that he regarded as his most important work.[26] Despite these disturbing influences, Mann's early writing displayed a perspective of its own (he was almost 40 when the war began), and it was rooted in a perceptive familiarity with the works of an astonishingly wide range of authors and leading philosophers.[27] To truly understand Mann's intellectual positions,

---

[23] This notion was used by other German writers then and expressed a variety of forms of disenchantment with contemporary trends. Mann's first use of this particular phrase may have been only in 1921, but he had held similar views for quite a while. See Hermann Kurzke, *Thomas Mann: Life as a Work of Art*, trans. Leslie Willson (Princeton: Princeton University Press, 2002), 263.

[24] See Ernst Bertram, *Nietzsche: Attempt at a Mythology* [1918], trans. Robert E. Norton (Urbana: University of Illinois Press, 2009). For an account of how close Mann and Bertram were during this period, see Steven E. Aschheim, *The Nietzsche Legacy in Germany, 1890–1990* (Berkeley: University of California Press, 1992), 148–51.

[25] In 1914 Mann contended, "It is his fight we are finishing" (T 497). Then, in 1915, Mann went out of his way to write a patriotic essay on Frederick II: "Friedrich und die große Koalition. Ein Abriß für den Tag und die Stunde," in *Thomas Mann: Politische Schriften und Reden 2* (Frankfurt: S. Fischer, 1960), 20–64. This essay assumed the questionable view that the powerful Berlin monarchy, in Frederick II's time as well as Mann's, was simply in a defensive position and had the right to use all sorts of aggressive means to defend itself. See also R 165–6 and 303. Like Nietzsche, Mann linked democratic ideals to Christianity (R 36) and, like Frederick II, he was often antipathetic to both. It should not be forgotten, however, that for centuries up to at least Bismarck's era, France and England had been much more aggressive than Germany, which up to that time was not even politically unified.

[26] See Ch. 3, and Houston Stewart Chamberlain, *Immanuel Kant: A Study and a Comparison with Goethe, Leonardo da Vinci, Bruno, Plato and Descartes* [1914], trans. Lord Redesdale (London: John Lane, 1915). Mann himself met not only with FDR but also with Wagner's daughter-in-law and Nietzsche's sister.

[27] The recent English edition of the *Reflections* gives no adequate indication of Mann's extensive and highly relevant references. See Hans Kurzke, *Thomas Mann, Betrachtungen eines Nichtpolitischen: Kommentar* (Frankfurt: S. Fischer, 2009), 781pp.

152   KANTIAN DIGNITY AND ITS DIFFICULTIES

early and late, and the unusual depth of his philosophical insights, it is essential to have a grasp of the tradition he was responding to, namely, the complex and interconnected sequence of tendencies in German thought that developed in Kant's aftermath, up to and including Nietzsche.

6.4 Mann's Intellectual Background: Essential Terminological Clarifications

On Mann's own account, the "intellectual foundations" (R 12) of his work are to be found in the writings of philosophers such as Kant, the Romantics, and Nietzsche. The positions of these figures themselves *differ*, however, in important ways from the questionable "isms" that are still often associated with them, and these differences need to be clarified before the details of Mann's position can be properly understood. First, there is the basic standpoint of Kant's *own* philosophy, which in this context can be characterized as a broadly rationalist and enlightened form of liberalism, with an ethical *content* that on many points overlaps with the philosophical position of contemporary philosophers such as Larmore. On this interpretation, Kant's work needs to be sharply distinguished from prevalent caricatures of it, such as either the subjective constructivist or the dogmatic rule-fetishist readings that are found in many contemporary discussions (including by MacIntyre and Larmore) and are often associated with the broad term "Kantianism."[28]

Similarly, the outlook commonly designated by the general term "Romanticism" needs to be distinguished from the specific Kant- and Enlightenment-oriented position called *Early* German Romanticism, which was developed by the all too briefly active "Jena circle" of the 1790s and the first years of the nineteenth century.[29] This group included an illustrious set of Friedrichs who all had the unusual gift of a combination of exceptional philosophical as well as literary skills:

---

[28] See above, Ch. 1, and Karl Ameriks, "On Two Non-Realist Interpretations of Kant's Ethics," in *Interpreting Kant's Critiques* (Oxford: Clarendon Press, 2003), 263–82; "A Commonsense Kant?" *Proceedings and Addresses of the American Philosophical Association* 79 (2005), 19–45; and "On the Many Senses of 'Self-Determination,'" in *Kantian Subjects*, 14–35. Larmore has held to a subjectivistic reading of the ground of Kant's ethics, but it can be argued his view rests on a common but all too uncharitable interpretation of Kant's notion of self-legislation. Sometimes a sharp distinction is made between "Kant's views" and "Kantian views," but I will be using the term "Kantian" in a variety of ways (so that it can also apply to Kant's own ideas), and will trust that the context will make clear whether the position that is being discussed is not to be regarded as a proper expression of Kant's doctrines. (Sometimes one might even understandably say, Kant himself was not "a good Kantian.") See Ch. 1, note 37.

[29] See *The Cambridge Companion to German Idealism*, 2nd edn, ed. Karl Ameriks (Cambridge: Cambridge University Press, 2017).

Friedrich Schleiermacher,[30] Friedrich Schlegel,[31] Friedrich Hölderlin,[32] and—eventually of most importance for Mann—Friedrich von Hardenberg, known as Novalis.[33] The Early Romantics had several important allies elsewhere[34]—the English Romantics, the American Transcendentalists, and Walt Whitman—and they eventually played a life-changing role in Mann's career. The interest in diversity, which was common to all these figures, influenced and broadened Mann's later appreciation of the Kantian tradition in a way that somewhat resembles Kant's own late gesture toward a rapprochement with Herder's diversity-oriented form of cosmopolitanism.[35] The Kant-inspired outlook of the Jena circle has to be sharply distinguished, however, from the irrationalist and reactionary attitudes that have often been attached to the term "Romanticism" in general. These attitudes are found primarily in instances of *Late* Romanticism, including Wagnerism, which heavily influenced decadent anti-Kantian movements near the end of the nineteenth century and beyond.[36] This vital distinction is still underappreciated in some circles, but Mann[37] and Nietzsche understood there was a

---

[30] Schleiermacher and Schlegel originally planned to translate Plato's dialogues together, but in the end the legendary translation was Schleiermacher's achievement. Schleiermacher's first publications were Spinoza-inspired critiques of Kant, but his lectures on ethics, from 1812 to 1817, combined Aristotle's views and Kant's.

[31] See, e.g., Fred Rush's account of Schlegel's philosophy in *Irony and Idealism: Rereading Schlegel, Hegel, and Kierkegaard* (Oxford: Oxford University Press, 2016). Schlegel took a conservative turn in later life, Hölderlin's literary career ended in 1806, and Novalis died in 1801.

[32] See Karl Ameriks, "Hölderlin's Kantian Path," in *Kantian Subjects*, 189–206, which argues that Hölderlin's main work was not a retreat to nostalgic aestheticism but primarily an advocacy of Kant's ethics. Mann occasionally suggested combining Hölderlin and Marx. See Bishop, "Mann's World," 36.

[33] See Jane Kneller's account of Novalis's close relation to Kant's philosophy, "The Copernican Turn in Early German Romanticism," in *Brill's Companion to German Romantic Philosophy*, ed. Elizabeth Millán Brusslan and Judith Norman (Leiden: Brill, 2018), 18–36. Mann knew György Lukács's work well, and Lukács gained recognition with an early essay on Novalis, which asserts, "Novalis's art and work...are a symbol of the whole of Romanticism" (*Soul & Form* [1907], trans. Anna Bostock, ed. John T. Saunders and Katie Terezakis (New York: Columbia University Press, 2010), 71).

[34] Ludwig van Beethoven, whose work became especially important for Mann, can also be considered an ally, in spirit, of the Early Romantics. Recent research has uncovered Beethoven's persistent and knowledgeable admiration for Kant's thought, which went back to his close association, in his early years in Bonn, with scholarly Kant enthusiasts and friends of Friedrich Schiller. See Hans-Joachim Hinrichsen, *Ludwig van Beethoven. Musik für eine neue Zeit* (Kassel and Berlin: Bärenreiter-Metzler, 2019); William Kinderman, *Beethoven: A Political Artist in Revolutionary Times* (Chicago: University of Chicago Press, 2020); and John E. Hare, "Kant, Aesthetic Judgement, and Beethoven," in *Theology, Music, and Modernity: Struggles for Freedom*, ed. Jeremy Begbie, Daniel K. L. Chua, and Markus Rathey (Oxford: Oxford University Press, 2021), 42–65. See also Piero Giordanetti, *Kant und die Musik* (Würzburg: Königshausen & Neumann, 2005); and Karl Ameriks, "Kant, Schiller, and Beethoven: Enlightened Connections of Aesthetics, Revolution, and Religion," *SGIR Review* (forthcoming).

[35] See Ch. 2.

[36] See Alex Ross, *Wagnerism: Art and Politics in the Shadow of Music* (New York: Farrar, Straus and Giroux, 2020).

[37] On the contrast of "magical" and "cynical" Romanticism, see GR 519 and 536, and R 261. On Mann's focus on the "forward looking elements" of Early Romanticism, see also Bishop, "Mann's World," 32. An extra complication of the era is that, in addition to the contrasting versions of nineteenth-century Romanticism, the publisher Eugen Diedrichs, in the early twentieth century,

154   KANTIAN DIGNITY AND ITS DIFFICULTIES

difference in the generations,[38] and the distinctiveness of Early Romanticism has now been extensively documented by numerous scholars.[39]

Finally, the basic position of Nietzsche himself, as an early admirer of Hölderlin and an enlightened *opponent* of chauvinism and irrationalism (as well as of hyper-rationalism) has to be sharply distinguished—as Mann observed in an insightful late essay (N)[40]—from the raving passages of Nietzsche's last year of writing. The term "Nietzscheanism" can be reserved, in contrast, for the still very popular characterization (implied even in some of Larmore's and MacIntyre's works) of Nietzsche's philosophy as tantamount to relativism, subjectivism, or even nihilism—all positions that he vigorously opposed from his position as basically an aesthetic elitist.[41] Mann's most judicious study, his post-World War II analysis, persuasively argues that Nietzsche's fundamental concept, from the beginning to the end, was "culture" as expressed in his basic claim that "only as an *aesthetic phenomenon* is existence and the world eternally *justified*."[42] Nietzsche had strong value commitments of his own and affirmed an "order of rank" to be led by humanity's "highest representatives," in a broadly aesthetic sense, instead of by democratic leaders concerned with justice for the masses (N 24–5).

The unfortunate fact is that, in many ways, the viewpoints that have just been characterized as subjectivist Kantianism, irrationalist Romanticism, and nihilist Nietzscheanism have probably had more influence (on many philosophers as well as on culture in general) than the genuine insights of the real Kant, Early Romantics, and sane Nietzsche. Although Mann's thought is remarkable in avoiding the common misinterpretations that occurred in reactions to the era of the Early Romantics and after, he still fell prey, for a long time, to some major misunderstandings of Kant and liberal democracy. Therefore, one especially relevant way to respond to MacIntyre's call for a critical consideration of the "genesis of

called for a "New Romanticism." This movement involved a number of different directions, some simply stressing myth or socialist ideas, but others supporting reactionary "folk" and racist positions. See George L. Mosse, "Bedeviled Conservatives," in *The Crisis of German Ideology: Intellectual Origins of the Third Reich* (New York: Grosset & Dunlop, 1964), 237–53.

[38] Mann often drew attention to Nietzsche's affinity with Romanticism (R 117). Nietzsche did not use the term "late" but he distinguished between Hölderlin and later Romantic figures that he came to regard as decadent, as well as between immediate negative and long-range beneficial effects of Romanticism. See Bishop, "Mann's World," 31–2, and Nietzsche, *Daybreak: Thoughts on the Prejudices of Morality* [1881] § 197.

[39] See especially the writings of Manfred Frank, e.g. *The Philosophical Foundations of Early German Romanticism* [1997], trans. Elizabeth Millán-Zaibert (Albany: State University of New York Press, 2004).

[40] Thomas Mann, "Nietzsche in the Light of Modern Experience," *Commentary* 6 (1948), 17–26 and 149–56.

[41] Cf. R. Lanier Anderson, "Nietzsche on Truth, Illusion, and Redemption," *European Journal of Philosophy* 13 (2005), 185–225; Tamsin Shaw, *Nietzsche's Political Skepticism* (Princeton: Princeton University Press, 2007); and Andrew Huddleston, *Nietzsche on the Decadence and Flourishing of Culture* (Oxford: Oxford University Press, 2019).

[42] Friedrich Nietzsche, *The Birth of Tragedy out of the Spirit of Music* [1872], in *The Birth of Tragedy and Other Writings*, trans. Ronald Speirs, ed. Ronald Speirs and Raymond Geuss (Cambridge: Cambridge University Press, 1999), § 5, 33.

reasons and beliefs about reasons" commonly offered in our culture is to carefully reexamine Mann's beliefs as a *paradigmatic*, and at times dangerously confused, instance of the great difficulty, even for an especially talented mind, of properly responding to one's own complex tradition. Furthermore, despite the notorious mistakes of the *first* half of his career (up to 1922), which sadly and vividly illustrate what was a widespread phenomenon in Germany, Mann's work remains equally worth reexamining as an example of how a surprising positive reversal in philosophical orientation is possible even after a long period of being committed to deep-seated errors. The *second* half of Mann's career is an exemplary and highly relevant vindication of much of what is still most valuable in the work of Kant as well as that of the Early Romantics and their cross-cultural allies.

As Mann noted in a letter to his eldest son, Klaus, on July 22, 1939: "to inherit something, one must understand it."[43] Unfortunately, it often takes a shocking development to generate adequate understanding and, as will become evident, the pattern of Mann's career shows that this can require a painful realization of deep flaws in common conceptions within one's own tradition, flaws that often involve "manipulated" and quite dangerous "reasons."

Kantian Dignity and its Difficulties. Karl Ameriks, Oxford University Press. © Karl Ameriks 2024.
DOI: 10.1093/9780198917656.003.0007

---

[43] Bishop, "Mann's World," 41.

7

Thomas Mann's Path, Part II: Intellectual Foundations in German Philosophy

> ...if an appreciation of the dignity of man is the moral definition of democracy, then its psychological definition arises out of its determination to reconcile and combine knowledge and art, mind and life, thought and deed.
>
> Europe has much to learn from America as to the nature of democracy. It was your American statesmen and poets such as Lincoln and Whitman who proclaimed to the world democratic thought and feeling, and the democratic way of life, in imperishable words.[1]

This chapter treats Thomas Mann as a serious philosophical figure who had an outstanding grasp of the complex development of post-Kantian thought. Mann held Kant and the Early Romantics in the highest regard, but in his early career he was especially fascinated by the trio of Schopenhauer, Wagner, and Nietzsche. An important influence on Mann's late work was Kierkegaard's critique of Hegel's excessive rationalism as well as his appreciation of the importance of aesthetics, combined with an incisive critique of an overly aesthetic orientation. Mann had an excellent understanding of the strengths and weaknesses of all of these post-Kantian figures, but only in his later career did he see that it is best to go beyond the whole sequence from Hegel to Nietzsche by returning to Kant's notion of dignity, and pure and democratic morality, supplemented by the creative insights that he always admired in the Early Romantics.

7.1 The Vocation Problem: Aesthetics, Ethics, or Religion?

A proper evaluation of the philosophical significance of Mann's work requires that one first engage in a fair amount of philosophical archaeology. The basic framework of the philosophical tradition that directly influenced Mann and his world was set by the main value options that were discussed at length by

---

[1] Thomas Mann, *The Coming Victory of Democracy*, trans. Agnes Meyer (New York: Alfred A. Knopf, 1938), 36 and 8.

G. W. F. Hegel and then, in quite different ways, by Søren Kierkegaard as well as Schopenhauer and Nietzsche. Schopenhauer, Wagner, and Nietzsche were the main *immediate* "intellectual foundations" of Mann's work but to make best sense of their thought and influence it is necessary to have a grasp of the main ideas of their predecessors, Hegel and Kierkegaard, and also to understand how these philosophers reacted to and departed from the positions of Kant and Early German Romanticism.

In this context, the most relevant point about Kant's system is the fact that the main later thinkers under discussion shared his concern with focusing ultimately on how the values of aesthetics, ethics, and religion are best to be characterized and ranked. Although Kant's theoretical philosophy is fundamental for all his work, his Critical revolution of the 1780s was motivated by a sharp practical turn that his thinking took after reading Rousseau in the early 1760s.[2] Thereafter, his main aim was to find a metaphysical system that could allow for an affirmation of absolute freedom, universal dignity, and moral autonomy—in contrast to his own early compatibilist and non-deontological writings. At the end of his 1781 first *Critique* (which he originally thought would be his last) Kant linked this project to an eventual system of ethics and a defense of a pure practical version of religion. By the time of his 1790 third *Critique* he came to see a need to thematize aesthetic experience as well, as a crucial component of any life ideally oriented toward a pure form of ethics and religion. (Like Kant, I will use the terms "ethics" and "morals" interchangeably, although others follow Hegel and employ a systematic distinction.) Kant's main successors were similarly committed to doing justice to these three spheres (which, for Kant, correspond to a threefold division of faculties: thought, will, and feeling), although in ways that used quite different definitions and had more radical intentions.

In contrast to mainstream contemporary philosophy, the value concerns of the major nineteenth-century European philosophers are most naturally understood in terms of their reactions to the central question that occupied Kant as well as other major eighteenth-century writers, from J. J. Spalding in 1748 through J. G. Fichte in 1800, namely, how best to define the *Bestimmung des Menschen*, that is, our ultimate human vocation as an individual and a species. Although this question was at first treated as a version of the Protestant issue of how best to define one's religious "calling," in the course of the Enlightenment the notion of a calling was radically broadened. For the first time in centuries it became a matter of public debate whether revealed religion should have primacy over other options, such as aesthetics, secular ethics, and reflective attitudes such as stoicism, deism, skepticism, scientism, and renunciation. (A version of this debate is continuing in discussions of "identity" in contemporary social contexts.) In European

---

[2] See Karl Ameriks, *Kant's Elliptical Path* (Oxford: Clarendon Press, 2012).

158   KANTIAN DIGNITY AND ITS DIFFICULTIES

thought after Kant, the basic options of leading primarily an *aesthetic, ethical,* or *broadly religious* (that is, including "cosmic" attitudes such as renunciation) individual life can best be understood philosophically in terms of reactions primarily to Hegel and to ideas that are most relevantly formulated in Kierkegaard's extensive account of "stages on life's way."[3] Before the significance of Kierkegaard's approach, and its relevance for understanding Mann, can be appreciated, it is therefore necessary to review some of the main features of Hegel's philosophy.

7.2 Hegel

In Hegel's system, the central option for citizens in a modern and scientifically-oriented society is to identify with one's station in the particular properly developed ethical realm (*Sittlichkeit*) that Hegel called the "objective spirit" of one's nation. This structured nest of concrete intersubjective institutions—family, civil society, and state (which also corresponds to the threefold division of faculties: feeling, will, and thought)—grounds the higher realm that he called a people's "absolute spirit," that is, its aesthetic, religious, and philosophical expressions. The phenomena of this realm are to be understood as, in order, the sensuous, mythical, and abstractly *representational superstructures* of our *base-level* life in objective spirit. In the most advanced cultures of late modernity, objective spirit supposedly allows for our self-realization as participants in a constitutional monarchy that systematically balances the needs of the individual and the community. It thereby also best fulfills what Hegel called "subjective spirit," that is, our psychological needs as feeling, willing, and thinking beings, seeking fulfillment in a balanced form of mutual recognition.

Even though Mann spent relatively little time with Hegel's work and was slow to turn to Kierkegaard directly,[4] it turns out that the best way to approach his most fundamental early concerns is to start with a reminder of the *reordering* of

---

[3] There are several English editions of many of Kierkegaard's works. All the main works are relevant but this chapter contains quotes from only two of them. See *On the Concept of Irony, with Constant Reference to Socrates* (1841); *Either/Or: A Fragment of Life* (1843); *Fear and Trembling: A Dialectical Lyric* [1843], ed. Silvia Walsh and C. Stephen Evans, and trans. by Silvia Walsh, with an introduction by C. Stephen Evans (Cambridge: Cambridge University Press, 2006); *Stages on Life's Way: Studies by Various Persons* (1845); *The Present Age: On the Death of Rebellion* (1846); *Concluding Unscientific Postscript to Philosophical Fragments* [1846], trans. David F. Swenson and Walter Lowrie (Princeton: Princeton University Press, 1941); and *The Sickness Unto Death: A Christian Psychological Exposition for Edification and Awakening* (1849). In this context it is not possible to address the additional complexities surrounding Kierkegaard's use of pseudonyms.

[4] In his late work, *The Story of a Novel: The Genesis of Doctor Faustus* [1949], trans. Richard and Clara Winston (New York: Alfred A. Knopf, 1961), 85 and 104, Mann refers to being enlightened by *Either/Or* and also Adorno's work on Kierkegaard. At N 156, there is a passing remark about Kierkegaard and the "rebellion" against "classical rationalism." See also the treatment of the relation of Mann's work to Kierkegaard's ideas in Erich Heller, *The Ironic German, A Study of Thomas Mann* (Chicago: Henry Regnery, 1979), 73, and 133–8.

Hegel's options that occurred in Kierkegaard's work.[5] Although Mann was, in large part, a defender of the "burgher" values of his Hanseatic background,[6] with a temperament that often remained close to the attitude of a conservative Hegelian, he was also very much a Romantic. Like the Early Romantics and Schopenhauer as well, Mann was skeptical of anything like the optimistic perfectionism and divinizing of the state that was common in the Hegelian attitude that was gaining strength in later nineteenth-century Prussia (R 123, 232). In this respect, in its initial concern with the development of an aesthetically sensitive *individual* rather than the so-called progress of universal history, Mann's approach resembled Kierkegaard's reaction to Hegel's system rather than that of the Prussian arch-conservatives.

According to Hegel, the development of culture has exhibited a *reconciling* historical and normative order, one with phases of emphasis that correspond roughly to the three spheres of absolute spirit: aesthetic, religious, philosophical (cf. R 211).[7] In his focus on the individual, Kierkegaard followed this ordering, except that (in addition to paying less attention to details of historical development), right after the aesthetic stage, he inserted the ethical, as the equivalent of Hegel's realm of objective spirit. In addition, at the end, Kierkegaard reversed priorities and, within the last stage, put orthodox faith in the highest place and above all forms of commitment to merely secular philosophy or rational religion. He insisted that only an acceptance of the basic revelations of Christianity can bring balance to the self and a true fulfillment of its fundamental infinite as well as finite concerns. The only catch was that he argued that this acceptance—unlike the appreciation of the genuine but also inevitably frustrating value of each of life's lower stages—requires a step that goes beyond rational *justification* and even has paradoxical components. Kierkegaard thereby reversed the rationalist and secular optimism behind Hegel's famous condemnation of traditional (that is, basically medieval) Christianity as alienated "unhappy consciousness" in the *Phenomenology of Spirit*.[8] For Kierkegaard, the last stage on life's way is full faith, and from that perspective modern agents should look back at all the lower stages

---

[5] According to Richard Rorty, "Hegel's philosophy of history legitimized and underwrote Whitman's hope to substitute his own nation-state for the Kingdom of God" (*Achieving our Country: Leftist Thought in Twentieth Century America* (Cambridge, MA: Harvard University Press, 1998), 20–1). Although it is true that Mann's hero, Whitman, may have seemed at times to endorse Hegel's triumphalist conception of history, it can also be argued that Rorty was projecting his own anti-religious preferences onto Whitman and—unlike Mann—doing injustice to his internationalism.

[6] Mann devoted a chapter to praising "Burgerly Nature" (R 83–122; see also 303, 322–5), and he contrasted it with what he criticized as the attitude of the bourgeoise.

[7] See, e.g., Michael Hardimon, *Hegel's Social Philosophy: The Project of Reconciliation* (Cambridge: Cambridge University Press, 1992).

[8] Compare the beginning of Kierkegaard, *The Sickness unto Death*, and the section on "Unhappy Consciousness" at the end of the "Self-Consciousness" chapter of Hegel's *Phenomenology of Spirit* (1807).

160 KANTIAN DIGNITY AND ITS DIFFICULTIES

as, by themselves, just the omnipresent but ultimately despairing forms of truly unhappy consciousness, "despairing" and "sick unto death" in "the present age."

Like Kierkegaard, Hegel regarded all these main orientations as, in some form, essential to human fulfillment, but he was more dismissive than Kierkegaard was in regard to the aesthetic and religious options. For Hegel, although at one time each of these options was of overriding significance, they have supposedly become not real options that fully reflective agents can any longer regard as *most* important. Commitment to the aesthetic option above all else, no matter how alluring it may be, should be treated as regression to a tendency of humanity's infancy. Hegel took the distinctive achievement of ancient cultures to be their unsurpassable aesthetic accomplishments, which culminated in the artistic shaping of an organically connected ethical and religious life in the magnificent, but merely finite, cultures of Athenian-style societies. The distinctive achievement of post-ancient cultures began, in dialectical contrast, with the medieval development of a universal religious appreciation of the inner value of each human soul, what Hegel called its self-reflective "infinity." This otherworldly era was succeeded by the modern, philosophical, and rational-ethical rather than aesthetic-ethical reorganizing of economic and political structures in the Enlightenment. For Hegel, the modern world had reached the beginning of a final era that satisfies human beings in the "spiritual daylight of the present."[9] It thereby combines the best tendencies of the "substance" of ancient society with the at first alienating, but dialectically essential, "reflection" of medieval thought. After human beings have come to understand themselves as each subjectively free within their own minds (in a sense that may appear Kantian but in fact is a form of rationalistic determinism), in the modern age their institutions can finally make them all objectively free in their external relations. Modernity is also marked by the development of uniquely reflective forms of aesthetic gratification, within the satisfying setting of an ethical restructuring of society along the lines of a post-French Revolution Prussian-style bureaucracy and constitutional monarchy. Philosophy, in our culminating era, simply provides the service of a systematic comprehension of this "end of history" situation.

In Hegel's final version of absolute spirit, some role was still given to art and religion, but their original meaning and prior status as the highest forms of individual life and culture were said to be transcended (*aufgehoben*). Understanding this feature of Hegel's system, which was typical of the German Idealists, is especially relevant because Early Romanticism presented itself from the start as an *alternative* to this kind of triumphalist and still popular attitude.[10] Matters are

---

[9] See Hegel, *Phenomenology of Spirit*, in the "Self-Consciousness" chapter, immediately before the "Master and Slave" section.

[10] See Karl Ameriks, "Hegel's Aesthetics: New Perspectives on its Response to Kant and Romanticism," *Bulletin of the Hegel Society of Great Britain*, 45/46 (2002), 72–92. As champions of diversity at the turn of the century, what the Early Romantics were reacting to, in particular, was the

THOMAS MANN'S PATH, PART II   161

complicated, however, because of the highly influential way that the Early Romantics were caricatured by Hegel—and then by Kierkegaard and many others[11] as well—as advocating *irrationalism* and not mere anti-rationalism. A proper appreciation of Mann, and of the related major movements of his time, needs to begin by employing, as he did, a more differentiated understanding of what comes under the heading of Romanticism.

7.3 Kant and the Early Romantics

Critics of the Early Romantics have tended to treat them as if their purpose was a reactionary or chaotic propagation of the values of earlier eras and exotic cultures. Contrary to these critics, the actual intent of these Romantics, at the most fundamental philosophical level, was to make use of what was best in the immediate pre-Hegelian era, namely, Kant's work in behalf of the Enlightenment, as well as the best ideas of his highly influential early student and literary innovator, J. G. Herder. Like the Early Romantics, Kant and Herder were enthusiastic champions of modern science. From the 1760s on, they focused, each in their own way, on "universal natural history"[12] and our status as living beings structured by fundamental natural laws. While Kant stressed the universal nature of scientific and moral law, Herder, like his Romantic successors, emphasized a new kind of appreciation for the variety of local cultures and the complexity of historical change. All these thinkers also held that, while the accomplishments of modern science are revolutionary, the *exact* sciences, even in their most developed form, have basic *limits*. Whatever a philosophical system is capable of, there will be fundamental truths—including those of aesthetics, ethics, and religion—that will escape its demonstrative capacities. These domains deserve to be treated not as irrational escapes from our science-oriented culture but as providing an essential supplement for it as well as a correction of scientism and philosophical hubris. The Early Romantics were enemies of irrationalism, for this goes beyond

---

overly ambitious character of Reinhold's and then Fichte's early Idealist systems. Hegel's system was not yet published, but the anti-systematic considerations of the Early Romantics can be applied against it just as much as against its Idealist predecessors.

[11] See, e.g., remarks by Troeltsch quoted in Robert E. Norton, *The Crucible of German Democracy: Ernst Troeltsch and the First World War* (Tübingen: Mohr Siebeck, 2021), 572.

[12] On the relationship of Kant and Herder, see Ch. 2. Kant's *Universal Natural History and Theory of the Heavens or an Attempt to Account for the Constitutional and Mechanical Origin of the Universe upon Newtonian Principles* (1755) offered a path-breaking cosmology, but it can also be read, like much of Herder's work, as a literary essay about the human condition within an amazingly well-organized cosmos. On the relevance for the Early Romantics of Herder's aesthetics, see Stephen Rumph, "Herder's Alternative Path to Musical Transcendence," in *Theology, Music, and Modernity: Struggles for Freedom*, ed. Jeremy Begbie, Daniel K L Chua, and Markus Rathey (Oxford: Oxford University Press, 2021), 327, n. 45. Rumph notes the importance of Herder's *Kalligone* (1800), which stresses that "true sublimity reposes in *the entire progressive work* of the poet."

162   KANTIAN DIGNITY AND ITS DIFFICULTIES

non-rationalism and is the rejection of rationality altogether.[13] Their work exemplified a kind of critical rationalism, for they affirmed the power of reason and experiment while also making clear that not every important truth for human beings can be expected to be provable by modern scientific procedures, let alone a traditional philosophical system.

The significance of this recognition of the limits of theoretical philosophy and science was well understood not only by the Jena Circle but also its successors—including, eventually, Thomas Mann as well. The main idea was well captured in an early remark by Nietzsche, who was especially inspired by Hölderlin and also affected by the impact of Kant's work: we "long to be completely truthful... this is *possible* only in a *very relative sense*.[14] That is tragic. That is *Kant's tragic problem*... Art now acquires an entirely *new* dignity. The sciences, in contrast, are *degraded* to a degree."[15] This limitation of science is not a matter of rejection but of noting the danger of its pretensions and of understanding the need to leave a significant "degree" of scope for something else—something with "entirely *new* dignity." This passage nicely makes explicit the epoch's cultural shift away from respect for dignity in the Kantian and strict moral sense and back to the earlier, aesthetic, and achievement-oriented sense. For Nietzsche the classicist, the problem of excess cognitive optimism was already a feature of decadent strands in late antiquity and the long-term influence of the rationalist Socratic–Platonic revolution. Nietzsche proposed at first to counteract this influence by campaigning on behalf of Wagner's aesthetic version of the ancients' tragic (so-called "Pre-Socratic") worldview. Although Nietzsche distanced himself from Wagner, after a few years of excessive enthusiasm, his primary attachment to an aesthetic perspective—in contrast to pure morality, religion, or mere science—did not disappear. It was always combined, however, with a project of spiritually rejuvenating what he understood as the legitimate value concerns of European culture (see *The Birth of Tragedy* § 23). This is why Mann admired what he called Nietzsche's early

---

[13] At times, Mann himself unfortunately lapsed into phrases such as "depth and irrationality suit the German soul" (T 506).

[14] This aspect of Nietzsche's thought is also noted in Lydia Goehr, *The Imaginary Museum of Musical Works: An Essay in the Philosophy of Music* (Oxford: Clarendon Press, 1992), 33. Nietzsche could have praised either Novalis or Friedrich Schlegel (who stressed the notion of the "relative") as well, but he never directly cited Schlegel, even though—or perhaps because—Schlegel anticipated the distinctive Dionysian notion in Nietzsche's treatment of the Greeks. This point is well documented now in Michael N. Forster, "Romanticism and *The Birth of Tragedy*," in *Romanticism, Philosophy, and Literature*, ed. Michael N. Forster and Lina Steiner (London: Palgrave-Macmillan, 2020), 265–95.

[15] Friedrich Nietzsche, "The Philosopher: Reflections on the Struggle between Art and Knowledge" [1872], in *Philosophy and Truth: Selections from Nietzsche's Notebooks of the Early 1870s*, ed. and trans. Daniel Breazeale (Atlantic Highlands, NJ: Humanities Press International, 1979), 28. It is striking that Nietzsche himself emphasizes the key terms in this passage. See Karl Ameriks, "On Some Reactions to 'Kant's Tragic Problem,'" in *Natur und Freiheit. Akten des XII. Internationalen Kant Kongresses*, ed. Violetta Waibel et al. (Berlin: De Gruyter, 2018), 3255–62. Nietzsche's claim about fundamental limits of science (and human cognition in general) did not, of course, rest solely on Kant's system (or Schopenhauer's) but was a commonplace in philosophy at that time (e.g., in English phenomenalism) and had distinctive roots in his own "perspectivism" as well.

"anti-fanatical" orientation, critique of hypocrisy, and interest in doing "justice" to nature, which saved him from escapist aestheticism (R 412–13).[16]

After directly praising Kant's Critical notion of the limits of theoretical reason (T 500), Mann, like Nietzsche, also professed a belief in the elevated significance of the aesthetic realm, although it is highly noteworthy that he discussed this at first by calling attention to Kant's notion of "postulates of *practical* reason" (R 156).[17] This statement was important—even though somewhat misleading[18]— not only because it reflected the attitude of a talented creative writer but also because Mann, quite properly, understood his primarily non-theoretical orientation as expressing a powerful tendency of the whole post-Kantian era. Appropriately defining that practical tendency requires further clarification of the quite different ways in which the main figures of the period understood the key terms: "aesthetic," "ethical," and "religious." Although these terms, in this very sequence, continued to correspond to the main concerns of the Hegelian era as reacted to by Kierkegaard in the 1840s, and then by Schopenhauer and Nietzsche as the domi- nant figures for the rest of the century in other circles, the terms took on very different meanings in the works of these post-Hegelians.

7.4 Kierkegaard and the Early Romantics

Even though he was primarily an advocate of a kind of orthodox Protestantism (which was also the childhood background of the other figures discussed here), Kierkegaard gave an exceptional amount of attention to the aesthetic stage. He understood this option in a much broader sense than as a mere orientation toward either art, in an appreciative or creative manner, or toward nature, which was primary for Kant as well as many earlier philosophers. Here Kierkegaard followed Schlegel, for he understood that, in the post-Kantian era, a focus on the aesthetic was, above all, a matter of carrying out an aesthetic *life* and crafting a maximally "interesting," and therefore often ironic, version of one's *self*. Devotion to this project can take many forms, some even compatible with actions that appear typical of highly ethical or religious people. For the true aesthete, however,

---

[16] See Paul Bishop, "The Intellectual World of Thomas Mann," in *The Cambridge Companion to Thomas Mann*, ed. Ritchie Robertson (Cambridge: Cambridge University Press, 2002), 22–42. Common claims that Nietzsche abandoned an aesthetically oriented position make too much of his later derogatory remarks about metaphysical-aesthetic approaches where what he primarily had in mind were weak aspects of Schopenhauer's and Wagner's positions, which Nietzsche was embarrassed about not having criticized earlier.

[17] What Mann meant by "practical" here was just a general orientation that contrasts with theoret- ical reason and was closer to Nietzsche's practical conception of life than to Kant's moral argument for God or the categorical imperative (on its standard reading).

[18] After his spectacular early success with *Buddenbrooks* in 1901, Mann took himself to be speak- ing "for many." See Heinrich Siefken, "Mann as Essayist," in *The Cambridge Companion to Thomas Mann*, ed. Ritchie Robertson (Cambridge: Cambridge University Press, 2002), 215.

164   KANTIAN DIGNITY AND ITS DIFFICULTIES

what is crucial is that such actions are pursued not for the sake of traditional ends themselves but for the satisfaction of the aesthete's own internal project. There are forms of this satisfaction that can be a matter of immediate sensual pleasure, but much more significant for Kierkegaard was a concern with a variety of sophisticated lifestyles that focus on the interesting,[19] even in contexts such as melancholy, which, with the right attitude, can give even a despondent person's life a kind of sustaining project.[20]

Kierkegaard himself was often captivated by the pull of an aesthetic life, as is obvious from his diaries and extensive literary expressions of a confessional nature. Nonetheless, Kierkegaard clearly held that it is a huge mistake for anyone to take an aesthetic life to be one's proper *vocation*, and he treated it as ultimately an all too self-focused, and therefore self-defeating, option. Here Kierkegaard was in part going along with the Hegelian school's slandering treatment of Romanticism,[21] which characterized Schlegel's kind of ironic perspective as a capricious individualism tantamount to an advocacy of evil.[22] Hegel's reaction became a common one, but it did serious injustice to the deeply communal orientation of the "symphilosophizing" Early Romantics.[23] It ignored their ethical commitment to the underlying ideals of Kant's system and the French Revolution as well as their openness to forms of cosmopolitan religiosity that go beyond dogmatism and superstition.

Fortunately, Kierkegaard's philosophy contained a critique of aestheticism that can be formulated in terms that are independent of Hegelian interpretive presumptions. Kierkegaard's basic point was that *if* one defines the aesthetic life in terms of mere individual satisfaction, then—no matter how true it is that some degree of satisfaction of that form remains essential to everyone—such a life, for any impartial judge, is much inferior to ones that recognize that there is much more to value than what is self-centered. Insofar as—but only insofar as—an

---

[19] The phenomenon of the interesting anticipated the "shock of the new," which eventually came to dominate modern art in place of the beautiful or sublime. See Karsten Harries, *The Meaning of Modern Art* (Evanston, IL: Northwestern University Press, 1968). Mann's critique of this trend in the period of Late Romanticism was expressed by a rejection of what he called the "irresponsibility of aesthetic gesture" (R 287, 450; cf. N 22).

[20] See, e.g., Richard Moran's discussion of grief in "Swann's Medical Philosophy," in *Proust's in Search of Lost Time: Philosophical Perspectives*, ed. Katherine Elkins (Oxford: Oxford University Press, 2023), 124–54.

[21] See Kierkegaard, *Concept of Irony*, and Hegel's critique of Schlegel in the section, "The Good and Conscience," in *Elements of the Philosophy of Right* (1817), §§ 140, 164. Hegel often repeated the main ideas of his critique, e.g., in his *Lectures on Fine Art* and *Lectures on the History of Philosophy*. Schleiermacher, a theologian, defended Schlegel's novel, *Lucinde* (1799), which was the work that caused most offense.

[22] Ironically, Schlegel had the last laugh, in a sense, when Kierkegaard's fiancé eventually married someone with the name "Johan Frederik Schlegel." Lukács discussed Kierkegaard, his fiancé, and the philosophy of Friedrich Schlegel, in *Soul & Form* [1907], trans. Anna Bostock, ed. John T. Saunders and Katie Terezakis (New York: Columbia University Press, 2010), 41–58.

[23] See Elizabeth Millán-Zaibert, *Friedrich Schlegel and the Emergence of Romantic Philosophy* (Albany: State University of New York Press, 2007).

underlying egoism defines what Kierkegaard basically meant by an aesthetic orientation, Mann could agree with its condemnation, while at the same time generally using a nobler concept of the aesthetic in his own work. In his enthusiasm at that time for German art (especially music and literature), Mann believed that the Reich was far above the "materialistic" business interests that he believed totally dominated the democracies of England and France. He even claimed (like many chauvinists then) that they deserved to be dismissed as not having a "culture" (R 206, 283, 299) but only a selfish "civilization," typical of "insipidly humane, trivially depraved, femininely elegant Europe" (R 53). Later though, especially when writing *Doctor Faustus*, Mann came to appreciate that Kierkegaard's worry about a connection between evil and a preoccupation with the aesthetic was in fact highly relevant, especially in the context of late modern German culture— and in this roundabout way he was also coming back to the true meaning of *Kant's* turn to practical reason.

7.5 Kierkegaard and the Aesthetic

Because Kierkegaard was so dramatic, especially in his masterpiece *Either/Or*, in depicting the varied charms of the aesthetic life, some of his readers have believed that he meant the contrast of the aesthetic and the ethical to amount to a stalemate, such that all an agent can do is take an irrational step beyond both and arbitrarily opt for a preference of one over the other. This interpretive reaction fits not only Hegel's dismissive picture of Romanticism but also the common suspicion that Kierkegaard's philosophy *in general* amounts to a kind of dangerous irrationalism. Fortunately, there is considerable evidence that this is a misreading, although it is true that, *if* one has nothing more to consider than either the mere aesthetic or ethical attitude as Kierkegaard's text at first described them, then it might understandably seem as if there is an impasse here that is without any rational solution.[24] To be taken in by this appearance, however, is to miss the larger point that Kierkegaard was operating all along, as one of his book's subtitles indicates, with a broad and "dialectical" conception of human beings, one that involves even more than general talk of traditional "aesthetic" or "ethical" options alone can reveal.

As works such as *Sickness unto Death* eventually made clear, Kierkegaard took it for granted that human nature has a complex, multilayered form, with a dynamic unity underlying the fact that, in various degrees, we are oriented in part

---

[24] Note that Kierkegaard gave his book the subtitle: *A Fragment of a Life*. See John J. Davenport, *Narrative Identity and Autonomy: from Frankfurt and MacIntyre to Kierkegaard* (New York and Abingdon: Taylor and Francis, 2012).

166   KANTIAN DIGNITY AND ITS DIFFICULTIES

to what is individual and in part toward what he often referred to simply as "the universal." This point is a commonplace, but it has several implications in Kierkegaard's story of stages on life's way. What it implies is that, as long as human beings avoid becoming crazy, they can and should recognize that, while they have many values that concern private and individual matters, they *inevitably* have others that concern public and "universal," that is, common, matters. (Kierkegaard, like Hegel, made use of the connection in Germanic languages—which is often lost is translation—between *gemein* (common), *Gemeinschaft* (community), and *allgemein* (universal)). Hence, even the aesthete, as an *entire person*, can be presumed not to be able to completely ignore that there is a universal side to its own existence that it would be inconsistent folly, as well as immoral, to deny altogether. This is a point that is highly relevant to understanding much of Mann's fiction, as well as, for example, Sartre's notion of bad faith.

Kierkegaard was well aware that, despite its fascinating appeal, there are deep problems with an aesthetic life. He stressed the obvious fact that, unlike ethical heroes, individuals trying to be *merely* aesthetic heroes must eventually realize that, in putting themselves absolutely first, they would eventually run into conflict with the much more powerful forces of the rest of the world. Therefore, any particular aesthetic success, even as a Caesar or Don Giovanni, is chancy and temporary at best.[25] Moreover, the problem here is not just that even aesthetic heroes cannot avoid the fact that others on the whole have much more power. As motivated agents, anyone opting for an aesthetic life should be able to recognize that their own life would suffer from emptiness if they really believed that all that is outside their own projects has no more value than what is bestowed on it from an individual perspective.[26] The more general point here is that, even though Kierkegaard ultimately endorsed, as a postulate-like "life-necessity,"[27] the move to a "leap of faith," he also made it clear that faith is still compatible with recognizing significant distinctions between all the lower stages of life orientation, distinctions that can be used in rational evaluations that accept external values and make no appeal to controversial religious beliefs. Thus, the ethical is *evidently* higher than the aesthetic, and what Kierkegaard called the stage of *infinite* resignation (a kind of reflectively unified and resilient monkishness) is presented as a last stage before faith that is *evidently* higher than even the ethical stage of tragic heroism (which dramatically exhibits something more fundamental than a mere empirical individual). Infinite resignation may sound negative, but it is rooted in

---

[25] See Kierkegaard, *Fear and Trembling*, "A Tribute to Abraham," 13, concerning "he who loved himself…the one who struggles with the world." See also, in *Sickness unto Death*, the discussion, throughout, of the despair of "lacking infinitude."

[26] Near the end of Part One of *Sickness unto Death*, Kierkegaard likened this to becoming a kind of "king without a country." Charles Larmore has made similar points in recent work.

[27] Kierkegaard, *Concluding Unscientific Postscript*, 179, note.

a deep, unified, and resilient self-conception, with a sense of infinite value that rises above all the still limited forms of aesthetic and social-ethical life.[28]

One reason Kierkegaard wrote as extensively as he did about aesthetic matters, despite his own reservations, is that he presumed—and, from all signs quite rightly, as Mann also believed—that, despite its limitations, the appeal of taking an aesthetic orientation as *primary* would become a growing problem, as popular versions of ethics and religion revealed their limitations. Even before Nietzsche, Mann, and MacIntyre, Kierkegaard foresaw that, in addition to the usual selfishness and short-sightedness of human beings, late modernity was increasingly marked by tendencies of disenchantment and misology. Many educated people were coming to believe both that "naturalist" considerations had shown that *any* value beyond the aesthetic—that is, any objective ethical or religious value—is mere superstition; and then also that complete adherence to science instead, or the so-called natural perspective of modern systematic philosophy as a guide to life, can also amount to its own kind of disappointing superstition. Kierkegaard, of course, was not tempted by naturalism, for he believed that, no matter what kind of completely "rational" house a modern system-builder might construct, human beings can still always get the sense that something crucial about life itself, and one's own life in particular, has been left out and has a claim that needs to be acknowledged, in however strange a form. This point was also memorably illustrated in much of Mann's fiction and, even before then, in the desperation of Fyodor Dostoevsky's characters (the depiction of which Nietzsche and Mann greatly admired). It is also relevant to Mann's later career because, despite his sympathy for deep individual feelings and the related "metaphysical" character of German culture (and it alone),[29] he eventually came to recognize that it was imperative for Germans finally to get beyond their aesthetic fascinations, and excess pride in their own culture, and accept, as fully essential, the humdrum ethical institutions of modern democracy and its core Kantian values.

7.6 Kierkegaard and "the Ethical"

The consideration that Kierkegaard had a sophisticated appreciation of the aesthetic life, but also a fairly traditional belief that its limits can be recognized without any especially controversial assumptions, let alone a leap to irrationalism, is

---

[28] Kierkegaard, *Fear and Trembling*, 39. Although the ethical stage is higher than the aesthetic even in its most advanced form, the willingness to be a tragic hero comes with a necessary connection to individual frustration. This is another reason why Kierkegaard believed it needed to be transcended by a higher stage that would *necessarily* provide some kind of satisfaction for the individual as such, as happens even in infinite resignation, and then also in full faith.

[29] Mann spoke of some kind of "metaphysical religion" as needed when politics leads to "despair" (R 269). Later, he realized that the Nazis, with their sham profundity, appealed to this need in a dangerous way when they insisted their movement had more than political aims.

168 KANTIAN DIGNITY AND ITS DIFFICULTIES

also relevant to avoiding some unnecessary mistakes in understanding his evaluation of what he treated as the significant limits of "the ethical"—at least in the quite specific sense that he tended to use the term in works such as *Fear and Trembling*. Here again there are some points that can help in properly understanding the complex attitude of Thomas Mann, who spoke for a while of being "nonpolitical" but also endorsed, even then, what were clearly all sorts of political and ethical values. There are numerous ways in which modern writers have *appeared* to be leaving value behind altogether, and yet a closer look at what most of them really meant can reveal that they were merely questioning various traditional approaches to value. For each of them there has usually been a kind of substantive ethical stance that was worth espousing.

These considerations are relevant to the somewhat complex textual analysis that is needed to explain Kierkegaard's notorious invocation of one example, the sacrifice that Abraham prepared for Isaac. Kierkegaard's discussion of this example in *Fear and Trembling: A Dialectical Lyric*, is still often taken as encouraging a relapse to a general irrationalism about value, a kind of anything goes attitude fueled by dogmatic superstition.[30] A close look at Kierkegaard's text *as a whole* shows that he was by no means trying to endorse any kind of fanaticism, and in fact he directly and effectively addressed this worry. Kierkegaard asks, "can one then speak candidly about Abraham without running the risk…"—and then he immediately explains, "it is no doubt permissible, then, to speak about Abraham." Why? Because "it is only by faith that one acquires a resemblance to Abraham, not by murder" and this faith essentially must develop through lower stages that prove a *thorough respect for rationality*, that is, for as far as it can go. Kierkegaard's account makes explicit the threefold *premise* that Abraham is to be understood as having "loved Isaac," as having been an exemplary "father," and as being "devout and God-fearing" in a unique way.[31] More generally, the point is that no one can claim to be in a position even to begin becoming a knight of *faith* who has not taken the prior steps of deep emotional, communal, and reflective maturity—in other words, the full aesthetic, ethical, and initial religious/rational stages. For Kierkegaard's readers then, the relevance of the story has nothing to do with knives but with the need to work through the first stages of life's way so as to be able, at the end, to prepare for the sacrifice of the general presumption that one must always hold on *only* to beliefs that are based on mere rationality.

The underlying aim of *Fear and Trembling* is to get the reader to consider not child sacrifice but the *general* problem of facing paradoxes in human life in the

---

[30] Similar interpretive misunderstandings have occurred in regard to other versions of existentialism—for example, in reactions to Sartre's story of the student who came to him with a question about how to act in wartime. See Karl Ameriks, "Kant, Sartre, and O'Neill: Vindicating Autonomy," in *Kant on Moral Autonomy*, ed. Oliver Sensen (Cambridge: Cambridge University Press, 2013), 53–70.

[31] See Kierkegaard, *Fear and Trembling*, "An Outpouring from the Heart," 25.

THOMAS MANN'S PATH, PART II   169

era *after* "paganism"—in other words, now that the significance of a full aware-ness of "spirit," that is, universal and absolute free choice, has become manifest. In particular, Kierkegaard presumes, like Kant, that the main problem for post-pagan life is avoiding despair and making sense of imagining possible forgiveness for *sin* as well as a future that has a real chance of moving toward the highest good, even after freely chosen evil. This is a possibility that, as even Kant argued, appears to defy *rational explanation* but points to a concern that persons cannot honestly avoid. A crucial footnote late in *Fear and Trembling* (in a typical bit of Kierkegaardian subtlety) explains the key point: "the whole work is aimed at Abraham," [but] "once sin is introduced, ethics runs aground precisely upon repentance, for repentance is the highest ethical expression but precisely as such the deepest ethical self-contradiction."[32] This does not mean that our standard ethical duties are to be considered as less than highly important. Kierkegaard's point is just the Lutheran and Kantian thought that, precisely for a conscientious agent, the problem of guilt always remains. Since no good works can by them-selves undo an agent's self-incurred evil, it appears "self-contradictory," from the standpoint of *mere reason*, to think one will be worthy of self-respect, let alone forgiven and "saved." It is simply in this sense that "ethics runs aground," and *not* that ethics altogether, as an ethics of religiously inspired love, is rejected. It is therefore not surprising that even Kant conceded, in *Religion within the Boundaries of Mere Reason*, that he could not avoid some reference to grace—although, of course, with Critical caveats about our knowing its actuality and being able to invoke it in any way *in place of* reforming ourselves. Like Kant, Kierkegaard insisted that a conversion toward morality by practical reason and one's own will first is still crucial, but this *alone*, if understood in purely secular terms, cannot ground an honest life without despair about matters overall. The project of faith and hope requires more than just appreciating the moral law.

What this shows is that the ultimate goal of the "Dialectical Lyric" was to ele-gantly construct, with Kierkegaard's typical ingenuity, a general reminder that there are deep paradoxes that must be faced even in *our* own value considerations and so, to that extent, our common situation as contemporary agents is similar—*but only in part*—to the challenge that was reserved for Abraham's unique

---

[32] Kierkegaard, *Fear and Trembling*, 86, note f. See the helpful discussion in Evans, "Introduction," vi–xxx. Kurzke, *Thomas Mann*, 548, points out that at the end Mann expressed a similar view, that nothing can remove the problem of sin, short of grace. It can be argued that naturalistic secular philosophies are in an at least as difficult a situation with regard to the future. None of them can pro-vide proof that immediate action on their directives will make matters *on the whole* better, let alone that any individual agent by itself can claim credit for improving the long run. Cf. John E. Hare, *The Moral Gap: Kantian Ethics, Human Limits, and God's Assistance* (Oxford: Clarendon Press, 1997). The long-range future all depends on what infinitely complex wave we are actually riding, and so some kind of extraordinary hope becomes relevant for every fully reflective agent. See Robert Merrihew Adams, "Moral Faith," *The Journal of Philosophy* 92 (1995), 75–95.

170 KANTIAN DIGNITY AND ITS DIFFICULTIES

situation.[33] Beyond all similarities, our *sinful* condition now makes us *unlike* Abraham's unique challenge, which did not concern the problem of facing up to prior sin. As the lengthier, but less well-known, second half of the book, the "Problemata," makes clear, the reason why Kierkegaard felt a need nonetheless to discuss Abraham so extensively is just that it gave him a chance to combat what he saw as the most dangerous *misconception* of duty in *his* era. The key point of this part of the text is that a *full identification* of highest duty with the Hegelian presumption of the demands of a particular community (which is "universal" insofar as it involves what is *allgemein* for the objective spirit of a specific group) cannot do justice to heroic religious figures who must be oriented, above all, to what is "absolute," that is, of *unconditionally* infinite value. Problem I, in the second part of Kierkegaard's book, begins by asking what follows *if* it is said that "the ethical, i.e., the ethical life [*der Saedelige*, a Danish version of Hegel's basic term, *Sittlichkeit*], is the highest." It is then immediately granted that, "If that is the case, then Hegel is right"—that is, *within* the Hegelian system, *teleological* suspension of the ethical qua apparent community good is nonsensical, since that is, by definition, the *highest* value.[34] But this fact does not entail that, in other contexts with a different conception of highest value, the *Hegelian* ethical could not be suspended, that is, teleologically trumped. In addition, as Kierkegaard pointed out with a number of examples, even the possible sacrifice of a family member, regrettable and tragic as it is, was considered ethically understandable (hence, a "teleological sacrifice") in numerous contexts in which there antecedently appeared to be a traditional overarching common good—as, for example, in a father's condemnation of his son in order for the laws of the Roman realm to be upheld.[35] The specific point that Kierkegaard was making about Abraham and

[33] An extra complication arises in Problem III, which concerns the Faustian sin that is found in conditions of asymmetry when one person introduces, in *direct* communication, considerations that can naturally raise doubts concerning paradoxical matters (e.g., of faith) which are such that it cannot be humanly expected that another person has the ability yet to know how to handle the doubts. This becomes a special problem in modern contexts, where rationality and transparency are highly valued. Hence Kierkegaard says, "Faust is too ideal a figure to be content with the nonsense that if he spoke [and tried to explain his complications] then the whole affair would come off without consequence" (*Fear and Trembling*, 97). This problem of "direct communication" has a parallel in the skeptical tendencies of philosophy in general, when specialists raise issues in ways that only tend to confuse others and can lead to misology and worse. Some philosophers have therefore preferred esoteric to exoteric expressions—and, ironically, one could argue that Hegel (albeit for different reasons than Kierkegaard's) also used this method in his discussions of religion. The answer to Problem III is therefore that in religious matters a kind of "silence"—i.e., indirect communication—*can* be warranted, especially in the complicated situations of our times.

[34] Kierkegaard, *Fear and Trembling*, "Problem I," 47. See also *Fear and Trembling*, "Preliminary Outpouring," 27, where the author's approach to faith is explicitly contrasted with "the Hegelian philosophy."

[35] See Kierkegaard, *Fear and Trembling*, "Problem I," 51. Kierkegaard means this as an example where something ethical is sacrificed but not the (Hegelian) ethical *as such*. Human sacrifice in fact continued to be practiced in some societies much later than modern readers might assume. In 1848, remarkable archaeological proof was found in Jerusalem of an ancient *pagan* leader's resort to human sacrifice, for political purposes, in a manner precisely as described in scripture but concerning an era

Isaac, however, was that "the universal" is "present in his loins,"[36] and so in *that* special case, from a simply rational perspective, the broader social good seemed just as directly endangered as the particular personal relation and its connected duties (and so *no* Hegelian "ethical" teleology can be anticipated to be satisfied).[37]

The immediate conclusion that Kierkegaard drew from all this is that there are examples in our own tradition that appear to challenge the key Hegelian presumption that the only way to understand the status of "*the* ethical" at any particular moment of choice is to say that there can be no higher *good* than the demands of a particular community as such, its "universal" *Sitten*—to use the German term that refers to "customs" as well as ethics.[38] The main point here is one that Kierkegaard went on to make most clearly in the very next section of *Fear and Trembling*, which argues that *if* there is such a thing as an "absolute" duty, then it cannot be equated with conditional duties to any *finite* community, no matter how enormous a value those duties can be acknowledged to have.[39] This is not dogmatism or fanaticism but is similar to the sensible point that Alan Donagan was making when he cited Franz Jägerstätter's firm refusal to go along with the Nazi command to recognize the *Führer* as the *absolutely* highest authority, even when practically all of Jägerstätter's Austrian community had vigorously insisted on it and his resistance would cost his own life.[40] This elementary distinction,

---

long after Abraham (2 Kings 3: 26–7). See James L. Kugel, *How to Read the Bible: A Guide to Scripture Then and Now* (New York: Free Press, 2007), 536.

[36] See Kierkegaard, *Fear and Trembling*, "A Tribute to Abraham," 16: "the promise in Abraham's seed."

[37] The hard lesson that the Abrahamic tradition drew after the "trial" was a point directly contrary to the beliefs behind what continued to be a standard practice in *other* cultures, for this tradition came to the innovative belief that the distinctive command of the one and only God is *precisely not* human sacrifice but something even more demanding: a long-term commitment to keeping faith in an eventual mind-boggling messianic fulfillment (along with, therefore, the "promise" of a bountiful following long after Isaac). A follower of Hegel's system might try to accommodate this point by explaining that what its social theory implies is not that the fulfillment of the standard norm of any traditional society is the highest after all, for that norm is just the highest for *that* age, and eventually, as with the disappearance of the sacrificial norms of ancient Greece as well, the dialectic of history would force into existence a new necessary norm. Kierkegaard does not consider this complication in detail, but it appears to be what he had in mind in rejecting attempts to explain situations such as Abraham's in terms of "the outcome" (*Fear and Trembling*, "Problem I," 55). Kierkegaard's point was that each of us has to live life "forwards," and we cannot pretend to escape existential stress by pretending to know the dialectic of history ahead of time.

[38] All this reflects Kierkegaard's presumptions about the Hegelian view. A defender of Hegel could argue, of course, that Hegel's philosophy has resources for a truly universal ethics, including principles that Kant also holds—but this would still leave a distinction between all merely rational philosophy and Kierkegaard's view.

[39] On "absolute duty," see Kierkegaard, *Fear and Trembling*, "Problem II," 59. *Given* the perspective of faith, Problems I (regarding teleological suspension) and II (regarding absolute duty) thus also have positive answers, like Problem III, for our situation as well as Abraham's. These answers are all presented not dogmatically but in a hypothetical manner, that is, as appropriate responses *if* someone is committed to the distinctive claims of traditional faith.

[40] See Alan Donagan, *The Theory of Morality* (Chicago: Chicago University Press, 1977), 15–17; and also Terence Malick's film, *A Hidden Life*, 2019.

172   KANTIAN DIGNITY AND ITS DIFFICULTIES

between duty as such and duty to one community, should not be difficult to appreciate philosophically, but its neglect was central to the tragic mistakes made when the supposedly most sophisticated citizens of Wilhelmine Germany, *including Mann*, believed they had perceived what Kant really meant, and they made their fateful chauvinistic decisions about what counts above all as duty (just as when, in the United States, self-proclaimed "Christian nationalists" have falsely assumed they understand what genuine duties are attached to those terms individually).[41]

7.7 Nietzsche

Kierkegaard's extensive treatment of the attractions of the aesthetic life anticipated the special significance granted to the broad realm of the aesthetic throughout the latter half of nineteenth-century Europe and beyond. Even though they were not advocates of art for art's sake, Schopenhauer, Wagner, and Nietzsche all gave the aesthetic life a new kind of elevated philosophical popularity and value. Nietzsche totally, rather than only partially, reversed the traditional ascending order: aesthetic, ethical, religious. He regarded the aesthetic option as the first stage normatively as well as historically, and he treated the others in their traditional forms as examples of increasing disvalue. He defined the aesthetic attitude, however, not in Kant's, Hegel's, or Kierkegaard's terms, but in a manner that transcended the traditional distinction between egoism and altruism. For Nietzsche, a proper aesthetic life and culture requires a balancing of rational-individual (Apolline) and affective-universal (Dionysian) concerns. This ideally culminates in a skilled celebrative affirmation, by creators and audience alike, and for the sake of *society as a whole*, of humanity's tragic status in the overall life-enhancing patterns of nature, along with a denial of the traditional independent powers ascribed to individual rational souls. In the aftermath of the Franco-Prussian war in 1870, Nietzsche and Wagner connected this *amor fati* view with a strong belief that its acceptance, when connected with events such as Wagnerian festivals (which, in their popularity and epoch-changing character in some circles, were similar to the festivals and widespread revolts of the late 1960s), could bring about a revolutionary ethical-cultural revitalization of Europe, an advance that would be the opposite of imperialist militarism. Hence, like Kierkegaard, even Nietzsche

---

[41] This totally community-oriented attitude is not limited to Fascism. In a typical ancient reaction to Christianity, the second-century Greek philosopher Celsus argued that religion is crucial as long as it simply reinforces a *particular* community's ancient traditions, but the new Christian attitude is a dangerous superstition because it makes people ultimately committed to something that transcends any particular local community. See Robert Wilken, "Celsus: A Conservative Intellectual," in *The Christians as the Romans Saw Them* (New Haven, CT: Yale University Press, 1984), 94–125.

never meant to suspend the ethical, that is, goodness, "altogether"; he simply had objections to taking *standard* conceptions of "the ethical" to be ultimate.

It is highly significant that Nietzsche's general procedure against the ethical views of his philosophical predecessors did not take the form of extended argument or conceptual analysis but was mostly a psycho-historical sketch expressed in a lively literary and *mocking* manner. This may have been simply the best strategy he was capable of, but it proved to be effective, indeed much more effective than the tangled debates that continued to mark the disharmony of academic authors. About the closest that Nietzsche came to a direct philosophical consideration, in his publications,[42] of Kant's ethical system appeared in the 1886 Preface that he added to a new edition of *Daybreak*. While the book itself considers morality primarily as a naturally conditioned manifestation of custom, the new Preface (§ 3) notes that Kant had offered an alternative, an embedding of ethics in a "critique of reason as a whole." At times it appears as if Nietzsche misunderstood this alternative, however, in the same way that Hegel and others had, and proceeded as if Kant had put into doubt the status of reason *in general*.[43] Such a strategy, of course, would have immediately undermined Kant's whole project, since the very tool that he would be relying on would itself be considered untrustworthy from the start. Kant indicated, however, in the very first sentence of the *Critique of Pure Reason* (A vii), that he was raising questions only "in one species" of reason's activities, and this turned out to basically concern just the problems that arise with the traditional aim of *demonstrating determinative theoretical* truths that transcend the realm of spatiotemporal experience.[44]

There was, in any case, a more relevant point that Nietzsche raised, namely, that the ultimate aim of Kant's Critical work was to provide a kind of "ground" for his practical philosophy. This part of Kant's system had been inspired, as Nietzsche

---

[42] Elsewhere, especially in private notes, Nietzsche challenged not only Kant but also the general rationalist tendency to claim certain and systematic knowledge of the mind—an issue that is too complex to explore here. No doubt Kant was often guilty of making overly dogmatic statements about theoretical reason's capacities for certain self-examination, but these claims contrast with his own path-breaking critiques of many traditional claims of self-knowledge, and they do not seem essential to his basic arguments. See Karl Ameriks, *Kant's Theory of Mind: An Analysis of the 'Paralogisms of Pure Reason'* (Oxford: Clarendon Press, 1982; expanded edn 2000).

[43] See the beginning of Hegel's "Introduction" in the *Phenomenology of Spirit*, and the critique in Karl Ameriks, *Kant and the Fate of Autonomy: Problems in the Appropriation of the Critical Philosophy* (Cambridge: Cambridge University Press, 2000), 287–94.

[44] Insofar as Kant concerned himself with a critique of reason "as a whole," this can be understood as involving, in part, "critique" simply as a matter of discrimination. This requires distinguishing the pure *theoretical* use of reason, which does, allegedly, face some genuine antinomies (but only when making *absolute* claims about spatiotemporal items), and the *pure* practical use of reason, which is *not* taken to have such acute problems—even though the philosophical overvaluation of *non-pure* uses of practical rationality can create difficulties, and was therefore made the focus of a second *Critique* in 1788. Misunderstandings of Kant's project are understandable because, in his haste to complete his massive work, he gave his first two *Critiques* misleading titles. He originally thought he could combine both projects within one book and, at first, he did not even anticipate that he would decide to write a *Groundwork of the Metaphysics of Morals* in 1785 as well as a third *Critique* in 1790.

174 KANTIAN DIGNITY AND ITS DIFFICULTIES

put it, by "the moral tarantula, Rousseau" (cf. R 11 and 21), and its "ground" seemed to require positing what Nietzsche called a "logical Beyond" (*Daybreak* § 3). It is not clear whether here Nietzsche was again committing the mistake (suggested by Reinhold and Hegel) of supposing that Kant's system required something beyond logic and reason *altogether*—which is false—or his philosophical point was simply that, as a necessary condition for its not being given up, Kant's pure ethics requires a *theoretical* argument showing that there really can be some relevant *non-spatiotemporal truths* beyond what we can theoretically determine. If this point was Nietzsche's basic worry, then he has had plenty of company. Here it is important, however, to distinguish: (1) the positive and difficult project of defending Kant's *own idealist arguments* for our not dismissing the *metaphysical possibility* of the specific nonspatial theoretical truths that he believed ethics requires—notably the existence of *absolute* freedom and dignity in human choice; and (2) the apologetic and modest project of focusing on the notion that an ethics with a *content* sharing Kant's basic principles can be regarded as attractive and innocent until proven not possibly true. The latter project would involve an argument that *necessary* ethical obligations, such as those involved in Kant's principles, have a kind of obvious normative force that sets them apart from scientific explanations, and that they can still be quite rational to accept as a "fact of reason" that "healthy understanding" always already affirms—as long as opponents have not established (and it appears that no one has yet) a closure argument proving that what we now *know* in our theoretical disciplines clearly excludes such principles.[45]

These basic philosophical issues are quite complicated and Thomas Mann showed no more interest in pursuing them at length than did Nietzsche. Mann was instead fascinated by Nietzsche's early Wagnerian work, *The Birth of Tragedy*, and its positive aesthetic conception of humanity's vocation, which he understood as involving a notion of "metaphysical supraindividuality" (R 172).[46] Mann accepted this notion, but his own view of the relation of art and life was somewhat more tragic than Nietzsche's, since he shared some ideas that are closer to Schopenhauer's resigned attitude. Mann did not advocate total resignation, but he was receptive to non-optimistic[47] aspects of Schopenhauer's basic doctrine that almost all that human beings can do is inevitably and painfully determined by the will, which is ultimately nonrational (R 165). Against Hegelians and others, Mann

[45] See Karl Ameriks, "Is Practical Justification in Kant Ultimately Dogmatic?", in *Kant on Practical Justification*, ed. Sorin Baiasu and Mark Timmons (Oxford: Oxford University Press, 2013), 153–75.

[46] Note that, at the very beginning of *The Birth of Tragedy* § 1, Nietzsche presented his leading idea as something to be obtained by "intuition" (*Anschauung*), not demonstration.

[47] The term "non-optimistic" rather than "pessimistic" is used here in order to avoid the fatalist implications often attached to Schopenhauer's view. See Ulrich Pothast, *The Metaphysical Vision: Arthur Schopenhauer's Philosophy of Art and Life and Samuel Beckett's Own Way to Make Use of it* (New York: Peter Lang, 2008). Mann respected what he called the "despair" of genuine "religious" views, which he found expressed in the writings of Dostoevsky (R 430).

always contended that human life does not *fundamentally* progress and, at first, he stressed that the best that can be done is to *temporarily resist* the liberal projects of the age (R 55, 205, 484). His "conservative revolution" was neither a revolution (although he said "militarism" was one way to "delay" democracy, R 205) nor a belief in some kind of reactionary restoration, but largely just an attempt to share vivid expressions of the full complexity of the human condition and, in so doing, to at least spread empathy with humanity's inevitable episodes of decline, disease, and suffering.

Born in 1875, Mann believed that the late nineteenth century was the beginning of an era of accelerating decadence (R 487) and that its so-called "progressive" movements would only lead, like the French Revolution, to anarchy (R 102, 211) and, possibly, a broad sense of alienation tending toward nihilism. Nietzsche had similar worries, but he went on to encourage the notion of developing the attitude of a positive *Übermensch* with a radically post-traditional perspective that can somehow still inspire better future generations. Mann, however, stayed resigned, in the first half of his career, to the task of just accurately displaying, with "lively ambiguity" (R 188), the tensions of the time, and thereby encouraging people to be tolerant and content with the fact (which Nietzsche and others had stressed) that human beings are a frequently frustrated but fascinating combination of opposed tendencies.

7.8 Mann and Nietzsche contra Schopenhauer

Despite this quasi-Schopenhauerian tendency, Mann agreed with some major modifications that characterized Nietzsche's reaction to Schopenhauer and Wagner. To understand this reaction in its full context, it helps to keep in mind how *they* understood Schopenhauer's main doctrines. They believed Schopenhauer's philosophy implied four main points: that human life is a complex of the contrasting tendencies of the (non-rational) supraindividual will to live and the (rational) individual-oriented power of representation; that, directly and indirectly, the will inevitably dominates all representation and individuation; that this duality of faculties parallels the duality of the musical and non-musical arts and therefore these have a "metaphysical," that is, universal and philosophical significance; and that humanity's mistaken focus on concrete individuality should be countered by a disinterested focus on ideal forms and values in art, and then practices of justice, compassion (R 17), and altruism. Ultimately, Schopenhauer endorsed an attitude of radical renunciation (*Entsagung*), which is somewhat like Kierkegaard's notion of infinite resignation but is oriented toward escaping from, rather than protecting, the individual self as such. Schopenhauerian renunciation aims at a cessation of individuality altogether, so that the errors and suffering that commonly attach to a focus on one's own life as an individual with ceaseless

176   KANTIAN DIGNITY AND ITS DIFFICULTIES

desires can at least be terminated—an idea that soon appeared eerily connected with a wave of suicides in highly educated families such as Mann's and Wittgenstein's.

At least in his early work, Nietzsche seemed very attracted to non-metaphysical versions of the first parts of the Schopenhauerian framework (as just defined), but he never accepted the view that resignation is a proper ideal. Mann agreed with Nietzsche on this point and, despite his general anti-optimism, he stressed that writers could still do a lot to prevent the spread of *unnecessary* diseases of the spirit—and that this was much more helpful than Christian campaigns of "social religion."[48] For Nietzsche, our will (nature) is not an at best zero-sum ("Darwinian") faculty concerned simply with sustaining the life of a species. On the contrary, it is a positive will that aims at qualitatively enhancing life and not merely serving lack-based desires. The will's expansion serves the aesthetic function of generating all kinds of developments that can make life *on the whole* more complex and fascinating, even though it has no *independent* ethical or religious value. Furthermore, inspired by the examples of ancient drama and German opera, Nietzsche, like Mann, stressed that the powers of will and representation (insofar as representation gives the temporarily satisfying illusion that individuality is independent of the will) need not be thought of as simply opposed but can be *combined* in ways that enhance each other and our appreciation of existence in general.

Here it is crucial to keep in mind that, although Nietzsche continued to use will as his prime notion, the concept had a variety of meanings for him. Most of these meanings are the opposite of how the term "will" has been understood throughout our mainline traditions as well as by many of his contemporary fans who reject those traditions. In affirming will, Nietzsche meant power in a sense modeled on displays of outstanding talent, but he *denied* absolute freedom of choice, determination by mere individual consciousness, and control by unconditional rational motives (all of which he regarded as no loss, since they are not essential to talent)—hence the fascination with Wagnerian notions such as the *Liebestod*. Yet Nietzsche also had strong positive commitments. These commitments were behind his attacks on irrationalism, militarism, anarchism, and any dismissal of all value, for overall he had a high regard for the powers of intellect and acts of "free-spirited" creativity (which is *not* literal, absolutely free causation) *insofar as* they create additional aesthetic meaning and variety in life in general. Nonetheless, belief in familiar basic values such as mere pleasure, peace, equality,

---

[48] Hermann Kurzke, *Thomas Mann: Life as a Work of Art*, trans. Leslie Willson (Princeton: Princeton University Press, 2002), 244. This may have been meant as a critique of the attitude of figures such as the leading liberal scholar, Ernst Troeltsch. In later life, however, Mann became surprisingly active at the First Unitarian Church of Los Angeles, which was an ally in his struggles against McCarthyism. See Heinrich Dietering, *Thomas Manns amerikanische Religion* (Frankfurt: Fischer, 2012).

free choice, pity, and distributive or retributive justice was dismissed by Nietzsche—and for the most part in Mann's *Reflections* as well—as unrealistic at best, and as tending toward shallowness, disenchantment, and nihilism.

When Nietzsche spoke of going "beyond good and evil" (in *On the Genealogy of Morals: A Polemic*, as well as in the title of a prior book) he simply meant rejecting the traditional "priestly" concept of "evil" as *freely* chosen immorality, and he was only dismissing the notion of "good" that is *defined* as the opposite of "evil" in that sense. This still left countless matters that Nietzsche regarded as correct for us to evaluate as good or bad in a broadly natural way and so, in this sense, he too never rejected the ethical *altogether*. The structure of his *Genealogy*, like that of Schopenhauer's work in general, mirrors, by a striking coincidence, the Kierkegaardian order: aesthetic, ethical, religious—but this time understood basically as involving a *decline* in value. This structure also mirrors the three-part order of *The Birth of Tragedy* (aesthetic birth, ethical-religious death, possible rebirth) except that the *Genealogy* (1887), unlike *The Birth of Tragedy*, does not contain a concluding positive section because that was already addressed in *Beyond Good and Evil: Prelude to a Philosophy of the Future* (1886). As with the other philosophers of the era, Nietzsche's preference for one "vocation" over another, in this case of the aesthetic over traditional ethical or religious options, did not mean that the other options were totally rejected; it just meant that their positive meanings had to be redefined in terms in line with the favored option.

In Schopenhauer's system there are metaphysical and ascetic versions of these three attitudes that are presented as laudable and *ascending* attempts (as long as religion is given something like a Buddhist rather than a theist meaning) to minimize the domination of the will. For Nietzsche, in contrast, any Schopenhauerian ethics of sympathy or quasi-religion of renunciation is a *condemnable* way of trying, improperly, to diminish the will. After having contrasted the positive aesthetic attitudes of the powerful and talented (for example, in practices such as magnanimous justice) with the negative ethical practices of "slave morality," Nietzsche devoted the third and final section of his *Genealogy* to giving, like Schopenhauer, special attention to the ascetic attitude—but this time in a highly critical way. Here Nietzsche spoke of an ascetic attitude that can be found even in art, but only in decadent forms where there is a reversion to honoring "priestly" ideas (in reconceived form, as in Wagner's *Parsifal*). Nietzsche then identified the primary modern forms of asceticism as the overly restrictive practices of scientism, rationalist philosophy, and moralistic religion. He condemned all of these for eventually leading to disenchantment and for failing to appreciate the value that is present in natural life, especially in non-decadent aesthetic variations that serve the achievement of what he called "unity in multiplicity."[49]

---

[49] Nietzsche, *Beyond Good and Evil* § 212. Nietzsche was thus a true friend of diversity and even a kind of cosmopolitanism, but this was not the same thing as endorsing the relatively liberal governments of modernity.

178 KANTIAN DIGNITY AND ITS DIFFICULTIES

7.9 Mann and Nietzsche's "Double Optic"

This overview of Schopenhauerian-Wagnerian-Nietzschean ideas has been necessary because, when Mann called these figures the "triple star" (R 58, 263) constellation that determined many of his early personal interests, he had to overcome the fact that their ideas were often misinterpreted, by alleged friends as well as foes. Despite the non-optimistic Schopenhauerian reservations discussed earlier, Mann still sided with Nietzsche's rejection of the life-denying attitude that he felt contaminated Schopenhauer's work and eventually Wagner's as well.[50] Nonetheless, both Mann (R 186) and Nietzsche could allow that, depending on context, an otherwise merely superstitious or unfortunate idea, such as "evil," extreme rationalism, or other forms of asceticism, could at times enrich society with the value of a new way of being different, as when Socrates *first* came on the scene. Mann agreed with Nietzsche's tendency to stress not so much the opposition of human powers of will and representation as the fact that, properly developed, the difference of these powers and their eventual *interaction* can lead to *positive* phenomena. This view of value resembles ideas found not only in the Romantics but also the liberal tradition, as in aspects of J. S. Mill's outlook after his reading of Coleridge.

In line with what he called Nietzsche's "double optic," or "stereoscopic vision," which he interpreted as encouraging due weight to both the "artistic and the burgherly" (R 89), Mann stressed that art and intellect are both needed (R 473), and therefore mere aestheticism is to be rejected just as strongly as mere intellectualism. Mann was fascinated (R 73–4) by how there is a constant will/representation tension within each individual (hence his novella *Tonio Kröger*, which, in his own view, best expressed Mann's own mixed parentage, a combination of Germanic and Latin roots, since his mother came from Brazil), as well as a contrast between some human beings and others who are much more aesthetic and creative, or more conformist, in a social or intellectual sense. Similarly, Mann focused, sometimes with unprecedented clinical attention, on the stimulating connection between growing and decaying tendencies within the minds and bodies of individuals[51] as well as within society as a whole. He clearly believed, like Nietzsche had, that even decadent factors can be crucial in generating *some* highly valuable effects, especially in works of genius.[52] We all have "ambiguous" (or, in the term from Novalis that Mann favored, "androgynous") characters, and the task of Mann's ironic work was, above all, to display this "lively ambiguity" (R 188). The term "lively" is crucial, for Mann took himself to be not merely documenting the familiar fact of the dual nature of human beings, but to be doing so in an

---

[50] See Bishop, "Mann's World," 31.
[51] In this regard, Mann's late novella, *The Black Swan* (1953), outdoes *Death in Venice* (1912).
[52] Kurzke, *Thomas Mann*, 460.

aesthetically influential, and ultimately life-enhancing and ethically valuable way, so that all kinds of readers could recognize, be reconciled with, and perhaps even come to further develop, each in their own manner, both of the ineliminable and contrasting sides of their nature.

7.10 Penultimate Overview

Despite his significant missteps, Thomas Mann can be credited with having eventually worked out, in his philosophical reactions, an impressive position that built on what was positively innovative in the work of his predecessors while eventually avoiding most of what was negative in it.

From the tradition of the *Early Romantics*, Mann learned, in later life, that writers can become properly influential exemplars when they combine their aesthetic talents with a progressive agenda and—unlike these Romantics—he fortunately managed to persevere so that his best insights could maintain an impact throughout a long career.

From the school of *Hegel*, Mann learned that even an artist's distinctive projects need to give full weight to modern politics and yet—unlike Hegel—he never fell prey to suggesting that a rationalist or optimistic system (even one that attends to the dialectic of modernity) can do full justice to life's basic difficulties.

From *Kierkegaard*, Mann gained essential insights, toward the end of his career, into how to portray the dangers inherent in the aesthetic perspective and—unlike Kierkegaard—he did so without channeling his writing in ways that might ultimately appeal only to those with a specific religious sensibility.

From *Schopenhauer*, Mann learned how deeply suffering and the absence of fundamental progress are essential features of human life even while—unlike Schopenhauer—he understood how not to let this fact encourage a thoroughgoing pessimism.

In *Nietzsche's* writings, Mann found an admirable concern with "an art for high and low" and "against the cleavage between educated and uneducated" (N 26) even while—unlike Nietzsche—he eventually recognized that this orientation needs to be monitored by respect for Kant's principles in their full democratic significance. The explanation of Mann's turn, eventually, to a proper appreciation of Kant and dignity will therefore be the topic of the next chapter.

If one looks back on Mann's entire philosophical trajectory one can see that it exhibits the pattern of one of Nietzsche's favorite thoughts, namely, that all great things perish of their own accord (see, for example, the account of the "suicide" of ancient tragedy in *The Birth of Tragedy* § 11, and *Genealogy*, Third Essay § 27). Ironically, in the context of Mann's thought, what ultimately perishes of its own accord is the influence of the whole sequence of post-Kantian thought, culminating in Nietzsche's extreme overvaluation of an aesthetic orientation—an overvaluation that Hegel and Kierkegaard had already warned of, even though they also fell prey, each in their own way, to an overemphasis on other candidates for humanity's main vocation. In the end, Mann's deep immersion in nineteenth-century German philosophy led him back, in a chastened but all the better educated manner, to the twin pillars at the very start of the century whose towering strength he had vaguely sensed in the first half of his career. Unfortunately, as the next chapter will explain, it was only the shock of tragic events within his own country that finally led him to reconsider the relevance of the expressive strategies of the Early Romantics and their connection to the genuine meaning of Kantian dignity. The end result was a new cosmopolitan orientation and lifework that finally did justice to the special merits of the ideas of his most valuable predecessors.

Kantian Dignity and its Difficulties. Karl Ameriks, Oxford University Press. © Karl Ameriks 2024.
DOI: 10.1093/9780198917656.003.0008

8

Thomas Mann's Path, Part III: Back to the Early Romantics and Kantian Dignity

> And, topping democracy, this most alluring record, that it alone can bind, and ever seeks to bind, all nations, all men, of however various and distant lands, into a brotherhood, a family. It is the old, yet ever-modern dream of earth, out of her eldest and her youngest, her fond philosophers and poets. Not that half only, individualism, which isolates. There is another half, which is adhesiveness or love, that fuses, ties and aggregates, making the races comrades, and fraternizing all.[1]

> For me this work is truly a God-given gift, since I can see clearly that what Whitman refers to as democracy is nothing other than what we, in a more old-fashioned manner, refer to as humanity.[2]

This chapter documents in detail two phases in Thomas Mann's thinking about dignity and duty. In its first phase, Mann's thinking was expressed in chauvinist terms that claimed that Germany's autocratic Reich and World War I position had a basis in Kant's philosophy. In 1922, however, political chaos led Mann to defend the new German republic. His defense invoked a genuinely Kantian notion of dignity and duty while appealing to the writings of Novalis as well as Walt Whitman and the example of the United States. This appeal has perplexed scholars, but the chapter argues that Mann's position is an appropriate expression of his enlightened philosophical trajectory. In conclusion, the chapter notes that, despite Mann's significant work in behalf of democracy and the fight against Fascism, there remained ambiguities in Mann's attitude, and his excessive admiration for Nietzsche's style of writing illustrates a serious general weakness in post-Kantian culture.

8.1 Duty: The Early View

Now that the relevant general background has been filled out, it is possible to compare in detail Mann's fascination with nineteenth-century German thought

---

[1] Walt Whitman, *Democratic Vistas* [1871], in *The Works of Walt Whitman*, vol. 2, ed. Malcolm Cowley (New York: Minerva Press, 1969), 223. Whitman adds: "Finally, at the core of democracy is the religious element."

[2] Thomas Mann in an open letter to Hans Reisinger, *Frankfurter Zeitung*, April 16, 1922.

182 KANTIAN DIGNITY AND ITS DIFFICULTIES

and his understanding of its main predecessor, Kant. Mann always accepted Goethe's judgment that Kant was the leading thinker of the modern era, someone whose outlook was by no means surpassed by later Idealists (R 143). Given this fact, it is remarkable that there are two central concepts in Kant's philosophy— duty and dignity—that Mann emphasized from the start but *at first* seriously misunderstood. Versions of these concepts had been of great importance for a long time, but in Kant's ethics they took on a distinctively universal meaning, one that eventually had a global impact, even determining United Nations declarations and numerous constitutions in the twentieth century. In this context it is shocking to see how simple—and how common—Mann's early mistakes were. The chaos of the immediate post-World War I era, however, brought him to his senses, and more quickly than it did most of his compatriots. The development of his views remains worthy of contemporary attention, although it must also be conceded that some backsliding can be detected in Mann's attitude. For this reason, a balanced evaluation needs to be presented of what is worst as well as of what is best in Mann's early as well as late understandings of Kant's key notions.

In the Preface of his *Groundwork of the Metaphysic of Morals* (4: [490–1]), Kant began his Critical ethics by insisting on a distinction between the familiar and contingent notion of "ought" (found in custom, positive law, and Wolff's philosophy) and the strict meaning of duty that the Critical philosophy is concerned with, which involves *necessary* rights and wrongs in a sense that can be understood independently of appeal to claims of revealed religion. Mainline German figures followed Kant insofar as they continued to use the term "duty" in a secular sense to express what human beings need to obey above all. Unfortunately, with the growth of nationalist and racist movements, there were many influential writers, such as Houston Stewart Chamberlain, who had a superficial and aggressive conception of duty as a fundamental normative notion. When they took it to express what agents are most basically called to do, they defined that calling in terms of belonging to the German nation and pure race. What is most shocking philosophically is that they went so far as to try to attach prestige to their view by claiming that it expressed the essence of Kant's thought.[3]

Chamberlain's philosophical and interpretive claims are clearly and dangerously wrong, but for a long time they were accepted by much of the educated German public—and the early Thomas Mann was, in large part (although he was never an anti-Semite), no exception. When Mann invoked the notion of a

---

[3] See Chs. 3 and 4. Mann remarked, "Well, Kant has also had an effect on me, simply because I am German" (R 143), and he called Kant's 1781 *Critique of Pure Reason* "a more radical break" than the 1789 French *Declaration of the Rights of Man* (T 500). See also R 25 and 222, and Mann's later Kantian remark: "There exists a caricature of this modern anti-intellectualism which has nothing to do with democracy, but which lands us in the middle of the base demagogic world of Fascism. This is the *contempt of pure reason* [emphasis added], the denial and violation of truth in favor of power" (*The Coming Victory of Democracy*, trans. Agnes Meyer (New York: Alfred A. Knopf, 1938), 36–7).

THOMAS MANN'S PATH, PART III   183

categorical imperative, he immediately used it to commend what he called "*Kant's warlike* [emphasis added] categorical intervention against the complete liberalization of the world...in the action of Bismarckian Germany of 1914" (R 143). In his view, with this war it was "as if it had been *precisely Kant* [emphasis added] in whom the social, preserving, constructive, organizational German spirit rose up against Western nihilism" (R 143-4). Moreover, Mann was not absolutizing duty in the sense of obligation to just any kind of state, for he claimed, "Germany as a republic, as a virtue-state with a social contract, a democratic people's government...this would be a fright! And especially it would no longer be Germany...The German has been free and unequal...that is aristocratic" (R 229).[4] In other words, for Mann at that time, being a dutiful Kantian was tied to being committed to an authoritarian society such as the one led by Kaiser Wilhelm II and his government's military maneuvers.

This was a widespread position that has long perplexed American commentators. As the American scholar Jennifer Ratner-Rosenberg notes:

> The question that vexed the economist Richard T. Ely and the psychologist G. Stanley Hall was why 'a great people' had 'gone wrong'. According to Ely it was partly due to the fact that German law had 'departed from the moral principles of Kant, and become brutalized by the spreading doctrines of Nietzsche and Treitschke and Bismarck.'[5]

Mann did not share Treitschke's right-wing Hegelian form of chauvinism, but the *Reflections* repeatedly goes out of its way to defend Bismarck's expansionist policies and later German aggression. Later, in a retrospective passage in the novel *Doctor Faustus*, one of Mann's characters tries to account for the strong enthusiasm for the war of 1914 (which definitely was shared by Mann himself) in terms of a feeling that Germany now had the right to take the lead after England, France, and others had each enjoyed their century of power and glory—that is, after what Mann describes as Germany's *Eckensteherei*, its being forced to sit in a corner. In addition to falling prey to a deplorable acceptance of the politics of imperialist nations, this attitude makes the typical blunder of the time of not realizing that, ironically, Germany's obsession with trying to make a "breakthrough" to hegemony

---

[4] Mann's rejection of this kind of republic depended on linking it with a project of "totalization" (R 190) in which *all* aspects of life would be subsumed into political service guided by an extreme party. In saying, "it was tried" (R 407), Mann may have had in mind Robespierre or early communist uprisings. For a vivid account of some especially chaotic events of the era, which Mann himself lived through, see Victor Klemperer's eyewitness report, *Munich 1919: Diary of a Revolution*, trans. Jessica Spengler (Cambridge: Polity, 2017).

[5] Jennifer Ratner-Rosenberg, *American Nietzsche: A History of an Icon* (Chicago: University of Chicago Press, 2012), 140, n. 86, quotation from Richard T. Ely, *The World War and Leadership in a Democracy* (New York: Macmillan, 1918), 174.

184 KANTIAN DIGNITY AND ITS DIFFICULTIES

would only make more likely the rise of a quite different country, the United States, as the powerhouse of the new century.[6]

Despite his skepticism about Hegel's notion of progress in universal history, Mann's mistake may have been influenced, in part, by a Hegelian infection. Mann quoted and praised an analysis by György Lukács: "burgherly calling as a life form means first of all the primacy of ethics in life; that life is dominated by what is systematically and regularly repeated, by what returns in line with one's duty, by what must be done without regard to desire" (R 84).[7] To believe that this analysis truly captures ethics is to make a mistake similar to one that Kierkegaard[8] pointed out, and that analytic philosophers still have fallen into when they have assumed that there was little more to a moral "ought," in Kant's sense, than the idea of a norm defined independently of an individual's desires. Kant and Kierkegaard, each in their own way, made it clear that there are *stages* of normativity and that, although the "ethical" realm of regular communal practice and even unanimous agreement may be a step above mere individual desire,[9] this alone is not enough to give "ought" its distinctive and *unconditional moral* meaning.[10]

8.2 Duty: The Later View

Here are two highly relevant and typically colorful observations by Walt Whitman:

> But the Scotchman [Carlyle] had none of the stomachic phlegm and never-perturb'd placidity of the Königsberg sage, and did not, like the latter, understand his own limits, and stop when he got to the end of them. He clears away the jungle and poison-vines and underbrush...Kant did the like in his sphere, and it was all he profess'd to do; his labors have left the ground fully prepared ever since—and greater service was probably never perform'd by mortal man.[11]

[6] See Thomas Mann, *Doctor Faustus: The Life of the Composer Adrian Leverkühn as Told by a Friend* [1947], trans. John E. Woods (New York: Alfred A. Knopf, 1997), ch. 30.

[7] György Lukács, *Soul & Form* [1907], trans. Anna Bostock, ed. John T. Saunders and Katie Terezakis (New York: Columbia University Press, 2010), 75.

[8] This philosophical point holds even though, as a matter of interpretation, Kierkegaard, like many others in Hegel's wake, misunderstood Kant's notion of moral self-legislation as a matter of arbitrary self-imposition by a willful individual.

[9] Mann called this the "predominance of ethics over aesthetics" (R 85), but in 1918 he still had not reached a cosmopolitan and relatively pure conception of ethics.

[10] In an all too neglected comment in his 1784 essay on enlightenment, Kant argued that the validity of even a unanimous decision by a church group depends on its content being such that it does not require individuals to make vows against conscience (Auf [8: 38–9]). Similarly, the authority of the sovereign depends on what a people "could will" ([Auf [8: 40]), in the sense of being in accord with the *necessary* principles of the moral law.

[11] Whitman, "Carlyle from American Points of View [1881]," in *The Works of Walt Whitman*, vol. 2, 171. Cf. 263, n. 12.

THOMAS MANN'S PATH, PART III   185

This is the American programme, not for classes but for universal man, and is embodied in the compacts of the Declaration of Independence...[12]

Mann's turn to a genuine appreciation of Kant came by means of the impact of two unanticipated events prior to his career-changing Berlin lecture of October 15, 1922, "On the German Republic." (The occasion was a celebration of the birthday of the progressive writer Gerhart Hauptmann, who at that time was so renowned that he was seriously considered as an appropriate President for the Republic. When Mann returned to Berlin for his 1930 lecture, "An Appeal to Reason," his talk was interrupted by Nazi stormtroopers.) One event was the assassination earlier in the year of two leading German politicians, a tragedy that was a shocking reminder of the precarious status of the new Republic. The other was Mann's decision to review a new German edition of work by Walt Whitman. Whitman's longest essay is *Democratic Vistas*, an extraordinarily passionate and perceptive plea on behalf of democracy and its mutually supportive relation to what Whitman called the diversity-oriented philosophy of "personalism."

In his talk, Mann grounded his defense of the German Republic on a reference to a set of ideals that he found best expressed in Whitman's vivid formulations of universalist and democratic doctrines, that is, doctrines that Whitman knew were common to what Kant's "labors left the ground fully prepared [for] ever since." To counter the worry at the time that the formation of the German Republic was an imposition by foreign powers, Mann presented Whitman's views as similar to those of a figure that he assumed his audience would be directly familiar with and sympathetic to, namely, Novalis. Novalis was a favorite Early Romantic author of Mann's, and Mann realized that—contrary to many reactionary misinterpretations— Novalis in fact addressed political issues in his era from a universalist and broadly democratic perspective. To this day, Mann's strategy has bewildered Anglophone readers. One editor of Mann's writings describes the talk in these terms: "And so Mann launched into an unexpectedly rhapsodic celebration of democracy as *somehow* [emphasis added] consistent with the deepest German traditions, connecting, in an inspired comparison, Novalis and Walt Whitman."[13] Another scholar is similarly perplexed: "...beginning with the pro-Republic speech of 1922...he tried to reconcile past German values with the new democratic principle, invoking somewhat *incongruously* [emphasis added] the German Romantic poet and *conservative* [emphasis added] thinker Novalis alongside the American democrat Walt Whitman."[14]

---

[12] Whitman, *Democratic Vistas*, 246.

[13] Mark Lilla, "Introduction," in Thomas Mann, *Reflections of a Nonpolitical Man* [1918], ed. Mark Lilla, trans. Walter D. Morris (New York: New York Review Books, 2021), xviii.

[14] T. J. Reed, in "Mann and History," in *The Cambridge Companion to Thomas Mann*, ed. Ritchie Robertson (Cambridge: Cambridge University Press, 2002), 11. These are not the only examples of the failure, among talented scholars, to appreciate the significant Kantian link between Whitman and

186 KANTIAN DIGNITY AND ITS DIFFICULTIES

A number of important connections are totally lost sight of here. Whitman was already well known to German readers in the late nineteenth century, and Mann had expressed awareness of his influence in Germany already in 1909.[15] Just as leading nineteenth-century American writers were quite familiar with German thought,[16] their German counterparts were familiar with Whitman, albeit to a lesser extent. In addition, there is the fact that, as been noted, Mann had been an admirer of the Romantics all his career and, as recent scholarship has argued in detail, Novalis was a well-known cosmopolitan pluralist, in regard to both art and politics, with a deep grounding in Kant's philosophy.[17] Whitman similarly combined a broadly Romantic perspective with a respect for Kant as having performed the "greatest service," since he knew well that Kant was the first of the revolutionary German thinkers, the original "transcendentalist" who championed the same modern "personalist" ideas that Whitman admired as proclaimed in the founding of the United States. All these writers challenged theological dogmatism, but the fact that they spoke respectfully of some positive connections between art, society, and religion hardly made them "conservative" in an inappropriate sense or "incongruous" to connect with each other.

It was thus precisely by reaching outward to democracy and America, and simultaneously turning back to an Early Romantic writer of his own country, one who was also raised on Kant's philosophy, that Mann came to fundamentally revise his conception of duty in a truly appropriate direction. The Early Romantics, like Kierkegaard, understood well that the "calling" of a human being as such should never be defined just by the state, let alone by either mere desire or the lack of desire. Mann found the same message in Whitman's *Democratic Vistas*, a post-"War of Secession" (as Whitman, unlike others to this day, properly called it) masterpiece that makes an inspiring case for art's ethical and political power. Mann could not help but have been struck by Whitman's highly relevant

---

Novalis that Mann perceived. Mark Mazower uses a pro-democracy passage from Walt Whitman as an epigraph, but he repeats the ill-founded presumption that Novalis's work amounts to a "turn away from philosophy and the Enlightenment" (*Governing the World: The History of an Idea* (New York: Penguin Press, 2012, 19, cf. 31). For an up to date and enlightened account of Novalis, see *Novalis: Philosophical, Literary, and Poetical Writings*, ed. James D. Reid (Oxford: Oxford University Press, 2024).

[15] See Hans Rudolf Vaget, *Thomas Mann, der Amerikaner: Leben und Werk im amerikanischen Exil 1938–1952* (Frankfurt: S. Fischer, 2011), 43.

[16] Kant and the post-Kantians were first directly introduced to the Transcendentalists in Concord by Karl Follen, who had studied in Jena and was in exile because of his radical politics. He was Harvard's first German instructor and died soon thereafter in a shipwreck, but his ideas reached a wider audience when he was immortalized as the model for the old professor in Louisa May Alcott's classic, *Little Women* (1868, 1869). I am indebted to Laura Dassow Walls for referring me to her work on Follen's significance and Alcott's relation to Kant's philosophy, in "The Cosmopolitan Project of Louisa May Alcott," *ESQ: A Journal of the American Renaissance* 57 (2011), 107–32.

[17] See, most recently, the compelling argument in Jane Kneller, "Novalis: The Art of Democracy," *Symphilosophie* 5 (2023), 53–70; and cf. Matthias Löwe, "Poetische Staaten: Frühromantik und Politik," in *Romantisierung von Politik: Historische Konstellationen und Gegenwartsanalysen*, ed. Sandra Kirshbaumer and Matthias Löwe (Paderborn: Brill, 2022), 45–58.

claim—which Mann surely understood as applicable to himself as well—that, "a few first-class poets, philosophs, and authors, have substantially settled and given status to the entire religion, education, law, sociology, etc. of the hitherto civilized world."[18] Whitman argued that "two or three really original American poets," writing in praise of democracy and the common humanity of *all* citizens in all parts of the country, could play a crucial role in giving "moral identity" to the States by inspiring a post-slavery campaign to guarantee fundamental equality of treatment for everyone.[19] It is not surprising that Mann could recognize the affinity between Whitman's self-understanding and the views of Novalis, who held that "everything national...and individual...can be transformed into the canonical and universal...This individual shading of the universal *is its romantic element*" (GR 516). Contrary to misconceptions that are still common, Mann understood that Novalis's values were not reactionary but progressive and cosmopolitan and involved, as with Herder, a recognition of the contributing role of diverse cultures in the flourishing of humanity in general.

Mann's argument used as its connecting concept a notion central to the work of Kant as well as Herder:

> ...the sense of *humanitas* as an idea, a feeling, an ethical and intellectual regulating principle, an unwavering awareness that the state is only 'a particular union of a group of people within the great state that humanity makes up for itself' (to borrow yet again an appropriate phrase from the poet...). (GR 516)

Mann was quoting Novalis, but when Mann praised "the idea of community residing in the recognition of the humanity in each of its individual members" (GR 533), his statements were clearly also an endorsement of the duties entailed by Kant's Formula of Humanity. Mann now combined this point with an echo of the main idea of Kant's essay on perpetual peace: "If our national feeling is not to fall into disrepute or not to become a curse, it will have to cease being a vehicle for anything warlike...it will be ever more unconditionally understood as the object of a cult of peace" (GR 517). In a later essay, he expressed the same point by endorsing Novalis's view that

> the ideal of ethics has no more dangerous competitor than the ethics of the strongest power, of the mightiest life...which has also been called the ideal of aesthetic greatness. It is the maximum ideal of the barbarian. (N 151)

Mann explained that the catalyst for his new public expression of these ideas, and his rereading of Novalis, was the "powerful effect" of having read Whitman,

---

[18] Whitman, *Democratic Vistas*, 211.
[19] Whitman, *Democratic Vistas*, 212. Whitman regarded himself, of course, as precisely the kind of poet that was needed.

188 KANTIAN DIGNITY AND ITS DIFFICULTIES

"the thunderer from Manhattan" (GR 530), who argued that "the new frame of democracy" cannot be held together "merely by political means" but needs a "hold in men's hearts, emotions, and belief" (GR 531). Mann understood this to require, as Novalis said, a new kind of writers, namely, "democratic-republican" "preachers of patriotism" (GR 531–2). All this was just a reiteration of Kant's notion of a realm of ends, combined with a call for it to be actualized by the fundamental Early Romantic doctrine of an alliance of philosophy and poetry (the "genius" of creative writing) in a manner that Novalis, once again, expressed best:

> Just as philosophy, by means of systematic thinking and the state, strengthens the powers of the individual with the powers of humanity and the world as a totality, so poetry, with respect to life. The individual lives in the whole and the whole in the individual. (GR 535)

Because Whitman himself, like the earlier American Transcendentalists, had read about Romanticism and German philosophy with great interest, it can be said that, *by turning to Whitman, Mann was finally going back, by a roundabout route, to what his most admired German predecessors, Kant and Novalis, had really meant* in their most basic doctrines. In feeling inspired to follow Whitman in proclaiming "the unity of humanity and democracy" (GR 530), Mann was acknowledging a fundamental value that he had severely discounted in his earlier understanding of the German tradition. He was finally beginning to recognize the errors in his own chauvinist views and thereby also becoming properly Kantian himself, as well as cosmopolitan in an extra direction by abandoning his ignorant condemnation (in which he had gone along with Schopenhauer) of democratic thought elsewhere, especially in the United States (R 105). Mann came to understand that the special strength of Whitman and the Romantic writers lay in their "real popularity" of the "most humane kind" (GR 515)—in other words, in their mastery of a style with which they could express values that had strong local roots and yet were also relevant, as Novalis said, to the "intimate community of finite and infinite" aspects that all human beings share (GR 535).[20]

Mann also admired Novalis's democratic notion of the ubiquity of genius, as well as his Kantian claim that—in a rebuke to the era of Frederick II—life was "plainly better in republics" (GR 535). In Whitman, Mann came to recognize the *reality* of someone who was at once a literary innovator and a broadly influential leader within society on account of his uniquely lively writing in behalf of genuine democracy and, in particular, on behalf of his own assassinated hero, Lincoln. Whitman knew how to make clear that, for all its glaring faults, his (relatively) democratically founded and war-torn republic has a significance that goes far

---

[20] See *The Early Political Writings of the German Romantics*, ed. Frederick C. Beiser (Cambridge: Cambridge University Press, 1996).

beyond national politics and involves an epoch-grounding pledge to fulfill a universal human calling: solidarity with all others. With Whitman, Mann had found a true cross-cultural brother, someone whose moral and literary approach was allied with the ideals and practice of the enlightened German Romantics of Mann's own tradition and the core values of Kant's doctrine of duties directed toward all of humanity. Mann added that, for Germany, the Early Romantics in general created "an era whose intellectual level was the highest ever reached in this land" (GR 531). He even went so far as to connect Romanticism with Modernism in a positive, creative sense (GR 536), and he illustrated this point with reference to Mahler's cross-cultural (part Asian) and romantic/modern *Lied von der Erde* (GR 539). The "intellectual discipline" (GR 536) that Novalis and other Romantics exhibited in concretely appealing to humanity's "simple good will" (GR 534) provided the crucial *Kantian* model of the needed middle ground that Mann had been seeking between the particularities of "aesthetic isolationism" (GR 547) and the generalities of abstract thought.

For precisely this reason, Mann could finally see an essential *public as well as liberal* role for the work of skilled popular writers like himself. As Novalis had noted, in this time of late modern "flux," such writers could provide society with its needed cultural "nucleus" (GR 528), what Kant would regard as an exemplary reminder of humanity's moral "compass" (GMS [4: 404]). Little could Mann, or anyone else then, realize how relevant this Early Romantic view about the universal role of democratic writers would become when Mann eventually emigrated to the United States. Just as important as Mann's 1930s westward move was the *prior* step that made it possible and fully meaningful, namely, his 1920s decision to engage in a reconsideration of the significance of his own Romantic tradition and to reverse his earlier disdainful attitude toward the United States. He thereby corrected a significant similar mistake of Kant's as well, one that had long-lasting consequences. One cannot help but imagine that Mann and other writers might have been inclined to move in a cosmopolitan direction much earlier if only Kant had lent his prestige to making an explicit link between enlightened German thinking and the path-breaking political ideas of the founders of the United States.[21]

---

[21] Ernst Troeltsch, a prominent leader whose liberal theology was never tempting to Mann, was also a supporter of the German war effort. He rationalized it with the odd idea that the massive use of the new *Volksarmee* would force the government, after a German victory, to reward a larger portion of the nation than before with special respect. Earlier, however, Troeltsch had written, "the declaration of human rights in the American and French revolutions is thus one of the most consequential... most ethically significant deeds in recent history" (*Politische Ethik und Christentum* (Berlin: De Gruyter, 1904), 13, quoted in Norton, *The Crucible of German Democracy: Ernst Troeltsch and the First World War* (Tübingen: Mohr Siebeck, 2021), 36). After the war, Troeltsch became an important supporter of the German Republic but, like many liberals, he maintained his prejudices, e.g. about Slavs and Asians, and he lacked an appreciation of the Early Romantics.

8.3 Dignity: The Early View

Similar complexities attach to Mann's relation to Kant's fundamental notion of dignity. Because of Kant's emphasis on rationality, numerous readers have made the mistake of assuming that Kant's ethics reserves the notion for agents who lead a life of self-absorbed and hyperreflective virtue.[22] In fact, for Kant, the character of a person with good will is world-oriented and such that there is precisely no need for this kind of constant reflection about duties. Moreover, at its most fundamental level, Kant's notion of the dignity of the human person is a *status* concept, and it requires simply that one have the *common capacity* to appreciate the moral law.[23] Human dignity thus applies not only to agents who already understand moral rules and act morally but even to those who are evil or are prevented, for example, by infancy or disablement, from acting very much at all. It is morally wrong for any human being to be *merely* instrumentalized by others, and this is why we provide legal and medical aid even for people who have severe special needs or who even, by all appearances, are villains.

Mann's early elitism was similar to Nietzsche's in rejecting Kant's pure and egalitarian notion of dignity. In accord with a hierarchical meaning that was common long before Kant,[24] Mann preferred to use the term only in nonmoral/nonpolitical contexts (R 322–3), such as those involving talent ("the dignity of the artist as a private person," R 11; cf. R 189), "burgerly" work (R 307), custom (a servant's bowing down, R 401), notable accomplishments (R 22, 371, 474), and the "dignity and charm" of culture (R 204). Unsurprisingly, Mann praised the honor orientation of a "German cadet" in contrast to what he called the "lackluster" notion of "democratic human dignity" (R 399). This attitude was also expressed in his early looking down on women (R 385), Americans ("who in America would understand anything of Dostoevsky?" (R 443)),[25] and Poles (R 218), and in the disgust he felt at the very notion of respect for a beggar (R 370).

Mann's life changed irreversibly when an honorary degree was taken away from him by pressure from the Nazis in 1936, and he realized that his entire

---

[22] For a careful general criticism of this presumption, see Melissa Merritt, *Kant on Reflection and Virtue* (Cambridge: Cambridge University Press, 2018).

[23] See Ch. 1. Here again it is important to keep in mind the distinction between basic human capacities, which involve *real* potential, grounded in the distinctive features common to all creatures born as human beings, and contingent abilities, which vary considerably from individual to individual and depend on training or special gifts. Dignity specifically involves the capacity in reason for appreciating moral law, which involves more than the mere rationality that comes with understanding. Although in cases of severe defect this capacity might not in fact ever be activated, a "dis-abled" human being is still a human being, with a given structure that reflects its species nature. Even if technical measures are not yet available to reverse the disablement, if they did become available and successful, we would not say the being had changed its basic identity or species.

[24] For a concise overview of the tradition, see Michael Rosen, *Dignity: Its Meaning and History* (Cambridge, MA: Harvard University Press, 2012), ch. 1.

[25] See also Tobias Boes, *Thomas Mann's War: Literature, Politics, and the World Republic of Letters* (Ithaca, NY: Cornell University Press, 2019), 47.

artistic career as a writer in Germany was fully vulnerable to the whims of an unethical state. He became an exile and overcame his naïve presumption that the "metaphysical" value of aesthetic culture was more fundamental than the negotiations of parliaments and mere "civilization." Because of his initial focus on "greatness," he had at one time even stated that, "one should not overestimate the significance of legal order for national life" (R 223). He had also believed it showed more respect for "human dignity" than "political revolt" (R 181) for writers to help humanity by simply providing lonely balm to divided, distressed individuals. Against his brother's early anti-war activism Mann's had only a limited retort in defense of himself: "politically irresolute art that seemed to exist only for itself…can still *help* the human being to *live*" (R 259).

8.4 Dignity: The Later View

By 1922, however, the aftereffects of the war had already begun to sink in, and Mann took the lead in proclaiming: "human decency and *dignity* [emphasis added] demand that we…declare Europe a republic" (GR 518). Mann had always thought that "authority is needed to keep the great majority of human beings in moral propriety" (R 207), but it was only in the second half of his life that he began to see that skilled voices in support of democratic principles—writers who can reach the heart as well as the head—can speak with authority and provide needed direction. This belated insight allowed Mann simultaneously to affirm values from both halves of his career: as a high-profile public figure, his campaign for democracy reconfirmed his old belief in the special value of literary genius, while it also served his newfound cosmopolitan commitment to protecting the essential conditions of tolerable life for humanity in general. As with Kant and the Early Romantics, this was not aestheticism but a productive combining of aesthetic and ethical vocations.[26]

In 1939, Mann wrote a provocative essay about Hitler called "A Brother."[27] Mann's point was not that he felt especially close to Hitler but that there was something in common even in this case. Mann recognized, in the trajectory of Hitler's life (his egomaniacal aspirations as artist, architect, musical aficionado, rhetorical orchestrator), a misfit's frustrated aestheticism, one that was especially forceful because it aimed not at mere politics but the creation of a whole new culture. Mann saw that this aim had some similarity to the general overevaluation of the aesthetic realm that he was now acknowledging had been a huge mistake in

---

[26] Mann understood this attitude as also the affirmation of a kind of religion, one defined as "reverence first of all for the mystery that is man" (N 156).

[27] Mann, "Ein Bruder," *Das Neue Tagebuch* 7 (1939), 306–9; "That Man is my Brother," *Esquire* 11 (1939), 31, 132–3. See Heinrich Siefken, "Thomas Mann's Essay, 'Hitler'," *German Life and Letters* 35 (1982), 165–91.

192 KANTIAN DIGNITY AND ITS DIFFICULTIES

Germany in general. As usual, though, Mann was not explicit and just assumed that his readers would recognize that he was acknowledging a personal error. He did concede, in 1928, that he had been wrong to oppose his brother Heinrich, whom he now admired as a champion of duty in Kant's universal sense.[28] Mann's final point, however, was that taking a wrong step toward making possible the murderous path of the Germans, inside as well as outside of the country, was not a matter of social or biological necessity. It was an error that each citizen had been responsible for (and that some of even Mann's earlier work may have encouraged) and, just as that choice had been freely made, so too an alternative, the democratic path, was also open and free to be chosen for the future.

In sum, in regard to *Kant*, the good news is that Mann learned, in the second half of his life, that the concepts of duty and dignity are most important when they are given a proper democratic meaning and—unlike Kant—he learned this lesson by looking outward and far away, by immersing himself in the best aspects of American culture.[29] Overall, Mann's reactions exhibit numerous still valid insights. The most striking point in these reactions, however, is the twofold truth that, in his crucial relation to Kant, Mann showed himself at first at his worst—like all too many of his German contemporaries—and yet also, shortly afterwards, at his best—like all too few of his German contemporaries then. It is this last feature of Mann's development that remains most relevant for our own uniquely troubled era.

8.5 Some Final Concerns

Even though Mann has often been regarded as "only" a literary figure, and one without a truly avant-garde or modernist orientation, the fact is that he eventually managed to develop a position that was in many ways more philosophically sophisticated than that of most of his leading contemporaries. His work amounts to an unusually well-balanced and underappreciated reaction to the whole complex tradition of modern Germanic thought, a tradition that had led his

---

[28] See Wolf Lepenies, *The Seduction of Culture in German History* (Princeton: Princeton University Press, 2006), 33. Unfortunately, Mann made another early error: he was spectacularly wrong in claiming to be sure that a "political seducer" would never find success in Germany (R 480). Shortly before World War II, Mann's early views were dredged up in the US by several writers who thought his anti-Fascist rhetoric was still much too elitist in tone. Mann responded gracefully and confessed that in 1918 he was still in an ignorant "bourgeois-intellectual" state in regard to the relation between cultural and political freedom. See T. J. Reed, "Mann and History," 19; and Stanley Corngold, *The Mind in Exile: Thomas Mann in Princeton* (Princeton: Princeton University Press, 2022), 61–76. Corngold calls the attack on Mann "absurdly unfair" (p. 76), given the clear change Mann made in his position in 1922, and he reprints Mann's entire response, "Culture and Politics" (pp. 68–74), as it originally appeared in *Survey Graphic* 28 (1939), 149–51.

[29] When Mann left to go back to Europe until the end of his life, it was in part precisely because, in the era of McCarthyism, he was disturbed that the United States was not living up to its own values.

predecessors and contemporaries into all sorts of bad misunderstandings and dangerous positions. This is not to deny that, at a personal and methodological level, matters did not entirely change and, in the end, Mann may have remained a kind of aristocrat at heart. He never *systematically* discussed the key values of duty and dignity in their pure philosophical meaning, or went into historical detail about the mystery of these values having been so widely rejected (although his general thesis about the dangers of overemphasizing an aesthetic attitude is certainly relevant). He was often so preoccupied with a revolt against hypocritical "Victorian" morality, which mostly involved issues surrounding his special concern with erotic matters,[30] that it was only on occasion that he explicitly thematized fundamental values such as respect for persons as ends in themselves in general, and he neglected the extensive virtue teachings of traditional philosophy. Mann regularly supported Social Democrats and many radical leftists, but he never aligned himself with the few committed followers of Kant in his day, such as his fellow émigrés, Ernst Cassirer and Hannah Arendt, who understood that protecting the traditional religious and Enlightenment idea that we are all "created equal" has nothing to do with prudishness.

Perhaps Mann's most revealing statement came in a letter of 1952: "My democratic reaction is not really genuine, it is merely an irritable reaction to German 'irrationalism' and the swindle of its profundity...and to any form of Fascism."[31] Earlier, upon reflecting on his turn towards "the intellectual world of democratic idealism," he remarked, "Do I believe in it? Largely."[32] Mann would probably not be disappointed if we are left wondering whether he himself was *always* something of a "confidence man."[33] Nonetheless, whatever we feel about his *private* complexes and ironic subtleties, this should not lead anyone to deny that his public life was an example of how significant cross-cultural progress is possible.

There remains, however, a disquieting fact that should not be ignored. However much Mann improved in the substance of his later views, the broader *methodological* tendencies of his early allegiance to the "triple star" constellation of Schopenhauer–Wagner–Nietzsche should not be forgotten. Mann deserves credit for not following most of the extreme proposals of these three "stars," but for a long time he went along with the preference they made fashionable for rhetorical flourishes rather than open-minded and detailed arguments that did full justice to earlier major figures. One mistake with regard to tradition is to accede to bad positions that happen to be long established (for example, slavery), but another is

---

[30] Mann noted that the revolt "against bourgeois morality belongs to the bourgeois age itself" (N 156)—but he left unspecified what our current "age" is.

[31] Mann, to Ferdinand Leon, March 3, 1952, quoted in Bishop, "Mann's World," 36.

[32] Mann, to Rene Schickele, Nov. 27, 1937, quoted in Kurzke, *Thomas Mann*, 420.

[33] Cf. Alex Ross, "Behind the Mask: The Ironic Genius of Thomas Mann," *The New Yorker*, Jan. 24 (2022), 26–31.

to sell short the gains that can come from pausing to take an extra close look at one's supposedly out of date predecessors.

Whatever one concludes about Mann as an individual, the most disturbing fact is that his early fall for a combined aesthetic and anti-democratic orientation was not a youthful or mere individual lapse but an especially clear symptom of a bizarre *general* cultural sickness, a whole educated generation that, with its adamant support for a world war, helped to create a disaster of the first order—only to repeat the mistake even more horribly and in larger numbers in the next generation. If we look for a common factor behind these disasters, a huge role surely has to be allotted to the broad and impatient turn away from basic ethical notions such as necessary duties and universal human dignity. Traditional religions and secular liberals shared a respect for the essence of these values, even if under other names and with other commitments, and yet *all* their most basic views— along with the principles of Kant's 1795 essay, *Perpetual Peace: A Philosophical Sketch*, which provided the most significant German formulations of truly worthy modern values—were swept aside by millions of war enthusiasts, educated as well as uneducated.

After the war, Mann wrote a careful two-part analysis of Nietzsche's philosophy for the new American journal *Commentary*. It might well have been called "Brother Nietzsche" because, like his earlier essay on Hitler, it did not shrink from confessing to an attraction (which was obvious from Mann's fiction) to an extreme valorization of an aesthetic calling. In just this respect, Mann certainly resembled the two "brothers" he discussed. Fortunately, he came to appreciate the significance of differences as well. Mann had started (R 75) with the belief that what was most important was the tension between *art* and *life* (including intellect), whereas Nietzsche stressed the conflict he felt between traditional *ethics* and *life*. In the end, though, Mann rightly concluded that Nietzsche was wrong to think "moral consciousness...threatens life" (N 149; cf. R 74), for "the real opposition is between ethics and aesthetics. Not morality but beauty is bound up with death" (N 149).[34] This does not mean that an aesthetic life should be avoided, but an overemphasis on it should be recognized as potentially dangerous and in need of respect for the rational guardrails of Kantian dignity and democratic order.

The full effect of Nietzsche's provocative style, combined with the growing non-literary power of mesmerizing music and the ever growing force of controlled and popular media, has yet to be adequately measured.[35] Nietzsche's

---

[34] In the best he could do to morally defend Nietzsche, Mann pointed out that Nietzsche at times expressed not only disgust with a merely profit-driven life but also a positive concern that working-men should become treated like servicemen, that is, as "the higher caste." Mann thought that this gave Nietzsche's view a "strongly socialist coloring" (N 153). Nonetheless, this "caste" conception still ignores the moral universalism captured by the notion of human dignity.

[35] See, e.g., Jonathan Haidt, "After Babel: How Social Media Dissolved the Mortar of Society and Made America Stupid," *The Atlantic* 329/4 (2022), 54–65.

writings were often taken in even much more radical ways than had been intended, but the careful as well as the not so careful readers who accepted the core of Nietzsche's outlook all had something clearly in common, namely, a too hasty rejection of philosophical doctrines aligned with core democratic values. The most shocking fact for philosophers to consider is that this broad rejection by extremists was not based on the offering of detailed plausible arguments, proven alternatives, or relevant evidence but instead was, in large part, the effect of what MacIntyre called "solicitations of power and interest."

This is a deeply disturbing pattern, and hence any appreciation of considerable cross-cultural progress, in the striking example of Mann's later career, must in the end be balanced by recognition of significant cross-cultural regress in the widespread disrespect for democratic values in our own time. If philosophical writing at the end of the nineteenth century and into the twentieth did not succeed in preventing disaster, one wonders how it will have any better chance now—especially if new "Democracy Will Win" campaigns fail to gain adequate support.[36]

Kantian Dignity and its Difficulties. Karl Ameriks, Oxford University Press. © Karl Ameriks 2024.
DOI: 10.1093/9780198917656.003.0009

[36] This chapter is especially indebted to encouraging help from colleagues and audiences in Mugla, Turkey (via Zoom), Portland, Oregon, and Riverside, California.

Afterword

> ...I note only that when we compare the thoughts that an author expresses about a subject, in ordinary speech as well as in writings, it is not at all unusual to find that we understand him even better than he understood himself...(KrV A 314/ B 370)

Philosophers looking back at the previous chapters may feel that they amount to something more like a cabinet of curiosities than a straightforward historical account, let alone the working out of a single main line of philosophical argument. Such an effect is not entirely unintended, for it is not clear that either history or philosophy should be presented as a matter of straightforward development. Philosophy has the special problem that it has repeatedly failed to live up to ambitious claims to be able to present itself as a rigorous science. In many ways, substantive philosophy is more like art than the sciences, given its rhapsodic methods of discovery and its often highly personal mode of presentation, which, for any substantive issue, cannot resolve matters by experimental methods or fully deductive procedures.[1] Like science, however, philosophy has an argumentative core, and it develops in its own manner by a complex process of retrieval and innovation, conjecture and refutation. Yet its potential for progress has often been overestimated by even the most critical revolutionary thinkers, such as Descartes, Kant, and Husserl. Whiggish legends of the "rise of scientific philosophy" or the unquestionable forward march of the human mind since the alleged idiocies of the ancients, medievals, and early moderns are still not uncommon. Will Durant, despite his sympathies with evolution as a philosophically fruitful notion, was closer to the truth when he chose to entitle his inspiring bestseller of 1926 simply *The Story of Philosophy*. A story, like a myth, need not be

---

[1] Kant preferred to limit the notion of genius to the arts, which are developed best when innovative masters go beyond mere imitation, no matter how talented. He liked to think that philosophy, like science, could eventually proceed simply by sound steps that can be easily followed by future students. This is to overlook the fact that acts of epochal discovery and innovation, even in science and philosophy as well as art, all require a genius-like ability to leap ahead of one's age. The founder of modern history of science, William Whewell, used Kant's notion of experience-transcending Ideas to account for the revolutionary shifts that occur when a new paradigm is introduced that goes "outside the box" and takes seriously, for example, the Idea of elliptical ("eccentric paths") rather than circular motion—an Idea that Kant himself used in illustrating his philosophical conception of history (Idee [8: 18]).

fully rational and progressive in form, but it can still contain considerable important truth.[2]

In addition to the uneven record of philosophy's general history, there are, as Herder understood especially well, more differences than are generally recognized because of geographical separation and the diversity of normative perspectives that are difficult to unite in a consistent, let alone adequate, perspective.[3] It has been tempting to think that it is only an incidental fact that philosophy is done (for example) in Asia and Europe, in England and on "the continent." It is all supposedly one and the same thing, philosophy, in all these contexts, and the phrase "German philosophy" should supposedly mean not a different subject but just something that incidentally is written in German, or by and/or for Germans at first. This convenient supposition is not easy to maintain in the face of the fact (which may well be a good thing) that there still do seem to be significantly different ways in which philosophers even in the larger European countries tend to approach issues, select topics, and express themselves—despite the homogenization that is definitely taking place as more philosophers everywhere now want to get their work published primarily in major English language venues.

Nonetheless, one point of the preceding chapters, such as the one comparing Kant and Price, was to document the fact that considerable overlaps and comparable innovations in philosophic ideas, at the highest level, can occur at the same time in different countries even without any direct interaction. This might be taken as some evidence for the validity, or at least worldwide significance, of the ideas that have independently developed. But this fact can also be taken as an indication that cultures are more out of touch with one another than is generally supposed. Another point of those chapters was that even philosophers who place a special emphasis on cosmopolitan sensitivity and respecting the dignity of persons everywhere can fall prey to shortsightedness or even severe prejudice, as when Kant looked down on the skills of many nationalities and failed to even seriously explore far away, but still accessible, philosophical writings in deep accord with his own work. Even more serious than these personal weaknesses, among outstanding philosophers, is the fact that some of the most basic ideas of leading modern philosophers have fallen prey to fundamental misunderstandings. Burke's reading of Price, Chamberlain's and the early Mann's reading of Kant

---

[2] See Robert B. Pippin's insightful discussion of the phenomenon of changes in "mattering" in Western culture, a "crisis in meaning" that is "relatively independent of, deeper than, and presupposed by arguments, evidence, and so forth." He highlights the key impact that Nietzsche and Heidegger had on many readers, in expressing the weakness of standard stories of philosophical progress, and in shaping the "declensionist narratives that have so influenced the collective mood of late modernity" ("The Curious Fate of the Idea of Progress," in *Kant and the Possibility of Progress: From Modern Hopes to Postmodern Anxieties*, ed. Samuel A. Stoner and Paul T. Wilford (Philadelphia: University of Pennsylvania Press, 2021), 222 and 232).

[3] For a concise and broadly Kantian overview of this problem, see Robert Audi, *Moral Value and Human Diversity* (New York: Oxford, 2007).

on duty, like many contemporary individualistic treatments of Kantian ideas of dignity and autonomy, can all be faulted for missing, or too quickly dismissing the complex, but not at all hidden, universal and unconditional meaning of Kant's moral doctrines. This is a perplexing phenomenon, but it is perhaps no more surprising than the fact that an assembly of some of the most gifted political thinkers of the age (in Philadelphia in 1776) could sincerely announce as "self-evident" a revolutionary claim about the equality of all persons at the same time that, as they surely knew, most people in other countries were probably willing to deny that the claim was even true. These different facts can, of course, be explained, but the explanations require uncovering complicated contextual factors that have been largely overlooked.

This is all a messy story and one reason why the difficulties in properly understanding Kantian dignity have been covered in earlier chapters in an episodic fashion. There is no simple and direct road from Kant's remarkable first major student, Herder, to the Fascist misappropriations by Chamberlain and his followers, or to those who have critically characterized Herder and Kant themselves largely in terms of reactionary ideas. Just as others could misunderstand Kant and Herder, they could misunderstand each other at times. Furthermore, Kant himself, and others who thought like him right at the same time, such as most of the signatories of the Declaration of Independence, could exhibit patterns of thought and behavior that went clearly against their own basic doctrine that human beings are all created equal and deserve open-minded manifestations of respect. Nonetheless, the words of a document with genuinely revolutionary ideas, and the elements of a complex and progressive philosophical theory, such as those in Kant's ethics, have a power that goes beyond the frailties of their authors. This is why, in a speech in Glasgow in 1860, Frederick Douglass could still eloquently assert:

> ...'we the people'; not we the white people, not even the citizens, not we the privileged class, not we the high, not we the low, but we the people; not we the horses, sheep, and swine, and wheel-barrows, but...we the human inhabitants; and if we Negroes are people, they are included in the benefits for which the Constitution of America was ordained and established.[4]

Unfortunately, despite the brave efforts of Lincoln, Whitman, and many others, the just benefits that Douglass noted were hardly delivered as they should have been. Political history has been the opposite of swift and steady progress, and the same has to be said for philosophy and the understanding of classical texts. As

---

[4] Frederick Douglass, as quoted in David Blight, "The Two Constitutions (review of *The Crooked Path to Abolition: Abraham Lincoln and the Antislavery Constitution*, by James Oakes)," *The New York Review of Books*, June 8 (2023), 34. See Ch. 5.4.

AFTERWORD 199

Kant suggested, even a philosopher of Plato's stature may not have understood the proper way to develop his own ideas (KrV A 313/B 370). There have in fact been an almost incredible number of difficulties in the history of reactions to Kant's basic doctrine of universal human dignity.[5] But this does not mean that the difficulty, that is, the problem, lies with the doctrine itself. Living up to this challenging doctrine is what remains the main difficulty for all of us. Above all, it should be kept in mind that with respect to the key figures of the past—Kant, Herder, Jefferson, Price, and Mann—the shortcomings in their life and work that have become apparent in our era are only part of the story. In several cases their faults are serious, but this still does not negate the fact that they each vigorously promoted numerous influential insights that remain crucial for the development of progressive movements concerning human dignity. In general, it is important not only to learn from the surprising number of ways in which the heroes of the past turn out to have been caught in the prejudices and confusions of their age, but also to appreciate that what is distinctive about them, as "our heroes," is how much they went beyond their era by stressing original ideas that continue to enlighten our times.[6]

Kantian Dignity and its Difficulties. Karl Ameriks, Oxford University Press. © Karl Ameriks 2024.
DOI: 10.1093/9780198917656.003.0010

---

[5] This is a general problem. See, e.g., Adam Gopnik, "The Biggest Losers: How the Bible Turned a History of Defeat into Triumph," *The New Yorker*, August 28 (2023), 66: "Think of books as books truly are, that is, badly reviewed, sporadically revived, occasionally rediscovered, and if any good at all, perpetually misread."

[6] Cf. Finton O'Toole, "Defying Tribalism (review of *Left is Not Woke*, by Susan Neiman)," *The New York Review of Books*, Nov. 2 (2023), 18–22.

References

Adams, Henry Mason. *Prussian-American Relations, 1775–1871*, Cleveland: Press of Western Reserve University (1960).

Adams, Robert Merrihew. "Moral Faith," *The Journal of Philosophy* 92 (1995), 75–95.

Adler, Anthony Curtis. *Politics and Truth in Hölderlin: "Hyperion" and the Choreographic Project of Modernity*, Rochester, NY: Camden House (2020).

Allais, Lucy. "Restorative Justice, Retributive Justice, and the South African Truth and Reconciliation Commission," *Philosophy and Public Affairs* 39 (2011), 331–63.

Allais, Lucy. "Kant's Racism," *Philosophical Papers* 45 (2016), 1–36, DOI:10.1080/0556864 1.2016.1199170.

Allais, Lucy. "Evil and Practical Reason," in *Kant on Persons and Agency*, ed. Eric Watkins, Cambridge: Cambridge University Press (2017), 83–101.

Allais, Lucy and Callanan, John J. (eds.). *Kant and Animals*, Oxford: Oxford University Press (2020).

Allen, Danielle S. *Our Declaration. A Reading of the Declaration of Independence in Defense of Equality*, New York: Liveright Publishing (2014).

Allison, Henry E. *Lessing and the Enlightenment: His Philosophy of Religion and its Relation to Eighteenth-century Thought*, Ann Arbor: University of Michigan Press (1966).

Allison, Henry E. *Kant's Groundwork of the Metaphysics of Morals: A Commentary*, Oxford: Oxford University Press (2011).

Allison, Henry E. *Kant's Conception of Freedom: A Developmental and Critical Analysis*, Cambridge: Cambridge University Press (2020).

Alznauer, Mark. "Hegel on the Conceptual Form of Philosophical History," in *Kant and the Possibility of Progress: From Modern Hopes to Postmodern Anxieties*, ed. Samuel A. Stoner and Paul T. Wilford, Philadelphia: University of Pennsylvania Press (2021), 165–84.

Ameriks, Karl. *Kant's Theory of Mind: An Analysis of the 'Paralogisms of Pure Reason,'* Oxford: Clarendon Press (1982; expanded edition 2000).

Ameriks, Karl. "Kant on the Good Will," in *Grundlegung zur Metaphysik der Sitten: Ein kooperativer Kommentar*, ed. Otfried Höffe, Frankfurt: Klostermann (1989), 45–65.

Ameriks, Karl. *Kant and the Fate of Autonomy: Problems in the Appropriation of the Critical Philosophy*, Cambridge: Cambridge University Press (2000).

Ameriks, Karl. "Hegel's Aesthetics: New Perspectives on its Response to Kant and Romanticism," *Bulletin of the Hegel Society of Great Britain*, 45/46 (2002), 72–92.

Ameriks, Karl. *Interpreting Kant's Critiques*, Oxford: Clarendon Press (2003).

Ameriks, Karl. "On Two Non-Realist Interpretations of Kant's Ethics," in *Interpreting Kant's Critiques*, Oxford: Clarendon Press (2003), 263–82.

Ameriks, Karl. "Reinhold, Systematicity, Popularity and 'The Historical Turn'," in *System and Context. Early Romantic and Early Idealistic Constellations/System und Kontext. Frühromantische und Frühidealistische Konstellationen*, ed. Rolf Ahlers, *The New Athenaeum* 7 (2004), 109–38.

Ameriks, Karl. "A Commonsense Kant?", *Proceedings and Addresses of the American Philosophical Association* 79 (2005), 19–45.

202 REFERENCES

Ameriks, Karl. "Kant, Hume, and the Problem of Moral Motivation," in *Kant and the Historical Turn: Philosophy as Critical Interpretation*, Oxford: Clarendon Press (2006), 89–107.

Ameriks, Karl. "Interpretation After Kant," *Critical Horizons* 10 (2009), 31–53.

Ameriks, Karl. "Ambiguities in the Will: Reinhold and Kant, *Briefe 2*," in *Studia Reinholdiana: Tagungsband der Reinhold-Tagung in Siegen 2010*, ed. Martin Bondeli and Marion Heinz, Berlin: De Gruyter (2012), 71–90.

Ameriks, Karl. "History, Idealism, and Schelling," *Internationales Jahrbuch des Deutschen Idealismus/International Yearbook of German Idealism* 10 (2012), 123–42.

Ameriks, Karl. "Kant, Human Nature, and History after Rousseau," in *Kant's 'Observations' and 'Remarks': A Critical Guide*, ed. Susan Meld Shell and Richard Velkley, Cambridge: Cambridge University Press (2012), 247–65.

Ameriks, Karl. *Kant's Elliptical Path*, Oxford: Clarendon Press (2012).

Ameriks, Karl. "Kant's Fateful Reviews of Herder's *Ideas*," in *Kant's Elliptical Path*, Oxford: Clarendon Press (2012), 221–37.

Ameriks, Karl. "Kant and the End of Theodicy," in *Kant's Elliptical Path*, Oxford: Clarendon Press (2012), 260–77.

Ameriks, Karl. "On the Extension of Kant's Elliptical Path in Hölderlin and Novalis," in *Kant's Elliptical Path*, Oxford: Clarendon Press (2012), 281–302.

Ameriks, Karl. "Vindicating Autonomy: Kant, Sartre, and O'Neill," in *Kant on Moral Autonomy*, ed. Oliver Sensen, Cambridge: Cambridge University Press (2013), 53–70.

Ameriks, Karl. "Is Practical Justification in Kant Ultimately Dogmatic?", in *Kant on Practical Justification*, ed. Sorin Baiasu and Mark Timmons, Oxford: Oxford University Press (2013), 153–75.

Ameriks, Karl. "History, Succession, and German Romanticism," in *The Relevance of Romanticism: Essays on German Romantic Philosophy*, ed. Dalia Nassar, Oxford: Oxford University Press (2014), 47–67.

Ameriks, Karl. "The Historical Turn and Late Modernity," in *Hegel on Philosophy in History*, ed. Rachel Zuckert and James Kreines, Cambridge: Cambridge University Press (2017), 139–56.

Ameriks, Karl (ed.). *The Cambridge Companion to German Idealism*, 2nd edn, Cambridge: Cambridge University Press (2017).

Ameriks, Karl. "In Graceland: Hope and History in Michael Collins' Fiction," *The Irish Times*, March 10 (2017). https://www.irishtimes.com/culture/books/in-graceland-hope-and-history-in-michael-collins-fiction-1.3005572.

Ameriks, Karl. "On Some Reactions to 'Kant's Tragic Problem'," in *Natur und Freiheit. Akten des XII. Internationalen Kant Kongresses*, ed. Violetta Waibel et al., Berlin: De Gruyter (2018), 3255–62.

Ameriks, Karl. "Once Again: The End of All Things," in *Kant on Persons and Agency*, ed. Eric Watkins, Cambridge: Cambridge University Press (2018), 213–30.

Ameriks, Karl. "On Herder's Hermeneutics," *SGIR Review* 1 (2018), 1–12.

Ameriks, Karl. *Kantian Subjects: Critical Philosophy and Late Modernity*, Oxford: Oxford University Press (2019).

Ameriks, Karl. "Beyond the Living and the Dead: On Post-Kantian Philosophy as Historical Appropriation," *Graduate Faculty Philosophy Journal* 40 (2019), 33–61.

Ameriks, Karl. "On the Many Senses of 'Self-Determination'," in *Kantian Subjects: Critical Philosophy and Late Modernity*, Oxford: Oxford University Press (2019), 14–35.

Ameriks, Karl. "Universality, Necessity, and Law in General in Kant," in *Kantian Subjects: Critical Philosophy and Late Modernity*, Oxford: Oxford University Press (2019), 103–19.

Ameriks, Karl. "Hölderlin's Kantian Path," in *Kantian Subjects: Critical Philosophy and Late Modernity*, Oxford: Oxford University Press (2019), 189–206.

Ameriks, Karl. "The Very Idea of Innovation: From Descartes to Post-Kantianism," *Symphilosophie* 2 (2021), 247–71.

Ameriks, Karl. "*Aufklärung über die Sittlichkeit. Zu Kants Grundlegung einer Metaphysik der Sitten*, by Bernd Ludwig" (review), *Archiv für Geschichte der Philosophie* 104 (2022), 786–90.

Ameriks, Karl. "*The Moral Habitat*, by Barbara Herman" (review), *Notre Dame Philosophical Reviews* (2022), 2022.08.05.

Ameriks, Karl. "Kant, Schiller, and Beethoven: Enlightened Connections of Aesthetics, Revolution, and Religion," *SGIR Review* (forthcoming).

Anderson, R. Lanier. "Nietzsche on Truth, Illusion, and Redemption," *European Journal of Philosophy* 13 (2005), 185–225.

Anderson, R. Lanier. "Transcendental Idealism as Formal Idealism: An Anti-Metaphysical Reading," in *Proceedings of the 13th International Kant Congress 'The Court of Reason' (Oslo, 6–9 August 2019)*, ed. Camilla Serck-Hanssen and Beatrix Himmelmann, Berlin and Boston: De Gruyter (2021), 49–67.

Arendt, Hannah. *On Revolution*, Harmondsworth: Penguin (1973).

Arendt, Hannah. *Lectures on Kant's Political Philosophy*, ed. Ronald Beiner, Chicago: University of Chicago Press (1992).

Armitage, David. *The Declaration of Independence: A Global History*, Cambridge, MA: Harvard University Press (2007).

Armitage, David and Subrahmanyam, Sanjay (eds.). *The Age of Revolutions in their Global Context, c. 1760–1840*, London: Palgrave Macmillan (2010).

Aschheim, Steven E. *The Nietzsche Legacy in Germany, 1890–1990*, Berkeley: University of California Press (1992).

Audi, Robert. *The Good in the Right: A Theory of Intuition and Intrinsic Value*, Princeton: Princeton University Press (2004).

Audi, Robert. *Moral Value and Human Diversity*, New York: Oxford University Press (2007).

Barzun, Jacques. *Race: A Study in Modern Superstition*, New York: Harcourt Brace and Co. (1937).

Beckert, Sven. "American Danger: United States Empire, Eurafrica, and the Territorialization of Industrial Capitalism, 1870–1950," *The American Historical Review* 122 (2017), 1137–70.

Beiser, Frederick C. *Enlightenment, Revolution, and Romanticism: The Genesis of Modern German Political Thought 1790–1800*, Cambridge, MA: Harvard University Press (1992).

Beiser, Frederick C. (ed.). *The Early Political Writings of the German Romantics*, Cambridge: Cambridge University Press (1996).

Beitz, Charles. "Human Dignity in the Theory of Human Rights: Nothing but a Phrase?," *Philosophy & Public Affairs* 41 (2013), 259–90.

Benjamin, Robert Spiers (ed.). *I am an American: By Famous Naturalized Americans*, with an Introduction by Archibald MacLeish, Forward by Francis Biddle, New York: Alliance Book Corporation (1941).

Bentham, Jeremy. "Short Review of the Declaration," in [John Lind and Jeremy Bentham] *An Answer to Declaration of the American Congress*, London (1776), 119–32. Reprinted in David Armitage, *The Declaration of Independence: A Global History*, Cambridge, MA: Harvard University Press (2007), 173–86.

Bergen, Doris. *Twisted Cross: The German Christian Movement in the Third Reich*, Chapel Hill: University of North Carolina Press (1996).

204 REFERENCES

Berman, Russell. *Enlightenment or Empire: Colonial Discourse in German Culture*, Lincoln: University of Nebraska Press (1998).

Bernhard, Thomas. *Immanuel Kant: Komödie*, Frankfurt: Suhrkamp (1978).

Bernstein, Richard J. *Why Read Hannah Arendt Now?*, Medford, MA and Cambridge: Polity (2018).

Bertram, Ernst. *Nietzsche: Attempt at a Mythology* [1918], trans. Robert E. Norton, Urbana: University of Illinois Press (2009).

Bieri, Peter. *Human Dignity: A Way of Living*, Cambridge: Polity (2017).

Biester, Johann Erich. "Etwas über Benjamin Franklin," *Berlinische Monatschrift* 2 (1783), 11–38.

Bird, Colin. *Human Dignity and Political Criticism*, Cambridge: Cambridge University Press (2021).

Bishop, Paul. "The Intellectual World of Thomas Mann," in *The Cambridge Companion to Thomas Mann*, ed. Ritchie Robertson, Cambridge: Cambridge University Press (2002), 22–42.

Blight, David. "The Two Constitutions (review of *The Crooked Path to Abolition: Abraham Lincoln and the Antislavery Constitution*, by James Oakes)," *The New York Review of Books*, June 8 (2023), 30–5.

Boes, Thomas. *Thomas Mann's War: Literature, Politics, and the World Republic of Letters*, Ithaca: Cornell University Press (2019).

Boes, Tobias. "'I'm an American': Thomas Manns Zusammenarbeit mit der amerikanischen Einwanderungsbehörde INS," *Thomas Mann Jahrbuch* 35 (2022), 73–85.

Botting, Eileen Hunt. *Wollstonecraft, Mill, and Women's Human Rights*, New Haven and London: Yale University Press (2016).

Boxill, Bernard and Hill, Thomas E., Jr. "Kant and Race," in *Race and Racism*, ed. Bernard Boxill, Oxford: Oxford University Press (2001), 448–71.

Boyle, Nicholas. *Goethe: The Poet and the Age, Volume I: The Poetry of Desire*, Oxford and New York: Oxford University Press (1992).

Brink, David O. "Normative Perfectionism and the Kantian Tradition," *Philosophers' Imprint* 19 (2019), 1–28.

Brookline Tab. February 16 (2018), 1.

Bubner, Rüdiger, *Innovations of Idealism*, trans. Nicholas Walker, Cambridge: Cambridge University Press (2003).

Budick, Sanford. *Kant and Milton*, Cambridge, MA: Harvard University Press (2010).

Burke, Edmund. *Reflections on the Revolution in France* [1790], ed. T. H. D. Maloney, Indianapolis: Hackett (1955).

Byrd, Sharon and Hruschka, Joachim (eds.). *Kant's 'Doctrine of Right': A Commentary*, Cambridge: Cambridge University Press (2010).

Cavallar, Georg. *Kant's Embedded Cosmopolitanism: History, Philosophy, and Education for World Citizens*, Berlin: De Gruyter (2015).

Chakravartty, Anjan. *Scientific Ontology: Integrating Naturalized Metaphysics and Voluntarist Epistemology*, Oxford: Oxford University Press (2017).

Chamberlain, Houston Stewart. *The Foundations of the Nineteenth Century* [1899], 2 vols., trans. John Lees, with an Introduction by Lord Redesdale, London: John Lane (1911).

Chamberlain, Houston Stewart. *Immanuel Kant: A Study and a Comparison with Goethe, Leonardo da Vinci, Bruno, Plato and Descartes* [1905], 2 vols., trans. Lord Redesdale, London: John Lane (1914).

Chamberlain, Houston Stewart. *Die Grundlagen des XIX Jahrhunderts*, vol. 2, Bruckmann: Munich (1919), 13th edn.

Commager, Henry Steele. *The Empire of Reason: How Europe Imagined and America Realized the Enlightenment*, Garden City NY: Anchor/Doubleday (1977).

Cone, Carl B. *Torchbearer of Freedom. The Influence of Richard Price on Eighteenth Century Thought*, Lexington, KY: University of Kentucky Press (1952).

Corngold, Stanley. "Mann as a Reader of Nietzsche," *boundary* 2/9 (1980), 47–74.

Corngold, Stanley. *The Mind in Exile: Thomas Mann in Princeton*, Princeton: Princeton University Press (2022).

Cramer, Katherine J. *The Politics of Resentment: Rural Consciousness in Wisconsin and the Rise of Scott Walker*, Chicago: University of Chicago Press (2016).

Cureton, Adam. "Treating Disabled Adults as Children: An Application of Kant's Conception of Respect," in *Respect: Philosophical Essays*, ed. Richard Dean and Oliver Sensen, Oxford: Oxford University Press (2022), 273–88.

Dahlstrom, Daniel. "The Aesthetic Holism of Hamann, Herder, and Schiller," in *The Cambridge Companion to German Idealism*, 2nd edn, ed. Karl Ameriks, Cambridge: Cambridge University Press (2017), 106–27.

Darwall, Stephen. *The British Moralists and the Internal "Ought": 1640-1740*, Cambridge: Cambridge University Press (1995).

Darwall, Stephen. "On a Kantian Form of Respect: 'Before a Humble Common Man . . . my Spirit Bows'," in *Respect: Philosophical Essays*, ed. Richard Dean and Oliver Sensen, Oxford: Oxford University Press (2022), 192–203.

Davenport, John J. *Narrative Identity and Autonomy: From Frankfurt and MacIntyre to Kierkegaard*, New York and Abingdon: Taylor and Francis (2012).

De Tocqueville, Alexis. *The Ancien Régime and the Revolution* [1856], trans. and ed. Gerald Bevan, London: Penguin (2008).

Dean, Richard. "Humanity as an Idea, as an Ideal, and as an End in Itself," *Kantian Review* 18 (2013), 171–95.

Dean, Richard. *The Value of Humanity in Kant's Moral Theory*, Oxford: Clarendon Press (2016).

Dean, Richard. "Abstract for The Value of Humanity," https://global.oup.com/acadeic/product/the-value-of-humanity-in-kants-moral-theory-9780199285723?cc=us&lang=en&

Dean, Richard. "The Peculiar Idea of Respect for a Capacity," in *Respect: Philosophical Essays*, ed. Richard Dean and Oliver Sensen, Oxford: Oxford University Press (2022), 140–56.

Debes, Remy (ed.). *Dignity: A History*, Oxford: Oxford University Press (2017).

Debes, Remy. "Respect: A History," in *Respect: Philosophical Essays*, ed. Richard Dean and Oliver Sensen, Oxford: Oxford University Press (2022), 1–25.

Deligiorgi, Katarina. "Interest and Agency," in *German Idealism Today*, ed. Markus Gabriel and Anders Roe Rasmussen, Berlin: De Gruyter (2017), 3–25.

Dietering, Heinrich, *Thomas Manns amerikanische Religion*, Frankfurt: Fischer (2012).

Dippel, Horst. *Germany and the American Revolution 1770-1800*, trans. Bernhard A. Uhlendorf, Chapel Hill: University of North Carolina Press (1977).

Donagan, Alan. *The Theory of Morality*, Chicago: Chicago University Press (1977).

Dwyer, Susan. "How Good is the Linguistic Analogy?" in *The Innate Mind: Structure and Contents*, ed. Peter Carruthers, Stephen Laurence, and Stephen P. Stich, Oxford: Oxford University Press (2006), 145–67.

Eggers, Daniel. "Moral Motivation in Early 18th Century Moral Rationalism," *European Journal of Philosophy* 27 (2019), 552–74.

Eigen, Sara and Larrimore, Mark (eds.). *The German Invention of Race*, Albany: State University of New York Press (2006).

206 REFERENCES

Ely, Richard, T. *The World War and Leadership in a Democracy*, New York: Macmillan (1918).

Engstrom, Stephen. "The Determination of the Concept of the Highest Good in Kant's Philosophy," in *The Highest Good in Kant's Philosophy*, ed. Thomas Höwing, Berlin: De Gruyter (2016), 89–108.

Evans, C. Steven. "Introduction," in Søren Kierkegaard, *Fear and Trembling: A Dialectical Lyric* [1843], ed. Silvia Walsh and C. Stephen Evans, trans. Silvia Walsh, Cambridge: Cambridge University Press (2006), vi–xxx.

Evans, C. Steven. "Patriotism and Love of the Neighbor: A Kierkegaardian View of a Contested Virtue," *Religions* 14 (forthcoming).

Eze, Emmanuel Chukwudi (ed.). *Race and the Enlightenment: A Reader*, Oxford: Blackwell (1997).

Fest, Joachim C. *The Face of the Third Reich: Portraits of the Nazi Leadership*, trans. Michael Bullock, London: Weidenfeld and Nicolson (1970).

Field, Geoffrey. *Evangelist of Race: The Germanic Vision of Houston Stewart Chamberlain*, New York: Columbia University Press (1981).

Fischer, Klaus. *Hitler & America*, Philadelphia: University of Pennsylvania Press (2011).

Fisher, Naomi. "Kant's Organic Religion: God, Teleology and Progress in the Third *Critique*," in *Kant and the Possibility of Progress: From Modern Hopes to Postmodern Anxieties*, ed. Samuel A. Stoner and Paul T. Wilford, Philadelphia: University of Pennsylvania Press (2021), 77–93.

Fisher, Naomi and Fisher, Jeffrey. "Schelling and the *Philebus*: Limit and the Unlimited in Schelling's Philosophy of Nature," *Epoché* 26 (2022), 347–67.

Flikschuh, Katrin and Ypi, Lea (eds.). *Kant and Colonialism: Historical and Critical Perspectives*, Oxford: Oxford University Press (2014).

Fontane, Theodor. *No Way Back* [1891], trans. Hugh Rorrison and Helen Chambers, New York: Penguin (2013).

Formosa, Paul. "Kant on the Radical Evil in Human Nature," *Philosophical Forum* 38 (2007), 221–45.

Formosa, Paul. *Kantian Ethics, Dignity and Perfection*, Cambridge: Cambridge University Press (2017).

Forster, Michael, N. "Introduction," in *Herder: Philosophical Writings*, ed. Michael N. Forster, Cambridge: Cambridge University Press (2002), vii–xxv.

Forster, Michael N. *Herder's Philosophy*, Oxford: Oxford University Press (2018).

Forster, Michael N. "Romanticism and *The Birth of Tragedy*," in *Romanticism, Philosophy, and Literature*, ed. Michael N. Forster and Lina Steiner, London: Palgrave-Macmillan (2020), 265–95.

Fraenkel, Carlos. *Philosophical Religions from Plato to Spinoza: Religion, Reason and Autonomy*, Cambridge: Cambridge University Press (2012).

Frank, Manfred. *The Philosophical Foundations of Early German Romanticism*, trans. Elizabeth Millán-Zaibert, Albany: State University of New York Press (2004).

Franks, Paul W. "Inner Anti-Semitism or Kabbalistic Heresy? German Idealism's Relation to Judaism," *Internationales Jahrbuch des Deutschen Idealismus/International Yearbook for German Idealism* 7 (2009), 254–79.

Franz, Michael. *Tübinger Platonismus. Die gemeinsamen philosophischen Anfangsgründe von Hölderlin, Schelling und Hegel*, Tübingen: Francke (2012).

Frege, Gottlob. *The Foundations of Arithmetic* [1884], trans. J. L. Austin, Evanston, IL: Northwestern University Press (1968), 2nd revised edn.

Frierson, Patrick R. "Richard Dean, *The Value of Humanity in Kant's Moral Theory* (review)," *Notre Dame Philosophical Reviews*, 2007.04.17.

Frierson, Patrick R. *What is the Human Being?*, Abingdon and New York: Routledge (2013).

Gentz, Friedrich. *The Origin and Principles of the American Revolution. Compared with the Origin and Principles of the French Revolution* [1800], trans. with a Preface by John Quincy Adams, ed. Peter Klosowski, Indianapolis: Liberty Fund (2009).

Geuss, Raymond. *Changing the Subject: Philosophy from Socrates to Adorno*, Cambridge, MA: Harvard University Press (2017).

Giordenetti, Piero. *Kant und die Musik*, Würzburg: Königshausen & Neumann (2005).

Gjesdal, Kristin. *Herder's Hermeneutics: History, Poetry, Enlightenment*, Cambridge: Cambridge University Press (2017).

Goebbels, Joseph. "Erkenntnis und Propaganda," in *Signale der neuen Zeit. 25 ausgewählte Reden von Dr. Joseph Goebbels*, Munich: Zentralverlag der NSDAP (1934), 28–52. Speech of January 9, 1928.

Goehr, Lydia. *The Imaginary Museum of Musical Works: An Essay in the Philosophy of Music*, Oxford: Clarendon Press (1992).

Goldenbaum, Ursula. "The Shift from Leibniz's Theodicy toward Protestant Philosophy of History as a Decrease in Religious Tolerance and Increase of Anti-Judaism." Templeton Conference Lisbon talk, October 2012. https://www.youtube.com/watch?v=VDyyLx06Qmk

Gopnik, Adam. "The Biggest Losers: How the Bible Turned a History of Defeat into Triumph," *The New Yorker*, August 28 (2023), 64–6.

Greene, Brian. *Until the End of Time: Mind, Matter, and Our Search for Meaning in an Evolving Universe*, New York: Alfred A. Knopf (2020).

Grey, Edward. *Twenty-Five Years 1892–1916*, New York: Frederick A. Stokes Company (1925).

Griffin, James. *On Human Rights*, Oxford: Oxford University Press (2008).

Grundmann, Thomas. "Progress and Historical Reflection in Philosophy," in *Philosophy and the Historical Perspective*, ed. Marcel von Ackeran and Lee Klein, Oxford: Proceedings of the British Academy 214 (2018), 51–68.

Guyer, Paul. "Kantian Perfectionism," in *Virtues of Freedom: Selected Essays on Kant*, Oxford: Oxford University Press (2016), 70–86.

Habermas, Jürgen. "Taking Aim at the Heart of the Present," in *A Critical Reader*, ed. David Couzens Hoy, Oxford and New York: Basil Blackwell (1986), 103–8.

Haidt, Jonathan. "After Babel: How Social Media Dissolved the Mortar of Society and Made America Stupid," *The Atlantic* 329/4 (2022), 54–65.

Hamburger, Michael. "The Sublime Art: Notes on Milton and Hölderlin," in *Contraries: Studies in German Literature*, Boston: E. P. Dutton (1970), 43–65.

Hampton, Jean. *The Intrinsic Worth of Persons: Contractarianism in Moral and Political Philosophy*, ed. Daniel Farnham, Cambridge: Cambridge University Press (2007).

Hardimon, Michael. *Hegel's Social Philosophy: The Project of Reconciliation*, Cambridge: Cambridge University Press (1992).

Hardimon, Michael. *Rethinking Race*. Cambridge, MA: Harvard University Press (2017).

Hare, John E. *The Moral Gap: Kantian Ethics, Human Limits, and God's Assistance*, Oxford: Clarendon Press (1996).

Hare, John E. "Kant, Aesthetic Judgement, and Beethoven," in *Theology, Music, and Modernity: Struggles for Freedom*, ed. Jeremy Begbie, Daniel K. L. Chua, and Markus Rathey, Oxford: Oxford University Press (2021), 42–65.

Harries, Karsten. *The Meaning of Modern Art*, Evanston, IL: Northwestern University Press (1968).

Hatfield, James Taft and Hochbaum, Elfriede, "The Influence of the American Revolution upon German Literature," *Americana Germanica*, 3 (1900), 348–5.

208 REFERENCES

Heller, Erich. *The Ironic German: A Study of Thomas Mann*, Chicago: Henry Regnery (1979).
Henrich, Dieter (ed.). *Kant-Gentz-Rehberg: Über Theorie und Praxis*, Frankfurt: Suhrkamp (1967).
Henrich, Dieter. "On the Meaning of Rational Action in the State," in *Kant & Political Philosophy: The Contemporary Legacy*, ed. Ronald Beiner and William James Booth, New Haven: Yale University Press (1993), 97–116. Translation of the Introduction in Henrich (1967).
Herder, Johann Gottlieb. "This, too, a Philosophy of History (excerpt) [1774]," in *Herder: On World History: An Anthology*, ed. Hans Adler and Ernest A. Menze, M. E. Sharpe: Armonk, NY and London (1997), trans. Ernest A. Menze with Michael Palma, 35–43.
Herder, Johann Gottlieb. "Tenth Collection," in *Letters for the Advancement of Humanity* [1793–7], in *Herder: Philosophical Writings*, ed. Michael N. Forster, Cambridge: Cambridge University Press (2002), 380–424.
Herman, Barbara. *The Practice of Moral Judgment*, Cambridge, MA: Harvard University Press (1993).
Herman, Barbara. *Moral Literacy*, Cambridge, MA: Harvard University Press (2007).
Herman, Barbara. "We are Not Alone: A Place for Animals in Kant's Ethics," in *Kant on Persons and Agency*, ed. Eric Watkins, Cambridge: Cambridge University Press (2018), 174–91.
Herman, Barbara. "Religion and the Highest Good: Speaking to the Heart of Even the Best of Us," in *Kant on Freedom and Spontaneity*, ed. Kate A. Moran, Cambridge: Cambridge University Press (2018), 214–30.
Herman, Barbara. *The Moral Habitat*, Oxford: Oxford University Press (2022).
Hill, Thomas E., Jr. *Dignity and Practical Reason in Kant's Moral Theory*, Ithaca: Cornell University Press (1992).
Hill, Thomas E., Jr. "The Dignity of Persons: Kant, Problems and a Proposal," in *Virtue, Rules, and Justice: Kantian Aspirations*, Oxford: Oxford University Press (2012), 185–202.
Hinrichsen, Hans-Joachim, *Ludwig van Beethoven. Musik für eine neue Zeit*, Kassel and Berlin: Bärenreiter-Metzler (2019).
Hitler, Adolf. *Mein Kampf* [1925–6], trans. Ralph Manheim, Boston: Houghton Mifflin (1971).
Höffe, Otfried. *Kant's Cosmopolitan Theory of Law and Peace*, trans. Alexandra Newton, Cambridge: Cambridge University Press (2006).
Hölderlin, Friedrich. *Patmos* [1802], trans. Michael Hamburger, in *Friedrich Hölderlin, Hyperion and Selected Poems*, ed. Eric L. Santner, New York: Continuum (1990), 245–57.
Huddleston, Andrew. *Nietzsche on the Decadence and Flourishing of Culture*, Oxford: Oxford University Press (2019).
Huseyinzadegan, Dilek. "For What Can the Kantian Feminist Hope? Constructive Complicity in Appropriations of the Canon," *Feminist Philosophy Quarterly* 4/1 (2018). Article 3. doi:10.5206/fpq/2018.1.3
Huseyinzadegan, Dilek. *Kant's Nonideal Theory of Politics*, Evanston, IL: Northwestern University Press (2019).
Huseyinzadegan, Dilek and Pascoe, Jordan. "A Decolonial, Intersectional, and Materialist Feminist Re-appraisal of Kant's Notion of the Enlightenment: Complicity, Accountability, and Refusal," in *The Palgrave Handbook of German Idealism and Feminist Philosophy*, ed. Susanne Lettow and Tuija Pulkkinen, London: Palgrave Macmillan (2023), 31–49.
Illies, Florian. *1913: The Year before the Storm*, trans. Shaun Whiteside and Jamie Lee Searle, New York: Melville House (2013).

Irwin, Terence. *The Development of Ethics: A Historical and Critical Study. Vol. 2: From Suarez to Rousseau*, Oxford: Oxford University Press (2008).

Irwin, Terence. *The Development of Ethics: A Historical and Critical Study. Vol. 3: From Kant to Rawls*, Oxford: Oxford University Press (2009).

Israel, Jonathan. *The Revolution of the Mind: Radical Enlightenment and the Intellectual Origins of Modern Democracy*, Princeton: Princeton University Press (2010).

Israel, Jonathan. *The Expanding Blaze: How the American Revolution Ignited the World, 1775-1848*, Princeton: Princeton University Press (2017).

Jackson, Timothy L. "The Image of God and the Soul of Humanity: Reflections on Dignity, Sanctity and Humanity," in *Religion in the Liberal Polity*, ed. Terence Cuneo, Notre Dame, IN: University of Notre Dame Press (2005), 43-73.

Kain, Patrick. "Kant's Defense of Human Moral Status," *Journal of the History of Philosophy* 47 (2009), 59-101.

Kain, Patrick. "Dignity and the Paradox of Method," in *Realism and Antirealism in Kant's Moral Philosophy: New Essays*, ed. Elke Elisabeth Schmidt and Robinson dos Santos, Berlin: De Gruyter (2017), 67-90.

Kakel III, Carroll P. *The American West and the Nazi East: A Comparative and Interpretive Perspective*, New York: Palgrave Macmillan (2011).

Kant, Immanuel. "An Answer to the Question: What is Enlightenment," trans. Mary J. Gregor, in *Immanuel Kant/Practical Philosophy*, ed. Mary J. Gregor, Cambridge: Cambridge University Press (1996a), 17-22.

Kant, Immanuel. *Critique of Practical Reason*, trans. Mary J. Gregor, in *Immanuel Kant/Practical Philosophy*, ed. Mary J. Gregor, Cambridge: Cambridge University Press (1996a), 139-271.

Kant, Immanuel. "On the Common Saying: 'This may be True in Theory, but it does not Apply in Practice,'" trans. Mary J. Gregor, in *Immanuel Kant/Practical Philosophy*, ed. Mary J. Gregor, Cambridge: Cambridge University Press (1996a), 273-309.

Kant, Immanuel. "Perpetual Peace: A Philosophical Sketch," trans. Mary J. Gregor, in *Immanuel Kant/Practical Philosophy*, ed. Mary J. Gregor, Cambridge: Cambridge University Press (1996a), 317-51.

Kant, Immanuel. *The Metaphysics of Morals*, trans. Mary J. Gregor, in *Immanuel Kant/Practical Philosophy*, ed. Mary J. Gregor, Cambridge: Cambridge University Press (1996a), 365-603.

Kant, Immanuel. *The Conflict of the Faculties*, trans. Mary J. Gregor and Robert Anchor, in *Immanuel Kant/Religion and Rational Theology*, ed. Allen W. Wood and George di Giovanni, Cambridge: Cambridge University Press (1996b), 233-327.

Kant, Immanuel, *Lectures on the Philosophical Doctrine of Religion*, trans. Allen W. Wood, in *Immanuel Kant/Religion and Rational Theology*, ed. Allen W. Wood and George di Giovanni, Cambridge: Cambridge University Press (1996b), 335-451.

Kant, Immanuel. *Critique of Pure Reason*, trans. Paul Guyer and Allen W. Wood, Cambridge: Cambridge University Press (1997a).

Kant, Immanuel. "Moral Philosophy: Collins Lecture Notes," trans. Peter Heath, in *Immanuel Kant/Lectures on Ethics*, ed. Peter Heath and J. B. Schneewind, Cambridge: Cambridge University Press (1997b), 41-222.

Kant, Immanuel. "Kant on the Metaphysics of Morals, Vigilantius's Lecture Notes," trans. Peter Heath, in *Immanuel Kant/Lectures on Ethics*, ed. Peter Heath and J. B. Schneewind, Cambridge: Cambridge University Press (1997b), 249-452.

Kant, Immanuel. *Philosophical Correspondence*, trans. and ed. Arnulf Zweig, Cambridge: Cambridge University Press (1999).

210   REFERENCES

Kant, Immanuel. *Critique of the Power of Judgment*, trans. Eric Mathews and Paul Guyer, ed. Paul Guyer, Cambridge: Cambridge University Press (2000).

Kant, Immanuel. "What Real Progress Has Metaphysics Made in Germany since the Time of Leibniz and Wolff?", ed. Friedrich Theodor Rink, trans. Ted Humphrey in *Immanuel Kant: Theoretical Writings after 1781*, Cambridge: Cambridge University Press, ed. Henry E. Allison and Peter Heath (2002), 351–424.

Kant, Immanuel. *Prolegomena to any Future Metaphysics that will Present Itself as a Science*, trans. and ed. Gary Hatfield, Cambridge: Cambridge University Press (2004a).

Kant, Immanuel. *Immanuel Kant: Vorlesung zu Moralphilosophie*, ed. Werner Stark, Berlin: De Gruyter (2004b).

Kant, Immanuel. *Immanuel Kant/Lectures on Logic*, ed. J. Michael Young, Cambridge: Cambridge University Press (2004c).

Kant, Immanuel. *Immanuel Kant/Notes and Fragments*, ed. Paul Guyer, trans. Curtis Bowman, Paul Guyer, and Frederick Rauscher, Cambridge: Cambridge University Press (2005).

Kant, Immanuel. "Essays Regarding the Philanthropinum," trans. Robert B. Louden, in *Immanuel Kant/Anthropology, History and Education*, ed. Günter Zöller and Robert B. Louden, Cambridge: Cambridge University Press (2007), 100–4.

Kant, Immanuel. "Idea for a Universal History with a Cosmopolitan Aim," trans. Allen Wood, in *Immanuel Kant/Anthropology, History and Education*, ed. Günter Zöller and Robert B. Louden, Cambridge: Cambridge University Press (2007), 108–20.

Kant, Immanuel. "Reviews of J. G. Herder's *Ideas for the Philosophy of the History of Humanity*," trans. Allen W. Wood, in *Immanuel Kant/Anthropology, History and Education*, ed. Günter Zöller and Robert B. Louden, Cambridge: Cambridge University Press (2007), 124–42.

Kant, Immanuel. "On the Use of Teleological Principles in Philosophy," trans. Robert B. Louden, in *Immanuel Kant/Anthropology, History and Education*, ed. Günter Zöller and Robert B. Louden, Cambridge: Cambridge University Press (2007), 195–218.

Kant, Immanuel. *Anthropology from a Pragmatic Point of View*, trans. Robert B. Louden, in *Immanuel Kant/Anthropology, History and Education*, ed. Günter Zöller and Robert B. Louden, Cambridge: Cambridge University Press (2007), 231–429.

Kant, Immanuel. "Postscript to Christian Gottlieb Mielcke's Lithuanian–German and German–Lithuanian Dictionary," trans. Günter Zöller, in *Immanuel Kant/Anthropology, History and Education*, ed. Günter Zöller and Robert B. Louden, Cambridge: Cambridge University Press (2007), 432–3.

Kant, Immanuel. "Lectures on Pedagogy," trans. Robert B. Louden, in *Immanuel Kant/ Anthropology, History and Education*, ed. Günter Zöller and Robert B. Louden, Cambridge: Cambridge University Press (2007), 434–85.

Kant, Immanuel. *Groundwork of the Metaphysics of Morals: A German–English Edition*, trans. Mary Gregor, ed. and revised Jens Timmermann, Cambridge: Cambridge University Press (2011a).

Kant, Immanuel. *Observations on the Feeling of the Beautiful and the Sublime*, trans. Paul Guyer, in *Observations on the Feeling of the Beautiful and the Sublime and Other Writings*, ed. Patrick Frierson and Paul Guyer, Cambridge: Cambridge University Press (2011b), 23–62.

Kant, Immanuel. "Remarks in the *Observations on the Feeling of the Beautiful and the Sublime*," trans. Thomas Hilgers, Uygar Abaci, and Michael Nance, in *Observations on the Feeling of the Beautiful and the Sublime and Other Writings*, ed. Patrick Frierson and Paul Guyer, Cambridge: Cambridge University Press (2011b), 65–202.

REFERENCES 211

Kant, Immanuel. "Anthropology Friedländer," trans. G. Felicitas Munzel, in *Immanuel Kant/Lectures on Anthropology*, ed. Allen W. Wood and Robert B. Louden, Cambridge: Cambridge University Press (2012a), 37–255.

Kant, Immanuel. "Anthropology Pillau," trans. Allen W. Wood, in *Immanuel Kant/Lectures on Anthropology*, ed. Allen W. Wood and Robert B. Louden, Cambridge: Cambridge University Press (2012a), 261–79.

Kant, Immanuel. "Menschenkunde (excerpts)," trans. Robert B. Louden, in *Immanuel Kant/Lectures on Anthropology*, ed. Allen W. Wood and Robert B. Louden, Cambridge: Cambridge University Press (2012a), 289–333.

Kant, Immanuel. "Anthropology Mrongovius," trans. Robert R. Clewis, in *Immanuel Kant/ Lectures on Anthropology*, ed. Allen W. Wood and Robert B. Louden, Cambridge: Cambridge University Press (2012a), 339–509.

Kant, Immanuel. "Continued Observations of the Terrestrial Convulsions that have been Perceived for Some Time," trans. Olaf Reinhardt, in *Immanuel Kant/Kant on Natural Science*, ed. Eric Watkins, Cambridge: Cambridge University Press (2012b), 367–73.

Kant, Immanuel. "Immanuel Kant's Physical Geography," trans. Olaf Reinhardt, in *Immanuel Kant/Kant on Natural Science*, ed. Eric Watkins, Cambridge: Cambridge University Press (2012b), 441–679.

Kant, Immanuel. "Natural Right Lecture Course Notes by Feyerabend," in *Immanuel Kant/Lectures and Drafts on Political Philosophy*, ed. Frederick Rauscher, trans. Frederick Rauscher and Kenneth R. Westphal, Cambridge: Cambridge University Press (2016), 81–180.

Kant, Immanuel. *Religion within the Boundaries of Mere Reason*, in *Religion within the Boundaries of Mere Reason and Other Writings*, ed. and trans. Allen W. Wood and George di Giovanni, revised edition with an Introduction by Robert Merrihew Adams, Cambridge: Cambridge University Press (2018), 37–229.

Kant, Immanuel. "The End of All Things," trans. Allen W. Wood in *Immanuel Kant/ Religion within the Boundaries of Mere Reason and Other Writings*, ed. and trans. Allen W. Wood and George di Giovanni, revised edition with an Introduction by Robert Merrihew Adams, Cambridge: Cambridge University Press, 2nd edition (2018), 231–46.

Kelly, Thomas and McGrath, Sarah. "Is Reflective Equilibrium Enough?", *Philosophical Perspectives* 24 (2010), 325–59.

Kershaw, Ian. *Hitler: A Biography*, New York: Norton (1998).

Kierkegaard, Søren. *Concluding Unscientific Postscript to Philosophical Fragments* [1846], trans. David F. Swenson and Walter Lowrie, Princeton: Princeton University Press (1941).

Kierkegaard, Søren. *Fear and Trembling: A Dialectical Lyric* [1843], ed. Silvia Walsh and C. Stephen Evans, and trans. by Silvia Walsh, Cambridge: Cambridge University Press (2006).

Killmister, Suzy. "Paul Formosa, *Kantian Ethics, Dignity and Perfection* (review)," *Ethics* 133 (2023), 420–4.

Kinderman, William. *Beethoven: A Political Artist in Revolutionary Times*, Chicago: University of Chicago Press (2020).

Klages, Ludwig. *Der Geist als Widersacher der Seele*, Leipzig: Johann Ambrosius Barth (1929–32).

Kleingeld, Pauline. "Kant and Wieland on Moral Cosmopolitanism and Patriotism," in *Kant and Cosmopolitanism: The Philosophical Ideal of World Citizenship*, Cambridge: Cambridge University Press (2012), 13–39.

Kleingeld, Pauline. "Kant's Second Thoughts on Colonialism," in *Kant and Colonialism*, ed. Katrin Flikschuh and Lea Ypi, Oxford: Oxford University Press (2014), 43–67.

212 REFERENCES

Kleingeld, Pauline. "On Dealing with Kant's Sexism and Racism," *SGIR Review* 2 (2019), 3–22.

Klemperer, Victor. *I Will Bear Witness: A Diary of the Nazi Years 1933–1941*, trans. Martin Chalmers, London: Weidenfeld & Nicolson (1998).

Klemperer, Victor. *Munich 1919: Diary of a Revolution*, trans. Jessica Spengler, Cambridge: Polity (2017).

Kneller, Jane and Axinn, Sidney (eds.). *Autonomy and Community: Readings in Contemporary Kantian Social Philosophy*, Albany: State University of New York Press (1998).

Kneller, Jane. "Kant on Sex and Marriage Right," in *The Cambridge Companion to Kant and Modern Philosophy*, ed. Paul Guyer, Cambridge: Cambridge University Press (2006), 447–76.

Kneller, Jane. "The Copernican Turn in Early German Romanticism," in *Brill's Companion to German Romantic Philosophy*, ed. Elizabeth Millán Brusslan and Judith Norman, Leiden: Brill (2018), 18–36.

Kneller, Jane. "Novalis: The Art of Democracy," *Symphilosophie* 5 (2023), 53–70.

Koonz, Claudia. *The Nazi Conscience*, Cambridge, MA: Harvard University Press (2003).

Korsgaard, Christine M. with G. A. Cohen et al. *The Sources of Normativity*, ed. Onora O'Neill, Cambridge: Cambridge University Press (1996).

Korsgaard, Christine M. *The Constitution of Agency: Essays on Practical Reason and Moral Psychology*, Oxford: Oxford University Press (2008).

Korsgaard, Christine M. *Creating the Kingdom of Ends*, Cambridge: Cambridge University Press (2016).

Kuehn, Manfred. *Kant: A Biography*. Cambridge: Cambridge University Press (2001).

Kugel, James L. *How to Read the Bible: A Guide to Scripture Then and Now*, New York: Free Press (2007).

Kumar, Apaar. "Kant on the Ground of Human Dignity," *Kantian Review* 26 (2021), 435–53.

Kurzke, Hermann. *Thomas Mann: Life as a Work of Art*, trans. Leslie Willson, Princeton: Princeton University Press (2002).

Kurzke, Hermann. *Thomas Mann, Betrachtungen eines Nichtpolitischen: Kommentar*, Frankfurt: S. Fischer (2009).

Kuzniar, Alice A. "Kant and Herder on the French Revolution," in *The French Revolution in the Age of Goethe*, ed. Gerhart Hoffmeister, Hildesheim: Georg Olms (1989), 15–29.

Laboucheix, Henri. *Richard Price as Moral Philosopher and Political Theorist*, trans. Sarah Raphael and David Raphael, Oxford: Oxford University Press (1982).

Lackey, Michael. *The Modernist God State: A Literary Study of the Nazis' Christian Reich*, New York and London: Continuum (2012).

Larmore, Charles. *The Romantic Legacy*, New York: Columbia University Press (1996).

Lear, Jonathan. *Radical Hope: Ethics in the Face of Cultural Devastation*, Cambridge, MA: Harvard University Press (2006).

Lepenies, Wolf. *The Seduction of Culture in German History*, Princeton: Princeton University Press (2006).

Lilla, Mark, "Introduction," in Thomas Mann, *Reflections of a Nonpolitical Man* [1918], ed. Mark Lilla, trans. Walter D. Morris, New York: New York Review Books (2021), vii–xxi.

Locke, John. *Second Treatise. An Essay Concerning the True Original Extent and End of Civil Government*, 3rd edn, London (1698).

Löwe, Matthias. "Poetische Staaten: Frühromantik und Politik," in *Romantisierung von Politik: Historische Konstellationen und Gegenwartsanalysen*, ed. Sandra Kirshbaumer and Matthias Löwe, Paderborn: Brill (2022), 45–58.

Löwith, Karl. *Meaning in History: The Theological Implications of the Philosophy of History*, Chicago: University of Chicago Press (1949).

Lu-Adler, Huaping. *Kant, Race, and Racism: Views from Somewhere*, Oxford: Oxford University Press (2023).

Lukács, György. *Soul & Form* [1907], trans. Anna Bostock, ed. John T. Saunders and Katie Terezakis, New York: Columbia University Press (2010).

McCarthy, Thomas. *Race, Empire, and the Idea of Human Development*, Cambridge: Cambridge University Press (2009).

McGrath, Sarah. "Moral Realism without Convergence," *Philosophical Topics* 38 (2009), 59–90.

McGrath, Sarah. *Moral Knowledge*, Oxford: Oxford University Press (2019).

McGregor, Neil. "Lost Capitals," in *Germany: Memories of a Nation*, London: Penguin Book (2016), 38–58.

MacIntyre, Alasdair. *A Short History of Ethics*, New York: Macmillan (1966).

MacIntyre, Alasdair. "Review of *The Morals of Modernity* and *The Romantic Legacy* by Charles Larmore," *The Journal of Philosophy* 94 (1997), 485–90.

MacIntyre, Alasdair. "Human Dignity: A Puzzling and Possibly Dangerous Idea," lecture at University of Notre Dame, November 2021.

McNaughton, David. "British Moralists of the Eighteenth Century," in *British Philosophy and the Age of Enlightenment*, ed. Stuart Brown, London and New York: Routledge (1996), 202–27.

McNaughton, David. "Michael Huemer, *Moral Intuitionism* (book review)," *Notre Dame Philosophical Reviews*, 2006.09.10.

Maliks, Reidar. *Kant's Politics in Context*, Oxford: Oxford University Press (2014).

Malter, Rudolf (ed.). *Immanuel Kant in Rede und Gespräch*, Hamburg: Meiner (1990).

Mann, Thomas. *The Coming Victory of Democracy*, trans. Agnes Meyer, New York: Alfred A. Knopf (1938).

Mann, Thomas. "Ein Bruder," *Das Neue Tagebuch* 7 (1939), 306–9; "That Man is my Brother," *Esquire* 11 (1939), 31, 132–3.

Mann, Thomas. "Culture and Politics," *Survey Graphic* 28 (1939), 149–51.

Mann, Thomas. "[I am an American by] D. [*sic*] Thomas Mann," in *I am an American: By Famous Naturalized Americans*, ed. Robert Spiers Benjamin, with an Introduction by Archibald MacLeish, Forward by Francis Biddle, New York: Alliance Book Corporation (1941), 30–5.

Mann, Thomas. "Nietzsche in the Light of Modern Experience," *Commentary* 6 (1948), 17–26 and 149–56.

Mann, Thomas. "Friedrich und die große Koalition. Ein Abriß für den Tag und die Stunde," [1915] in *Thomas Mann: Politische Schriften und Reden 2*, Frankfurt: S. Fischer (1960), 20–64.

Mann, Thomas. *The Story of a Novel: The Genesis of Doctor Faustus* [1949], trans. Richard and Clara Winston, New York: Alfred A. Knopf (1961).

Mann, Thomas. *Doctor Faustus: The Life of the Composer Adrian Leverkühn as Told by a Friend* [1947], trans. John E. Woods, New York: Alfred A. Knopf (1997).

Mann, Thomas. *Reflections of a Nonpolitical Man* [1918], ed. Mark Lilla, trans. Walter D. Morris, New York: New York Review Books (2021). Includes "Reflections of a Nonpolitical Man," 1–489; "Thoughts in War Time [1914]," trans. Mark Lilla and Cosima Mattner, 491–506; "On the German Republic," [1922] trans. Lawrence Rainey, 507–47.

Maser, Werner (ed.). *Hitler's Lectures and Notes*. trans. Arnold Pomerans, Evanston IL, San Francisco, and London: Northwestern University Press (1974).

214 REFERENCES

Mazower, Mark. *Governing the World: The History of an Idea*, New York: Penguin Press (2012).

Merritt, Melissa. *Kant on Reflection and Virtue*, Cambridge: Cambridge University Press (2018).

Mertel, Kurt. "Historicism and Critique in Herder's *Another Philosophy of History*: Some Hermeneutic Reflections," *European Journal of Philosophy* 24 (2014), 397–416.

Micheli, Giuseppi. "The Early Reception of Kant's Thought in England 1785–1805," in *Kant and His Influence*, ed. George Macdonald Ross and Tony McWalter, Bristol: Thoemmes (1990), 202–14.

Mikkelsen, Jon M. (ed.). *Kant and the Concept of Race*, Albany: State University of New York Press (2013).

Millán-Zaibert, Elizabeth. *Friedrich Schlegel and the Emergence of Romantic Philosophy*, Albany: State University of New York Press (2007).

Miles, Jack. *Religion As We Know It: An Origin Story,* New York: Norton (2020).

Mills, Charles W. *The Racial Contract*, Ithaca, NY: Cornell University Press (1997).

Mills, Charles W. "Dark Ontologies: Whites, Jews, and White Supremacy," in *Autonomy and Community: Readings in Contemporary Kantian Social Philosophy*, ed. Jane Kneller and Sidney Axinn, Albany: State University of New York Press (1998), 131–68.

Mills, Charles W. *Black Rights/White Wrongs: The Critique of Racial Liberalism*, Oxford: Oxford University Press (2017).

Mills, Charles W. "Reflection: A Time for Dignity," in *Dignity: A History*, ed. Remy Debes, Oxford: Oxford University, Press (2017), 263–8.

Miniger, J. D. "Nachschrift eines Freundes: Kant, Lithuania, and the Praxis of Enlightenment, " *Studies in East European Thought* 57 (2005): 1–25.

Moran, Richard. "Williams, History, and the 'Impurity of Philosophy'," *European Journal of Philosophy* 24 (2016), 315–30.

Moran, Richard. "Swann's Medical Philosophy," in *Proust's in Search of Lost Time: Philosophical Perspectives*, ed. Katherine Elkins, Oxford: Oxford University Press (2023), 124–54.

Morgan, Edmund S. *The Birth of the Republic, 1763–1789*, 4th edn, Chicago: University of Chicago Press (2012).

Mosse, George L. "Bedeviled Conservatives," in *The Crisis of German Ideology: Intellectual Origins of the Third Reich*, New York: Grosset & Dunlop (1964), 237–53.

Mozart, Wolfgang Amadeus, *Mozart's Letters: An Illustrated Selection*, trans. Emily Anderson, Boston: Little, Brown and Co. (1938).

Nagel, Thomas. *Moral Feelings, Moral Reality, and Moral Progress*, New York: Oxford University Press (2024),

Nash, Gary. "Sparks from the Alter of '76: International Repercussions and Reconsiderations of the American Revolution," in *The Age of Revolutions in their Global Context, c. 1760–1840*, ed. David Armitage and Sanjay Subrahmanyam, London: Palgrave Macmillan (2010), 1–19.

Neumann, Peter. *Jena 1800: The Republic of Free Spirits* [2017], trans. Shelley Frisch, New York: Farrar, Straus and Giroux (2022).

Nietzsche, Friedrich. *Philosophy and Truth: Selections from Nietzsche's Notebooks of the Early 1870s)*, trans. and ed. Daniel Breazeale, Atlantic Highlands, NJ: Humanities Press International (1979).

Nietzsche, Friedrich. *The Birth of Tragedy out of the Spirit of Music* [1872], in *The Birth of Tragedy and Other Writings*, trans. Ronald Speirs, ed. Ronald Speirs and Raymond Geuss, Cambridge: Cambridge University Press (1999), 1–116.

Norton, Robert E. "The Myth of the Counter-Enlightenment," *Journal of the History of Ideas* 68 (2007), 635–58.

Norton, Robert E. "Isaiah Berlin's 'Expressionism,' or: 'Ha! Du bist das Blökende!'," *Journal of the History of Ideas* 69 (2008), 339–47.

Norton, Robert E. *The Crucible of German Democracy: Ernst Troeltsch and the First World War*, Tübingen: Mohr Siebeck (2021).

Novalis (Friedrich von Hardenberg). *Novalis: Philosophical, Literary, and Poetical Writings*, ed. James D. Reid, Oxford: Oxford University Press (2024).

O'Neill, Onora. *Constructions of Reason: Explorations of Kant's Practical Philosophy*, Cambridge: Cambridge University Press (1989).

O'Neill, Onora. *Towards Justice and Virtue: A Constructive Account of Practical Reasoning*, Cambridge: Cambridge University Press (1996).

O'Neill, Onora. *Constructing Authorities: Reason, Politics and Interpretation in Kant's Philosophy*, Cambridge: Cambridge University Press (2015).

O'Neill, Onora. *A Philosopher Looks at Digital Communication*, Cambridge: Cambridge University Press (2022).

Ord, Toby. *The Precipice: Existential Risk and the Future of Humanity*, New York: Hachette (2021).

O'Toole, Finton. "Defying Tribalism (review of *Left is Not Woke*, by Susan Neiman)," *The New York Review of Books*, Nov. 2 (2023), 18–22.

Ostaric, Lara. "Absolute Freedom and Creative Agency in Early Schelling," *Philosophisches Jahrbuch* 119 (2012), 69–93.

Outram, Dorinda. *The Enlightenment*, 4th edn, Cambridge: Cambridge University Press (2019).

Palmer, R. R. *The Age of the Democratic Revolution: A Political History of Europe and America*, 2 vols., Princeton: Princeton University Press (1959).

Papish, Laura. *Kant on Evil, Self-Deception, and Moral Reform*, Oxford: Oxford University Press (2018).

Peach, Bernard. "Preface and Introduction," in *Richard Price and the Ethical Foundations of the American Revolution: Selections from his Pamphlets, with Appendices*, ed. Bernard Peach, Durham, NC: Duke University Publications (1979), 9–40.

Peterson, Susan Rae. "The Compatibility of Richard Price's Politics and Ethics," *Journal of the History of Ideas* 45 (1984), 537–47.

Pinkard, Terry. *Does History Make Sense?* Cambridge, MA: Harvard University Press (2017).

Pippin, Robert B. "The Curious Fate of the Idea of Progress," in *Kant and the Possibility of Progress: From Modern Hopes to Postmodern Anxieties*, ed. Sam A. Stoner and Paul T. Wilford, Philadelphia: University of Pennsylvania Press (2021), 217–32.

Plantinga, Alvin. *Warrant and Proper Function*, New York: Oxford University Press (1993).

Pothast, Ulrich. *The Metaphysical Vision: Arthur Schopenhauer's Philosophy of Art and Life and Samuel Beckett's Own Way to Make Use of it*, New York: Peter Lang (2008).

Price, Richard. *A Review of the Principal Questions in Morals* [1758], ed. D. D. Raphael, Oxford: Oxford University Press (1974).

Price, Richard. *Richard Price and the Ethical Foundations of the American Revolution: Selections from his Pamphlets, with Appendices*, ed. Bernard Peach, Durham, NC: Duke University Publications (1979).

Price, Richard. *Observations on the Importance of the American Revolution and the Means of Making it a Benefit to the World* [1784], in *Political Writings/Richard Price*, ed. D. O. Thomas, Cambridge: Cambridge University Press (1991), 116–51.

216 REFERENCES

Price, Richard. *Political Writings/Richard Price*, ed. D. O. Thomas, Oxford: Oxford University Press (1991).

Purviance, Susan. "Richard Price's Contextual Rationalism," *Studies in the History of Ethics* (2005), 1–21.

Putnam, Hilary. *Jewish Philosophy as a Guide to Life: Rosenzweig, Buber, Levinas, Wittgenstein*, Indianapolis and Bloomington: Indiana University Press (2008).

Rashdall, Hastings. *The Theory of Good and Evil*, Vol. 2, Oxford: Oxford University Press (1924).

Ratner-Rosenberg, Jennifer. *American Nietzsche: A History of an Icon*, Chicago: University of Chicago Press (2012).

Rawls, John. *Political Liberalism*, New York: Columbia University Press (1993).

Rawls, John. *Lectures on the History of Moral Philosophy*, ed. Barbara Herman, Cambridge, MA: Harvard University Press (2000).

Redesdale, Lord (David Bertram Ogilvy Freeman-Mitford). "Introduction," in Houston Stuart Chamberlain, *Immanuel Kant: A Study and a Comparison with Goethe, Leonardo da Vinci, Bruno, Plato and Descartes* [1905], trans. Lord Redesdale, London: John Lane (1914), i–xi.

Reed, T. J. "Mann and History," in *The Cambridge Companion to Thomas Mann*, ed. Ritchie Robertson, Cambridge: Cambridge University Press (2002), 1–21.

Rees, Laurence. *Hitler's Charisma: Leading Millions into the Abyss*, New York: Penguin Random House (2012).

Reichl, Pavel. "Kant's A Priori History of Metaphysics: Systematicity, Progress, and the Ends of Reason," *European Journal of Philosophy* 29 (2020), 811–26.

Reiss, Hans. "Postscript," in *Kant: Political Writings*, 2nd edn, ed. Hans Reiss, Cambridge: Cambridge University Press (1991), 250–72.

Rex, Richard. *The Making of Martin Luther*, Princeton: Princeton University Press (2017).

Rodriguez, Facundo. "Reconstructing Kant: Kant's Teleological Moral Realism," *Kant Yearbook* 14 (2022), 71–95.

Roosevelt, Theodore. "The Foundations of the Nineteenth Century," *History as Literature*, New York: Charles Scribner's Sons (1913), 233–43.

Rorty, Richard. *Philosophy and the Mirror of Nature*, Princeton: Princeton University Press (1979).

Rorty, Richard. *Achieving our Country: Leftist Thought in Twentieth Century America*, Cambridge, MA: Harvard University Press (1998).

Rorty, Richard. *Philosophy and Social Hope*, London: Penguin (1999).

Rorty, Richard. *Philosophy as Poetry*, Charlottesville: University of Virginia Press (2016).

Rosen, Michael. *Dignity: Its History and Meaning*, Cambridge, MA: Harvard University Press (2012).

Rosenberg, Alfred. *Houston Stewart Chamberlain als Verkünder und Begründer einer deutschen Zukunft*, Munich: H. Bruckmann (1927).

Rosenberg, Alfred. *Der Mythos des 20. Jahrhunderts. Eine Wertung der seelisch-geistigen Gestaltkämpfe unserer Zeit*, Munich: Hoheneichen (1930).

Rosenberg, Alfred. *Race and Race History and Other Essays by Alfred Rosenberg*, ed. Robert Pois, New York: Harper & Row (1970).

Rosenfeld, Sophia. *Common Sense: A Political History*, Cambridge, MA: Harvard University Press (2011).

Ross, Alex. "The Hitler Vortex: How American Racism Influenced Hitler," *The New Yorker*, April 30 (2018), 66–73.

Ross, Alex. *Wagnerism: Art and Politics in the Shadow of Music*, New York: Farrar, Straus and Giroux (2020).

Ross, Alex. "Behind the Mask: The Ironic Genius of Thomas Mann," *The New Yorker*, Jan. 24 (2022), 26–31.

Rousseau, Jean-Jacques. *Emile, on Education* [1762], trans. Barbara Foxley, London: J. M. Dent and Sons [1911], repr. (1974).

Rumph, Stephen, "Herder's Alternative Path to Musical Transcendence," in *Theology, Music, and Modernity: Struggles for Freedom*, ed. Jeremy Begbie, Daniel K. L. Chua, and Markus Rathey, Oxford: Oxford University Press (2021), 317–35.

Runciman, David. "Schockingly Worldly," *London Review of Books*, 25 October (2003), 7–10. Review of *Emmanuel Sieyès: Political Writings*, ed. Michael Sonenscher, Indianapolis: Hackett (2003).

Rush, Fred. *Irony and Idealism: Rereading Schlegel, Hegel, and Kierkegaard*, Oxford: Oxford University Press (2016).

Sieyès, Emmanuel. *Emmanuel Sieyès: Political Writings*, ed. Michael Sonenscher, Indianapolis: Hackett (2003).

Schafer, Karl. "Kant: Constitutivism as Capacities-First Philosophy," *Philosophical Explorations* 2 (2019), 177–93.

Schafer, Karl. "Transcendental Philosophy as Capacities-First Philosophy," *Philosophy and Phenomenological Research* 103 (2020), 661–86.

Schama, Simon. *Patriots and Liberators—Revolution in the Netherlands, 1780–1813*, New York: Alfred A. Knopf (1977).

Schlegel, Friedrich. "Versuch über den Republikanismus" [1796], in *Kritische Schriften und Fragmente [1794–1797]*, ed. Ernst Behler and Hans Eichner, Paderborn: Ferdinand Schöningh (1988), 51–61.

Schlegel, Friedrich. "Athenaeum Fragments," in *Theory as Practice: A Critical Anthology of Early German Romantic Writings*, ed. Joachim Schulte-Sasse, Minneapolis: University of Minnesota Press (1997), 319–26.

Schneewind, Jerome B. (1998): *The Invention of Autonomy: A History of Modern Moral Philosophy*, Cambridge: Cambridge University Press (1998).

Schönecker, Dieter and Schmidt, Elke Elisabeth, "Kant's Ground-Thesis: On Dignity and Value in the Groundwork," *Journal of Value Inquiry* 52 (2018), 81–95.

Schott, Robin May (ed.). *Feminist Interpretations of Kant*, University Park, PA: Penn State University Press (1997).

Schulz, Kathryn. "You Name it: Carl Linnaeus and the Effort to Label all Life," *The New Yorker*, August 21 (2023), 50–4.

Sen, Amartya. "Equality of What?", in *Equal Freedom*, ed. Stephen Darwall, Ann Arbor: The University of Michigan Press (1995), 307–30.

Sensen, Oliver. *Kant on Human Dignity*, New York and Berlin: De Gruyter (2011).

Sensen, Oliver. "Dignity: Kant's Revolutionary Conception," in *Dignity: A History*, ed. Remy Debes, Oxford: Oxford University Press (2017), 237–62.

Shaw, Tamsin. *Nietzsche's Political Skepticism*, Princeton: Princeton University Press (2007).

Shell, Susan Meld. "*Nachschrift eines Freundes*: Kant on Language, Friendship, and the Concept of a People," *Kantian Review* 15 (2010), 88–117.

Sherratt, Yvonne. *Hitler's Philosophers*, New Haven, CT: Yale University Press (2013).

Siefken, Heinrich. "Thomas Mann's Essay, "Hitler," *German Life and Letters* 35 (1982), 165–91.

Siefken, Heinrich. "Mann as Essayist," in *The Cambridge Companion to Thomas Mann*, ed. Ritchie Robertson, Cambridge: Cambridge University Press (2002), 213–25.

218 REFERENCES

Sloan, Phillip. "The Essence of Race: Kant and Late Enlightenment Reflections," *Studies in the History of Biological and Biomedical Sciences* 47 (2014), 191–5. Review of Mikkelsen (2013).

Smith, Page. *John Adams, vol. 1: 1735–1784*, Garden City, NY: Doubleday (1962).

Snyder, Timothy. *Bloodlands: Europe Between Hitler and Stalin*, New York: Basic Books (2010).

Sorel, Georges. *Reflections on Violence* [1908], trans. Thomas Ernest Hulme, ed. Jeremy Jennings, Cambridge: Cambridge University Press (1999).

Spencer, Vicki C. "Unity and Diversity: Herder, Relativism, and Pluralism," in *The Emergence of Relativism: German Thought from the Enlightenment to National Socialism*, ed. Martin Kusch et al., London: Routledge (2019), 20–15.

Stark, Cynthia. "The Rationality of Valuing Oneself: A Critique of Kant on Self-Respect," *Journal of the History of Philosophy* 35 (1997), 65–82.

Stebbing, Jada Twedt. "Attributability, Weakness of Will, and the Importance of Just Having the Capacity," *Philosophical Studies* 173 (2016), 289–307.

Steigmann-Gall, Richard. *The Holy Reich: Nazi Conceptions of Christianity, 1919–1945*, Cambridge: Cambridge University Press (2003).

Stoner, Samuel A. and Wilford, Paul T. "Realizing the Ethical Community: Kant's *Religion* and the Reformation of Culture," in *Kant and the Possibility of Progress: From Modern Hopes to Postmodern Anxieties*, ed. Samuel A. Stoner and Paul T. Wilford, Philadelphia: University of Pennsylvania Press (2021), 94–114.

Tasioulas, John. "Human Dignity and the Foundations of Human Rights," in *Understanding Human Dignity*, ed. Christopher McCrudden, Oxford: Oxford University Press (2013), 293–314.

Taylor, Charles. "The Importance of Herder," in *Isaiah Berlin: A Celebration*, ed. Edna and Avishai Margalit, Chicago and London: University of Chicago and Hogarth Press (1991), 40–64.

Thomas, D. O. "Introduction," in *Richard Price/Political Writings*, ed. D. O. Thomas, Oxford: Oxford University Press (1991), vii–xxii.

Troeltsch, Ernst. *Politische Ethik und Christentum*, Berlin: De Gruyter (1904).

Vaget, Hans Rudolf. *Thomas Mann, der Amerikaner: Leben und Werk im amerikanischen Exil 1938–1952*, Frankfurt: S. Fischer (2011).

Valdez, Inés. "It's Not about Race: Good Wars, Bad Wars, and the Origins of Kant's Anti-Colonialism," *American Political Science Review* 111 (2017), 819–34.

Valdez, Inés. *Transitional Cosmopolitanism: Kant, DuBois, and Justice as a Political Craft*, New York: Cambridge University Press (2019).

van der Linden, Harry. *Kantian Ethics and Socialism*, Indianapolis: Hackett (1988).

Velkley, Richard. *Freedom and The End of Reason*, Chicago: University of Chicago Press (1989).

Velkley, Richard. *Being After Rousseau: Philosophy and Culture in Question*, Chicago: University of Chicago Press (2002).

Velkley, Richard. "Language, Embodiment, and the Supersensuous in *Fichte's Addresses to the German Nation*," in *Kant and the Possibility of Progress: From Modern Hopes to Postmodern Anxieties*, ed. Samuel A. Stoner and Paul T. Wilford, Philadelphia: University of Pennsylvania Press (2021), 153–64.

Waldron, Jeremy. *One Another's Equals: The Basis of Human Equality*, Cambridge, MA: Harvard University Press (2017).

Wall, John. "The American Revolution and German Literature," *Modern Language Notes* 16 (1961), 163–76.

Walls, Laura Dassow. "The Cosmopolitan Project of Louisa May Alcott," *ESQ: A Journal of the American Renaissance* 57 (2011), 107–32.

Watkins, Eric and Fitzpatrick, William. "O'Neill and Korsgaard on the Construction of Normativity," *The Journal of Value Inquiry* 36 (2002), 349–67.

Watkins, Eric. *Kant on Laws*, Cambridge: Cambridge University Press (2019).

Watson, Peter. *The German Genius: Europe's Third Renaissance, the Second Scientific Revolution and the Twentieth Century*, New York: HarperCollins (2010).

Weinberg, Gerold (ed.). *Hitler's Second Book: The Unpublished Sequel to Mein Kampf*. New York: Enigma Books (2003). Trans. Krista Smith from a 1928 manuscript.

Wessling, Jordan. "A Dilemma for Wolterstorff's Theistic Grounding of Human Dignity and Rights," *International Journal for Philosophy of Religion* 76 (2009), 277–95.

White, Morton G. *The Philosophy of the American Revolution*, Oxford: Oxford University Press (1981).

Whitman, James Q. *Hitler's American Model: The United States and the Making of Nazi Race Law*. Princeton: Princeton University Press (2017).

Whitman, Walt. *Democratic Vistas* [1871], in *The Works of Walt Whitman*, vol. 2, ed. Malcolm Cowley, New York: Minerva Press (1969), 208–63.

Wilken, Robert. "Celsus: A Conservative Intellectual," in *The Christians as the Romans Saw Them*, New Haven, CT: Yale University Press (1984), 94–125.

Wollstonecraft, Mary. *A Vindication of the Rights of Men* [1790]; *A Vindication of the Rights of Woman* [1791], ed. D. L. MacDonald and Kathleen Sherff, Peterborough, ON and Orchard Park, NY: Broadview Press (1997).

Wolterstorff, Nicholas. *Justice: Rights and Wrongs*. Princeton: Princeton University Press (2008).

Wood, Allen W. *Kant's Moral Religion*, Ithaca: Cornell University Press (1970).

Wood, Allen W. "Harry van der Linden, *Kantian Ethics and Socialism* (review)," *Idealistic Studies* 19 (1989), 271–3.

Wood, Allen W. *Kant's Ethical Thought*, Cambridge: Cambridge University Press (1999).

Wood, Allen W. *Unsettling Obligations: Essays on Reason, Reality, and the Ethics of Belief*, Stanford, CA: CSLI Publications (2002).

Wood, Allen W. "Kant and Herder: Their Enlightenment Faith," in *Metaphysics and the Good: Themes from the Philosophy of Robert Merrihew Adams*, ed. Samuel Newlands and Larry M. Jorgensen, Oxford: Oxford University Press (2009), 313–42.

Wood, Allen W. *Kant and Religion*, Cambridge: Cambridge University Press (2020).

Wood, Gordon S. *The Radicalism of the American Revolution*. New York: Random House (1991).

Wulf, Andrea. *Magnificent Rebels: The First Romantics and the Invention of the Self*, New York: Knopf Doubleday (2022).

Zagarri, Rosemary. "Scholarship on the American Revolution since *The Birth of the Republic*," in Edmund S. Morgan, *The Birth of the Republic, 1763–1789*, 4th edn, Chicago: University of Chicago Press (2012), 193–209.

Zammito, John H. *Kant, Herder, and the Birth of Anthropology*, Chicago: University of Chicago Press (2002).

Zoeller, Guenter. "Law and Liberty: Immanuel Kant and James Madison on the Modern Polity," in *Revista de Estudios Kantianos* 3 (2018), 1–13.

Zöller, Günter. "Genesis und Klima. Naturgeschichte und Geo-Anthropologie bei Kant und Herder," in *Proceedings of the XI International Kant-Congress 2010*, ed. Claudio LaRocca and Margit Ruffing, Berlin: De Gruyter (2013), 551–64.

220 REFERENCES

Zuckert, Rachel. "History, Biology, and Philosophical Anthropology in Kant and Herder," *Internationales Jahrbuch des Deutschen Idealismus/International Yearbook of German Idealism* 8 (2010), 38–59.

Zuckert, Rachel. *Herder's Naturalist Aesthetics*, Cambridge: Cambridge University Press (2019).

Zylberman, Ariel. "The Relational Structure of Human Dignity," *Australasian Journal of Philosophy* 96 (2018), 738–52.

Zylberman, Ariel. "*Human Dignity and Political Criticism*, by Colin Bird (review)," *Notre Dame Philosophical Reviews*, 2022.08.03.

Index

Since the index has been created to work across multiple formats, indexed terms for which a page range is given (e.g., 52–53, 66–70, etc.) may occasionally appear only on some, but not all of the pages within the range.

Abegg, J F 101 n.24, 108 n.49, 112 n.56
Abraham 87, 168–72
achievement (accomplishment) 5, 16, 22–3,
    25 n.21, 31, 32 n.42, 39 n.63, 40 n.65, 42–5,
    51, 55, 73 n.9, 74, 80, 83 n.32, 98, 112–13,
    116, 136 n.69, 143, 162, 177, 190
Adams, J 56, 92, 94, 98, 105–6, 118, 124
Adams, J Q 105 n.40, 121 n.15
Adams, R M 136 n.72
Adorno, T 158 n.4
Alcott, L M 186 n.16
Allais, L 9, 80 n.23, 93, 114–16
Allen, D 9, 117, 132–3, 135
Allison, H E 20 n.7, 36 n.53
American Revolution 9, 55–7, 58 n.26, 97–8,
    102–9, 112–14, 120–4, 131–2, 144, 189 n.21
animals 23, 26, 48, 78–9, 82
antinomies 19 n.6, 173 n.44
anti-Semitism 7, 55, 62, 71, 75–6, 83–95,
    112 n.56, 116, 135, 182–3
Aquinas 4
Arendt, H 32 n.39, 54, 56, 102–3, 105, 193
Aristotle 4–5, 34, 36, 132, 153 n.30
Armitage, D 97 n.11, 102–3
Aschheim, S 151 n.24
Asians (Orientals) 111–13, 116, 189
Audi, R 9, 122 n.17, 135–6, 197 n.3
Augustine 66 n.50, 67, 87, 88 n.51
Australia 83 n.30
autonomy (moral self-legislation) 33–4, 41, 55,
    64, 69, 76–7, 81, 83–5, 90, 101, 123, 132–3,
    139, 157, 184 n.8, 198

Baltics 7, 14, 54, 59–60, 94–7, 100–1
Bancroft, G 56
Bayes, T 118
Beauvoir, S de 149
Beethoven, L van 65 n.47, 153 n.34
Behler, E 65
Beiser, F C 65, 108 nn.50, 51
Bentham, J 94, 104–5, 135–6, 144

Berlin, I 58
Berman, R 96 n.8
Bernhard, T 111 n.54
Bertram, E 151
Bieri, P 71 n.2, 105 n.38
Biester, J E 105 n.40
Bird, C 46–7
Bismarck, O 151 n.25, 183–4
Bormann, M 86
Brandom, R 67 n.53
Brink, D 9, 129
Brusslan, E 65
Bubner, R 64 n.42, 67 n.52
Budick, S 66 n.48, 107 n.45
Burke, E 105, 117–18, 121–2, 144
Butler, J 125
Byrd, S 96 n.8

capabilities 25 n.21, 30–1, 74, 104–5
capacity, of human species 2, 5, 16, 19–23,
    25–33, 36 n.53, 36–44, 46–8, 50–2, 73–4,
    76 n.18, 76–8, 80–3, 84 n.36, 98, 104–5,
    112, 119–20, 125–6, 129–30, 132–3,
    136 n.69, 190
Carlyle, T 184
Cartesianism 2, 46, 78, 130, 196
Cassirer, E 54, 84, 193
Catholics 63 n.40, 84 n.39, 87, 103–4
Celsus 172 n.41
Chakravartty, A 69 n.56
Chamberlain H S 3, 8, 71–3, 76, 80 n.22,
    82–7, 90 n.56, 93, 95, 113, 144, 151,
    182, 197–8
character, individual 20–1, 45, 82, 91–3, 100–1,
    126, 190
Charles I 107 n.45
Chinese 111, 116
Christianity 71, 83 n.32, 84–91, 100, 132 n.25,
    151 n.25, 159–60, 171–2, 176
Cicero 119
Clarke, S 118, 125

222 INDEX

Cohen, H 84, 91
Coleridge, S 145, 178
colonialism 3, 6, 8–9, 55, 60 n.35, 72, 81, 92,
    94–111, 113, 115, 121, 135
common sense 2, 25, 44–5, 47–8, 123, 132 n.55,
    135–8, 140, 142
Comte, A 53
Condorcet, N de 106
conservative revolution 151, 175
constitutions
    American 55–6, 92, 97, 102 n.27, 103, 105,
        107 n.46, 108, 110, 126, 198
    German 16 n.1, 38, 48 n.85, 95, 103–4, 120
    modern 94, 102 n.27, 126, 158, 160, 181
constructivism 1, 5, 29 n.30, 33–8, 125 n.26, 152
Corngold S 147–8, 192 n.28
Crèvecoeur, J H S de 102 n.26
Cudworth, R 118, 125
Cureton, A 44 n.74

Dahlstrom, D 60 n.32
Darwall S 43
Darwinism, C 34, 87, 141, 176
Dean, R 16, 23 n.14, 38–45, 73 n.9
Debes, R 16 n.1
Declaration of Independence 8–9, 81, 94, 97–8,
    102–5, 108–9, 117, 132–9, 142, 150,
    185, 198
Deligiorgi, K 26 n.23
DeWitt, J 28 n.29
Diedrichs, E 153 n.37
Dippel, H 107 n.47, 121
Donagan, A 171–2
Dostoevsky, F 167, 174 n.47, 190
Douglass, F 198
Durant, W 196
Dutch 9, 56–7, 102 n.26, 104 n.34, 106, 107 n.47,
    109–10, 120
Dwyer, S 81 n.26

Early Romantics 10–11, 14, 49 n.2, 52–3, 61,
    62 n.39, 63–8, 143, 152–65, 178–81,
    186–9, 191
Ely, R T 183
end in itself 17, 27, 36, 39–41, 119, 127
English Revolution 9, 109, 117–18
English Romantics 153
Engstrom, S 4 n.7
equality 2, 8–9, 18–19, 23–4, 29, 32–8, 50, 55,
    61–2, 68, 71–2, 77, 80–1, 98–9, 104–5, 112,
    117, 119, 124–7, 131–40, 147, 176, 183, 187,
    190, 192–3, 198
Erhard, J G 56

Establishment Attitude 108, 111–16
Ethiopia 99
Euclid 24, 112
Evans, C S 59 n.29, 169 n.32
evident 9, 23–4, 48, 69, 98, 104 n.36, 117–19,
    123–7, 130, 132–42, 166–7, 198
evil 17, 21–2, 27, 42, 46, 66 n.50, 74, 78–9,
    80 n.23, 82, 84, 88, 93, 100, 112–15, 128–9,
    164–5, 169, 177–8, 190

Faktum der Vernunft (fact of reason) 30,
    130, 174
Fascists 6–7, 13, 24, 38, 48 n.85, 71–96, 99–100,
    104, 115, 149–51, 167 n.29, 172 n.41,
    181–2 n.3, 185, 190–1, 192 n.28, 193
Faust 170 n.33
feeling 17, 46 n.82, 58, 66, 76, 78–80, 86, 125–8,
    143, 156–8, 167, 181, 183, 187
feminism 3
Feuerbach, L 53
Fichte, J G 3, 32 n.41, 53, 67, 157, 160 n.10
Fischer K 97 n.9
Fisher, J 67 n.52
Fisher, N 62 n.38, 67 n.52
Flikschuh, K 96
Follen, K 186 n.16
Fontane, T 49–50
Formosa, P 16, 20 n.7, 21 n.9, 22, 24 n.18,
    25–39, 41–2
Formula of Humanity 26, 187
Formula of Universal Law 26–7
Forster, G 56, 108 n.51, 113
Forster, M N 60 n.33, 162 n.14
Foucault, M 65, 94 n.1
Fraenkel, C 90 n.57
Franco-Prussian War 172
Frank, M 65, 154 n.39
Frankfurt, H 41 n.68
Franklin, B 92, 101–2, 105–6, 118, 124, 133–5
Franks, P W 8, 71, 75–6, 85 n.40, 89–91
Franz, M 67 n.52
Frederick II 56–7, 110, 151, 188
freedom (absolute free choice) 1–2, 18–22,
    25–9, 32, 35 n.49, 42–3, 46–7, 71–2,
    76–9, 84, 86, 126, 128–57, 169, 174,
    176–7, 192
Frege, G 35
French 57, 65, 104 n.34, 105–6, 118, 121 n.12,
    124, 148 n.13, 182 n.3, 183
French and Indian War 109
French Revolution 7, 9, 50, 52, 56, 75–6, 102,
    107, 117–18, 120–1, 121 n.15, 133,
    148 n.13, 160, 164, 175, 189 n.21

INDEX

Freud, S 24
Friedman, M 54
Frierson, P R 39 n.64

Gadamer, H-G 54, 68
genius 51, 63, 66, 86 n.42, 178, 188, 191, 196 n.1
Gentz, F 105–6, 121 n.15
Gerhardt, V 20 n.7
German Idealism 8, 11, 66–7, 75, 89, 160–1, 181–2
German Republic (Weimar) 147–8, 150–1, 181–3, 185, 188–9
Geuss, R 70
Gjesdal, K 51, 93 n.64
God 18 n.4, 19 n.6, 34, 42 n.69, 84–7, 126–7, 131, 145, 159 n.5, 163 n.17, 168, 171 n.37, 181
Goebbels J 73, 84
Goehr, L 162 n.14
Goethe, J W 32 n.39, 51, 54, 182
Goldenbaum, U 85 n.41
good predisposition, seed, or germ 21, 39 n.64, 40, 42–3, 65, 71, 73, 80, 98, 112, 130
good will 21 n.8, 39 n.64, 189–90
Gopnik, A 199 n.5
Great Britain 23, 57, 73, 96–7, 102 n.26, 104, 107–9, 111, 117–18, 119 n.5, 121–2, 125–6, 140, 151, 165, 183–4, 197
Green, J 56, 108
Green, T H 130
Grey, E 150 n.20
Griffin, J 82 n.28
Grundmann, T 75 n.14

Habermas, J 94 n.1
Hall, G S 183
Hamann, J G 60 n.35
Hamburger, M 67 n.51
Hampton, J 74 n.12
Händel, G F 140
Hare, J 32 n.40, 131 n.51
Hatfield, J T 56 n.18
Hauptmann, G 185
Hegel, G W F 3, 11, 32 n.39, 47 n.83, 53–4, 63, 66–8, 75, 90, 102 n.27, 136, 156–61, 163–6, 170–74, 179–80, 183–4
Heidegger, M 54, 65, 92 n.61, 197 n.2
Heller, E 148 n.13
Herder, J G 3, 7, 49–70, 93, 121 n.12, 144, 153–4, 161, 187, 197–9
Herman, B 125
highest good 4, 16, 32, 42 n.69, 82 n.28, 86, 131–2, 136, 169
Hill Jr, T H 17 n.2, 32 n.42, 74 n.12

Hitler, A 8, 72–3, 82–7, 95 n.5, 97, 99, 104 n.37, 111, 151–2, 191–2, 194
Hochbaum, E 56 n.18
Hölderlin, F 63–5, 67, 153–4
Höffe O 110 n.53
Hottentots 110
Hruska, J 96 n.8
Huemer, M 29 n.30
Hume, D 79, 106, 145
Husserl, E 196

idealism 1, 8, 35, 46 n.79, 71–2, 82–4, 86 n.42, 87
identity, personal 29 n.32, 30, 37, 58, 73, 80 n.22, 101, 120, 129, 190 n.23, 193
Illies, F 54 n.15
Immortality 130–1, 136–7, 144–5
intuitionism 35, 122, 125, 127, 138 n.77
Irish 58, 108 n.49
Irwin, T 125 n.26, 129 n.46
Isaac 168–71
Israel, J 107 n.47, 121 n.10, 122–3

Jackson, T 74 n.12
Jacobi, F H 91
Jägerstetter, F 171
Japan 111
Jefferson, T 3, 57, 92, 94, 98, 105–6, 110, 117–18, 131, 133–5, 140, 149, 199
Jenisch, D 61, 62 n.37
Jesus 66, 85, 87–8, 90–1, 131
Job 66, 90
justice 1, 4, 84, 126, 131, 134, 136, 154, 163, 175–7

Kain, P 42 n.70
Kästner, A G 67
Kelly, T 9, 138 n.77
Kierkegaard, S 11, 156–61, 163–72, 175–7, 179–80, 184, 186
Killmister, S 28 n.28
King, M L 149 n.17
King Jr, M L 149
Klages, L 54 n.14
Kleingeld, P 57 n.25, 72 n.3, 81
Klemperer, V 84 n.39, 183 n.4
Klopstock, F G 67 n.51
Kneller, J 65, 153 n.33, 186 n.17
Korsgaard, C 29–30, 138 n.77
Kosciuszko, T 106
Kuhn, T 65
Kumar, A 44 n.74

Laboucheix H 124, 125 n.25
Lackey, M 8, 71–89, 93

224 INDEX

Lafayette, M de 106
La Fontaine, J de 70
Lagarde, P de 83 n.34, 151
Langton, R 20 n.7
Larmore, C 146–7, 152, 154, 166 n.26
late modernity 64, 66 n.50, 67, 147, 158, 167, 197 n.2
Late Romanticism 10–11, 152–4, 164 n.19
Latvians 101
Leibniz, G W 67, 70, 113
Lessing, G E 52 n.11
Lincoln, A 73 n.7, 149, 156, 188, 198
Lind, J 104, 135–6
Linnaeus, C 55
Lithuanians 7, 49, 58–62, 66, 93, 100–1
Locke, J 63, 98, 125, 135, 149
Louis XVI 107, 118 n.3
Löwith, K 53 n.13
Lu-Adler, H 91 n.58
Lukaçs, G 54, 153 n.33, 164 n.22, 184
Luther, M 66, 85, 88 n.51, 169

MacIntyre, A 4, 65, 118 n.3, 140, 146–9, 152, 154–5, 167, 195
Madison, J 126 n.34
Mahler, G 189
Maliks, R 96 n.7
Mandela, N 150
Mann, F 14, 143 n.2
Mann, H 148 n.13, 191–2
Mann, K 155
Mann, T 1, 3, 7, 9–15, 51, 62 n.39, 101 n.24, 104 n.34, 111 n.54, 143–99
  Buddenbrooks 163 n.18
  Death in Venice 168 n.31
  Doktor Faustus 12–13, 148, 158 n.4, 165, 183–4
  Mario and the Magician 149
  The Black Swan 168 n.31
  The Magic Mountain 144
  Tönio Kröger 178
Maritain, J 1 n.1
Marx, K 53, 68, 75, 153 n.32
materialism 11, 83–4, 130, 165
McGrath, S 9, 137 n.76, 138–42
McNaughton, D 29 n.30
Mendelssohn, M 89–91, 105 n.40
Merritt, M 190 n.22
Micheli, G 119 n.5
Mill, J S 3, 76, 124, 145, 178
Mills, C W 8–9, 71–2, 83 n.30, 114–16
Milton, J 66–7, 107 n.45, 124, 144–5
Miniger, J D 60 n.35

Mirabeau 118
Moore, G E 138 n.77, 145 n.3
Moran, R 164 n.20
Moses 87
motivation 80, 120 n.7, 124–5, 127–8, 130–1
Mozart, W A 123–4
Murdoch, I 32 n.39, 34 n.45

Nagel, T 120 n.7
Nash, G 103
nationalism 3, 51, 58–9, 71, 75–6, 84, 86–7, 113, 131–2, 171, 182, 187, 189, 191
Native Americans 9, 92, 96, 99, 102, 110–12, 135
Natorp, P 73
Neumann, P 49 n.2
Newton, I 35 n.49
Nietzsche, F 10–11, 24, 46, 64–5, 75, 86–7, 143, 147–57, 162–3, 167, 172–81, 183, 190, 193–5, 197 n.2
Novalis 9–10, 63–5, 152–4, 162 n.14, 178, 181, 185–9

Obama, B 150
O'Neill, O 4 n.6, 22 n.13, 34 n.45, 51 n.8, 54, 74 n.12, 98 n.14, 100 n.22, 125 n.24
Ostaric, L 67 n.52

Pacific Islanders 66
Paine, T 92, 105, 124
Palmer, R R 103
Papish, L 114 n.58
patriotism 59, 88, 117–18, 188
Paul 87
Peach, B 104 n.34, 121, 134
perfectionism 36, 112, 129, 159
Peterson, S R 118 n.4
Philo 90
Pietism 49, 85
Pinkard, T 102 n.27
Pippin, R B 197 n.2
Pitt, W 108 n.49
Plato 67, 69, 146–51, 153 n.30, 163, 199
play (games) 17, 27–8, 80 n.24, 129–30
Poles 55, 58, 97, 106, 111, 190
Pope, A 144
Price, R 3, 9, 59, 94, 102 n.26, 104, 117–42, 144, 149, 197–9
Priestley, J 118, 130
Prometheus 102 n.26
prudence 28, 29 n.32, 30–1, 37–8, 126–8
Prussia 7, 50, 54, 56–7, 60 n.35, 61–2, 98–101, 110–13, 115, 159–60, 172

psychopaths 37–8, 42
Purviance, S 125 n.23
Putnam, H 120 n.7

race 3, 8, 55–8, 71–96, 99–100, 109, 111–16,
    135, 140–1, 144, 151, 153 n.37, 182
rank 16, 23, 25, 84 n.36, 119, 154
Rashdall, H 73 n.7, 122 n.16
Ratner-Rosenberg, J 183
Rawls, J 34–5, 54, 103–4, 138–9
realism, moral 16, 33–7, 122 n.17, 125–6,
    138 n.77, 139
realm of ends 17–19, 47, 188
Rees, L 84 n.38
Reinhold, K 2 n.3, 3, 19 n.6, 63–5,
    160 n.10, 174
Reid, T 138 n.77
Reiss, H 108
religion 3, 6, 11, 21, 31–3, 57–8, 66, 71, 79,
    85–93, 103, 105 n.39, 114, 124–7, 131–2,
    141–2, 145–6, 148 n.15, 156–72, 174 n.47,
    176–7, 179, 182, 184 n.10, 186–7,
    191 n.26, 194
respect for persons 3, 6, 13, 16, 18–21, 29–33,
    37–40, 43–4, 46–8, 52, 58–9, 62, 66, 73–4,
    81–2, 89–93, 95, 98–9, 103–5, 115–16, 119,
    127–8, 130–1, 133, 136, 147, 162,
    190–3, 197–8
revolution, personal 21, 65
Rilke, R M 92 n.61
rights, moral 3–5, 32 n.42, 56–7, 71, 77, 94,
    97–8, 103–4, 106–9, 117–18, 120 n.7, 144,
    182 n.3, 189 n.21
Rodriguez, F 36 n.53
Roosevelt, F D 149–51, 151 n.26
Roosevelt, T 73, 149
Rorty, R 70, 148 n.15, 159 n.5
Rosen, M 16 n.1, 45 n.77, 82 n.28, 95 n.4,
    190 n.24
Rosenberg, A 73, 86 n.43, 87
Rosenfeld, S 132 n.55
Ross, W D 122
Rousseau, J-J 18, 27, 46, 50–1, 52 n.11, 55, 59,
    66, 69, 75–8, 80–2, 92, 104, 108, 112–14,
    119 n.5, 131 n.53, 149–50, 157, 174
Rumpf, S 161 n.12
Runciman, D 56 n.20
Rush, F 65, 153 n.31
Russians 14, 53–5, 100, 109, 111

Sambians 61–2, 100–1
Sartre, J-P 166, 168 n.30
Schelling, F W J 3, 63, 66–7

Schiller, F 60, 65, 153 n.34
Schlegel, A W 63
Schlegel, F 63–5, 69, 152, 162 n.14, 163–4
Schleiermacher, D F 63–4, 153–4, 164 n.21
Schmidt E E, 23 n.14
Schönecker, D 23 n.14
Schopenhauer, A 10–11, 148, 156–9, 162 n.15,
    163, 172–9, 188, 193
Schulz, K 55 n.17
Schurman, J 145 n.4
science 9, 11–13, 44 n.73, 45–6, 50, 52, 55–60,
    64, 67, 69–70, 75 n.14, 77, 82, 86, 88, 99,
    101 n.26, 113, 124, 130, 132–3, 140, 144–5,
    147, 157–8, 161–2, 167, 174, 196
Scots 108 n.49
Sellars, W 54
Sen, A 25 n.21
Sensen, O 23 n.14, 77 n.20
Shaftesbury (Cooper, A A) 145
Shakespeare, W 51, 68, 105
Shelbourne (Petty, W) 118
Shell, S M 60–2
Sidgwick, H 3
Shelley, M 102 n.26
Siep, L 20 n.7
Sieyès, E J 56, 102 n.27
slavery 24, 48, 68, 81, 92, 99, 106, 109, 113,
    134–5, 139–40, 187, 193
Sloan, P 80 n.22
Smith, P 56 n.22, 106
Socrates 162, 178
Sorel, G 12
South Africa 83 n.30, 115 n.59
Soviet Revolution 107
Spalding, J J 157–8
Spencer, V 60 n.34
Spinoza, B 63, 153 n.30
Stark, C 114 n.58
Stebbing, J W 41 n.68
Steigmann-Gall, R 84 n.39
Strawson, P F 54
Stresemann, G 145 n.4
style, philosophical 12, 55, 59, 63–4, 64–5,
    68–70, 80 n.24, 124, 132–7, 148–50, 173,
    181, 188, 194
Swiss 109

Tasioulas, J 4 n.5, 82 n.28
Taylor, C 65
Timmermann, J 20 n.7
Tocqueville, A de 118 n.3
transcendental idealism 35, 46, 111 n.54, 119,
    129, 173–4

226   INDEX

Transcendentalists, American 153, 186, 188
Treitschke, G F 183
Troeltsch, E 161 n.11, 176 n.48, 189 n.21
Truman, H 73 n.7
Tungusi 110
Turgot, A R J 118, 124
Turks 55

United Nations 14, 16 n.1, 104, 141, 182
United States of America 7–10, 12–15, 55,
 81, 83 n.30, 92, 94–116, 118, 120–4, 126,
 131, 135, 143–5, 148–51, 156, 171, 183–90,
 192, 198

Vaihinger, H 73
Valdez, I 113 n.57
van den Berghe, P 83 n.30
van der Linden, H 4 n.7
Velkley, R 146 n.5
Vernunftglaube (postulates of pure practical
 reason) 2, 31–3, 65, 86, 130, 163
virtue 22, 32, 39–40, 45–6, 61, 84, 100, 126, 131,
 137, 149, 183, 193
vocation 32–3, 143, 156–8, 164, 174–5, 177,
 179–80, 191

Wagner, R 10–11, 73, 151–4, 156–7, 162–3,
 172–8, 193
Waldron, J 95 n.4
Wall, J 58 n.26
Walls, L D 186 n.16
War of (attempted) Secession 107 n.46, 186
Washington, G 57, 92, 110, 118
Watson, G 41 n.68

Weber, M 149
Weil, S 149
Whewell W 141, 196 n.1
White, M 97–8, 137–8
Whitman, W 10, 62 n.39, 107 n.46, 143,
 148 n.15, 149, 153, 156, 159 n.5, 181,
 184–9, 198
Wieland, C M 56, 63 n.40, 108 n.51
Wilhelm II 72, 111, 151, 183
Williams, B 65
will (*Wille*) 42, 119, 127–9
Wilson, W 73 n.7
Winckelmann, J J 67
Wittgenstein, L 54, 176
Wlömer, J H 61
Wolff, C 36, 67, 113, 182
Wöllner, J C 107 n.44
Wollstonecraft, M 102 n.26, 117 n.2, 124, 149
Wolterstorff, N 73 n.9, 120 n.7
Wood, A W 4 n.7, 60 n.32, 80 n.23
Wood, G 103, 107
Wordsworth, W 145
World War I 7, 9–10, 14, 54, 150–1, 181–3, 194
World War II 3, 6–7, 10, 14, 48 n.85, 54, 143 n.2,
 149, 154, 192 n.28, 194
worth, moral 17–18, 21–2, 29–30, 39–41, 43–5,
 51–5, 79, 82, 90, 119, 136, 168–9

Ypi, L 96–7

Zagarri, R 102 n.28
Zeller, E 145 n.4
Zoeller, G 126 n.34
Zylberman, A 47